50 YEARS

OF

ASEAN

AND

SINGAPORE

50 YEARS

OF

ASEAN

AND

SINGAPORE

Editors

Tommy Koh, Sharon Seah Li-Lian
and Chang Li Lin

World Scientific

NEW JERSEY · LONDON · SINGAPORE · BEIJING · SHANGHAI · HONG KONG · TAIPEI · CHENNAI · TOKYO

Published by

World Scientific Publishing Co. Pte. Ltd.

5 Toh Tuck Link, Singapore 596224

USA office: 27 Warren Street, Suite 401-402, Hackensack, NJ 07601

UK office: 57 Shelton Street, Covent Garden, London WC2H 9HE

Library of Congress Cataloging-in-Publication Data

Names: Chang, Li Lin, editor of compilation. | Koh, Tommy T. B. (Tommy Thong Bee),
    1937– editor of compilation. | Seah, Sharon, editor of compilation.
Title: 50 years of ASEAN and Singapore / [edited] by Chang Li Lin, Tommy Koh and Sharon Seah Li-Lian.
Other titles: Fifty years of ASEAN and Singapore
Description: Hackensack, NJ : World Scientific, 2017. | Includes bibliographical references and index.
Identifiers: LCCN 2017013740| ISBN 9789813225114 (hardcover : alkaline paper) |
    ISBN 9789813225121 (paperback : alkaline paper)
Subjects: LCSH: ASEAN--History. | Singapore--Relations--Southeast Asia. |
    Southeast Asia--Relations--Singapore. | Regionalism--Southeast Asia. |
    Peace--Political aspects--Southeast Asia. | Political stability--Southeast Asia. |
    East Asian cooperation.
Classification: LCC DS525.8 .A14 2017 | DDC 341.24/73--dc23
LC record available at https://lccn.loc.gov/2017013740

British Library Cataloguing-in-Publication Data
A catalogue record for this book is available from the British Library.

First published 2017

Cover: The ASEAN emblem and ASEAN 50th anniversary logo are reproduced with permission from the ASEAN Secretariat. © ASEAN

Foreword

ASEAN marks its 50th anniversary in 2017. Founded in 1967 at the height of the Cold War, ASEAN was conceived by Indonesia, Malaysia, the Philippines, Thailand, and Singapore as a collective response against threats to peace and development of our region. Against the odds, ASEAN not only survived, but thrived, with regional peace and the enormous economic progress of the original founding states being self-evident. ASEAN subsequently added Brunei, Cambodia, Laos, Myanmar, and Vietnam to its ranks. Today, Southeast Asia is a region of peace, prosperity, and stability. ASEAN has become a vibrant, inter-connected economic community of 630 million people with great prospects for the future.

Consequently, ASEAN is a key pillar of Singapore's foreign policy. It enlarges our political and economic space, providing us access to expanding markets and opportunities. Over the years, regular interactions amongst ASEAN Leaders and officials have built personal rapport, expanded cooperation, broadened engagement, and deepened mutual understanding. This has created a conducive environment for regional countries to maintain peace and stability and resolve differences peacefully despite our great diversity. Our pioneer generation of leaders, diplomats, civil servants and private sector understood ASEAN's value and worked tirelessly to deepen integration and interdependence between ASEAN Member States, while ensuring that Singapore remained relevant and credible. Their good work continues to be carried out by the current generation.

From my personal experience attending ASEAN meetings over the past 15 years, I have benefitted from the exchange of ideas, cultures, and friendships which the region has to offer. I have witnessed how the interests and concerns of Member States are amplified internationally when ASEAN speaks with one voice. ASEAN is also capable of summoning a spirit of unity which is unparalleled. Even when faced with the thorniest of issues, leaders and officials work tirelessly to find common ground, and achieve agreement by consensus. This is not a trivial undertaking, given the diversity of the region we sit in.

This book is a meaningful endeavour to celebrate ASEAN's values and achievements, and to help Singaporeans gain a better appreciation of ASEAN. It is a treasure trove of experiences, lessons and memories, which will hopefully give you some insight into the growth and development of ASEAN, as well as the significant contributions that Singapore and Singaporeans have made to ASEAN. I am happy that Ambassador-at-Large Tommy Koh, Sharon Seah at the National University of Singapore's Centre for International Law and Chang Li Lin have taken the opportunity of ASEAN's 50th anniversary to persuade such a varied and distinguished group of Singaporeans who have served the ASEAN cause, to share their reflections through this book.

While 50 years is but a blink of an eye in human history, ASEAN has achieved much that we can be proud of during this time. I hope that you will enjoy the potpourri of tales and adventures that this book has to offer.

Dr. Vivian Balakrishnan
Minister for Foreign Affairs, Singapore

Contents

ASEAN's Landmark Achievements

ASEAN's External Relations

Making of the ASEAN Charter

ASEAN and Civil Society

Singaporeans in ASEAN

Post-Charter ASEAN

ASEAN Historical Timeline

1961 The Viet Nam War begins in 1955 and ends only in 1975. During this period of instability, Philippines, Malaysia and Thailand forms the Association of Southeast Asia (ASA) in 1961. The Non-Aligned Movement (NAM) is also established in the same year.

1967 Association of Southeast Asian Nations (ASEAN) comprising Indonesia, Malaysia, Philippines, Singapore and Thailand is established by the signing of the Bangkok Declaration on 8 August 1967 by the foreign ministers of the five countries. Mr. Adam Malik, Foreign Minister of Republic of Indonesia, coined the term "ASEAN".

(From left to right): Signing of the historic Bangkok Declaration on 8 August 1967 by Narciso Ramos, Foreign Secretary of the Republic of the Philippines, Adam Malik, Foreign Minister of the Republic of Indonesia, Thanat Khoman, Foreign Minister of the Kingdom of Thailand, Tun Abdul Razak, Deputy Prime Minister of Malaysia and S. Rajaratnam, Foreign Minister of the Republic of Singapore.

1971 The Zone of Peace, Freedom and Neutrality Declaration (ZOPFAN) is signed in Kuala Lumpur, Malaysia.

1973 The Member States agree to establish an ASEAN Secretariat. Indonesia offers to host it.

1974 Australia becomes ASEAN's first Dialogue Partner.

1975 New Zealand becomes an ASEAN Dialogue Partner.

1976   ○   Following the Viet Nam War, the Indochina Refugee Crisis takes place and only resolved in 1995.

In February, the first ASEAN Summit is held in Bali, Indonesia. ASEAN Heads of State/Government meet to discuss and resolve regional issues. The Treaty of Amity and Cooperation (TAC) and the Declaration of ASEAN Concord are signed. The ASEAN Secretariat is established within the Department of Foreign Affairs of the Republic of Indonesia in Jakarta.

Inaugural ASEAN Summit (or the ASEAN Heads of Government Meeting as it was initially called) held in Bali, Indonesia on 23 and 24 February 1976. The Treaty of Amity and Cooperation and the Declaration of ASEAN Concord were signed at this inaugural meeting.
(Ministry of Information and the Arts Collection, courtesy of National Archives of Singapore)

1977   ○   Dialogue relations are established between ASEAN and Canada, the European Union (EU), Japan, United States, and United Nations Development Programme (UNDP). The UNDP is the only multilateral aid organisation to be accorded status of Dialogue Partner.

A special Meeting of ASEAN Foreign Ministers takes place in Manila, Philippines to commemorate ASEAN's 10th Anniversary.

1978   ○   Vietnam invades Cambodia in December 1978 and overthrows the Khmer Rouge regime. ASEAN condemns the Vietnamese invasion and occupation of Cambodia at the UN and other international fora.

1979   ○   The UN Security Council meets in February and considers a resolution submitted by ASEAN on the Cambodian situation. USSR vetoes the resolution.

In July, the First UN meeting on Refugees and Displaced Persons in Southeast Asia is held in Geneva, Switzerland. Singapore produces a 32-page booklet "Vietnam and the Refugees".

1981   The UN convenes an International Conference on Kampuchea which was boycotted by Vietnam, USSR and their allies.

The leaders of the three Cambodian factions — Prince Sihanouk, Son Sann and Khieu Samphan meet in Singapore and agree to form a coalition government.

1984   Brunei joins ASEAN as its Sixth Member State.

1988   In July, Indonesia hosts the First Jakarta Informal Meeting on Cambodia.

1989   In February, Indonesia hosts the Second Jakarta Informal Meeting on Cambodia that eventually leads up to the Paris Peace Agreement on Cambodia which is convened in August. Singapore and ASEAN play an active role.

1991   ASEAN Free Trade Area (AFTA) negotiations begin. ASEAN also launches a dialogue process with the People's Republic of China. The Republic of Korea (ROK) becomes an ASEAN Dialogue Partner. In October, the Paris Peace Agreement on Cambodia is finally signed.

1992   In February, Singapore hosts the Fourth ASEAN Summit. ASEAN agrees to establish the AFTA. In July, the ASEAN Declaration on the South China Sea is adopted in Manila, Philippines.

1993   In July 1993, the 26th ASEAN Ministerial Meeting and Post-Ministerial Conference, held in Singapore, agrees to establish the ASEAN Regional Forum (ARF), a multilateral platform for Asia-Pacific countries to foster dialogue and consultation, promote confidence-building and preventive diplomacy in the region.

1994   In July, the inaugural meeting of the ASEAN Regional Forum (ARF) is held in Bangkok, Thailand. There are currently 27 ARF members: Australia, Bangladesh, Brunei Darussalam, Cambodia, Canada, China, Democratic People's Republic of Korea, European Union, India, Indonesia, Japan, Lao PDR, Malaysia, Mongolia, Myanmar, New Zealand, Pakistan, Papua New Guinea, Philippines, ROK, Russia, Singapore, Sri Lanka, Thailand, Timor-Leste, United States and Vietnam.

1995   Vietnam joins ASEAN as its Seventh Member State. India becomes an ASEAN Dialogue Partner. The Southeast Asian Nuclear-Weapon-Free Zone Treaty (SEANWFZ) of the Bangkok Treaty is signed in December.

1996   People's Republic of China and Russia become ASEAN's Dialogue Partners.

1997   The Asian Financial Crisis hits.

Lao PDR and Myanmar join ASEAN as its Eighth and Ninth Member State at the 30th ASEAN Ministerial Meeting in Subang Jaya, Malaysia.

ASEAN Plus Three cooperation between ASEAN, China, Japan and ROK is initiated.

1999   Cambodia joins ASEAN as its Tenth Member State on 30 April.

In June, Singapore hosts the inaugural meeting of the ASEAN Eminent Persons Group (EPG) on VISION 2020.

2000   In November, Singapore hosts the Fourth Informal ASEAN Summit. The Initiative for ASEAN Integration (IAI) to narrow the CLMV countries' development gap, proposed by then Singapore Prime Minister Goh Chok Tong, is endorsed.

Prime Minister Goh Chok Tong interacts with ASEAN counterparts at the Fourth ASEAN Informal Summit held in Singapore on 25 November 2000. The Summit endorses Singapore's proposal to narrow the development gap through the Initiative for ASEAN Integration (IAI). (*Source*: MFA Archives)

2001   Declaration on Joint Action to Counter Terrorism is adopted. The ASEAN Leaders agree to launch negotiations for an ASEAN-China FTA.

2003   In April, ASEAN+3 Leaders convene an unprecedented meeting in Bangkok to contain the spread of Severe Acute Respiratory Syndrome (SARS) that erupted in late 2002.

In October, ASEAN Leaders adopt the Declaration of ASEAN Concord II (also known as the Bali Concord II) to establish an ASEAN Community comprising three pillars, namely the ASEAN Political-Security Community, ASEAN Economic Community and the ASEAN Socio-Cultural Community at the Ninth ASEAN Summit.

2005   In December, the Inaugural East Asia Summit (EAS) is held in Kuala Lumpur, Malaysia. The EAS is an annual forum to foster political and security dialogue and cooperation among initially ASEAN, Australia, China, India, Japan, ROK and New Zealand. Its current membership now includes the United States and Russia.

ASEAN is accorded observer status at the United Nations General Assembly.

ASEAN Leaders adopt a declaration to develop the ASEAN Charter. The ASEAN Eminent Persons Group (EPG) comprising one distinguished representative from each ASEAN Member State is tasked to draft the Charter.

2007   ASEAN Convention on Counter Terrorism (ACCT) is adopted.

In November, the ASEAN Charter is adopted at the 13th ASEAN Summit. ASEAN Leaders also endorse the ASEAN Economic Community (AEC) Blueprint and sign the Declaration on the Acceleration of the Establishment of an ASEAN Community by 2015.

2008   In January, Singapore is the first ASEAN Member State to ratify the ASEAN Charter.

In May, ASEAN hosts an unprecedented international aid conference in Yangon to discuss relief measures for recovery efforts in Myanmar after Cyclone Nargis devastated Myanmar.

In December, the ASEAN Charter enters into force after Thailand delivers the tenth and final instrument of ratification.

Noeleen Heyzer with ASEAN Secretary-General Surin Pitsuwan with local children affected by Cyclone Nargis in Myanmar.

2009   Formation of the ASEAN Intergovernmental Commission on Human Rights (AICHR).

2010   The ASEAN Commission on the Promotion and Protection of the Rights of Women and Children (ACWC) is established. The Masterplan on ASEAN Connectivity is adopted.

2011   The Agreement on the Establishment of the ASEAN Coordinating Centre for Humanitarian Assistance on Disaster Management is signed.

2012   Brazil becomes the first Latin American country to accede to the TAC.

AICHR adopts the ASEAN Human Rights Declaration.

ASEAN issues the Six-Point Principles on the South China Sea.

Regional Comprehensive Economic Partnership (RCEP) negotiations launched in November.

2014   Myanmar assumes Chairmanship of ASEAN for the first time. Nay Pyi Taw Declaration on the Realisation of the ASEAN Community by 2015 is adopted.

2015   In January, Indonesia deposits the final Instrument of Ratification of the ASEAN Agreement on Transboundary Haze Pollution.

The ASEAN Convention on Trafficking in Persons Against Women and Children (ACTIP) — the first ASEAN regional convention and legally binding instrument on combating human trafficking, is signed by ASEAN Leaders in November.

ASEAN Leaders announce the establishment of the ASEAN Economic Community on 31 December 2015.

2016

Lao PDR takes ASEAN Chairmanship.

40th Anniversary of the Treaty of Amity and Cooperation (TAC).

Accession of Chile, Egypt and Morocco to the TAC in September.

Foundational Documents of ASEAN

The Founding of ASEAN*

⁕

First of all, on behalf of my Delegation and the Government of Singapore, I would like to thank the Government of Thailand and its people for hosting this Conference of what is today, five countries and in the course of years to come of many more countries of Southeast Asia. Secondly, on behalf of my Delegation, I would like to extend particular thanks to our Chairman for the tactful, judicious and patient way in which he guided our not always coherent deliberations towards a more than successful conclusion. I would like to take this opportunity to thank the officers who did excellent work in translating our intentions into more concrete form by way of documents and papers.

So, today, after four days of rather pleasant and friendly discussions, we are about to launch the new ASEAN. It is easy to give birth to a new organisation but the creation of an organisation of this nature is the most simple of all tasks. It is a mere skeleton that we have erected. Now the really difficult task is to give flesh and blood to this concept. We, in Singapore, are not unmindful of the fact that schemes for regional cooperation will run into more rocks than calm waters. Nevertheless, having had four or five days of discussions with my ministerial colleagues, there is one thing that is uppermost in my mind and that is the conviction of my ministerial colleagues in regard to both the

*Full text of the statement by Mr. S. Rajaratnam, Minister for Foreign Affairs, in Bangkok on August 8, 1967. Reproduced with permission from the National Archives of Singapore.

inevitability and the desirability of regional cooperation. However, it would be necessary not only for ministers or leaders to take this new regional scheme seriously but also to transmit to its people the need for a new kind of thinking.

For 20 years each of us in this region had been compelled to do things purely on the basis of nationalist fervour. And many of us know that after 20 years of decolonisation, nationalism alone has not provided or fulfilled the expectations by way of happier life, more fruitful life, better living standards to our countries and for our peoples. This realisation has grown and, therefore, it is necessary for us if we are really to be successful in giving life to ASEAN to marry national thinking with regional thinking. We must now think at two levels. We must think not only of our national interests but posit them against regional interests: That is a new way of thinking about our problems. And that is two different things and sometimes they can conflict. Secondly, we must also accept the fact, if we are really serious about it, that regional existence means painful adjustments to those practices, and thinking in our respective countries. We must make these painful and difficult adjustments. If we are not going to do that, then regionalism remains a Utopia.

The last point that I would like to stress is that there may be, as has happened to other associations of this kind, misunderstanding as to what ASEAN is all about. So, I would like to stress that those who are outside the grouping should not regard this as a grouping against anything, against anybody. We have approached ASEAN as standing for something, not against anything. If there are people who misunderstood the proposed regional grouping, or manifest hostility against it, let us explain that it can only be because as in Europe and in many parts of the world, outside powers have vested interests in the balkanisation of this region. We ourselves have learn the lessons and have decided that small nations are not going to be balkanised so that they can be manipulated, set against one another, kept perpetually weak, divided and ineffective by outside forces.

So, as far as we are concerned, we want to ensure a stable Southeast Asia not a balkanised Southeast Asia. And those countries who are interested, genuinely interested, in the stability of Southeast Asia, the prosperity in Southeast Asia, and better economic, and social conditions will welcome small countries getting together to pool their collective resources and their collective wisdom to contribute to the peace of the world. The more unstable Southeast Asia is, the more the peace of the world is also threatened.

So, I would urge people outside the region not to misunderstand this coming together of our five and other Southeast Asian countries. We want to ensure that ASEAN stands for the interests of ASEAN and therefore by implication for the peace and prosperity of the world. That is all we are interested in. And if other countries think of tomorrow and are willing to help us to achieve this objective, they will be welcomed as friends. And we will also be worthwhile friends to them.

However, in order to win over regard and respect from the outside world, we must first take ASEAN seriously ourselves. There are a lot of people watching what all this is going to amount to. So first we must take our own child seriously. We must convince those that are watching us that we are prepared to make the adjustments and sacrifices necessary to achieve our objective and we are serious about it. The message must get through that this time the Southeast Asian countries are not going to be like the Balkans during the last two World Wars; that they are not going to be pushed around; once other nations take us seriously, just as we take ourselves seriously; once there is acceptance of our role as a united grouping of Asian countries, then we can bring peace and prosperity to this region as well as to the rest of the world.

1967 ASEAN Declaration

Adopted by the Foreign Ministers at the First ASEAN Ministerial Meeting in
Bangkok, Thailand on 8 August 1967
http://asean.org/the-asean-declaration-bangkok-declaration-bangkok-8-
august-1967/

⌒ ﻌ ⌒

The Presidium Minister for Political Affairs/ Minister for Foreign Affairs
of Indonesia, the Deputy Prime Minister of Malaysia, the Secretary of
Foreign Affairs of the Philippines, the Minister for Foreign Affairs of
Singapore and the Minister of Foreign Affairs of Thailand:

MINDFUL of the existence of mutual interests and common problems
among countries of South-East Asia and convinced of the need to
strengthen further the existing bonds of regional solidarity and cooperation;

DESIRING to establish a firm foundation for common action to promote regional cooperation in South-East Asia in the spirit of equality
and partnership and thereby contribute towards peace, progress and
prosperity in the region;

CONSCIOUS that in an increasingly interdependent world, the cher-
ished ideals of peace, freedom, social justice and economic well-being
are best attained by fostering good understanding, good neighbourliness
and meaningful cooperation among the countries of the region already
bound together by ties of history and culture;

CONSIDERING that the countries of South East Asia share a primary
responsibility for strengthening the economic and social stability of the
region and ensuring their peaceful and progressive national development, and that they are determined to ensure their stability and security

from external interference in any form or manifestation in order to preserve their national identities in accordance with the ideals and aspirations of their peoples;

AFFIRMING that all foreign bases are temporary and remain only with the expressed concurrence of the countries concerned and are not intended to be used directly or indirectly to subvert the national independence and freedom of States in the area or prejudice the orderly processes of their national development;

DO HEREBY DECLARE:

FIRST, the establishment of an Association for Regional Cooperation among the countries of South-East Asia to be known as the Association of South-East Asian Nations (ASEAN).

SECOND, that the aims and purposes of the Association shall be:
1. To accelerate the economic growth, social progress and cultural development in the region through joint endeavours in the spirit of equality and partnership in order to strengthen the foundation for a prosperous and peaceful community of South-East Asian Nations;
2. To promote regional peace and stability through abiding respect for justice and the rule of law in the relationship among countries of the region and adherence to the principles of the United Nations Charter;
3. To promote active collaboration and mutual assistance on matters of common interest in the economic, social, cultural, technical, scientific and administrative fields;
4. To provide assistance to each other in the form of training and research facilities in the educational, professional, technical and administrative spheres;
5. To collaborate more effectively for the greater utilization of their agriculture and industries, the expansion of their trade, including the study of the problems of international commodity trade, the improvement of their transportation and communications facilities and the raising of the living standards of their peoples;

6. To promote South-East Asian studies;
7. To maintain close and beneficial cooperation with existing international and regional organizations with similar aims and purposes, and explore all avenues for even closer cooperation among themselves.

THIRD, that to carry out these aims and purposes, the following machinery shall be established:

(a) Annual Meeting of Foreign Ministers, which shall be by rotation and referred to as ASEAN Ministerial Meeting. Special Meetings of Foreign Ministers may be convened as required.

(b) A Standing committee, under the chairmanship of the Foreign Minister of the host country or his representative and having as its members the accredited Ambassadors of the other member countries, to carry on the work of the Association in between Meetings of Foreign Ministers.

(c) Ad-Hoc Committees and Permanent Committees of specialists and officials on specific subjects.

(d) A National Secretariat in each member country to carry out the work of the Association on behalf of that country and to service the Annual or Special Meetings of Foreign Ministers, the Standing Committee and such other committees as may hereafter be established.

FOURTH, that the Association is open for participation to all States in the South-East Asian Region subscribing to the aforementioned aims, principles and purposes.

FIFTH, that the Association represents the collective will of the nations of South-East Asia to bind themselves together in friendship and cooperation and, through joint efforts and sacrifices, secure for their peoples and for posterity the blessings of peace, freedom and prosperity.

DONE in Bangkok on the Eighth Day of August in the Year One Thousand Nine Hundred and Sixty-Seven.

For the Republic of Indonesia :

ADAM MALIK
Presidium Minister for Political
Minister for Foreign Affairs

For the Republic of Singapore :

S. RAJARATNAM
Minister of Foreign Affairs

For Malaysia :

TUN ABDUL RAZAK
Deputy Prime Minister,
Minister of Defence and
Minister of National Development

For the Kingdom of Thailand :

THANAT KHOMAN
Minister of Foreign Affairs

For the Republic of the Philippines :

NARCISO RAMOS
Secretary of Foreign Affairs

2007 Singapore Declaration on the ASEAN Charter

Adopted in Singapore on 20 November 2007

❧

WE, the Heads of State/Government of Brunei Darussalam, the Kingdom of Cambodia, the Republic of Indonesia, the Lao People's Democratic Republic, Malaysia, the Union of Myanmar, the Republic of the Philippines, the Republic of Singapore, the Kingdom of Thailand and the Socialist Republic of Viet Nam, Member Countries of ASEAN, on the occasion of the 40th Anniversary of ASEAN and the 13th ASEAN Summit in Singapore;

REAFFIRMING our conviction, as expressed in the Kuala Lumpur Declaration on the Establishment of the ASEAN Charter on 12 December 2005 and the Cebu Declaration on the Blueprint of the ASEAN Charter on 13 January 2007, that the Charter shall serve as a legal and institutional framework, as well as an inspiration for ASEAN in the years ahead;

REITERATING our full resolve and commitment to narrow the development gap and to advance ASEAN integration through the creation of an ASEAN Community in furtherance of peace, progress and prosperity of its peoples; and

HAVING SIGNED the ASEAN Charter;

DO HEREBY DECLARE:

To faithfully respect the rights and fulfil the obligations outlined in the provisions of the ASEAN Charter;

To complete ratification by all Member Countries as soon as possible in order to bring the ASEAN Charter into force; and

To undertake all appropriate measures in each Member Country to implement the ASEAN Charter.

ADOPTED in Singapore, this Twentieth Day of November in the Year Two Thousand and Seven.

https://cil.nus.edu.sg/2007/2007-charter-of-the-association-of-southeast-asian-nations-signed-on-20-november-2007-in-singapore-by-the-heads-of-stategovernment/

Key ASEAN Acronyms

༄༅

Selected ASEAN Institutions

ACC	ASEAN Coordinating Council
ACB	ASEAN Centre for Biodiversity
ACE	ASEAN Centre for Energy
ACWC	ASEAN Committee on Women and Children
ADF	ASEAN Development Fund
ADMM	ASEAN Defence Ministers' Meeting
AEC	ASEAN Economic Community
AEM	ASEAN Economic Ministers
AF	ASEAN Foundation
AFMM	ASEAN Finance Ministers Meeting
AFTA	ASEAN Free Trade Area
AHA Centre	ASEAN Coordinating Centre for Humanitarian Assistance on Disaster Management
AHMM	ASEAN Health Ministers Meeting
AICHR	ASEAN Inter-Governmental Commission on Human Rights
AIF	ASEAN Infrastructure Fund
AIPA	ASEAN Inter-Parliamentary Assembly (formerly ASEAN Inter-Parliamentary Organization)
AIPR	ASEAN Institute for Peace and Reconciliation
ALAWMM	ASEAN Law Ministers Meeting

ALMM	ASEAN Labour Ministers Meeting
AMAF	ASEAN Ministerial Meeting on Agriculture and Forestry
AMBDC	ASEAN Mekong Basin Development Coordination
AMCA	ASEAN Ministers Responsible for Culture & Arts
AMEM	ASEAN Ministers on Energy Meeting
AMM	ASEAN Foreign Ministers' Meeting (formerly ASEAN Ministerial Meeting)
AMMDM	ASEAN Ministerial Meeting on Disaster Management
AMME	ASEAN Ministerial Meeting on Environment
AMMin	ASEAN Ministerial Meeting on Minerals
AMMS	ASEAN Ministerial Meeting on Sports
AMMST	ASEAN Ministerial Meeting on Science and Technology
AMMSWD	ASEAN Ministerial Meeting on Social Welfare and Development
AMMTC	ASEAN Ministerial Meeting on Transnational Crime
AMMW	ASEAN Ministerial Meeting on Women
AMMY	ASEAN Ministerial Meeting on Youth
AMRDPE	ASEAN Ministers Meeting on Rural Development and Poverty Eradication
AMRI	ASEAN Ministers Responsible for Information
APSC	ASEAN Political-Security Community (formerly ASEAN Security Community, ASC)
ARC	ASEAN Resource Centre
AREPG	ASEAN-Russia Eminent Persons Group
ARMAC	ASEAN Regional Mine Action Centre
ARF	ASEAN Regional Forum
ASC	ASEAN Standing Committee
ASCC	ASEAN Socio-Cultural Community
ASMC	ASEAN Specialised Meteorological Centre
ASEANAPOL	Chiefs of ASEAN Police
ASEAN-ISIS	ASEAN Institute of Strategic and International Studies
ASEANTOM	ASEAN Network of Regulatory Bodies on Atomic Energy

ASEC	ASEAN Secretariat
ASED	ASEAN Education Ministers Meeting
ASOD	ASEAN Senior Officials on Drugs
ATM	ASEAN Transport Ministers Meeting
AUN	ASEAN University Network
CPR	Committee of Permanent Representatives to ASEAN
LSAD	ASEAN Secretariat Legal Services and Agreements Division
M-ATM	ASEAN Tourism Ministers Meeting
TELMIN	ASEAN Telecommunications and IT Ministers Meeting

Selected Documents

AADMER	ASEAN Agreement on Disaster Management and Response (2005)
AATHP	ASEAN Agreement on Transboundary Pollution (2002)
AC	ASEAN Charter (2007)
ACCT	ASEAN Convention on Counter Terrorism (2007)
ACTIP	ASEAN Convention on Trafficking in Persons (2015)
AHRD	ASEAN Human Rights Declaration (2012)
API	Agreement on the Privileges and Immunities of ASEAN (2009)
BC	Bali Concord, or Declaration on ASEAN Concord (BC I 1976, BC II 2003, BC III 2011)
COC	Code of Conduct on the South China Sea
DOC	Declaration on the Conduct of Parties in the South China Sea (2002)
HPA	Hanoi Plan of Action 1999–2004
MPAC	Master Plan on ASEAN Connectivity (2010)
SEANWFZ	Southeast Asian Nuclear Weapons-Free Zone (1995)
TAC	Treaty of Amity and Cooperation (1976)
ZOPFAN	Zone of Peace, Freedom and Neutrality Declaration (1971)

VAP   Vientiane Action Programme 2004–2010
V2020   Vision 2020 (1997)

Selected Terms

AMC/AMS   ASEAN Member Country/State
ASEAN-6   Brunei Darussalam, Indonesia, Malaysia, Singapore,
                   Philippines, Thailand
ASEAN-10   Brunei Darussalam, Cambodia, Indonesia, Lao
                   PDR, Malaysia, Myanmar, Singapore, Philippines,
                   Thailand, Viet Nam
CEP   Comprehensive Economic Partnership
CLMV   Cambodia, Laos, Myanmar, Viet Nam
COP   Conference of the Parties
DG   Director-General
DSG   Deputy Secretary-General (of ASEAN)
EPG   Eminent Persons Group
GSP   Generalised System of Preferences
HLTF   High Level Task Force
HOS/G   Heads of State/Government
IAI   Initiative for ASEAN Integration
NDG   Narrowing the Development Gap
PMC   Post-Ministerial Conference
ROP   Rules of Procedure
SG   Secretary-General (of ASEAN)
SOM   Senior Officials' Meeting
TOR   Terms of Reference
WG   Working Group

External Relations

AANZFTA   ASEAN-Australia-New Zealand Free Trade Area
ACFTA   ASEAN-China Free Trade Agreement (Also CAFTA)
AIFTA   ASEAN-India Free Trade Agreement
AJCEP   ASEAN-Japan Comprehensive Economic Partnership
                   Agreement

AKFTA	ASEAN-Korea Free Trade Agreement
APT/ASEAN+3	ASEAN Plus Three (China, Japan, Republic of Korea)
CMI	Chiang Mai Initiative
EAS	East Asia Summit
ERIA	Economic Research Institute for ASEAN and East Asia
RCEP	Regional Comprehensive Economic Partnership
TPP	Trans Pacific Partnership

ASEAN Economic Community

AATIP	ASEAN Air Transport Integration Project
ABAC	ASEAN Business Advisory Council
ABIF	ASEAN Banking Integration Framework
ACIA	ASEAN Comprehensive Investment Agreement (2009)
ACB	ASEAN Compliance Body (formerly ASEAN Compliance Monitoring Body)
ACT	ASEAN Consultation to Solve Trade and Investment Issues
AFAFGIT	ASEAN Framework Agreement on the Facilitation of Goods in Transit (1998)
AFAFIST	ASEAN Framework Agreement on the Facilitation of Inter-State Transport (2009)
AFAS	ASEAN Framework Agreement on Services (1995)
AHTN	ASEAN Harmonised Tariff Nomenclature
AIA	ASEAN Investment Area
AIPS	ASEAN Framework Agreement for the Integration of Priority Sectors (2004)
ASA	ASEAN Swap Arrangement
ASW	ASEAN Single Window
ATIGA	ASEAN Trade in Goods Agreement (2009)
CEPT	Common Effective Preferential Tariff (1992)
EDSM	Protocol on Enhanced Dispute Settlement Mechanism (2004)

MAAS	ASEAN Multilateral Agreement on Air Services (2009)
MAFLAFS	ASEAN Multilateral Agreement on the Full Liberalisation of Air Freight Services (2009)
MAFLPAS	ASEAN Multilateral Agreement on the Full Liberalisation of Passenger Air Services (2010)
MRA	Mutual Recognition Arrangement
PTA	Agreement on ASEAN Preferential Trading Arrangements (1977)
ROO	Rules of Origin
SEOM	Senior Economic Officials Meeting

ASEAN's Challenges

The 1976 Bali Summit: ASEAN Shifts Gears

Barry DESKER

The first ASEAN Summit (or ASEAN Heads of Government Meeting as it was initially called) was held in Bali, Indonesia, on 23–24 February 1976. This Summit led to the transformation of ASEAN and the decisions taken by the Summit have set a benchmark in ASEAN's evolution. A discussion of the decision to hold the Summit and its outcomes requires an appreciation of the genesis for the establishment of ASEAN in 1967, a recognition of the challenges faced by ASEAN in its formative years and the climate of uncertainty in the region following the emergence of communist regimes in Indochina in 1975, and an awareness that bilateral relationships among ASEAN Member States (AMS) at that time were uneasy and characterised by mutual suspicions.

Low Initial Expectations for ASEAN

ASEAN's establishment in August 1967 was marked by low expectations among its founding fathers. They were aware of the failed experiments in regional integration which preceded ASEAN, including the American-sponsored Southeast Asia Treaty Organization (SEATO) established in Manila in September 1954, the Association of Southeast Asia (ASA) formed in July 1961 by Malaya, Thailand and the Philippines, the still-born MAPHILINDO which linked Malaya, the Philippines and Indonesia formed in Manila in July 1963 as well as the British-supported Federation of Malaysia established in September 1963 which originally intended to unify peninsula Malaya, Singapore, Sarawak, Sabah and

Brunei. Brunei pulled out of the negotiations while Singapore, in an acrimonious split, separated from the Malaysian Federation in August 1965.

With the emergence of an anti-communist government in Indonesia led by President Suharto following the failed coup attempt by the Indonesian Communist Party (PKI) and dissident elements of the Indonesian armed forces on 1 October 1965, it was recognised that efforts should be made to integrate Indonesia into the region. For Malaysia and Singapore, Indonesia's policy under President Sukarno of *Konfrontasi* had resulted in a low intensity conflict from 1963 to 1966. This was highlighted by Indonesia's active campaign against international recognition of Malaysia, especially in the Third World, accompanied by improvised explosive devices laid by Indonesian saboteurs in Singapore and Malaysian towns, failed parachute and seaborne landings by Indonesian commandos in Johor and an armed conflict on the Borneo border between Indonesia and Malaysia. ASEAN was seen as a means of integrating Indonesia into the region and laying the foundations for a stable regional relationship. As a treaty partner of the United States, Thailand was worried about the possible spillover of the ongoing American war in Vietnam and the bloody civil war in Laos and it sought support from a group of neighbours who were themselves battling communist insurgency movements. The Philippine leadership in the early 1960s under President Diosdado Macapagal had a romantic vision of re-integrating with the Malay world, a perspective which underpinned Manila's interest in ethnic regional associations. His successor, President Ferdinand Marcos, was keen on a foreign policy more independent of the United States and ASEAN provided such a vehicle.

The difference in 1967 was that the establishment of ASEAN was seen as reinforcing the ability of these relatively weak, newly independent states to overcome external threats and to stabilise bilateral relationships. Mutual suspicions among the member states did not bode well for the future of the new organisation. The backdrop included the Philippines' territorial claim to Sabah, which had joined the Federation of Malaysia, Malaysian support for Muslim separatists in southern Thailand and Thai connivance with Malayan Communist Party insurgents who had taken refuge in southern Thailand and were engaged in a renewed insurgency south of the border, continuing Malaysian suspicions of Indonesian ambitions for a greater Indonesia (Indonesia Raya) while Indonesia was fearful of Singapore, perceived to be a Third China. Since independence, Malaysia and Singapore had relied on the British military presence as a security shield. The British Labour Government's decision in January 1968 to withdraw British military forces by spring 1971 highlighted the need for alternative arrangements by Malaysia and Singapore and the desirability of improved links with their immediate neighbours. Finally, the gel which linked these states was the concern that the region was a cockpit of conflict and ASEAN's establishment came at a time when there was considerable discussion of the "domino theory", the belief that a successful communist take-over of Vietnam would lead to the fall of the other states in the region to communist regimes. As pro-Western states, there was apprehension among the AMS that the combination of domestic communist insurgencies and external communist advances could undermine their security and stability.

External Threats Fostered Closer Cooperation

In its early years, ASEAN learnt the habit of cooperation. At independence, the ties of each of its member states were stronger with their former colonial powers than with its neighbours, while Thailand which was nominally independent during the colonial era, was an ally of the United States. ASEAN was essentially an instrument of the foreign ministries of the five member states and ASEAN's focus in its formative years was on foreign policy issues. There was very little contact among the other Ministries and Heads of Government/State only met bilaterally outside the ASEAN framework. While ASEAN had few significant achievements, the absence of conflict among its member states in a region regarded as the Balkans of the East led ASEAN's promoters to commend its founding fathers for their vision. For Singapore, emerging from its traumatic exit from Malaysia, ASEAN meetings provided an opportunity to engage Malaysian foreign policy makers at a time when bilateral ties were strained. After Singapore's hanging of two Indonesian marines in 1968 for the MacDonald House bombings in 1964, ASEAN provided a cover for informal Indonesia-Singapore bilateral contacts. Similarly, other ASEAN members used the umbrella provided by ASEAN meetings to maintain their ties with neighbours, even in the worst of times in their bilateral relationships, as seen in the Malaysia-Philippines contacts despite their frosty relationship arising from the Philippines' claim to Sabah.

The conflicts in Indochina weighed heavily on the ASEAN countries and were a major focus of attention during meetings of the ASEAN Foreign Ministers. While Malaysia adopted a pro-Western policy under Prime Minister Tunku Abdul Rahman, his successor, Tun Abdul Razak Hussein called for the neutralisation of Southeast Asia and convened a meeting of the ASEAN Foreign Ministers in Kuala Lumpur in November 1971, which proposed the establishment of a Zone of Peace, Freedom and Neutrality in Southeast Asia (ZOPFAN). In the Kuala Lumpur Declaration, the Ministers agreed to keep South East Asia "free from any form or manner of interference by outside Powers". While Malaysia joined Indonesia in seeking the exclusion of major powers from the region, Thailand and the Philippines, which were participating as American allies in the war in Vietnam, were intent on maintaining the status quo. Singapore argued for a continuing role for major powers to ensure a balance of power in the region. ASEAN foreign policy experts spent the next four years negotiating the ZOPFAN framework.

While Singapore had minimal diplomatic links with the competing Vietnamese groupings, Singapore enjoyed excellent relations with the Prince Sihanouk's Cambodian regime. His overthrow by a pro-American military coup led by Lon Nol in March 1971 presaged the widening of the Indochinese war. Although Indonesia pressed its ASEAN partners to join in intervening in the Cambodian conflict at the April 1971 Jakarta Conference on Cambodia, Singapore resisted these pressures. As domestic pressures led the United States towards seeking a face-saving negotiated peace settlement followed by American military withdrawal, the ASEAN states recognised that they needed to adjust to the changing regional environment. Following the Paris Peace Accords in January 1973, all ASEAN countries established diplomatic relations with Vietnam, which had previously only had ties with Indonesia.

The changing dynamics in the region can be seen in Malaysia's decision to establish diplomatic relations with China in 1974, following the visit of US President Nixon to China in February 1972. US-China relations rapidly improved. The Philippines and Thailand followed Malaysia in establishing diplomatic relations in June and July 1975 respectively. By contrast, Singapore took the view that it would be the last country in ASEAN to establish relations with China and would do so "after Indonesia" to allay Indonesian fears that Singapore was a Third China, even though Foreign Minister S. Rajaratnam made his first visit to China in June 1975, followed by Prime Minister Lee Kuan Yew in May 1976. Developments in Indochina and American withdrawal from the region influenced the turn towards China by Singapore and the other AMS.

Responding to the Emergence of Communist States in Indochina

When the Khmer Rouge took over Phnom Penh on 17 April 1975, Thailand pushed ASEAN members for a joint recognition of the new regime by 0700 hours (Bangkok time) the following morning. This was done. On 30 April 1975, when Saigon fell to the Democratic Republic of Vietnam (DRV) forces, Thailand once again took the lead in seeking joint ASEAN recognition of the Provisional Revolutionary Government (PRG) of South Vietnam by 0700 hours (Bangkok time) the following morning. Lee Chiong Giam and I were the senior officers in the Foreign Ministry handling the issue (although we were barely 34 and 28 years old respectively) and went to the home of the Minister for Foreign Affairs, Mr. S. Rajaratnam, at 1.00 am in the morning. Mr. Rajaratnam took the firm view that ASEAN should respond in a measured style, without the appearance of panic or fear. He opposed an immediate joint recognition, arguing against acceptance of the political fiction represented by the PRG. For Mr. Rajaratnam, a contest of political wills was beginning in Southeast Asia and ASEAN should not be seen as caving in at the very onset of the struggle. By taking a firm position in the discussions among the ASEAN countries, a critical aspect in shaping a discussion in a situation of uncertainty, Singapore helped to shape the ASEAN position against separate recognition of the PRG. All five ASEAN states had already established diplomatic relations with the DRV. The failure of the manoeuvre led Vietnam to eventually push for unification as the Socialist Republic of Vietnam and a single application for membership in the United Nations.

President Marcos of the Philippines proposed the holding of an ASEAN Summit in April 1975 as the DRV swept south towards Saigon in a rapid advance. At the Eighth ASEAN Ministerial Meeting in Kuala Lumpur held from 13 to 15 May 1975, the Foreign Ministers agreed to convene the inaugural ASEAN Heads of Government Meeting. Although the public statements of the Ministers "expressed their readiness to enter into friendly and harmonious relationships with each nation in Indochina", the ASEAN states were concerned that the communist victories would embolden their domestic communist parties and lead to a flow of weapons and ammunition. There was a sharp increase in insurgent activities in north and north-eastern Thailand as well as southern Thailand. In Malaysia, the Inspector General of Police was killed in a drive-by shooting in June 1974, assassinations of Special Branch officers occurred and the National Monument in Kuala Lumpur commemorating the end of the Malayan Emergency (the communist insurrection) was blown up in August 1975. In Singapore, a car bomb exploded prematurely killing two of the bombers in December 1974. The establishment of martial law in the Philippines in September 1972 was Marcos' response to the rise of the pro-Maoist New People's Army insurgency, which gained support as the tide turned in Indochina.

Negotiations Leading to the First ASEAN Summit

In the lead-up to the Summit, Malaysia and Thailand pushed for ASEAN's expansion to encompass the Indochinese countries and Burma. Malaysia saw such a move as an extension of its neutralisation policy while Thailand under Prime Minister Kukrit Pramoj was keen on rapidly adjusting to the communist victories in Indochina. Kukrit Pramoj set a deadline of 31 January 1976 for the closure of the American air bases and the withdrawal of US personnel, which was eventually extended to

20 July 1976. By contrast, President Suharto of Indonesia was suspicious of all communist regimes and the Indonesian military was pushing for ASEAN defence and security cooperation to counter external threats. Although security concerns underpinned ASEAN cooperation, all five ASEAN Leaders emphasised enhanced economic cooperation as the justification for the Summit. The Philippines and Singapore pushed for the establishment of an ASEAN Free Trade Area (AFTA), with across the board tariff cuts, but there was strong resistance from Indonesia, which was wary of opening the Indonesian market and feared that domestic Indonesian industry was uncompetitive.

Senior Foreign Affairs officials met regularly from September 1975, generally for a week, followed by two weeks at home, to discuss and draft the Summit declarations and documents. As there was no permanent ASEAN Secretariat (ASEC) at that time, each country took turns to host these meetings. As one of the young officers involved in drafting, together with See Chak Mun and Kishore Mahbubani, these frequent meetings and informal exchanges over meals with our counterparts, such as Nitya Pibulsonggram and Sawanit Kongsiri of Thailand, Zain Azraai and Bertie Talalla of Malaysia, Brigadier General Adenan, Major General R. H. Purnomo and Janner Sinaga of Indonesia, and Rosario Manalo, Alberto Encomienda, Sonia Brady and Alicia Ramos of the Philippines, created bonds of friendship and mutual understanding. From 1968, ASEAN meetings tended to be attended by the ASEAN Directorates in each of the capitals, which were staffed by relatively weak officers in each country, reflecting the low emphasis placed on ASEAN in its early years. By comparison, the participants in the Summit drafting groups were among the best in their own services and their paths frequently crossed over the next 30 years. They recognised that ASEAN faced major challenges and that new policy approaches were necessary.

Major Outcomes of the Summit

A major outcome of the Summit was the conclusion of the Treaty of Amity and Cooperation. Three aspects should be highlighted as TAC became a foundational instrument for ASEAN in the following decades. First, in a gesture towards the non-ASEAN members, it included a proviso that the Treaty "shall be open for accession by other States in Southeast Asia". Accession to TAC was part of the process of integrating Cambodia, Laos, Myanmar and Vietnam into TAC after the end of the Cold War in 1990 and as a peace settlement was reached on the conflict in Cambodia. Second, a critical aspect was the inclusion of a provision for the peaceful settlement of disputes through the establishment of a ministerial-level High Council of the parties to the Treaty. As Malaysia feared that the Philippines would use this clause of the Treaty to advance its claim to Sabah, it insisted that issues could only be taken up with the agreement of all parties to the dispute. In practice, the AMS avoided the use of regional mechanisms and did not use the Treaty provisions in intra-regional disputes, preferring to turn to bilateral negotiations and international fora such as the International Court of Justice (ICJ) and the International Tribunal for the Law of the Sea (ITLOS). Third, Indonesia expended considerable political capital to promote the idea of national and regional resilience in the Treaty as the underpinning for enhanced regional cooperation. While initially presented largely within a security framework, which concerned Malaysia and Singapore, in particular, the concept of national resilience was eventually defined in Article 11 of the TAC as cooperation "in their political, economic, socio-cultural as well as security fields in conformity with their respective ideals and aspirations, free from external interference as well as internal subversive activities in order to preserve their respective national identities". In later years, the concept of national resilience won wide acceptance within ASEAN policy elites, despite earlier misgivings.

The key document resulting from the Summit was the Bali Declaration of ASEAN Concord. The ASEAN Leaders were focused on ensuring stability and the Declaration committed each member state to resolve to eliminate threats posed by subversion to their stability. The political provisions included a commitment to settle intra-regional dif-ferences by peaceful means, immediate consideration of initial steps towards recognition of, and respect for, the ZOPFAN, a reference to the possibility of an ASEAN Extradition Treaty as well as the establishment of the machinery for ASEAN cooperation.

While Indonesia pushed for a substantive section on security cooperation which included regular meetings of ASEAN defence ministers and senior officials, joint ASEAN training exercises, coordination in procurement, exchanges of defence personnel and establishment of an ASEAN defence college, the final document only referred to "cooperation on a non-ASEAN basis between the member states in security matters in accordance with their mutual needs and interests." This provision led to the long delay in the convening of meetings of the ASEAN Defence Ministers, which only occurred in 2006 after the adoption of the Plan of Action of the ASEAN Security Community (ASC) at the 10th ASEAN Summit in November 2004. This reflected the wariness in 1976 of the other AMS, especially Malaysia and Singapore, that Indonesia would attempt to play the role of the dominant regional power in ASEAN after American military withdrawal in the region, while Thailand was concerned that a confrontational approach would be taken towards the victorious Indochinese powers, especially Vietnam.

The economic provisions were severely watered down. Singapore led the push for an AFTA, with 10 to 15% tariff cuts, which was supported by the Philippines, Thailand and Malaysia but was strongly opposed by Indonesia. President Suharto feared that Indonesia would be flooded with foreign imports, undermining its efforts to build its domestic industries. Although President Suharto did not throw his weight around and sought consensus decisions, he won the trust and respect of Prime Minister Lee Kuan Yew and other ASEAN Leaders because he could be relied upon to uphold his commitments. At the Summit-level, the Leaders sought what was possible, not the ideal outcomes, for their own countries. Thus President Suharto's objections led to the derailing of proposals for an AFTA at this first ASEAN Summit in 1976 (but his support resulted in the declaration at the fourth ASEAN Summit held in Singapore in 1992 that an AFTA would be established within 15 years). The Summit also agreed on regular meetings of economic ministers, cooperation in the establishment of large-scale industrial plants, collaboration in facing global economic issues, especially in the supply of basic commodities such as food and energy, while a preferential trading arrangement was seen as a long-term objective. While these results were a let-down for Singapore, the placing of economic issues firmly on the ASEAN agenda at the Summit and Ministerial levels was seen as an opportunity to build on the results of the Bali discussions. One immediate result was that ASEAN increasingly coordinated on economic issues at international meetings such as the annual conference of the International Labour Organization (ILO), meetings of the General Agreement on Tariffs and Trade in Geneva and the United Nations Conference on Trade and Development (UNCTAD).

The expansion beyond the political, economic and security realm was seen in references to cooperation against drug trafficking, support for Southeast Asian studies through collaboration among national institutes and calls for cooperation in social development. Institutionally, such references provided the basis for meetings of ministers or senior officials in these areas after 1976.

On the administrative front, the Leaders agreed to establish a secretariat in Jakarta. This marked a major shift in ASEAN as there was earlier resistance to a permanent secretariat and the seat of the secretariat rotated annually, following the current Chair of ASEAN. One weakness was the reluctance to fund the secretariat. Instead of adopting the UN formula for the payment of annual contributions, it was finally agreed at the Bali Summit that Member States would make equal contributions, resulting in low levels of secretariat funding. While Indonesia nominated itself as the host country and offered an impressive building as the site of the secretariat, the lack of funding resulted initially in a thinly manned secretariat staffed by officers who were still coming to grips with what ASEAN stood for and what could be achieved. The first ASEAN Secretary-General (SG) was Lieutenant General H. R. Dharsono from Indonesia, who was introduced at the Summit and subsequently appointed for a five-year term. But Dharsono only served until early 1978 as he incurred the wrath of President Suharto for supporting Indonesian student demands opposing Suharto's re-election for a third term as President. Indonesia pushed successfully for his removal from office.

Progress by ASEAN — Slowly but Surely

What started as a fledging organisation, ASEAN, in its own ways, began to make important contributions. Tan Sri M. Ghazali Shafie, Malaysia's

Minister of Home Affairs from 1973 to 1981 and Minister of Foreign Affairs from 1981 to 1984, revealed in a speech at the Fletcher School of Law and Diplomacy in November 1981 that the Bali Declaration of ASEAN Concord had a confidential companion paper. According to Ghazali, this paper "described the developments in Southeast Asia following the American withdrawal from the region, and which examined ways on how ASEAN could respond to them. Special attention was focused on the situation in Kampuchea (Cambodia), particularly to the position of the Chinese and Soviets which seemed to have brought Kampuchea to a new stage of fluidity. ASEAN decided in favour of prudence and to wait a little longer before taking a definite position collectively."

Ghazali went on to argue that "ASEAN used this confidential document extensively in formulating the ASEAN Concord, and the Heads of Government alluded to it in the Joint Press Statement in the following manner:

> "They discussed developments affecting the ASEAN region. They reaffirmed the determination of their respective Governments to continue to work for the promotion of peace, stability and progress in Southeast Asia, thus contributing towards world peace and international harmony. To this end, they expressed the hope that other powers would pursue policies which would contribute to the achievement of peace, stability and progress in Southeast Asia."

Ghazali concluded that "ASEAN was becoming an important political force for stability in Southeast Asia".

Underlying Tensions at the Bali Summit

Besides Malaysian suspicions as a result of the Sabah Question, the Singapore-Indonesia relationship was also strained at that time over Singapore's abstention in a vote on Indonesia's invasion and occupation of East Timor in December 1975. All other AMS had voted against, following Indonesia. The Indonesian military had pushed for the invasion of East Timor as it was perceived as a security threat because of the replacement of the Portuguese colonial administration by the left wing Fretelin movement sympathetic to African revolutionary movements. Fretelin's take-over was regarded by President Suharto as a communist thrust into the soft underbelly of Indonesia. This resulted in a cool Indonesian reception of Singapore in Bali compared to an earlier visit to Bali by Prime Minister Lee Kuan Yew for a bilateral meeting with President Suharto in September 1975.

The Philippines under President Marcos focused more on the glitzy aspects of conference decisions. Marcos was more interested in the presentation and the publicity and was less concerned with the policy outcomes and the longer term impact of decisions at the Summit. Malaysian Prime Minister Hussein Onn had just assumed office after the passing away of Tun Abdul Razak in January 1976. He was wary of Marcos and stiff in responding to President Suharto. His officials pushed for strong references to ZOPFAN, suggesting a continuity of policy with Tun Abdul Razak, and strongly opposed Indonesian efforts to include defence cooperation within the ASEAN framework. Thai Prime Minister Kukrit Pramoj took a firmer position in Bali compared to earlier bilateral meetings in Bangkok and on his visits to ASEAN countries. He was focused on the threats posed by the emergence of communist regimes in Indochina. Following negative interactions with a Vietnamese delegation that had visited Bangkok and his visit to China in July 1975 which led to the establishment of diplomatic relations with China. Kukrit appeared confident of Chinese support in the event of a threat from Vietnam, China's erstwhile ally during the Vietnam War. There was a sense that Thailand was moving towards seeking a closer alignment with China.

President Suharto had a critical role in the success of the Summit. He played the gracious host but was firm in underlining areas of concern to Indonesia. The ASEAN Leaders began to recognise that he would uphold commitments that he had made. At this point, however, he listened more to his officials and was closely guided by them, especially on economic issues. When he saw that there was strenuous opposition to Indonesian initiatives such as the bid for formal ASEAN defence cooperation, he did not push the Indonesian position and agreed to set aside their proposals. Because of his approach, other ASEAN Leaders regarded Indonesia as the first among equals and deferred to him, as seen in the decisions to locate the ASEC in Jakarta and to agree that an Indonesian would be the first ASEAN SG.

A Game Changer

In retrospect, the first ASEAN Heads of Government Meeting, or the Bali Summit as it was called later, marked a shift in ASEAN's trajectory. While ASEAN had been on the back burner in its capitals in the initial years, after Bali in 1976, the pace of ASEAN political cooperation intensified. Although economic, social and cultural cooperation was the avowed objective of ASEAN, economic cooperation would proceed at a slow pace while socio-cultural cooperation was accorded an even lower priority. The perceived challenge from the emergence of a communist Indochina in 1975 shaped ASEAN's response. Closer political cooperation created a sense of security and stability in the region. Although critics derided ASEAN for failing to embark on substantial economic cooperation, the Bali Summit laid the groundwork for closer political cooperation and the emergence of ASEAN as the most successful regional organisation after the European Union.

Barry DESKER is Distinguished Fellow at the S. Rajaratnam School of International Studies (RSIS), Nanyang Technological University. He is a Member of the Presidential Council for Minority Rights, Singapore, a Member of the Board of Directors of the Lee Kuan Yew Exchange Fellowship and Singapore's Representative to the ASEAN Inter-Governmental Commission on Human Rights (AICHR). From 2000 to 2014, he was the Director, Institute of Defence and Strategic Studies and served as founding Dean of RSIS from 2007 to 2014. He was the Chief Executive Officer of the Singapore Trade Development Board from 1994 to 2000 and Singapore's Ambassador to Indonesia from 1986 to 1993. Ambassador Desker is currently also Non-Resident Ambassador of Singapore to the Holy See and Spain. A President's Scholar, he was educated at the University of Singapore, University of London and Cornell University. He was awarded an honorary Doctor of Letters by Warwick University in 2012 and Doctor of Laws by the University of Exeter in 2013.

ASEAN and the Cambodian Conflict, 1978–1991[1]

ANG Cheng Guan

෴

Vietnam invaded Kampuchea on 25 December 1978. On 8 January 1979, the Vietnamese-installed government in Phnom Penh announced the formation of the Khmer People's Revolutionary Party (KPRP) that included Heng Samrin as the President, Hun Sen as Minister of Foreign Affairs and Chea Sim as Minister of the Interior. It was clearly against international law. The Vietnamese, however, calculated that, as Ha Van Lau the Vietnamese Permanent Representative to the United Nations, told his Singapore counterpart at the United Nations, Tommy Koh, "in two weeks, the world will have forgotten the Kampuchean problem".[2] Hanoi had envisaged an invasion that resembled the Soviet invasions of Hungary and Czechoslovakia — "a quick blitzkrieg operation, destruction of all resistance, rapid establishment of a *fait accompli* that would survive the (brief) world condemnation…"[2] Hanoi further believed that the horrors of the Khmer Rouge regime under Pol Pot would also soften international criticisms and objections. Unfortunately for the Vietnamese, it was not to be because of ASEAN's determined efforts over the next decade to foil the Vietnamese plan.

---

[1] This essay is summarised from Ang Cheng Guan, *Singapore, ASEAN and the Cambodian Conflict, 1978–1991* (Singapore: NUS Press, 2013).

[2] K. Mahbubani, "The Kampuchean Problem: A Southeast Asian Perspective", *Foreign Affairs*, Vol. 62, No. 2, 1983–1984.

ASEAN sprang into action almost immediately after the invasion. On 12 January 1979, a special ASEAN Foreign Ministers closed-door meeting was convened in Bangkok, capital of Thailand, the country most anxious about the implications of the Vietnamese invasion given its geographical proximity and its role during the Vietnam War, to discuss the invasion. Although the Bangkok meeting was called by the Thai Prime Minister Kriangsak Chomanan, the idea of the meeting was initiated by S. Rajaratnam, the Foreign Minister of Singapore — the other Southeast Asian country which was most distressed by the invasion. For Singapore, "Cambodia's problems could become Singapore's problems in the future".[3] Singapore and Thailand played key roles in leading the rest of the ASEAN members to ensure that the invasion would not be forgotten in two weeks as the Vietnamese had hoped.

ASEAN did not envisage an eventual military solution to the Kampuchean problem. As S. R. Nathan, then-Permanent Secretary, Singapore Ministry of Foreign Affairs noted, "it was a political, rather than a military war which was waged in Kampuchea",[4] a view similarly expressed by the Minister for Defence Goh Keng Swee who predicted that the Vietnamese would have to seek a political settlement in Kampuchea,[5] and the Minister for Foreign Affairs S. Rajaratnam who explained that "all wars must end through a political act" thus the political warfare in Kampuchea needed to be maintained. The Vietnamese, he said, would only give up the fight when they were convinced that they were not winning the war, and it would be a matter of time before losing it.[6]

It was recognised from the very beginning that the Kampuchean problem was complex and would take time to resolve, but no one was sure of how long it would be. The immediate priority was to deny the

[3]Notes of conversation between PS Mr. Chia Cheong Fook and Mr. Sam Rainsy (Advisor to Prince Sihanouk), Ministry of Foreign Affairs, 4 March 1983.
[4]Notes of conversation between 1PS and Edith Lenart, journalist for *The Economist* and *Sunday Times* (Paris), 18 December 1979.
[5]"The Vietnam War: Round 3", in *Wealth of East Asian Nations: Speeches and Writings by Goh Keng Swee*, ed. Linda Goh (Singapore: Federal Publications, 1995), 312.
[6]Notes of meeting between Minister and Madam Ieng Thirith, Minister of Social Affairs of DK, Delegate Lounge of the UN in Geneva, 27 May 1980.

Vietnamese legitimacy; it was "one step at a time, one battle at a time."[7] As Nathan described, "there could be no solution as long the PRC and the Soviet Union were involved in protecting their respective interests". Nathan thought that it would be up to the Soviets to decide the cost factor; there was a possibility that they would decide at some point in the future to put a stop as the Soviets were known not to put everything into one basket. Without Soviet assistance, Vietnamese determination would reach its limits.[4]

ASEAN believed that the United States was the only country which could provide aid to the non-communist side which could match that of the Soviet Union to Vietnam or China to the Khmer Rouge.[8] However, there were little expectations of the American role at the initial stage. The United States had not overcome the "Vietnam syndrome", American officials were both doubtful of the capabilities of the non-communist forces and ASEAN's ability to stay the course. Washington also did not want to complicate US-China relations despite Singapore's repeated argument that United States should do more to increase Thai options and reduce Bangkok's dependence on the Chinese for its security against Vietnam. In 1981, the top priority was to initiate the flow of funding and then attempt to gain commitment from Washington. Since 1981, Singapore had been lobbying for increased American assistance to the non-communist forces. Both Singapore's foreign minister Rajaratnam and his successor Dhanabalan, during their visits to Washington, stressed to American leaders and officials the vital role of the US in building up a credible non-communist force in Cambodia.[9]

It is often misunderstood that ASEAN supported the Khmer Rouge. The reality was that the Khmer Rouge was the only effective fighting force against the Vietnamese and it would have been impossible to oust the invaders without a tactical alliance with the Khmer

---

[7] Dhanabalan interview, 1994, B 001500/09, Senior ASEAN Statesmen Oral History Interviews (Singapore: Oral History Centre, 1998).

[8] Visit of PM Son Sann to Singapore (9–14 March 1984), *Information Note on Kampuchea*, 22 March 1984.

[9] US Support for Non-communist Khmer Groups, *Information Note on Kampuchea*, 23 October 1981.

Rouge. In fact, neither the Pol Pot regime nor the Heng Samrin government were acceptable to the major powers, including ASEAN. This was
why Singapore felt the most urgency to form a united front or coalition
government — what came to be known as the CGDK or Coalition
Government of Democratic Kampuchea. Lee Kuan Yew argued that by
forming a coalition, and by receiving ASEAN support, Sihanouk's and
Son Sann's forces could offer the Kampuchean people alternative lead-
erships to Pol Pot or Heng Samrin. Although a Democratic Kampuchean
coalition government would help the Khmer Rouge gain international
acceptability, in the longer term, it would increase the likelihood of the
non-communist forces returning to Phnom Penh through free elections and a political settlement acceptable to both Vietnam and China
and diminish the chances of the Khmer Rouge returning to power by
force. Lee emphasised that ASEAN would not be a party to any plan to
restore the Khmer Rouge to power by force and against the will of the
Cambodian people.[10]

The resolution of the Cambodian problem is generally considered a
diplomatic triumph for ASEAN. It tested ASEAN's solidarity from 1978
to 1991.[11] Over those years, there was broad agreement within ASEAN,
but there were also deep divisions which the members did manage to
overcome. The situation in Bangkok was complex. When Prem
Tinsulanonda became Prime Minister in April 1980, Thai policy towards
Cambodia shifted from a policy of détente with the communist
Indochinese states, as practiced by his predecessor Kriangsak Chomanan,
to a strongly anti-Vietnamese one.[12] Lee believed that "without Prem as
prime minister and Siddhi Savetsila as foreign minister, we would not
have been able to cooperate so closely and successfully to tie the

---

[10]Text of an interview with Prime Minister Lee Kuan Yew by Derek Davies, editor,
and Susumu Awanohara, correspondent of *Far Eastern Economic Review*, Istana Office
Wing, 16 October 1981.

[11]Lee Kuan Yew, *From Third World to First: The Singapore Story: 1965–2000*
(Singapore: Times Editions, 2000), 374.

[12]Lau Teik Soon, "ASEAN and the Cambodian Problem", *Asian Survey* 22, no. 6 (1982):
548–60.

Vietnamese down in Cambodia." Lee remembered that both Prem and Siddhi "were a good team that secured Thailand's long-term security and economic development. Without them, the Vietnamese could have succeeded in manipulating the Thai government."[13] However, there remained a strong group in Thailand who believed that Siddhi was taking too strong a position against the Vietnamese.[14] Unlike Singapore, Thailand was less concerned about preventing the Khmer Rouge from returning to power after a Vietnamese withdrawal. While Thailand and Singapore strongly supported the united front comprising KPNLF, FUNCINPEC and the Khmer Rouge, both Indonesia and Malaysia were greatly suspicious of Beijing and the Chinese-backed Khmer Rouge. The Malaysians, under Prime Minister Hussein Onn, and Foreign Minister Ahmed Rithauddin were somewhat skeptical of the effectiveness of the united front arrangement. In March 1980, Hussein Onn and President Suharto met in Kuantan and announced what is popularly known as the Kuantan Formula. There were, however, various interpretations of the formula. The official version was that Malaysia and Indonesia had urged Vietnam to free itself from the influence of China and the Soviet Union. The unofficial version, which both sides denied, was that both Kuala Lumpur and Jakarta had considered recognising the Heng Samrin regime in return for Vietnamese troop withdrawal from Kampuchea.[15] Whichever is the correct interpretation, the essential point to note is that both Indonesia and Malaysia were especially concerned and wary of China — a concern which continued until the resolution of the Cambodian problem — and wanted to ensure that in the long run, Vietnam would not be weakened to the extent that it would not have been able to serve as an effective bulwark against possible Chinese aggression.[16] That said, support for the ASEAN strategy grew firmer

---

[13] Lee Kuan Yew, *From Third World to First: The Singapore Story: 1965–2000* (Singapore: Times Editions, 2000), 334.

[14] Notes of dinner conversation between Son Sann, 1DPM and 2DPM, Sri Temasek, 2 April 1983.

[15] Brief on the Indochina Conflict, 31 January 1981 — Brief on Kampuchea.

[16] Suharto/Hussein Onn Meeting at Kuantan, 31 March 1980.

under Mahathir's premiership with Ghazalie Shafie as Foreign Minister.[17] Professor Tommy Koh emphasised that over the years, Kuala Lumpur contributed significantly to the ASEAN cause on Cambodia.[18]

Jakarta also became more supportive of the ASEAN strategy in 1983 after its own attempts to open a separate line to Hanoi were frustrated, especially when the Vietnamese brought in East Timor as an issue against Indonesia. As Singapore's former Ambassador to Indonesia, Barry Desker, noted, the difference between Indonesia and Singapore was that Jakarta wanted a regional solution to the Cambodia problem whereas Singapore was focused on an international solution. That said, Suharto must be credited for keeping ASEAN solidarity over the Cambodia issue, despite the differences amongst the member countries,[18] and the pressures within Indonesia, as significant elements of the Armed Forces, such as intelligence chief and later Commander-in Chief of the Armed Forces General Benny Moerdani, regarded Indonesia and Vietnam as sharing similar revolutionary backgrounds.[19]

The Philippines was largely indifferent to the issue. The Philippines was on the fringe of ASEAN. In terms of its history, culture and approach to life, the Philippines did not seem to be seized with the problem as the other ASEAN countries were. The presence of US bases there also made it feel safe as also did its physical separation from Vietnam. Even though it was less enthusiastic about the Kampuchean problem, Manila was nonetheless generally supportive of the ASEAN strategy.[20] It must be noted that the much respected Foreign Minister Carlos Romulo played a significant role in the early years of the Cambodia problem. Romulo who had been in ill-health in the 1980s stepped down as Foreign Minister in 1984, died in 1985.

The progress of efforts to bring a comprehensive solution to the Cambodia crisis was influenced by, and quickened in tandem with

---

[17]Ghazalie Shafie became Foreign Minister from 18 July 1981.

[18]Notes of lunch meeting hosted by 2PS Bilahari Kausikan, Tanglin Room, MFA, 5 August 2009.

[19]Email correspondence with Barry Desker, 22 October 2009.

[20]Extract of notes of conversation between Minister, S. Dhanabalan and Stephen Solarz, Chairman of House Sub-committee on Asia and the Pacific, 23 August 1983.

developments in the East-West Cold War as well as the Sino-Soviet conflict. The process of glasnost and perestroika initiated by Gorbachev and the eventual withdrawal of Soviet force from Eastern Europe leading to the collapse of the Soviet Union in 1990, transformed the global geopolitical situation against which the Cambodia problem had been played out. The Soviet defeat and withdrawal from Afghanistan presaged the Vietnamese withdrawal from Cambodia in 1989.[21] But had it not been for ASEAN's persistent efforts lobbying and bringing its case to international fora year after year,[22] it is very likely that the Cambodia issue would have been forgotten (as the Vietnamese had hoped) long before the end of the Cold War.

ANG Cheng Guan is Head of Graduate Studies at the S. Rajaratnam School of International Studies. He specialises in the international history of modern Asia, with a focus on Southeast Asia. His publications include *Southeast Asia and the Vietnam War* (London: Routledge, 2010); *Lee Kuan Yew's Strategic Thought* (London: Routledge, 2013); and *Singapore, ASEAN and the Cambodia Conflict, 1979–1991* (Singapore: NUS Press, 2013). His forthcoming book is *Southeast Asia's Cold War: An Interpretative History* (Hawaii University Press, 2017). He is currently working on the sequel *Southeast Asia after the Cold War: The Pursuit of an ASEAN-centred Order.*

---

[21] Email correspondence with Mushahid Ali, 29 August 2009.
[22] See, for example, Barry Desker, *Against All Odds: Singapore's Successful Lobbying on the Cambodia Issue at the United Nations* (Occasional Paper, ISEAS Yusof Ishak Institute, 2016).

The Role of ASEAN in the Resolution of the Indochinese Refugee Outflow in the 1970s and 1980s

Janet LIM

During the 1970s and 1980s, conflicts in Vietnam, Laos and Cambodia brought about great political and social upheavals. Particularly after 1975, with the communist take-overs and withdrawal of the United States from these countries, one of the most serious consequences was the outflow of hundreds of thousands of refugees. The refugee outflows were to last for almost two decades and impacted heavily on the neighbouring countries in Southeast Asia, especially Thailand, Malaysia, Indonesia, Philippines and Singapore, the then five members of ASEAN.

The most dramatic of these outflows were the refugees from Vietnam who took to boats in their attempts to reach the countries of Southeast Asia. They became known as the "boat people". Most of the departures were organised clandestinely, with the refugees having to pay big sums of money and gold for unseaworthy boats. They became prey to pirates, which were then very prevalent in the South China Sea, Gulf of Thailand and the Straits of Malacca. Many cases of robbery, terror, violence, rape and murder by pirates came to light and brought international attention and outcry to the extent of this humanitarian crisis. As an illustration of how horrific the situation was, statistics from UNHCR showed that in 1981 alone, 452 boats arrived in Thailand, carrying 15,479 refugees, of which 349 boats had been attacked an average of three times each, 578 women had been raped, 228 women had been abducted and 881 people were dead or missing. A typical incident reported at the time would read as follows — '*18 persons leave in a small craft and in crossing the Gulf of Thailand are attacked by pirates, one girl who resists being raped is killed and another young girl of 15 is abducted. The remaining 16 persons who are of no use to the pirates have their boat rammed repeatedly and all perish at sea.'* (UNHCR Press Release, "UNHCR Expresses Grave Concern at Continuing Plight of Refugees in Distress at Sea", 14 Nov. 1983)

By mid-1979, there were more than half a million refugees who sought asylum in Southeast Asia, since 1975. Given the United States' role in Vietnam during the war and in the context of the Cold War, there was general sympathy in Western countries for the refugees. These countries opened their doors to the refugees for resettlement. It was on this basis that countries in Southeast Asia, including Singapore, agreed to host refugees who were rescued from sea. By 1979, some 200,000 refugees had been resettled in third countries, but some 350,000 still remained in the region. As the outflow continued, the situation became untenable for the hosting countries in the region and member states of ASEAN announced that they would not accept any more new arrivals. The number of boats that were not allowed to land and pushed back to sea hit an all-time high. It was against this backdrop that an international conference on Indochinese refugees was called by the UN Secretary-General in July 1979. Attended by some 65 UN member states, the conference resulted in some significant outcomes: Vietnam agreed to crack down on illegal departures, while resettlement countries agreed to more than double the number of resettlement places from 125,000 to 260,000, in return for temporary asylum to be provided by countries in the region. In a spirit of regional solidarity, Indonesia and the Philippines also agreed to the establishment of Regional Processing Centers in Galang and Bataan respectively to speed up resettlement processing for the region. Critically, Vietnam agreed to the establishment of an orderly departure Programme, which allowed those with legitimate reasons to leave directly from Vietnam in a safe and dignified manner. The impact was immediately felt as between 1980 to 1986, the number of arrivals fell, while departures for resettlement increased, and temporary asylum in the Southeast Asian states, with some notable exceptions, was largely preserved, thus bringing some respite to those still arriving.

Just as it was thought that the refugee problems in the region were being resolved, the tide turned in 1987 as arrivals from Vietnam started to surge again. Resettlement could not keep pace, despite the fact that a record 430,000 refugees had been resettled over an 18-month period, and there was a return to push backs by countries of first asylum. The ASEAN Foreign Ministers called for the convening of another international conference in July 1988. It was clear by then that the consensus reached between the countries of origin, countries of first asylum and countries of resettlement in 1979, had essentially collapsed and that a new formula had to be found. In June 1989, exactly ten years after the first international conference, the UN Secretary-General opened the second International Conference on Indochinese refugees, with the participation of 75 UN member states. It came after a year of intense preparatory work, where the ASEAN Member States and Vietnam and Laos were closely engaged with the UNHCR to design a new agreement. Chaired by the Foreign Minister of Malaysia, the conference adopted this new agreement, known as the Comprehensive Plan of Action (CPA). The plan reaffirmed and strengthened the key elements agreed at the 1979 conference, but introduced two new requirements. First, it required that after a certain cut-off date, all new arrivals were to be subjected to a screening process to determine if they were fleeing for reasons of persecution. This ended effectively the *prima facie* (automatic) refugee recognition so far accorded to the Indochinese refugees. Second, the plan provided for the eventual return of those who were screened out as refugees. This was a sensitive step, as there was then still a strong lobby for Indochinese refugees. With the UNHCR acting as the honest broker, Vietnam was persuaded to increase its efforts to discourage dangerous and clandestine departures and to expand the orderly departure programme already in place. In return, countries in the region agreed to safeguard temporary asylum for those who seek it, while resettlement countries undertook to expand resettlement of all those who arrived before the cut-off dates and rapid resettlement for those screened in as refugees.

Despite the fact that, with the exception of the Philippines, none of the countries in the region were party to the 1951 Refugee Convention, and had no prior experience with refugee status determination, a credible process with proper safeguards were established by all the major asylum countries in the region, with the support of UNHCR. Overall, after the implementation of screening, only about 28% of all new arrivals were recognised as refugees. This enabled the resettlement countries to keep to their commitments of resettling all those who arrived before the cut-off date, as well as all subsequent arrivals recognised as refugees. The solution for those screened out was provided through an orderly return program, established bilaterally between the resettlement countries and Vietnam. Assistance was provided to the returnees and monitoring access was given to the UNHCR. Over the next eight years, the implementation of this plan was scrupulously followed through a number of coordinating mechanisms with a steering committee and subcommittees involving the UNHCR and participating states. By the time the CPA was declared over in 1997, the arrival rates, which were as high as 70,000 in 1979, had been reduced to a trickle. More than 530,000 Vietnamese and Laotians were resettled in more than 15 third countries, led by the United States, and 109,000 Vietnamese persons were returned home. The screening procedures and expanded orderly departure program proved to be effective in discouraging those who planned to leave for economic or resettlement reasons. Singapore played its role in allowing more than 32,000 Vietnamese refugees rescued at sea to pass through the Hawkins Road camp, between 1978 and 1996, on their way to resettlement.

There are important lessons to be learned from the resolution of the Indochinese refugees outflow. The CPA was a remarkable achievement in many senses, even if there were ups and downs in its very long journey. It was a demonstration of true international solidarity, premised on the need to share responsibility and made it possible to finally resolve the biggest humanitarian crisis at the time. The process was long and challenging and yet there was sustained engagement and commitment on the part of all parties. It was unique in bringing about agreement among countries of origin, the countries of asylum, and the international community. Based on the principle of *quid pro quo* and interlocking commitments by the stakeholders, it was a good example of a win-win solution. It was a plan which dealt with the root causes, related to the government policies and political situation in the countries of origin, as well as focused on the immediacy and scale of the humanitarian crisis which could not be ignored. Although ASEAN was then still in its infancy, the member states recognised the importance of a regional approach and benefited from the substantial support of the international community.

In today's tumultuous world where conflicts in different parts of the world have brought about the forced displacement of more than 65 million people, the highest number since World War II, the very same principles of international solidarity and responsibility sharing are more needed than ever. In a globalised and interconnected world, no region in the world can be immune from the conflicts in any other part of the world, however distant.

ASEAN today has doubled its membership in the region. As such, it could provide the opportunity for more effective regional cooperation on which similar problems, if it occurs in the future, could be prevented or resolved. In the past, the Western countries, were willing for a number of historical and other reasons, to accept refugees from the region for resettlement, in addition to providing financial support. With the changed circumstances of today, it is likely that the ASEAN region, being one of the better developed regions in the world, would be expected to provide solutions to refugee problems originating in its own region.

Janet LIM has spent 34 years at the United Nations, serving in various positions both in the UN Refugee Agency (UNHCR) headquarters in Geneva and in the field. Her field assignments have included UNHCR's country and emergency operations in different parts of the world, including Thailand, Malaysia, Sri Lanka, Turkey, Western Sahara and Syria. In Geneva, she served in senior positions which included being Director of the Emergency and Security Services, Director of the Bureau for Asia and the Pacific, and during her last 5 years, she was the Assistant High Commissioner (Operations). During her career, she has also been seconded at a senior level to UNAIDS and to UNAMA, the peacekeeping operation in Afghanistan.

After graduating from the University of Singapore, she served briefly in the Administrative Service of the Singapore Civil Service before pursuing postgraduate studies at the University of Bielefeld, Germany. She is currently a Fellow, School of Social Sciences, as well as an Advisory Board member of the Institute for Societal Leadership in the Singapore Management University. She has also been appointed as Executive-in-Residence with the Geneva Center for Security Policy (GCSP), an international foundation concerned with inter-national affairs and security issues.

ASEAN and the South China Sea Disputes:
An Appraisal

Tara DAVENPORT

The South China Sea, the largest sea in Southeast Asia, is also the stage for one of the most complex disputes in contemporary times. At the heart of these disputes are the competing sovereignty claims over the maritime features[1] scattered throughout the South China Sea between China/Taiwan, Vietnam, the Philippines, Malaysia and Brunei (the Claimants).[2] Maritime disputes over which Claimant has control over the resources surrounding the disputed features also exist, stemming partly from the possibility that some of these features are capable of generating exclusive economic zones (EEZs) and continental shelves under the 1982 United Nations Convention on the Law of the Sea (UNCLOS).[3]

---

[1] The generic term "features" is used to refer to high-tide features (natural areas of land which are above water at high tide), low-tide elevations (natural areas of land, submerged at high-tide and above water at high tide), and submerged features.

[2] There are five distinct groups of features in the South China Sea: the Pratas Islands (claimed by China/Taiwan), the Paracel Islands (China/Taiwan and Vietnam), Macclesfield Bank (claimed by China/Taiwan), Scarborough Shoal (claimed by China/Taiwan and the Philippines) and the Spratly Islands (claimed by China/Taiwan, Vietnam, the Philippines, Malaysia and Brunei).

[3] Article 121(3) provides that only islands capable of sustaining human habitation or an economic life of their own are entitled to an exclusive economic zone and continental shelf. Much uncertainty exists on the nature and status of many of the features in the South China Sea, and while the 2016 *Award of the Annex VII Arbitral Tribunal in the matter of the South China Sea Disputes between the Philippines and China* has removed some of this uncertainty. China has rejected the Award as

The South China Sea disputes (SCS disputes) are viewed as a major flashpoint in post-Cold War Southeast Asia and have been a perennial source of tension.[4] These tensions are periodically exacerbated by actions taken by the various Claimants to bolster their territorial claims to the features and their maritime claims in the South China Sea. Such actions have included occupation, sometimes through force, of disputed features, as well as national legislation asserting sovereignty and proclaiming maritime zones.[5] More recently, China has been increasingly assertive and has interfered with resource exploration and exploitation activities in the EEZs of the Philippines and Vietnam, as well as embarked on large-scale island-building activities on features in the Spratly Islands which it occupies. Further complicating the disputes are its geopolitical overtones: the disputes have been perceived as a proxy for US-China regional hegemony[6] as well as a "litmus test of China's attitudes and long-term intentions as a rising power ... towards its smaller Southeast Asian neighbours."[7]

The disputes inevitably have implications for ASEAN. Six ASEAN members (Malaysia, Brunei, the Philippines, Indonesia, Singapore and Vietnam) surround the South China Sea and four of the Claimants are ASEAN members. The South China Sea hosts a series

---

null and void. It also remains to be seen whether and how the Award will impact the maritime claims of the other Claimants.

[4] Amitav Acharya, *Constructing a Security Community in Southeast Asia: ASEAN and the Problem of Regional Order, 3rd Edition* (London and New York: Routledge, 2014), 128.

[5] Nguyen Hong Thao and Ramses Amer, "A New Legal Arrangement for the South China Sea?", *Ocean Development and International Law* 40(2009): 333, 335–340.

[6] Bilahari Kausikan, "Consensus, Centrality & Relevance: ASEAN and the South China Sea", (Speech, ASEAN Summit 2016 *Charging Through the Complexities: Emboldening SMEs for the AEC* organised by RHT Law Taylor Wessing and RHT Academy, Singapore, August 14, 2016).

[7] Aileen S.P. Baviera, "An ASEAN Perspective on the South China Sea: China-ASEAN Collision or China-US Hegemonic Competition", in *Entering Unchartered Waters? ASEAN and the South China Sea*, ed. Pavin Chachavalpongpun (Singapore: ISEAS Publishing, 2014), 88–89.

of Sea Lines of Communication (SLOCS) between the Indian and Pacific Oceans that are economically and strategically important to ASEAN members, as well as the economies of Northeast Asia, the United States and Europe.[8] Oil and gas resources, as well as extensive fisheries, are found in the South China Sea, the majority of which falls within the EEZ of ASEAN members.[9] It is thus unsurprising that ASEAN has emerged as an important actor in the South China Sea arena.

ASEAN and the South China Sea: Key Milestones

The genesis of ASEAN's role in the South China Sea disputes was borne out of a conflict, namely the 1988 naval clash between China and Vietnam over South Johnson Reef. Although Vietnam was not an ASEAN member at that time, the other ASEAN members were alarmed at the potential threat to regional peace and security.[10] Thus, Indonesia and Canada launched a series of regional Track 2 workshops described as the "Managing Potential Conflicts in the South China Sea Workshops."[11] The Workshop series avoided dealing with territorial disputes and focused on issues such as cooperation and confidence-building. During the second workshop held in Bandung, Indonesia, and attended by China, Taiwan, and Vietnam, the participants agreed on six principles as the basis for cooperation.[12] These six principles ultimately formed the basis for the **1992 ASEAN Declaration on the South China Sea**, the first formal declaration adopted by the Foreign Ministers of ASEAN

---

[8] Sam Bateman *et al.*, "Good Order at Sea in Southeast Asia", *RSIS Policy Paper*, (April 2009): 11.

[9] Clive Schofield, "What's at Stake in the South China Sea? Geographical and Geo-political Considerations", in *Beyond Territorial Disputes in the South China Sea: Legal Frameworks for the Joint Development of Hydrocarbon Resources,* eds. Robert Beckman *et al.* (Cheltenham: Edward Elgar, 2013), 11, 34–46.

[10] See Thao and Amer, *supra* n. 5, 336.

[11] Hasjim Djalal, "Indonesia and the South China Sea Initiative", *Ocean Development and International Law* 32(2001): 97–103.

[12] Djalal, *ibid.*, 99.

on the South China Sea.[13] The principles affirmed, *inter alia,* the need to resolve sovereignty and jurisdictional issues by peaceful means without resort to force, the need for all parties to exercise restraint and explore the possibility of cooperation in the South China Sea. It also called for the application of the Treaty of Amity and Cooperation (TAC)[14] as the basis for establishing a code of international conduct over the South China Sea.

Since then, the South China Sea has been on the agenda of ASEAN, and has been included in a variety of statements, declarations and communiques issued during ASEAN Summits, ASEAN Ministers Meetings, ASEAN Senior Official Meetings or ASEAN-China Meetings.

Arguably, ASEAN's most notable achievement is the **2002 ASEAN-China Declaration on a Code of Conduct in the South China Sea** (DOC).[15] The catalyst was China's occupation of the Philippines' claimed Mischief Reef in 1995, which prompted ASEAN Foreign Ministers to express serious concern and urge the parties to "refrain from taking actions that de-stabilize the situation."[16] In 1997, negotiations on a proposal for a framework for political and economic cooperation, which included "norms of conduct" and guidelines for peaceful settlement of disputes began between China and ASEAN. After five years of negotiations, it proved impossible to agree on a binding code of

---

[13] ASEAN, 1992 ASEAN Declaration on the South China Sea (25th ASEAN Ministerial Meeting in Manila, Philippines, July 22, 1992).

[14] The TAC was adopted in 1976 by the founding members of ASEAN. Other ASEAN Members signed it upon or before joining the organisation. China signed the treaty in 2003. Significantly, the TAC introduces a specific mechanism for the settlement of disputes between parties, namely that a High Council comprising representatives at the ministerial level from each of the contracting parties can recommend to parties appropriate means of settlement of disputes including good offices, mediation, inquiry or conciliation: See Articles 14 and 15, 1976 Treaty of Amity and Cooperation in Southeast Asia signed on 24 February 1976 in Bali, Indonesia.

[15] ASEAN, 2002 Declaration on the Conduct of Parties in the South China Sea (8th ASEAN Summit, Phnom Penh, Cambodia, November 4, 2002).

[16] ASEAN Statement by the ASEAN Foreign Ministers on the Recent Developments in the South China Sea (March 18, 1995).

conduct and thus, as a compromise, the DOC was adopted at the 8th ASEAN Summit in Cambodia.[17]

Under the DOC, the parties undertook to resolve their territorial and jurisdictional disputes by peaceful means, without resorting to the threat or use of force, through friendly consultations and negotiations by sovereign states directly concerned, in accordance with universally recognised principles of international law including UNCLOS.[18] Most critically, the parties also undertook to "exercise self-restraint in the conduct of activities that would complicate or escalate disputes and affect peace and stability including, among others, refraining from action of inhabiting on the presently uninhabited islands, reefs, shoals, cays and other features and to handle their differences in a constructive manner."[19] The DOC went on to identify confidence-building measures and cooperative activities, and reaffirm the commitment to adopt a code of conduct in the South China Sea.[20] The DOC did not specify any geographical limit[21] and was also not intended to be a binding legal document.[22]

The DOC has remained the centrepiece of ASEAN/China discussions on the South China Sea. In 2004, the **Joint Working Group on the Implementation of the DOC**[23] was established to "study and

---

[17] Carlyle A. Thayer, "ASEAN, China and the Code of Conduct in the South China Sea", *SAIS Review of International Affairs* 33, no. 2 (Summer–Fall 2013): 75, 76–77.

[18] 2002 Declaration on the Code of Conduct, para. 4.

[19] 2002 Declaration on the Code of Conduct, para. 5.

[20] 2002 Declaration on the Code of Conduct, paras. 5, 6 and 10.

[21] Vietnam had suggested that the DOC apply specifically to the Paracel Islands. This was opposed by China but as a compromise, the Philippines recommended dropping any references to the geographical boundaries of the Declaration: See Acharya, *supra* n. 4, 130.

[22] During the negotiations of the DOC, the Philippines had wanted a more binding framework but this was not accepted by China: See Acharya, *supra* note 4, 129.

[23] ASEAN and China agreed to establish a Joint Working Group on the Implementation of the DOC in the 2004 Plan of Action to Implement the Joint Declaration on ASEAN-China Strategic Partnership for Peace and Prosperity, adopted in Vientiane, Laos, 29 November 2004.

recommend measures to translate the provisions of the DOC into concrete cooperative activities that will enhance mutual understanding and trust" and Terms of Reference were adopted.[24] In 2011, ASEAN and China agreed on the **Guidelines for the Implementation of the DOC** which stipulated that the implementation of the DOC should be carried out on a step-by-step basis; the initial activities should be confidence-building measures; and implementation should lead to an eventual realisation of a Code of Conduct (COC).

Negotiations on the confidence-building activities to be carried out under the DOC are still ongoing. China proposed establishing an ASEAN-China Maritime Cooperation fund in 2011 (worth about US$470 million) to implement practical projects under the DOC although this has yet to be operationalised.[25]

Another notable document is the **ASEAN's Six-Point Principles on the South China Sea**[26] issued in 2012. In July 2012, ASEAN failed to issue its usual joint communique at the ministerial meeting in Cambodia for the first time in its history due to Cambodia's unwillingness to accept certain references to the SCS disputes, despite the efforts of Singapore and Indonesia to negotiate a compromise.[27] The other ASEAN Member States (AMS) were concerned at the potential damage to ASEAN unity, and as a result of intensive diplomatic efforts by Indonesian's foreign minister at the time, Dr. Marty Natalegawa, the ASEAN Foreign Ministers issued a joint Statement on "ASEAN's Six-Point Principles on the South China Sea" several

---

[24] ASEAN, Terms of Reference of the ASEAN-China Joint Working Group on the Implementation of the Declaration on the Conduct of Parties in the South China Sea (Kuala Lumpur, Malaysia, December 7, 2004).

[25] Sam Bateman, "Existing and Previous Maritime Cooperative Arrangements in the South China Sea" (Conference on Maritime Confidence Building Measures in the South China Sea, Australian Strategic Policy Institute, Sydney, August 11–13, 2013), 13–21.

[26] ASEAN, Statement of the ASEAN Foreign Ministers (Phnom Penh, Cambodia, July 20, 2012).

[27] Thayer, *supra* n. 17, 75–84, 78–79.

days later.[28] The six points reflected the commitment of ASEAN Member States to the DOC, the Guidelines for the Implementation of the DOC, the early conclusion of a COC, respect for international law including UNCLOS, the continued exercise of self-restraint and non-use of force by all parties; and the peaceful resolution of disputes, in accordance with universally recognised principles of international law.[29]

A further development which warrants note is the joint statement by the Heads of States of ASEAN Members and China on **the Application of the Code for Unplanned Encounters at Sea in the South China Sea** (CUES) on 7 September 2016,[30] which amongst other things, provided for the improvement of operational safety of naval ships and the establishment of a diplomatic hotline to respond to maritime emergencies[31] This was an express acknowledgement by China that it would observe CUES in the South China Sea where previously it was not clear, although it has been criticised for being non-binding and for not applying to coast guard vessels which were involved in the majority of incidents in the South China Sea.[32]

A binding code of conduct between ASEAN and China is the ultimate goal of ASEAN-China negotiations on the SCS disputes. ASEAN presently has a draft COC which includes a mechanism for dispute settlement.[33] Negotiations between ASEAN and China have been slow

---

[28] Acharya, *supra* n. 4, 131–132.

[29] ASEAN, Statement of the ASEAN Foreign Ministers (Phnom Penh, Cambodia, July 20, 2012).

[30] ASEAN, Joint Statement on the Application of the Code for Unplanned Encounters at Sea in the South China Sea (Vientiane, Lao People's Democratic Republic, September 7, 2016).

[31] Sam Bateman, "CUES and Coast Guards", East Asia Forum, October 7, 2016, http://www.eastasiaforum.org/2016/10/07/cues-and-coast-guards/

[32] Hoang Thi Ha, "Making the CUES Code Work in the South China Sea", *Today*, September 8, 2016, http://www.todayonline.com/commentary/making-cues-code-work-south-china-sea

[33] Acharya, *supra* n. 4, 133.

and in 2012, China maintained that it would only sign a code of conduct when conditions were ripe and instead, wanted to focus on the implementation of the DOC.[34] However, in a positive development, China agreed to start formal negotiations on the COC in April 2013.[35] In August 2016, ASEAN and China agreed to finish a draft framework for a Code of Conduct by mid-2017.[36] This goal was achieved in May 2017 at the meeting of ASEAN and Chinese senior officials in Guiyang, China.

ASEAN's Role in the South China Sea Disputes: An Appraisal

An evaluation of ASEAN's role in the South China Sea disputes has garnered mixed reactions. To some, ASEAN is at best, a mere "talk shop"[37] with no real traction to make an impact in the disputes. Critics point to the glacial pace of the negotiations of the COC;[38] the fact that the DOC is non-binding and has not prevented the Claimants from fortifying the features they presently occupy;[39] and the failure of ASEAN in curtailing China's assertive behavior.[40] At worst, the South China Sea disputes expose the fault lines dividing ASEAN members in a manner that shatters any illusion of regional unity. As one observer succinctly

---

[34] *Ibid.*

[35] Thayer, *supra* n. 17, 80.

[36] Prashanth Parameswaran, "Beware the Illusion of China-ASEAN South China Sea Breakthroughs", *The Diplomat*, August 17, 2016, http://thediplomat.com/2016/08/beware-the-illusion-of-china-asean-south-china-sea-breakthroughs/

[37] Arif Havas Oegroseno, "ASEAN as the Most Feasible Forum to Address the South China Sea Challenges", *American Society of International Law Proceedings* 107 (2013): 290.

[38] Tang Siew Mun, "ASEAN Must Speak Up More on South China Sea Matter", *The Straits Times*, August 13, 2015.

[39] Robert C. Beckman, "ASEAN and the South China Sea Dispute", in *Entering Unchartered Waters? ASEAN and the South China Sea*, ed. Pavin Chachavalpongpun (Singapore: ISEAS Publishing, 2014), 15, 29–30.

[40] Ralf Emmers, "The Changing Power Distribution in the South China Sea: Implications for Conflict Management and Avoidance", *Political Science* 62, no. 2 (2010): 118–131.

put it, "if ASEAN cannot take a position on such a crucial matter in its own region, why should anyone take us seriously?"[41] Examples of such disunity can be seen in the failure of the Foreign Ministers to issue a joint statement on the South China Sea in 2012 discussed above; and the failure of ASEAN to issue a joint response on the Philippines/China South China Sea Arbitral Award in 2016.[42]

These criticisms can sometimes overshadow the very real and positive impact that ASEAN has on the South China Sea disputes despite its inherent limitations. Not all the Member States of ASEAN are claimants in the South China Sea disputes, and not all the ASEAN Claimants will have the same position on the South China Sea disputes. Further, ASEAN members and China are increasingly economically interdependent and taking too strong a position on the SCS disputes could jeopardise this. The ASEAN principle of consensus has meant that ASEAN members with diverse interests and positions must be able to unanimously agree on how to handle the SCS disputes. This has and will inevitably create challenges. Notwithstanding this, ASEAN has played a significant role in two aspects, namely, conflict management and facilitating China's acceptance of multilateralism.[43]

ASEAN's role in conflict management

Conflict management refers to the processes, methods, devices, techniques and strategies employed to manage a conflict.[44] It includes norm-

---

[41] Kausikan, *supra* n. 6, 2.

[42] Prashanth Parameswaran, "What Really Happened at the ASEAN-China Special Kunming Meeting", *The Diplomat*, July 21, 2016; "ASEAN deadlocked as South China Sea split deepens at Laos Summit", *The Straits Times*, July 24, 2016; Elinor Noor, "ASEAN not so divided on the South China Sea", *East Asia Forum*, August 17, 2016.

[43] Bama Andika Putra, "China's Assertiveness in the South China Sea: Have ASEAN's Endeavours in Establishing Regional Order Truly Failed?", *Journal of Politics and Law* 8 (2015): 178.

[44] Mely Caballero-Anthony, *Regional Security in Southeast Asia* (Singapore: ISEAS Publishing, 2005), 22.

setting, assurance, community-building, deterrence, non-intervention, isolation, mediation, enforcement and internationalisation.[45] ASEAN has played a significant role in alleviating the possibility of conflict in the SCS disputes. A simple testament to this is the fact that "Southeast Asia is at peace with itself, at peace with the world and prospering,"[46] something which would not have seemed likely in the tumultuous period leading up to the establishment of ASEAN. The disputes have not resulted in a serious military conflict despite characterisations of the disputes as a serious flashpoint in Asia (although, of course, there have been a few military skirmishes and some sabre-rattling).[47]

ASEAN has contributed to conflict management in several ways. First, ASEAN provides an important forum for community-building amongst its Member States and between AMS and China. These interactions are not limited to ASEAN meetings or ASEAN-China meetings, but also extend to the ASEAN Plus Three processes, East Asia Summit, and the ASEAN Regional Forum. As noted by one scholar:

> The unprecedented number of meetings has led to a situation where top leaders, officials and other regional elites have extensive points of contact. Through the socialisation in these meetings, webs of personal networks have been built among the participants. The socialisation and the networks have not only increased confidence and trust among their members; it has also contributed to the building of a nascent regional identity.[48]

---

[45] Muthiah Alagappa, "Regionalism and Conflict Management: A Framework Analysis", *Review of International Studies* 21 (1995): 359–97.

[46] Kausikan, *supra* n. 6, 8.

[47] Mikael Weissmann, "Why Is There a Relative Peace in the South China Sea?", in *Entering Unchartered Waters? ASEAN and the South China Sea*, ed. Pavin Chachavalpongpun (Singapore: ISEAS Publishing, 2014), 36–37.

[48] *Ibid.*, 43.

Indeed, these meetings have been described as "institutionalised frameworks of consultative mechanisms"[49] and instill habits of dialogue and consultation between AMS and China which "deepen the process of socialisation of ASEAN political leaders and officials, hence inducting into the overall ASEAN mechanisms of cooperation."[50]

Second, these meetings also serve as a critical platform for discussion of the SCS disputes, particularly as and when incidents occur. This communication can and has prevented disputes from escalating into something more serious.

Third, the various statements, communiques and declarations issued after these meetings are also vital tools of conflict management. The 1992 Declaration, 2002 DOC, the ASEAN Six-Point Principles all reiterate the importance of international law, the peaceful settlement of disputes, self-restraint and the non-use of force. While one could argue that these are just statements with no legal effect and no mechanisms of enforcement, these documents provide assurance to the relevant stakeholders, set out norms and establish modalities for dispute management. At the very least, they provide a baseline for acceptable behaviour in the South China Sea which functions as an effective moral constraint on the Claimants.

Thus, ASEAN has provided an effective forum for conflict management in the South China Sea in small, incremental but no less vital steps. This is an example of the "ASEAN Way" *par excellence*, with its emphasis on negotiations, consensus and compromise.[51]

China and multilateralism

China has always expressed preference for a bilateral approach to discussing the SCS disputes. This is to its advantage as its economic and

---

[49] Caballero-Anthony, *supra* n. 44, 55.

[50] *Ibid.*, 57.

[51] Gillian Goh, "The ASEAN Way: Non-Intervention and ASEAN's Role in Conflict Management", *Stanford Journal of East Asian Affairs* 3 (2003): 113.

military might put it in a superior bargaining position. However, China has accepted ASEAN as a legitimate multilateral framework to discuss aspects of the SCS disputes, in particular, those aimed at the conduct of the relevant parties. It is remarkable that China agreed to instruments such as the DOC and is still continuing to engage in negotiations on a COC as both purport to restrain China's behavior in the South China Sea to a certain extent. Thus, the multilateral framework provides an important bulwark against China's military and economic power particularly for the smaller Southeast Asian nations. Further, China's engagement with multilateral institutions such as ASEAN has undoubtedly moderated China's regional behavior and has made it cognizant of its' neighbours' interests. As observed by one scholar, there has been a "reciprocal process between China's soft power diplomacy" and ASEAN's "constructive engagement policies".[52]

Conclusion

ASEAN will not be the forum for the resolution of the underlying sovereignty and jurisdictional issues, and neither the DOC nor the COC should be seen as panaceas for the disputes. Indeed, it has always faced considerable obstacles in playing a meaningful role in the SCS disputes, including the diverse interests and positions of the different ASEAN members, the growing economic interdependence between ASEAN members and China and China's development as a future super-power. Despite this, ASEAN has played a valuable and sometimes underappreciated role in the South China Sea disputes, particularly in the way it has endeavoured to manage the conflicts and has compelled China to engage in multilateral frameworks. While there are always ways in which any organisation can improve, the important achievements of ASEAN in the context of the SCS disputes should not be discounted, and instead, should be highlighted and built upon.

---

[52] Weissman, p. 53.

Tara DAVENPORT is presently an instructor at the Faculty of Law, National University of Singapore (NUS) and is also pursuing her doctorate at Yale Law School, under a Fulbright Scholarship and a NUS Scholarship. She previously worked as a Research Fellow at the Centre for International Law, NUS where her main research interests were oceans law and policy, with a specific focus on the South China Sea disputes, submarine cables and maritime piracy.

ASEAN and Pandemic Challenges

Vernon LEE

◦ ◖ ◦

Over the years, ASEAN countries have been affected by numerous public health threats from emerging infectious diseases. The 1998/1999 Nipah virus outbreak among pigs affected pig handlers in Malaysia, resulting in 257 human cases and 105 deaths, and the culling of more than one million pigs. The 2003 Severe Acute Respiratory Syndrome (SARS) outbreak, which originated in southern China, spread rapidly to Vietnam resulting in 63 human cases and 5 deaths, and to Singapore resulting in 238 cases and 33 deaths. The H5N1 avian influenza virus, first introduced to poultry in Southeast Asia in 2004, had spread widely despite efforts to control the virus through the culling of infected poultry flocks. It resulted in more than 350 human cases and 250 deaths. ASEAN countries were also substantially affected by the 2009 H1N1 influenza pandemic, which spread rapidly from the Americas through global trade and travel routes. Other re-emerging threats such as the mosquito-borne dengue and Zika viruses are also seeing a resurgence.

The threat from these emerging and re-emerging infectious diseases will continue to grow due to a combination of challenges. If left unchecked, these diseases may result in severe epidemics, engulfing the region and causing substantial and lasting health, social, and economic damage.

Among the challenges facing ASEAN, zoonotic diseases (diseases transmitted from animals to humans) pose substantial risk because many emerging diseases have animal origins such as the Nipah virus, SARS, and avian influenza. Increasing economic development and urbanisation, especially if poorly planned, have resulted in encroachment on natural animal habitats, and the need for more food sources and increased farming have resulted in greater interaction between animals and humans than ever before. This increases the risk that animal diseases may develop and cross the species barrier to infect humans. This problem is often compounded by the previous lack of collaboration between the animal and human health sectors in surveillance of zoonotic diseases, prevention programs, and response measures during outbreaks.

In addition, the increasing connectivity of travel and trade within and outside of ASEAN has resulted in economic advantages and regional development, but also increases the risk of rapid disease spread. Infectious diseases do not respect borders, and the high volume and efficient speed of travel may result in the spread of diseases between countries if undetected — SARS in 2003 is one example. In an ever-interconnected region, protection against infectious diseases is only as good as the weakest link. No matter how good the disease prevention and control programs in one country, if other countries do not have the same level of protection, diseases that arise from those countries will spread and the damage will be collectively felt.

Coordinating regional capacity building activities have also been challenging. The structuring of the World Health Organization (WHO) regions, a remnant of political divides of a previous era with three ASEAN countries (Thailand, Indonesia, and Myanmar) in the WHO South East Asia Region, while others are in the WHO Western Pacific Region, makes coordination of capacity building and regional response activities challenging. This has improved with the establishment of the Asia Pacific Strategy for Emerging Diseases (APSED) in 2005, which brings together both WHO regions to work towards a common goal. The ASEAN-WHO Memorandum of Understanding for 2014–2017, signed by the Secretary-General of ASEAN and the Regional Directors of both WHO regions, provides further opportunities to address these issues.

The consistent reporting of infectious disease events through the national international health regulations (IHR) focal points is a good example of regional collaboration under a WHO policy instrument. Another example of regional collaboration is the ASEAN-Japan project on regional stockpiling of oseltamivir (Tamiflu) and personal protective equipment. This stockpile can be rapidly deployed to countries in need during an influenza outbreak, negating the need for each country to maintain their own costly stockpiles.

ASEAN platforms have also provided an opportunity to collaborate on infectious diseases. This includes high-level meetings such as the ASEAN Health Ministers Meeting (AHMM) and Senior Officials Meeting on Health Development (SOMHD), and infectious diseases-specific platforms including the ASEAN Expert Group on Communicable Diseases (AEGCD), and the ASEAN Technical Working Group on Pandemic Preparedness and Response (ATWGPPR). These have resulted in the development of programmes such as the ASEAN Regional Cooperation in Communicable Diseases and Pandemic Preparedness and Response, and the ASEAN Plus Three Emerging Infectious Diseases Programme, which work towards collaborative activities to reduce the risk and impact of these diseases.

To mitigate the risks posed by the above challenges, ASEAN countries need to collaborate to adopt an all-hazards approach to preparedness and response planning, to strengthen local and regional platforms to build core public health capacities, and to engage all sectors in a whole-of-government and all-of-society approach. At the ASEAN Health Ministers' Meeting in 2014, ASEAN outlined the Post-2015 Health Development Agenda, which structures health priorities into four clusters, with cluster two focusing on "responding to all hazards and emerging threats", illustrating the emphasis of an all-hazards approach. This forms part of the new ASEAN Strategic Framework on Health Development, in which ASEAN countries aim to adopt an all-hazards approach to promote resilient health system responses to communicable diseases, emerging tropical diseases, as well as environmental health threats, hazards and disasters.

Adopting an all-hazards approach means that instead of focusing myopically on specific events, countries can focus on overall risks and build plans that are flexible in responding rapidly to threats. This includes capabilities that are critical in any emergency such as command and control structures, internal and public communications platforms, and logistics systems, all of which are generic and can deal with a range of emergencies. At the same time, plans will need to include consideration for specific hazards in the local context. For example, protection against influenza may include stockpiles of specific anti-viral drugs, while smallpox preparedness plans may include stockpiling of smallpox vaccines.

ASEAN countries have made progress towards adopting an all-hazards approach and have incorporated pandemic preparedness planning into disaster preparedness. One example is Singapore's pandemic preparedness plan, a generic framework that enables immediate response to any disease with pandemic potential. The local and international disease situation, and the potential public health impact based on risk assessment, will determine the type and strength of response. The responses are not hard-wired to a specific disease, but are building blocks that can be mixed and matched to provide the flexibility to adopt responses that are tailored to each unique scenario — not too little and not too much.

Capacity building is another challenge. Local and regional risk assessment, preparedness, and response programs need to be strengthened. The WHO revised the IHR in the wake of the SARS outbreak to strengthen global and national capacities to respond to infectious disease threats. The IHR (2005), a binding instrument of international law, came into force in 2007 and requires countries to have core capacities across key public health domains. This was supposed to have been achieved by 2012 but globally, as of 2015, countries that have responded to the WHO IHR core capacity implementation survey have only achieved 75% of the required attributes. In 2015, the IHR Review Committee recommended including peer review and voluntary external evaluations, in addition to self-evaluation. In collaboration with the Global Health Security Agenda (GHSA) initiative, WHO developed the Joint External Evaluation (JEE) process where countries can volunteer to be assessed by a group of international experts after conducting a self-evaluation. In 2016, Cambodia was the first country in ASEAN to undergo the JEE process, with several other ASEAN countries joining soon.

Capacity-building requires substantial investment, but competition for resources from pressing national and regional developmental priorities often mean that public health takes a back seat. It is important to support capacity-building activities through multilateral activities such as training and development programs, and to have sustainable financing models based on local support supplemented by donor resources as needed. Effective programs require long-term and sustainable funding to stand the tests of time and disease. Donor resources may be required as a catalyst to fund hardware and train local expertise. However, local resources are needed to ensure sustainability, including funding, human resources, and government and community support. ASEAN should continue to work with WHO and international partners and donor organisations to ensure that regional capacity building is seamlessly achieved.

In addition, ASEAN has to work together beyond the health sector due to the substantial non-health impact of health security threats. The billions of dollars lost from culling pigs during the Nipah virus outbreak or poultry during the avian influenza outbreaks, and the significant drop in travel and trade to countries affected by the SARS outbreak are reminders of these non-health impacts. Building robust preparedness and response programs requires the collaboration of all government agencies in a whole-of-government approach. This will avoid gaps that are not addressed, or wastage of resources due to duplication. For example, combating zoonotic diseases require close collaboration between the health and agricultural agencies. Support from non-governmental stakeholders and the community are also critical as part of an all-of-society approach to ensure that policies are contextualised and implemented on the ground. Indonesia, for example, has done well through the formation of KOSNAS Zoonosis, a national multi-sectoral committee that addresses the risk of zoonotic infections.

In 2007, a study of pandemic response plans in ASEAN found that most plans dealt with the health issues but that multi-sector pandemic preparedness plans were lacking. The ASEAN-USAID Project on Multi-Sectoral Pandemic Preparedness and Response is one program that encouraged ASEAN member states to look at an all-of-society approach, and this has led to various multi-sector preparedness and response activities including readiness exercises. ASEAN countries have also developed a detailed ASEAN Multi-sector Pandemic Preparedness and Response Work Plan to fill the gaps in multi-sector pandemic preparedness.

Many ASEAN countries have now included multi-sector planning, and broad emerging infectious diseases or all hazards approaches, in their pandemic preparedness plans. For example, Indonesia conducted multi-sectoral pandemic readiness field exercises in Bali and Makassar in 2008, and regularly conducts tabletop preparedness exercises. Cambodia, in collaboration with ASEAN and WHO, held PanStop, a multi-sectoral pandemic readiness exercise in 2007; while Laos and the Philippines held similar exercises in late 2007 and 2008 respectively. Malaysia also held a series of exercises, ExPanFlu, to evaluate its preparedness against an influenza outbreak. Myanmar and Thailand have also held several tabletop exercises on pandemic preparedness to ensure whole of government coordination. Singapore regularly conducts multi-sectoral tabletop and field exercises to test its readiness and preparedness systems. Vietnam, one of the early countries to be affected by H5N1 avian influenza, has also conducted multi-sectoral simulation exercises.

In conclusion, ASEAN countries have taken substantial collective steps to address the threats posed by infectious diseases, and these should continue to be strengthened. Many of the aforementioned programs will likely be folded into cluster two on "responding to all hazards and emerging threats" of the new Post-2015 Health Development Agenda, Adopting an all hazards approach, working across sectors, and building local and regional capacities can help ASEAN countries response to these challenges. While the basic building blocks are good, ASEAN countries must continue to strengthen them to reduce the threat and impact of diseases on society.

I would like to thank Dr. Wee Liang En for assisting with research on the ASEAN infectious disease platforms.

Vernon LEE is a preventive medicine physician and adjunct Associate Professor at the Saw Swee Hock School of Public Health, National University of Singapore. He conducts translational infectious diseases research, and has 80 publications on infectious diseases and public health.

He was previously Advisor to the Assistant Director General for Health, Security and Environment at the World Health Organization (WHO) headquarters; and has also worked in the WHO Office in Indonesia on avian and pandemic influenza preparedness. He continues to contribute to WHO working groups on infectious diseases epidemiology and preparedness.

A/Prof Lee graduated from medical school at the National University of Singapore and is a Fellow of the Academy of Medicine, Singapore. He also holds a PhD in epidemiology from the Australian National University, and the Master in Public Health and Master of Business Administration degrees from the Johns Hopkins University, USA.

ASEAN and Singapore's Partnership in Disaster Response

Kadir MAIDEEN

◦ ✍ ◦

Introduction

ASEAN has a current combined GDP of US$2.5 trillion, making it the seventh-largest economy in the world. It has a population of 630 million people, which represents the third-largest labour force in the world. However, the ASEAN region is one of the world's most disaster-prone regions.

The UN Economic and Social Commission for Asia and the Pacific (ESCAP) reported[1] that disaster-induced deaths in ASEAN rose by more than three-fold in the period between 2004 and 2013. During this time, ASEAN suffered 41.2 per cent of all global natural disasters, such as typhoons, earthquakes and floods, and bore 50.5 per cent[2] of all disaster-related fatalities. Economic damage was valued at over US$560 billion.[3]

As trends have shown that future disasters may occur with increasing magnitude and frequency, ASEAN will need to ensure that it is prepared to mitigate against these events.

---

[1] "ESCAP Statistical Database", UN ESCAP, http:/ /www.unescap.org/stat/data/.

[2] The number of fatalities was approximately 354,000, out of a total of 700,000 deaths worldwide. (*Source*: Global Disaster Database @emdat.be)

[3] "Building Resilience: Enhancing the Role of ICT for Disaster Risk Management (DRM)", *UN ESCAP*, http://www.unescap.org/sites/default/files/Enhancing%20 the%20role%20of%20ICTs%20for%20D RM.PDF

ASEAN's Efforts in Disaster Management

The Indian Ocean tsunami which occurred in December 2004 triggered ASEAN's effort in disaster management. 280,000 lives[4] were lost and 5 million[5] people were affected by the tsunami, with an estimated US$10 billion[6] in damages. The ASEAN Committee on Disaster Management (ACDM), represented by the National Disaster Management Offices[7] of all ten ASEAN Member States (AMS), formulated the ASEAN Agreement on Disaster Management and Emergency Response (AADMER) in 2005.

The AADMER

The AADMER is a proactive and holistic regional disaster management framework that facilitates cooperation, coordination, technical assistance, and resource mobilisation during a disaster. It also affirms ASEAN's commitment to the Hyogo Framework of Action (HFA) and is the first legally-binding HFA-related instrument in the world.

This Agreement continues to be in effect, and serves as a legally-binding framework upon which all AMS are guided when responding to regional disasters. The AADMER was signed by all the ASEAN foreign ministers in July 2005 and entered into force in December 2009.

All AMS have pledged to cooperate and dovetail efforts to build up a robust, region-wide framework to address the effects of a natural disaster. By complementing each other's strengths and mutually-reinforcing each other's weaknesses, ASEAN's collective resilience against the catastrophic effects of natural disasters can be leveled-up.

---

[4] "Indonesia quake toll jumps again", *BBC News*, January 2005, http://news.bbc.co.uk/1/hi/world/asia-pacific/4204385.stm

[5] "Facts and Figures: Asian Tsunami Disaster", *New Scientist,* January 20, 2005, https://www.newscientist.com

[6] Asian Disaster Preparedness Center, "Social and Economic Impact of December 2004 Tsunami", *IUCN*, http://cmsdata.iucn.org/

[7] Singapore is represented by the Singapore Civil Defence Force (SCDF) in the ACDM.

The AADMER Work Programme

The AADMER Work Programme[8] was also developed to operationalise the AADMER into tangible, implementable action plans. In addition,
the ASEAN Coordinating Centre for Humanitarian Assistance on disaster management (AHA Centre) was established in November 2011 to
oversee this effort and facilitate cooperation and coordination amongst
the AMS during a disaster.

The AADMER Work Programme of 2010–2015 laid the regional
mechanisms for joint response and disaster risk reduction at the
macro level. From 2016 to 2020, the focus will now be on fostering
participative collaboration and inclusive partnerships between the
private and public sector to develop joint response to disaster
management.

Singapore's Contributions to ASEAN

While Singapore is free from natural disaster, it is located within one of
the most natural disaster-prone regions in the world. Besides, Singapore
cannot insulate itself from the disaster management efforts due to the
increased interconnectivity between the AMS. The effects of a natural
disaster on a particular member state will inevitably be felt by the
others, as the devastation effects ripple downstream throughout the
entire ASEAN system (such as in areas of trade and economy). ASEAN
solidarity is even more important with the establishment of the ASEAN
Community in 2015.

The Singapore Civil Defence Force (SCDF), as Singapore's representative in the ACDM, is responsible for institutionalising the AADMER
in Singapore. For instance, Singapore has established a ready pool of

---

[8] The Work Programme seeks to translate AADMER's spirit and intent into concrete
actions and initiatives to be implemented in order to attain the ASEAN vision
of disaster-resilient nations and safe communities. Under the Work Programme,
Working Groups has been formed to look into different aspects of disaster
management, such as early warning, preparedness and response, prevention and
mitigation, recovery as well as knowledge and innovation.

trained Emergency Response and Assessment Team (ERAT) officers who are on 24/7 standby to respond at the onset of a disaster in the region.

As the lead shepherd for several components of the AADMER Work Programme, Singapore has contributed to building up ASEAN's collective capabilities in disaster management through: (a) provision of training in leadership development, firefighting, rescue and disaster management; (b) hosting of disaster-related events such as the Strategic Policy Dialogue on Disaster Management; and (c) sharing of knowledge and expertise through joint exercises and exchange programmes.

Singapore has made several significant contributions to enhance the disaster management capacity of ASEAN, which include:

1. *Standard Operating Procedure for Regional Standby Arrangements and Coordination of Joint Disaster Relief and Emergency Response Operations (SASOP)*

   As part of the effort to operationalise the AADMER Work Programme, SCDF played a key role in crafting the SASOP in 2008. The SASOP serves to: (a) provide the guides and templates to initiate the establishment of the ASEAN Standby Arrangements for Disaster Relief and Emergency Response; (b) the procedures for joint disaster relief and emergency response operations; (c) the procedures for the facilitation and utilisation of military and civilian assets and capacities; and (d) the methodology for the periodic conduct of the ASEAN Regional Disaster Emergency Response Simulation Exercises (ARDEX), which test the effectiveness of the procedures. The SASOP was adopted by all AMS.

   Since then, SASOP has been tested, fine-tuned and revalidated at subsequent ARDEX platforms. It will continue to be refined and adapted to fit current-world exigencies.

2. *Establishment and Operationalisation of the ASEAN Coordinating Centre for Humanitarian Assistance on Disaster Management (AHA Centre)*

   The AHA Centre's mandate is to facilitate coordination and cooperation amongst the AMS, United Nations and other international organisations to promote regional collaboration in disaster management. It serves as the operational engine of the aforementioned AADMER Work Programme by translating its desired outcomes into action plans, and overseeing its subsequent implementation.

Singapore played an instrumental role in the establishment and operationalisation of the AHA Centre in 2011. In serving as the regional hub for disaster monitoring and analysis, Singapore assisted in the development of the communications technology (satellite communications capability, internet connectivity, Global System for Mobile Communications, and PSTN (voice-enabled calls) and support plan to ensure seamless connection between the AHA Centre and all AMS on a 24/7 basis.

Since its establishment, the AHA Centre has consistently demonstrated its value through its successful monitoring of disaster situations and disaster response coordination. The Centre also consistently produces situational reports and updates for dissemination, and has proven its worth in facilitating ASEAN's response to disasters. To date, the AHA Centre has responded to 17 disasters in the region.

3. *ASEAN Emergency Response and Assessment Team (ASEAN-ERAT)*
   Singapore was pivotal in the establishment and training of the ASEAN-ERAT which is a rapid deployment and response mechanism that serves to conduct immediate needs assessment of the disaster area.

   ERAT members are deployed at the onset of a disaster in the region to assist the affected country in damage assessment and disaster relief coordination. ASEAN-ERAT roles also include providing support on logistics, emergency communications and coordination. Once at the disaster area, the team will report their findings to the AHA Centre, so as to sharpen subsequent response efforts to achieve maximum effectiveness on the ground. To date, there are 118 ERAT members in ASEAN, of which 12 are from Singapore.

4. *Disaster Emergency Logistics Stockpile (DELSA)*
   Due to the increased frequency and magnitude of disasters in ASEAN, there was a pressing need for a regional mechanism that would ensure the timely delivery of emergency relief logistics to the affected area.

This led to the establishment of the DELSA, under the stewardship of Singapore and Malaysia, where a stockpile of relief supplies are stored at the UN Humanitarian Response Depot in Subang, Malaysia.

In addition, workshops have been held to familiarise logistics officers on logistics management and crisis communications. Currently, the project team is in the midst of establishing two more satellite warehouses in the Philippines and Thailand.

One ASEAN, One Response (OAOR)

ASEAN Leaders signed and adopted the Declaration on One ASEAN One Response: ASEAN Responding to Disasters as One in the Region and Outside the Region during the 28th ASEAN Summit in Lao PDR in September 2016. The OAOR aims to achieve faster response, mobilise greater resources and establish stronger coordination amongst different humanitarian actors to ensure a synergised and collective ASEAN response to disasters.

In subscribing to the spirit of this Declaration, Singapore, as a responsible member of ASEAN and the international system, will continue to invest efforts and resources to develop the capabilities and capacities of other nations to better safeguard themselves against the effects of a natural disaster.

Conclusion

As globalisation inevitably continues unabated, nations can no longer be fully insulated from the far-reaching devastating effects of natural disasters. As technological progress, climate change, environmental damage brought forth by urbanisation, and evolving extreme weather patterns combine potently together, it will become increasingly difficult to accurately forecast the devastating impact of a future natural disaster.

It is for this reason that all countries should strive towards building up a comprehensive suite of disaster management measures to contain and mitigate against the effects of a natural disaster. In being ably prepared, countries will be able to avoid the considerable loss of lives and properties that typically follow in the wake of a natural disaster.

In so doing, a safe and secure home for all in ASEAN, in the spirit of a One ASEAN Community, can and will be achieved.

Kadir MAIDEEN joined the Singapore Civil Defence Force (SCDF) in 1994 and is currently the Director of the National Service Training Institute. He ensures the basic training of SCDF National Service enlistees and the In-Camp Training (ICT) of SCDF NSmen.

He has also served as the Officer Commanding of a Fire Station specialising in Hazardous Material (HAZMAT) response, commanded SCDF's elite Disaster Assistance and Rescue Team (DART), attached to the ASEAN Secretariat in 2007 as an Expert in Disaster Management and successfully commanded the second Civil Defence Division as its Division Commander.

He is an active member of the ASEAN Emergency Rapid Assessment Team (ERAT) and United Nations Disaster Assistance and Coordination (UNDAC) team that is ready for immediate deployment to any sudden on-set disasters regionally and worldwide.

He has been conferred the State Medal of Valour in 2004 for the rescue operations at the Nicoll Highway collapse. He has also been awarded the SCDF Overseas Service Medal on six occasions for being part of the overseas operations to Taiwan, Pakistan and Indonesia.

Narrowing the Development Gap:
Singapore and the Initiative for ASEAN Integration

Sharon SEAH Li-Lian[1]

✦

Concerns about the emergence of a "two-tier ASEAN" arose after the successive admission of four new ASEAN Member States (AMS) in the 1990s — Vietnam in 1995, Lao PDR and Myanmar in 1997 and finally, Cambodia in 1999. By then, the economic levels of the original six members were already sufficiently high, having enjoyed nearly three decades of relatively uninterrupted growth. The development levels of the ten ASEAN Member States were vastly different. Cambodia, Laos and Vietnam had just emerged after decades of civil war and Myanmar was still facing severe trade sanctions from the West.

But it was not only differences in economic terms that the grouping faced. There were significant differences in basic infrastructure, human resource development and institutional capacities. Cambodia, Laos, Myanmar and Vietnam — or the CLMV in short, faced severe limitations, having suffered devastation due to long years of war and civil strife. Roads, railways and airports were destroyed and local populations had no healthcare access or educational opportunities. In fact, just to give an example of the severity of the challenges faced, Laos had

---

[1] The author is indebted to Mr. Lee Chiong Giam for his generous time in sharing his experiences spear-heading Singapore's efforts in the Initiative for ASEAN Integration (IAI) and who had personally visited and established the IAI Training Centres in the CLMV countries and to the Technical Cooperation Directorate of the Ministry of Foreign Affairs as well as the Ministry of Education for their kind assistance.

more bombs dropped on it than in the whole of Europe during World War II. Of the more than 250 million cluster bombs dropped in Laos by the United States during the Vietnam War, more than a third of the ordnance remain unexploded today! Clearing cluster munitions in the Lao countryside, which has taken more than three decades and millions of dollars, still remains unfinished work.

Singapore's Initiative

Against these challenges, ASEAN knew that it had to narrow the development gap if it were to realise its ambitions for regional economic integration. Then Prime Minister Goh Chok Tong, who had advocated at home that the better-off should help the less well-off, applied the same principle in ASEAN. Mr. Goh felt that the six founding members, being the better-off countries, had an obligation to assist Cambodia, Laos, Myanmar and Vietnam and pushed his fellow ASEAN Leaders into action.

The ASEAN Leaders at the fourth informal Summit in November 2000 in Singapore launched the "Initiative for ASEAN Integration" (IAI) to narrow the development gap, enhance ASEAN's competitiveness as a region and accelerate the regional integration process. The next year, the ASEAN Foreign Ministers adopted the 2001 Hanoi Declaration on Narrowing the Development Gap for Closer ASEAN Integration stressing the need to "devote special efforts and resources to promoting the development of the new Member Countries of ASEAN (Cambodia, Laos, Myanmar, and Viet Nam or CLMV)". That the 2003 Declaration of the ASEAN Concord (the Bali Concord II) was signed demonstrated the priority and urgency that the ASEAN Leaders accorded to deepening and strengthening ASEAN integration through technical assistance. This was quickly followed through with the Vientiane Action Programme 2004–2010, drawn up to guide the AMS to achieve its collective ASEAN Vision 2020.

Setting up IAI Training Centres

The Ministry of Foreign Affairs of Singapore was tasked immediately to carry out the tasks set out by PM Goh. The mission was to set "clear and achievable goals" and Singapore felt that the best way to help the CLMV countries was to capitalise on areas where Singapore had considerable experience and expertise. MFA's Deputy Secretary Mr. Lee Chiong Giam led separate assessment missions to the CLMV countries in 2001 to determine their training needs and assess how and where Singapore could offer assistance that would be most relevant to the needs and interests of the CLMV countries. Mr. Lee felt that there was no point harbouring lofty ideas and imposing on the CLMV countries with training courses that may be irrelevant. This tended to be a common mistake of well-meaning international organisations and NGOs. Through these needs assessment missions, Singapore determined that training in the English language, information and communication technologies (ICT), airport and sea port management, road-building and maintenance was most urgent. An effective way to reach more trainees was to send trainers to the CLMV countries rather than to fly the trainees to Singapore.

Under the IAI, Singapore established four training centres in Phnom Penh, Vientiane, Hanoi and Yangon in 2001. In the early years, courses in the English-language, aviation management, port management and public administration were highly sought after. Demand for training in the English language was especially high because there was a recognition that ASEAN's working language was English and that learning English helped to open the world to the newer ASEAN members. It was the best way to help the CLMV countries to level up and open up access to further educational opportunities. Lao Prime Minister Thongloun Sisoulith himself took a three-month course in English language and communications at the Nanyang Polytechnic in November 1998. He renewed his ties with his lecturers when he returned to Singapore for an official visit in May 2017.[2] The courses have evolved over the years to meet the needs of the CLMV countries to include topics such as urban planning, sustainable development, food security, trade facilitation strategies and smart nation technologies, to name a few. To date, Singapore has committed more than S$170

---

[2] "Laos PM Thongloun Sisoulith recalls days spent at Nanyang Poly; meets former teachers", *The Straits Times*, 3 May 2017, accessed May 8, 2017, http:/ /www.straitstimes.com/singapore/pm-thongloun-recalls-days-spent-at-nanyang-poly-meets-formerteachers

million to the IAI and trained more than 35,000 participants from the CLMV countries.[3]

As an extension of these capacity-building programmes, Singapore also started Train-the-Trainer programmes where CLMV trainers would come to Singapore to be trained so that they can in turn go back to their home countries to train others. The Train-the-Trainer programme was successful in extending technical assistance to an even larger number of officials who needed skills training.

ASEAN Scholarships

Singapore's efforts at narrowing ASEAN's development gap did not stop at capacity-building for government officials. The ASEAN Scholarships were first introduced by then Minister for Education Mr. Ong Pang Boon in 1969. Since then, the Ministry of Education awards around 80 to 120 ASEAN Scholarships annually to outstanding students from the nine ASEAN countries at the pre-tertiary level and another 200 to 240 scholarships at the undergraduate level. The only condition for the fully expenses paid, bond-free scholarships was that students had to return home to serve in their countries. Students who came to Singapore to study were matched with a local foster family who would host them on weekends and during the school holidays. Many ASEAN students later found it difficult to leave Singapore afterwards but many of them eventually returned to contribute to their countries and to the region. Many of the ASEAN scholars who spent many of their schooling years hold many fond memories of Singapore and of the friendships they made here. I met a group of ex-ASEAN scholars in Bangkok when I served as First Secretary in the Embassy who called themselves "WIS" (Was In Singapore). They had spent their secondary school days in Singapore and subsequently left for Australia, the United Kingdom or United States to continue their studies but they would meet regularly to trade stories and tell Singaporean jokes. The reservoir of goodwill they had for Singapore was evident.

---

[3] Singapore Cooperation Programme, https://www.scp.gov.sg/content/scp/our_courses/initiative_for_asean_integration.html

Progress of the IAI

The IAI has worked through two six-year work plans — the IAI Work Plan I (2002–2008) which comprised 232 projects in four key areas of human resource development, infrastructure, ICT and regional economic integration and the IAI Work Plan II (2009–2015) which comprised 182 actions focused on the key programme areas in the ASEAN Community Blueprints. Unfortunately, the ASEAN Secretariat (ASEC) reports that although over 280 projects worth US$40 million had been undertaken, the implementation rate was less than 45%.[4] In 2016, the ASEAN Leaders adopted the Vientiane Declaration on the adoption of the IAI Work Plan III "to assist the CLMV countries to meet ASEAN-wide targets and commitments to realise the goals of the ASEAN Community". The IAI Work Plan III (2016–2010) offers a strategic framework to guide the IAI agenda and a detailed implementation schedule for the next five years. The IAI Work Plan III will focus on five priority areas: (1) food and agriculture, (2) trade facilitation, (3) micro, small and medium enterprises (MSMEs), (4) education and (5) health and well-being. The IAI Task Force which comprises the Committee of Permanent Representatives to ASEAN (CPR) is tasked to "coordinate, monitor and report the progress of implementation of the IAI Work Plan III to the ASEAN Summit annually". The ASEC has also established a dedicated unit to assist the CPR's work of tracking implementation progress.

Conclusion

There is no doubt that there has been significant progress made since 2000. According to the ASEC, the average GDP growth rate of the CLMV countries between 2006 and 2015 was between 6% to 8.7%, higher than the regional average of 5.2%. Foreign direct investment (FDI) flows into CLMV countries also more than doubled between 2007 and 2015 amounting to US$17.4 billion. While the CLMV countries

---

[4] See ASEAN Secretariat, "Initiative for ASEAN Integration (IAI) Work Plan III", http://asean.org/storage/2016/09/09rev2Content-IAI-Work-Plan-III.pdf

have made broad improvements in physical infrastructure, access to education, access to basic services like clean water, sanitation and health-care and experienced rapid economic growth in the last decade, achieving the vision of ASEAN integration cannot depend solely on technical assistance through the IAI framework. Implicit to all of the work that is going on in the CLMV countries to help them to level up is also the realization that the countries themselves must continue to implement broad policy changes and reforms that are necessary for them to keep up with the pace of change. The rapidly changing global economy, a rise in protectionist sentiments and the riskier geo-political environment will pose challenges and it will seem like a race that never meets its end point but hopefully with greater political determination and collective effort, ASEAN will be able to achieve its Vision 2025.

An Inclusive ASEAN for Enhanced Economic Growth

Cassandra CHIU

ASEAN is a ten-member state international body that is home to an estimated 630 million people. 17,102,139 people or 2.7% of the ASEAN population are reported to suffer from a disability. And this is a conservative figure. As well as the Southeast Asian culture of keeping disability care-giving within the family, there is also no established standard for measuring the prevalence of disability in the population. Data gathered from both developed and developing countries indicate that an estimate of 10% to 12% is not unrealistic. This matches the figure of 10% that is often cited by the United Nations. In truth, the figure in ASEAN is likely to be much larger than the reported 17 million people.

The 12.65% employment rate in Singapore's disabled population is not unique in the region. A recent study showed that People With Disabilities (PWD) in sheltered employment can earn as little as US$130 per month and are likely working well below their capabilities. Those who are fortunate enough to be in mainstream employment also often accept remuneration that is lower than market value, as there are no other options. This is compared to a median salary in Singapore of US$2,800 per month in the same period.

The estimated 17 million PWD in ASEAN tend to be unseen, unheard, uncounted and unrepresented. They face discrimination and barriers in many spheres and stages of life. In day-to-day life, PWD are often excluded from access to the physical environment, information and social networks. They also face barriers to equal and appropriate education and opportunities to fair employment. Most if not all are trapped in a vicious cycle of poverty. Being disabled is an expensive way of life that one does not choose. Besides the added medical cost of living with a disability, PWDs also have to foot the cost of adapting mainstream products and transport to mitigate their disability. This is exacerbated by either disproportionately low income or no employment at all.

Traditionally Southeast Asians consider disability as shameful and something to hide. Disability represents misfortune for an individual and their family. It is considered one's or one's family's failure. Whilst this archaic view is no longer prominent, the stigma remains. The culture within the region still considers family as the central and primary unit and emphasizes loyalty within the family. As such, family is often the first and only line of support for PWD. In addition, many of the religions in the region promote the value of charity and kindness, which results in sympathy towards the less fortunate. This societal environment raises PWD to be dependent on family and leaves them feeling like they do not have the skills and capabilities to thrive. A lack of relevant opportunities further reduces the impetus to step out of that self-limiting cycle and strive towards self-sufficiency.

In recent years, all ten ASEAN countries have adopted and ratified the United Nations Convention on the Rights of Persons with Disabilities. Governments have been turning their attention to including PWD in policies. However, legislative help in leveling the playing field is limited in scope and depth. More importantly, it lacks the buy-in of PWD, their families and the general public as the attitude towards disability is very much focused on the "dis" in their abilities.

ASEAN is still developing socio-economically and now is the best time to lay the right foundation for sustainable change. While supportive legislations and policies are vital, it is just as important — if not more — to shift the mindset of society from sympathy to empathy and empowerment.

For this to happen, PWD need to take responsibility to acquire the skills needed to be accountable for their success in life. When society gives PWD the opportunity to participate fully and equally in all spheres and stages of life, PWD can be contributing members of family, community and society. This will foster a new societal culture where PWD are no longer treated as lesser members of society who require charity, but can instead be respected as equals.

If US$10 per month was allocated as handout or as social support for each PWD, it would amount to an annual burden of US$2.04 billion to ASEAN collectively. Wouldn't it be better to put this money towards appropriate education, skill upgrading and creating opportunities for PWD, allowing them to achieve independence and thrive in life? PWD can only succeed when society wills it so and are ready to provide the opportunities.

The United Nations Economic and Social Commission for Asia and the Pacific estimates that if PWD were paid the same as their able bodied peers, the GDP of these countries could increase by 1% to 7%. If we take even the most conservative estimate, that would be an increase in GDP-PPP of approximately US$80 billion for ASEAN.

As ASEAN celebrates its golden jubilee, let's work towards ASEAN's centennial anniversary where we can envisage PWD stepping up and being an integral part of society, mushrooming social enterprises and inclusive employers, world class rehabilitation that would give our PWD the skills to flourish, and be a beacon for other regions in significantly reducing the effects that disability causes society.

Disability is neither alien nor distant in ASEAN. It affects 17 million Southeast Asians and their families. Why should we allow disability to continue to be seen as a liability to society? ASEAN's economic growth has outpaced that of many other regional and global economies. When ASEAN can truly include even a fraction of the 17 million PWD in the labour force, we can look forward to reaping the rewards of this inclusiveness. It could be the ingredient that brings ASEAN to its next economic peak.

Let the ASEAN motto of "One Vision, One Identity, One Community" lead the way forward in reversing the economy of disability.

A version of this essay originally appeared in the World Economic Forum on ASEAN 2017.

Cassandra CHIU founded and manages The Safe Harbour Counselling Centre. She graduated with a Master's in Professional Counselling from Swinburne University of Technology (Australia). She also lectures postgraduate students on "counselling the disabled". Cassandra was honoured with The Singapore Woman Award (2012), a fellowship at The Social Innovation Park (2012) and conferred as a Young Global Leader (2014) by the World Economic Forum. Outside of counselling, Cassandra is a passionate advocate of equal opportunities for persons with disabilities. As a consultant, she has worked with various agencies and private organisations to develop policies and services that offer equal opportunities for their employees, customers and the public. She is expanding on this area of her work. Her vision as a person living with blindness is to change what it means to be disabled in Asia for the individual, his or her family, the community and society at large.

ASEAN's
Landmark Achievements

Myanmar and ASEAN: From Isolation to Engagement

Robert CHUA

✧ ❧ ✧

When my wife Hisayo and I joined the diplomatic reception on board the United States Navy transport ship "River Fall" which made a port call in Yangon on 21 March 2017, I was glad to see a new phase of Myanmar-US relations in Myanmar's foreign policy of confidence in engaging the international community. Eleven years ago, when I started my Myanmar posting, this would have been an impossible scenario given the military government's suspicions of the outside world interfering in Myanmar's development. The foreign media missed the significance of this port call which the Myanmar media noted was the first US Navy ship to visit Myanmar since World War II. Thirty years ago, Myanmar was in a different international environment. Observers in Myanmar noted the military government's distrust of the outside world after seeing US Navy ships offshore responding to the unrest of August 1988 in Rangoon and standing by to evacuate US citizens in the city.

Why Myanmar Joined ASEAN?

Academic Mya Than noted that after ASEAN was formed in 1967, Myanmar was approached by its friends in ASEAN to join the regional organisation.[1] However, as a founding member of the Non-Aligned Movement (NAM), Myanmar adhered to the principles of peaceful co-

---

[1] Mya Than, *Myanmar in ASEAN: Regional Cooperation Experience* (Singapore: Institute of Southeast Asian Studies, 2005).

existence and neutrality and decided not to do so. It was against hosting foreign military bases and some ASEAN members then as members of the military bloc Southeast Asia Treaty Organization had allowed foreign bases on their land. Subsequently, Myanmar decided to join ASEAN in 1997.

From my conversations with Myanmar civil servants including U Aung Lynn, currently Myanmar's Ambassador to the United States, Myanmar's decision to join ASEAN was made by the State Law and Order Restoration Council (SLORC) that came into power in the 1988 coup d'état. To promote its image, the SLORC government started an initiative to increase engagement with its neighbours, regional and international organisations. Myanmar re-joined the NAM in 1992 under Indonesia's Chairmanship.[2] It took further steps to join ASEAN. Necessary preparations were made in the country and meetings with the ASEAN Member States (AMS) were conducted in the following years. The end of Cold War rivalry, socio-economic developments in the region, and the ASEAN way of addressing issues were the main factors for Myanmar to join the ASEAN. Observers in Myanmar recalled that the SLORC government was then under international pressure to release opposition leader Daw Aung San Suu Kyi and other political prisoners from imprisonment and to democratise Myanmar. They needed the regional support of ASEAN. Also, as the Cold War was over, Myanmar sought ASEAN membership to emerge from its isolation and to become a part of the regional economic community. Historically, there was a desire in Myanmar to be part of a regional organisation. Institute of Southeast Asia Studies Fellow Daw Moe Thuzar noted that independence hero General Aung San (father of Daw Aung San Suu Kyi) had envisaged in 1946 that Burma together with French Indochina, Thailand, Malaya and Indonesia might some-day form a "United States of Indochina" working together for peace and progress, based on ethnic, strategic and economic "points of affinity".[3] In General Aung San's view, an independent Burma would need to

---

[2] Myanmar left the Non-Aligned Movement in 1979.

[3] Thuzar, Moe, "Myanmar and ASEAN: New Beginnings, New Directions?", September 2016, https:/ /media.wix.com/ugd/ df6fb8_24cdf40493134aa7a lc52f986 1 4d6206.pdf

"cooperate and form friendships with other nations for mutual or mul-tilateral interests of defence or economics."

In the 1990s, ASEAN was ready to accept Myanmar together with Vietnam, Laos and Cambodia as members. ASEAN would then com-pletely represent the whole of Southeast Asia. ASEAN accepted Myanmar as a member despite protests from the Western countries. The ASEAN Secretariat (ASEC) noted that Myanmar was technically ready to join ASEAN in terms of its obligations for political, economic and functional cooperation. Myanmar had also set up a national ASEAN secretariat in its Foreign Ministry and ASEAN units in other Ministries to coordinate ASEAN-related activities. Since its entry, Myanmar has participated fully in ASEAN activities.

ASEAN's engagement with Myanmar from 1997 to 2007 was marked by constructive engagement to support its domestic reforms and integration into the regional community. Its collective position was conveyed in the annual ASEAN Foreign Ministers' Meetings and their joint statements which had paragraphs on the situation in Myanmar, urging Myanmar to release opposition leader Daw Aung San Suu Kyi and political prisoners, forge national reconciliation, hold free, fair and inclusive general elections and achieve its "Seven Step Roadmap to Democracy". Responding to international concerns, Myanmar continually informed fellow ASEAN members on its politi-cal developments. Myanmar decided to relinquish its turn to be the Chair of ASEAN in 2006 to focus on its ongoing national reconcilia-tion and democratisation process. The constructive engagement of AMS helped Myanmar in implementing its "Seven Step Roadmap to Democracy" for regional peace and stability which was completed with the general elections in 2010 and the convening of its Parliament in 2011.

Two key events in 2007 and 2008 marked the turning point of Myanmar-ASEAN relations. From August to September 2007, there was an uprising in Yangon sparked by growing economic hardships. Thousands of monks and civilians protested against the military govern-ment in downtown Yangon which ended with the use of police and mili-tary force and was widely reported by the media and netizens. The ASEAN

Chair's Statement issued by Singapore Foreign Minister Mr. George Yeo in New York on 27 September 2007 with the agreement of the other ASEAN Foreign Ministers, in response to the military's crackdown on the civilian protestors in Yangon reflected the frank interaction within the ASEAN family on the Myanmar situation which had troubled Myanmar-ASEAN relations: "The ASEAN Foreign Ministers expressed their concern to (Foreign) Minister Nyan Win that the developments in Myanmar had a serious impact on the reputation and credibility of ASEAN."

This frank spirit of ASEAN's constructive engagement with Myanmar was replayed after Cyclone Nargis devastated Myanmar from 2 to 3 May 2008. The military government was criticised by the international community for its slow response to help the thousands of disaster victims and to receive emergency international aid. It was also distracted by foreign naval ships sailing towards Myanmar to intervene and help the disaster victims under the "Right to Protect" doctrine. ASEAN collectively responded to the humanitarian disaster. The ASEAN Foreign Ministers discussed and worked with the United Nations Secretary-General to convene the ASEAN-UN Pledging Conference in Yangon on 25 May 2008 following which a consultative mechanism Tripartite Core Group (TCG) comprising Myanmar, ASEAN and the UN with three senior representatives each, was set up in Yangon on 31 May 2008 to find a way to help the military government to overcome its concerns and facilitate the inflow of emergency international aid and aid workers to help the Cyclone victims. As Singapore was then the ASEAN Chair, I was assigned by the Singapore Foreign Ministry to serve as the Senior ASEAN Member in the TCG chaired by Myanmar's Deputy Foreign Minister U Kyaw Thu who was supported by officials from Foreign and other Ministries in the crisis management. Dr. Puji Pujiono, UN Regional Disaster Response Adviser seconded to ASEAN for the post-Nargis work, and Ms. Adelina Kamal, Head of the ASEAN Secretariat's Disaster Management Unit, supported me. The UN side was led Mr. Daniel Baker, Acting UN Humanitarian Coordinator and Head of United Nations Population Fund (UNFPA) office in Yangon, who was later succeeded by Mr. Bishow Parajuli, UNDP Resident Representative in Yangon as UN

Humanitarian Coordinator, and supported by Mr. Ramesh Shrestha, UN Children's Fund (UNICEF) Representative in Myanmar and Mr. Chris Kaye, World Food Programme Representative in Myanmar.

ASEAN played an important role in the coordination of emergency international aid for the Cyclone Nargis victims in the Ayeyarwaddy region. ASEAN led and coordinated the international aid efforts through the TCG mechanism bridging cooperation and building trust between the Myanmar government and the UN representing the international community. The TCG was like a jazz band which I told my Myanmar, ASEAN and UN colleagues, as much of our work was improvisation as we did not have a precedent to work with. Our first meeting was held in the Myanmar Foreign Ministry's office in Yangon. We enjoyed good chemistry and honest and frank discussions on doing as much as we could in the critical emergency relief phase in our weekly meetings at the Chatrium Hotel in Yangon. Our common aim was to save and rebuild the lives of the survivors. Deputy Foreign Minister Kyaw Thu trusted the ASEAN team as an honest broker and in the first month of the TCG's work, he asked me to stand-in and chair the meetings for him when he went overseas on official duty. Two aspects of the emergency humanitarian work showed the trust ASEAN had built in the TCG.

Without satellite capability, the Myanmar government did not know the massive devastation caused by Cyclone Nargis in the Ayeyarwaddy region. Over 138,000 lives were lost in this natural disaster and about 2.4 million people were severely affected. The only way was to send joint assessment teams comprising Myanmar, ASEAN and UN officials quickly by helicopters, boats and cars to ground zero. I was capably supported by Colonel Kadir Maideen Mohamed and Major Ow Yong Tuck Wah of the Singapore Civil Defence Force who were sent to Yangon by Singapore's Ministry of Foreign Affairs. With their extensive experience in disaster management, they quickly set up the TCG's 24/7 Control Room in the Chatrium Hotel to guide the 32 five-member joint assessment teams and record their feedback from ground zero. Major Ow Yong Tuck Wah jointly led a damage assessment team comprising Myanmar government, ASEAN and UN officials to Labutta, the most affected township in the Ayeyarwaddy region, from 5 to 7 June 2008. The ASEAN Embassies in a collective show of solidarity deployed their diplomatic staff to help man the 24/7 Control Room until the joint assessment teams which were united with high team spirit safely returned to Yangon from their two-week exercise without casualties. The UN also deployed its assets from its Country Team in Myanmar to support this exercise. The Myanmar government was significantly cooperative in facilitating unrestricted access to the affected areas, and providing over 50 portable sets of CDMA[4] phones (based on military communications technology with wide coverage from the Ayeyarwaddy region to Yangon) to the joint assessment teams to communicate with the TCG's Control Room. This iconic bread box size handy set was the debut of CDMA handphones in Myanmar which are still used for countrywide communication by the public.

The TCG's damage assessment report gave the international community a clear picture of the urgent humanitarian needs in the Ayeyarwaddy region, and subsequently formed the basis of the landmark Post Nargis Joint Assessment (PONJA) which was a credible joint rapid assessment of recovery needs and development of a shared post-disaster recovery and reconstruction plan done by the TCG with the methodologies of the UN's village tract assessment and the World Bank's damage and loss assessment. The PONJA was submitted in time for the ASEAN Foreign Ministers Meeting in July 2008 as a progress report of the TCG's work. As recorded in detail by Pavin Chachavalpongpun and Moe Thuzar in their book *Myanmar: Life After Nargis*, based on interviews with all the key TCG participants, the PONJA exercise involved about 350 persons comprising international staffers and national staffers of ASEAN, UN agencies, World Bank, Asian Development Bank, Myanmar civil servants and local civil society volunteers, and NGOs in a systematic assessment of the impact of Cyclone Nargis. The Myanmar government also deployed 20 officers from the 18 Ministries involved in the emergency relief work to join the PONJA exercise.

---

[4] Code Division Multiple Access (CDMA), a competing cell phone service technology to Global System for Mobile Communication (GSM) that is used more widely.

Besides teamwork fostered by the TCG, PONJA's successful mission was also due to the availability of ten foreign helicopters leased by the World Food Programme and initially deployed to supply emergency food aid to the Cyclone victims in the Ayeyarwaddy region. The entry of these helicopters was initially blocked by the military government as encroaching on the country's sovereignty. ASEAN broke the deadlock. As the Senior ASEAN Member in the TCG, I urged the Myanmar government to allow these ten UN-leased helicopters on temporary deployment to complement the limited resources of the Myanmar Air Force in bringing the huge amount of international relief aid arriving daily by the air bridge from Bangkok, which was facilitated by Air Attache Colonel David Dahl of the US Embassy in Yangon who had built trust with the Myanmar authorities. I also suggested that the Myanmar government could deploy a military intelligence officer in each helicopter flight into the Ayeyarwaddy region to track its flight path and humanitarian deliveries. My inputs were accepted by the Myanmar government and the ten helicopters were allowed to be deployed at Yangon International Airport for six months.

The handling of the tonnes of emergency relief aid arriving daily at Yangon International Airport became a logistics bottleneck, with many diligent Myanmar personnel and volunteers lining up on the tarmac to manually unload the boxes of aid from each plane. Deputy Transport Minister Colonel Nyan Tun Aung asked me for technical support from Singapore. The Singapore government responded promptly with the donation of ground handling equipment and the dispatch of a technical team to help the Myanmar airport personnel to operate the equipment. This cleared the logistics bottleneck. Brigadier-General Zin Yaw, Commander of Mingaladon Air Base located next to Yangon International Airport, played an important role in transferring the emergency international aid to the Ayeyarwaddy region with the limited number of helicopters under his charge. The arrival of the ten UN-leased helicopters accelerated the aid delivery to the Cyclone survivors.

I believe that the experience of Cyclone Nargis disaster management opened the isolationist mindset in Myanmar to engage with the international community. Nargis was the worst natural disaster in the history of Myanmar. The then military government did not fully know the extent of the damage and did not have enough capacity for disaster management. ASEAN collectively helped Myanmar in this humanitarian disaster management via the TCG. The starting point was that this disaster happened in an AMS. Firstly, Myanmar had confidence in ASEAN as a family and as Southeast Asian neighbours. It had a comfort level with ASEAN and the ASEAN way of working together since Myanmar joined ASEAN in 1997. There was a natural dynamic for crisis management from the hundreds of annual ASEAN meetings which built rapport. When the ASEAN Foreign Ministers proposed this ASEAN-led TCG mechanism to the Myanmar government, there was quick acceptance and implementation. Secondly, having the presence of the ASEC office in Yangon backed by ASEAN volunteers was a practical gesture that ASEAN wanted to help on the ground, putting politics aside. In addition, ASEAN knows the UN well and vice versa. The UN represented the international community's concerns and there were occasional differences with Myanmar which were bridged by ASEAN in the post-Nargis disaster management such as approval for the ten helicopters with foreign pilots to be deployed in the emergency relief phase. In the future, this TCG mechanism could be replicated in areas of severe natural disasters facing similar issues of trust and cooperation.

Outlook

ASEAN membership has brought Myanmar out of its isolation, though not without its difficult moments when Myanmar was under military rule. Its crackdown on the monks' protests in September 2007 was firmly chided by the ASEAN family in their press statement issued in New York. Significantly, the TCG experience opened mindsets throughout the Myanmar civil service towards international engagement as benefiting the country's development. Former ASEAN Secretary-General Dr. Surin Pitsuwan addressing a Myanmar Times Forum in Yangon on 22 March 2017 recalled from his experience of working with Myanmar during the post-Cyclone Nargis emergency and reconstruction phases that

Myanmar was a "problem" for ASEAN, and presently, Myanmar was at a turning point and needed to decide how it wanted to contribute to ASEAN.

In the past five years of its active engagement with ASEAN and the outside world, I see Myanmar growing in confidence after it capably completed its first Chairmanship of ASEAN in 2014. While there were some skeptics among ASEAN's Dialogue Partners on Myanmar's capacity to be Chair, they did not know that Myanmar had an experienced ASEAN team led by President U Thein Sein who had been attending ASEAN Summits since he was Prime Minister in 2007, Foreign Minister U Wunna Maung Lwin who had extensive experience from attending UN General Assemblies in New York and Geneva, and Permanent Secretary U Aung Lynn who was in the Foreign Ministry's ASEAN Department since it was set up and led their delegation to the ASEAN Senior Officials' Meetings. It was significant that US President Barack Obama attended the ASEAN-East Asia Summit and ASEAN-US Summits in Nay Pyi Taw, marking a new chapter of Myanmar-US relations which were upgraded to a partnership with the lifting of US sanctions and the restoration of Generalised System of Preferences in 2016 after State Counsellor Daw Aung San Suu Kyi's visit. The experience of Myanmar and the US working together in post-Cyclone Nargis disaster management fostered by the ASEAN-led TCG, and Myanmar's subsequent rotational role as Dialogue Coordinator of ASEAN-US relations catalysed Myanmar-US rapprochement.

2017 marks ASEAN's 50th anniversary and the 20th anniversary of Myanmar's membership of ASEAN. I believe ASEAN through its annual meetings and Initiative for ASEAN Integration (IAI) capacity building programmes, will continue to support Myanmar to be an active and responsible member of the regional and international community as it grapples with the challenges of forging peaceful national reconciliation to end six decades of ethnic conflict, and the racial and religious divide in its Rakhine State. In its one-year performance report under the new Myanmar government and marking the 20th anniversary of its membership, the Myanmar Ministry of Foreign Affairs stated:

For nearly two decades, continued criticism and pressure were exerted on ASEAN because of Myanmar's human rights and de-

mocracy record. It was thus believed within ASEAN that Myanmar was a hindrance to ASEAN's efforts for the promotion of
cooperation with Western countries. Now, Myanmar has transformed into a democratic nation, and has become the countries (*sic*) with the most political and media freedoms among
AMS, it may have been seen that the participation of Myanmar
in ASEAN has gained the high regard of other countries in the
world.

— *The Global New Light of Myanmar*, 31 March 2017

A career diplomat, **Robert CHUA Hian Kong** has been serving as Singapore's
Ambassador to the Republic of the Union of Myanmar since May 2006. His
previous postings were the USA, Japan, Philippines and Vietnam. He served
as the Senior ASEAN Member in the Myanmar-ASEAN-UN Tripartite Core
Group in 2008 which was set up by the ASEAN Foreign Ministers to facilitate
the distribution of international humanitarian assistance to the victims of
Cyclone Nargis. He is currently also serving as Dean of the Diplomatic Corps
in Myanmar. He graduated with a Bachelor of Social Sciences Honours degree
in Political Science from the University of Singapore in 1979, and a Master
of Arts degree in International Relations from the Fletcher School of Law
and Diplomacy, Tufts University, Boston, USA in 1985 under a Fulbright
Scholarship. He was awarded the Singapore Armed Forces Good Service Medal
in 1981 after the completion of national service, the Civil Service Long Service
Medal in 2002 and the Public Administration Medal (Silver) in 2004.

Weathering the Storm: ASEAN's Humanitarianism in the Aftermath of Nargis

Noeleen HEYZER

Introduction

While it is only in recent years that ASEAN has begun to play an active humanitarian role, the roots of ASEAN's humanitarianism in fact go back to the founding of the regional body in 1967. According to ASEAN's founding document, the Bangkok Declaration, ASEAN's main objectives are to maintain regional stability, promote economic cooperation and regional integration and to protect social and cultural development of its people. The concepts of peace and protection are, at the core, humanitarian concepts, that put the well-being of people at the centre and recognise the imperative of protecting those in need.

ASEAN did not, however, consciously assume a humanitarian role until the late 2000s, following several massive disasters in the region. The first was the Aceh tsunami of December 2004, which contributed to the acceleration of ASEAN's ratification of a legally binding framework on disasters, the AADMER or in full, the ASEAN Agreement on Disaster Management and Emergency Response, the fastest agreement to ever be passed in ASEAN. The second was Cyclone Nargis in May 2008, the massive cyclone in Myanmar that set the stage for the first-ever humanitarian coordination mission led by ASEAN, an experience that provided the momentum for the establishment of the ASEAN Coordinating Centre for Humanitarian Assistance in disaster response (AHA Centre). It was a defining experience for ASEAN, described by then Secretary-General of ASEAN, Dr. Surin Pitsuwan, as ASEAN's "baptism by cyclone". Singapore was chair of ASEAN when Cyclone Nargis struck and Foreign Minister George Yeo played a critical role in the decision by ASEAN Foreign Ministers to allow ASEAN to take the lead in the coordination of assistance to the victims of Cyclone Nargis.

A Cyclone Like No Other

Cyclone Nargis struck Myanmar on 2 May 2008, causing widespread destruction and devastation across the Ayeyarwady Delta. The cyclone was the deadliest ever recorded in the North Indian Ocean Basin and the second-deadliest named tropical storm of all time. It left more than 140,000 people dead or missing and more than 800,000 homeless, with an estimated 2.4 million people — one-third of the entire population of Ayeyarwady and Yangon divisions — were affected by the disaster. The cyclone devastated farming and fishing communities, destroying over 700,000 homes and causing severe damage to critical infrastructure, including the destruction of schools and three-quarters of the hospitals and clinics in the area. Damage was estimated at US$4 billion, with total economic losses amounting to approximately 2.7 percent of Myanmar's projected gross domestic product (GDP) in 2008.

In the immediate aftermath of the cyclone, then Myanmar Prime Minister U Thein Sein activated the National Disaster Preparedness Central Committee. However, the Government of Myanmar was reluctant to allow access to international assistance and aid workers. While some bilateral aid, including from neighbouring countries, was accepted, the majority of international humanitarian workers were prevented from entering the country. Pressure mounted from the international community, with some diplomats calling for lifesaving assistance to be delivered without the consent of the government. Myanmar's relationship with many Western countries had been tense for about two decades before the Cyclone struck. The presence of a United States naval ship and a French warship created great suspicion from Myanmar as to the nature of international humanitarian intervention, particularly as there was talk around invoking the "Responsibility to Protect".

I was in Jakarta on 8 May at a meeting with Bill Gates when I received news that the numbers of those who had died or were missing had reached 100,000. No public statement from any of our countries had been issued at that time and the Government made it clear that they did not welcome outside help. What crossed my mind immediately was how isolated the country had become, that there was a complete lack of trust of the outside world that had to be bridged, but the outside world had no idea how best to engage. Many people worked behind the scenes and on the ground to find solutions that could work. As an initial step, ASEAN had invoked AADMER for the first time in its history. After obtaining agreement from member states, an ASEAN Emergency Rapid Assessment Team (ERAT) comprising disaster management experts from ASEAN countries was deployed from 9 to 18 May 2008. In my capacity as UN Under-Secretary-General and Executive Secretary of the Economic and Social Commission for Asia and the Pacific (ESCAP), I felt, like many others, that ASEAN and the UN could together play an even stronger role to build trust and facilitate humanitarian cooperation. This chapter captures my small contribution in the context of this bigger effort.

Bridge of Trust

Since I was in Jakarta, I immediately contacted Dr. Pitsuwan to hear his views and discuss possible options. Since he was traveling, he suggested that I speak on both our behalf when I met with various Indonesian officials. I approached Dr. Kuntoro Mangkusubroto, the Executive Director of the Indonesian Bureau for Rehabilitation and Reconstuction Agency for Aceh and Nias (BRR) to ask whether he and his team could offer assistance based on the agency's experience in the 2004 tsunami recovery. They were eager to help and Pak Kuntoro promised to discuss the matter with the President. However, even the Indonesian Government could not get all their aid into Myanmar, much of which was held up in Singapore. During my meeting with Indonesian Foreign Minister, Dr. Hassan Wirajuda, I added my voice to those who stressed that Indonesia would have to make a strong stand to support the Government of Myanmar through ASEAN. There were similarities between the situation in Aceh and Myanmar. In fact, Dr. Kuntoro's Director of International Relations, Mr. Heru Prasetyo, trusted me to deliver a book to the Prime Minister of Myanmar on the transformation of the Indonesian Army and the relief operation in Aceh after the tsunami, which PM Thein Sein later told me he found very useful.

ASEAN's collective response to Nargis was confirmed on 19 May when an emergency meeting of foreign ministers chaired by Singapore decided on an ASEAN-led coordinating mechanism. Singapore's Foreign Minister George Yeo and Indonesian Foreign Minister Dr. Wirajuda made a strong plea for ASEAN to play a leading role in the humanitarian response. This was based on the ERAT recommendation that a humanitarian coalition be formed to 'facilitate effective distribution and utilisation of assistance from the international community, including the expeditious and effective deployment of relief workers, especially health and medical personnel". The decision of the Singapore meeting was immediately conveyed to the UN Secretary-General, Mr. Ban Ki Moon and led to the ASEAN-UN cooperation that followed. ASEAN would now be able to build a bridge of trust to encourage Myanmar to work with the outside world in a coherent and coordinated way. Without ASEAN's willingness to play this bridging role, Myanmar would have remain isolated and continued dealing with the massive disaster internally, while the outside world would have been kept out of the relief and recovery efforts.

A New Humanitarian Partnership

Over the following week, the ASEAN Secretariat, in consultation with experts from member states, worked on designing an appropriate mechanism, drawing on Indonesia's experience in the 2004 Indian Ocean tsunami recovery effort. A two-tiered structure with a two-year mandate was agreed to. The ASEAN Humanitarian Task Force (AHTF), functioned as the diplomatic and policy-level body of the ten ASEAN countries. Following the first AHTF meeting on 25 May, an operational mechanism, the Yangon-based Tripartite Core Group (TCG) was established to oversee the everyday operations of the relief and recovery efforts chaired by Myanmar's then Deputy Foreign Minister, U Kyaw Thu. It consisted of nine representatives, three each from ASEAN, the Myanmar government and the United Nations. Singapore Ambassador Robert Chua, Thai Ambassador Barnsarn Bunnag, and Vietnam Ambassador Chu Cong Phung served on the TCG on behalf of ASEAN.

It was a historic first for ASEAN's collective humanitarian engagement. It was also the first time ASEAN and the UN worked together on disaster management. The partnership was built on strong personal relationships and trust; and ASEAN provided that bridge of trust while the United Nations engaged with its expertise and material resources. The UN Secretary-General played a major role when he attended the ASEAN-UN International Pledging Conference on 25 May in Yangon chaired by Singapore Minister George Yeo. I was part of the Secretary-General's delegation and witnessed his announcement after meeting with Senior General Than Shwe that he had obtained agreement for full humanitarian access for the international community. It was a real breakthrough that took everyone by surprise, and one that helped the TCG achieve some early successes. For instance, the TCG was able to facilitate access for humanitarian workers through the granting of nearly 4,000 visas during the emergency relief period. Aid workers' requests for visas, visa extensions and permits to travel were channeled through the TCG's fast-track process.

Following a visit to cyclone-affected areas in late July 2008, then UN Emergency Relief Coordinator Sir John Holmes remarked that "Nargis showed us a new model of humanitarian partnership, adding the special position and capabilities of ASEAN to those of the UN in working effectively with the government". ASEAN leadership, Holmes continued, was "vital in building trust with the government and saving lives". Local organisations also felt that ASEAN had played a much-needed role. Its engagement helped to open up an unprecedented level of humanitarian space in the country, and allowed for the establishment of a more permanent humanitarian presence to facilitate humanitarian assistance.

Benchmarks of Progress

ASEAN also worked with the government of Myanmar and international partners to establish benchmarks to monitor progress in the recovery effort. I was pleased to be a member of the AHTF's Advisory Group assisting them to make policy decisions and establish the priorities and targets with regard to the implementation of the ASEAN-led initiative. Over the next two years, this unprecedented international relief effort pooled together the resources of ASEAN Member States, UN organisations and the international community and progress was made on several fronts.

The Post-Nargis Joint Assessment (PONJA) was launched on 8 June 2008, involving staff and volunteers from the government of Myanmar, ASEAN, the UN, international and local NGOs, and the private sector. The Asian Development Bank and the World Bank also took part. Divided into 32 teams, more than 300 people spent ten days assessing cyclone-affected areas that had previously been effectively closed to foreigners. The results of the needs assessment provided the comprehensive understanding of the damage and loss, and the resources needed for post disaster relief and reconstruction.

To guide recovery efforts, the AHTF and the TCG also facilitated the formulation of the Post-Nargis Recovery and Preparedness Plan (PONREPP), which set out a three-year recovery strategy running from 2009 to 2011. The economic sanctions against Myanmar created a complicated backdrop for donors who struggled to fund the activities beyond the immediate relief efforts. Against many odds, I co-chaired a donor conference in Bangkok with ASEAN Secretary-General Dr. Pitsuwan on 25 November 2009 and together we succeeded to raise 90 percent of the requested US$103 million urgently needed by the affected communities in the Delta as identified by the PONREPP. It made a difference that we had visited these communities together and knew the realities on the ground.

In addition, the TCG Chair U Kyaw Thu, Dr. Pitsuwan, and I worked together to explore good practices and lessons learned from the region of how Governments successfully managed complex post-disaster reconstruction efforts to help Myanmar with knowledge and guiding principles in preparing recovery plans. This culminated in the ESCAP-ASEAN Regional High-level Expert Group meeting on Post-Nargis Recovery, October 2008, attended by more than 100 regional experts and high-ranking decision-makers from governments, international partners and the United Nations. Much of the discussions guided the preparation of the PONREPP. Deputy Minister U Kyaw Thu found that the experience "went beyond all expectations" and requested that I explore possibilities to work beyond the cyclone-affected areas to support the longer-term economic and social development of Myanmar. This eventually led to an unprecedented dialogue with Myanmar's leaders on development and poverty reduction that allowed eminent international scholars, such as Nobel Laurate Joseph Stiglitz, and local researchers to exchange experiences and ideas with government leaders in December 2009. This has been regarded by many as helping to catalyze the early opening-up of the country from its former isolation.

ASEAN's Future Humanitarian Role

Cyclone Nargis occurred at a defining moment, as Member States had adopted the first ASEAN Charter only months earlier. It was the first humanitarian mission in which ASEAN played a coordinating role and set an important precedent for the organisation's role in crisis management in the region. It was a test for ASEAN's solidarity and relevance. The collective leadership of our Foreign Ministers and Ambassadors, working closely with Myanmar, and in partnership with the international humanitarian community, delivered and made meaningful progress on the goals of the Charter to bring ASEAN closer to the people. As ASEAN turns 50, this is an achievement to be proud of and celebrated. It is my hope that the experience from Nargis will encourage ASEAN to make similar progress when the region faces new challenges and humanitarian emergencies. Then only will we be able to further celebrate the Charter's commitment to "place the well-being, livelihood and welfare of the peoples at the centre of the ASEAN community-building process". The current humanitarian challenge for ASEAN is for its Member States to commit to consistent cooperation for alleviating human suffering and for the facilitation of humanitarian assistance to people in need in all humanitarian crises, whether natural or man-made. Such commitment would ensure that ASEAN's humanitarianism is in line with international humanitarian principles of humanity and impartiality, and that ASEAN will continue to show leadership in regional humanitarian action. ASEAN's role in the Nargis response has shown that an effective people-centred ASEAN can work and when it does, it brings stability and peace not just to our region but the world.

Noeleen HEYZER served as UN Under-Secretary-General (2007–2015). She was the first woman to head the UN Economic and Social Commission for Asia and the Pacific (ESCAP). She was also the UN Special Adviser to Timor-Leste. She worked closely with ASEAN, Myanmar, and the UN in the recovery efforts assisting cyclone-affected people in the Ayeyarwady Delta. In 2009, she led an unprecedented dialogue with Myanmar's leaders on development and poverty reduction. She was the first UN official to address the East Asia Summit convened by ASEAN, and led on regional connectivity together with ADB President, Mr. Haruhiko Kuroda. Dr. Heyzer was the first Executive Director from the South to lead the UN Women's Fund (1994–2007) and is widely recognized for her work on Women, Peace and Security.

Journey Towards an ASEAN Free Trade Area for Trade in Goods: An Exercise in Mutual Accommodation

David CHIN Soon Siong

ASEAN was established in 1967 by Indonesia, Malaysia, Philippines, Singapore and Thailand primarily for political reasons. It was the five countries' aim to foster closer political association in response to increasing geopolitical tensions in Southeast Asia.

Towards the late 1980s it was apparent that such political closeness had evolved satisfactorily. This enabled the five countries to bond even further and an economic relationship was the next logical area for closer cooperation.

ASEAN's first move was to work towards freeing up trade in goods among the six countries, as Brunei had joined ASEAN by 1984.

The Common Effective Preferential Tariff (CEPT) scheme was the main mechanism through which tariffs were reduced in ASEAN. The Agreement on the CEPT for the ASEAN Free Trade Area (AFTA-CEPT) was signed in 1992 and came into effect in 1993. ASEAN adopted a process that accommodated the differing stages of development amongst the original six ASEAN Member States (AMS) and subsequently evolved an even more accommodating formula for the four newer AMS. This process was deemed necessary so that those countries that were able to liberalise their tariffs could lead by example. It was hoped that this would encourage the other AMS by showing the effects of positive gains in their economic development due to trade liberalisation.

Singapore's Role in the AFTA-CEPT

In Singapore, tariffs are practically non-existent. Singapore's role in the AFTA-CEPT was therefore to lead by example and effectively become the first to achieve all the targets set while awaiting the rest of the AMS to reach their targets at their own pace within the accommodating approach described below. Singapore's legendary negotiator, Mr. Ridzwan Dzafir chaired the Committee of Trade and Tourism (COTT) in the early years of ASEAN. Singapore initiated many of the approaches described below and strived to work towards a gradual process that the other ASEAN countries could accept.

Mr. Ridzwan Dzafir was the Director-General of Singapore's then Trade Development Board[1] when he took on the chairmanship of COTT. The negotiation for AFTA-CEPT started in COTT. When the five Economic Committees were reorganised into the Senior Economic Officials' Meeting (SEOM), he, as Singapore's SEOM Leader continued to lead discussions on all economic issues, but his heart was mainly with the AFTA-CEPT.

A very soft-spoken man, Mr. Dzafir would often quietly persuade compromises amongst the ASEAN negotiators through a combination of formal interventions in negotiations coupled with behind-the-scenes discussions with the negotiators holding opposing positions. He had never been known to react angrily during the negotiations, however difficult some negotiators were. As Chairman of COTT, he would always continue talking and in the process point out very clearly the implications of the issues. In so doing, he was able to show to a negotiator pushing an unfair approach the implications of his position and demonstrate the unfairness of his position without having to argue or shame him. This had helped in many instances where the negotiator then realised the folly of his approach and changed his position. Ridzwan therefore allowed that negotiator to abandon his position by agreeing with Ridzwan rather than having to lose the argument with a "loss of face".

---

[1] Established in 1983, the Trade Development Board was later restructured to form the International Enterprise Singapore (IE Singapore) in 2002.

As a very fair man, Ridzwan seemed to keep track of who he had helped in the negotiations and he would often balance this by helping the opposing party the next time round. Since Singapore often was not a party to these disagreements, he was therefore always the "Honest Broker". Over the years, his reputation as a fair and honest chairman of COTT enabled him to be instrumental in moving the AFTA-CEPT forward.

A main reason for the respect that all ASEAN negotiators had for Ridzwan was his clear goal that all the negotiators not find themselves in big trouble when they returned back to their countries after a round of negotiations. There had been many instances where a position pushed by one ASEAN country resulted in major difficulties for another ASEAN country. Ridzwan would, in that case, very diplomatically allude to those results so that it awakened the affected party who otherwise did not object earlier. He had saved many of his fellow ASEAN negotiators this way.

These negotiators would always come up to Ridzwan to thank him afterwards for helping them understand the implications of what could have been a very difficult position for them.

After years, the respect that all ASEAN negotiators had for "Pak Ridzwan" was demonstrated by the fact that an assurance by Ridzwan of a fair proposal was what could lead to an agreement. I had the privilege to be Ridzwan's deputy for many years and succeeded him as Singapore's SEOM Leader and would always remember his advice to never forget that our fellow negotiators all had to return home to face their bosses, and had to report what they have achieved. Hence, often Ridzwan's Chairmanship of COTT was one where he tried to ensure that every ASEAN country gained something that they can claim on their return home. The other negotiators got to know this over the years and this led to a more collegial relationship in the AFTA-CEPT negotiations. This was therefore the main reason why the AFTA-CEPT evolved from such a friendly, mutually helpful and understanding approach, rather than the usual intense bargaining and conflicts that was more typical of trade negotiations elsewhere in the world.

In the record of Singapore's role in ASEAN, we must acknowledge the contributions of the late Mr. S. Tiwari, Principal Senior State

Counsel, International Affairs Division of Singapore's Attorney-General's Chambers.

Tiwari was involved in the negotiation of all ASEAN Agreements since the start of ASEAN.

He used to be the legal right hand man of Pak Ridzwan during Ridzwan's 30 years as Singapore SEOM Leader. He made sure that whatever we did was properly and legally documented.

Singapore had always been asked by ASEAN member countries to draft ASEAN Trade Agreements and practically all of them were drafted by Tiwari himself.

He is really Mr. Legal ASEAN Trade Agreements.

ASEAN Secretariat did not have a legal department or legal officers until the early 2000s, hence ASEAN had always relied on Singapore and Tiwari to put up the first draft. Then all the lawyers from the other AMS would comment and it was always Tiwari who chaired the Legal Drafting Committee to clean up the negotiated text for the Ministers to sign. Tiwari therefore had drafted all the AFTA-CEPT Agreements and hence contributed significantly to ASEAN.

The process to achieve agreement comprises the following very gradual and accommodating steps:

A. ASEAN's Process of Negotiated Accommodation

In the 1992 AFTA-CEPT Agreement, the founding ASEAN countries committed to reducing tariffs between zero to five per cent over 15 years. ASEAN countries were free to decide on the rate and extent of their tariff reduction as long as the target of all tariffs at zero to five per cent was achieved at the end of the 15 years i.e. by the year 2008. ASEAN countries then voluntarily decided on their own liberalisation programmes, and staging of their tariff reductions.

B. Rate of Liberalisation of Goods Tariffs

Initially the rate of tariff reductions was minimal and there were con-cerns that too many tariff lines would be left to be concluded in the later stages. Also, there was too slow a reduction in effective percentages in the initial years. Concerns about the risk of a large "cliff jump" in tariff reductions towards the end of the process — causing unacceptable economic effects — were very real. Attempts were then made to accelerate liberalisation during the earlier years in order to pre-empt that situation. This would be to prevent the process from becoming far too difficult in the later years for ASEAN to accomplish.

C. Negotiated Targets for Liberalisation

The Senior Economic Officials' Meetings (SEOM) then agreed on setting targets for the ASEAN countries to comply with, while maintaining the flexibility that countries could select tariff lines for liberalisation to suit their own development needs. The initial target was for countries to make a reduction in respect of an agreed percentage of tariff lines by a certain year. The formula was then improved — to one where the percentage of tariff lines committed for reduction would need to account for an agreed percentage of the individual ASEAN country's intra-ASEAN trade. This meant that reductions were to be made only to those items actually traded within ASEAN. These agreed percentages were periodically and gradually increased.

D. Acceleration of Overall Target

In tandem with the gradual increases in the percentage of lines for tariff reduction, ASEAN Ministers and Heads of Government also agreed on accelerating the overall timeframe. In 1994, the original timeframe of 15 years (2008) was reduced to ten years (2003). In 1998, this timeframe was further reduced to nine years (2002) such that the original six ASEAN countries were committed to reduce all their tariffs to zero to five per cent by 2002. The next most important development in ASEAN's tariff liberalisation efforts was the November 1999 decision by ASEAN's Heads of Government that all import tariffs on all products under the AFTA-CEPT scheme would be eliminated (zero per cent or no tariffs) for the original six ASEAN countries by 2010 and for the remaining four newer ASEAN countries (Cambodia, Lao PDR, Myanmar and Vietnam) by 2015.

E. Safety Valves to Underpin Accelerated Liberalisation

Realism had a role. In order to obtain agreement for accelerated liberali-sation, the negotiators had to cater for sensitivities that may be peculiar to different countries. Failure or unwillingness to address this would have resulted in no agreement for acceleration, especially if countries felt that such sensitivities were not catered for. To build in these safety valves, ASEAN agreed that tariff lines that were progressively reduced would be deemed to form an "Inclusion List" (IL). The AFTA-CEPT mechanism then classified the non-included tariff lines of products into four other categories; namely the "Temporary Exclusion List" (TEL), the "Sensitive List" (SL), and the "Highly Sensitive List" (HSL) as well as a "General Exceptions" List (GE). Items in these four lists were taken out of the percentages committed for liberalisation.

1. Temporary Exclusion List (TEL)

Items in the TEL refer to products receiving protection from a delay in tariff reductions. These products can be held at tariffs higher than 20% until 1 January 2000, at which time they would all have to be brought into the Inclusion List (IL). Entry into the Inclusion List must be at the tariff rate of 20% or lower for the original six ASEAN countries.

2. Sensitive List (SL)

The SL comprises unprocessed agricultural products which were given a longer timeframe for liberalisation. These products have until 2010 to meet the reduction of tariffs to within the zero to five percent range.

3. Highly Sensitive List (HSL)

The HSL consists of unprocessed agricultural products, namely sugar and rice, which have been given a longer timeframe before being phased into the AFTA-CEPT. These products have up to 2010 to reach a reduction of tariffs to not more than 20% tariff rate.

4. General Exceptions (GE)

Items in the GE Lists refer to products which a country deems necessary for the protection of national security, public morals, protection of human, animal and plant life and health and the protection of artistic, historic or archaeological value. These products designated as GE are permanently excluded from the AFTA-CEPT scheme. Initially countries are free to put an agreed limited number of products into this list to cover special sensitivities. Notwithstanding this liberal allowance, ASEAN countries have now agreed to review their respective GE lists with a view towards phasing them into the AFTA-CEPT scheme. What this means is that only those items in accordance with the WTO General Exceptions rules can in future remain in the GE list.

F. Encouraging the Liberalisation Process through an Interim Reciprocity Rule

To encourage faster liberalisation and phasing into the Inclusion List, ASEAN negotiators agreed that an item is only deemed to be in the IL when its tariff has been reduced to 20%, and that an ASEAN country can only enjoy the tariff reductions of other countries' included items if its own tariff is also in the Inclusion List. This effectively means that if an ASEAN country wants to enjoy the 20% or less for item A of another ASEAN country, it must reduce its own tariff for item A to 20% at least. This is a departure from the WTO's Most-Favoured Nation (MFN) principle, but as it is only for the interim process of liberalisation, it serves as a motivating factor and an accelerator. This was accepted by all ASEAN countries and is the main reason for ASEAN accelerating its process of liberalisation by encouraging the entry of the TEL into the IL list and by driving tariffs down to 20%. Once the process is completed, full MFN principle will be automatically reinstated.

G. Setting of Interim Targets for Tariff Lines in the Inclusion List to Reach 0–5% Tariff and Later to Reach Zero Tariff

The ASEAN Economic Ministers then agreed that once a product's line has been put into the Inclusion List at 20% tariff or below 20% tariff, the tariff will be further reduced to a 0–5% tariff rate within two years of its entry into the Inclusion List.

Interim targets were then set to ensure an orderly phase-in of the target elimination of tariffs by 2010 for the original six ASEAN countries and by 2015 for the four newer ASEAN countries. After the six original ASEAN countries achieved the bulk of tariff commitments at the 0–5% rate, an additional set of targets was agreed on for the four newer ASEAN countries to arrive at the 0–5% tariff rate level.

The four newer ASEAN countries were given three more years from 2015 to 2018 to keep some of their tariffs at the 0–5% tariff rate instead of reducing all the Inclusion List tariffs to zero by 2015.

These interim targets were agreed to by the ASEAN Economic Ministers in September 2002 and are set out in Table 1 and Table 2 below.

Through this method of gradually accommodating the interests of AMS, coupled with the use of fixed negotiated targets, the ten ASEAN countries were able to target all the tariffs in the Inclusion List for a reduction down to zero for the six original ASEAN countries by 2010 and by 2015 for the four newer ASEAN countries. Given the large difference in the development levels of ASEAN, this was a unique approach towards liberalisation of trade in goods.

Table 1.   Percentage of tariff lines in Inclusion List (IL) to reach 0–5% tariff.

	ASEAN-6	Vietnam	Laos and Myanmar	Cambodia
80%	—	2003	2005	2007
100%	2003	2005, with flexibility to 2006	2007, with flexibility to 2008	2009, with flexibility to 2010

Table 2.   Percentage of tariff lines in Inclusion List (IL) to reach zero tariff.

	ASEAN-6	Vietnam	Laos and Myanmar	Cambodia
60%	2003	2006	2008	2010
80%	2007	2010	2012	—
100%	2010	2015, with flexibility up to 2018	2015, with flexibility up to 2018	2015, with flexibility up to 2018

Source: Author's own, Year 2001.

H. Adherence to WTO Principles

While the process adopted by ASEAN was unique and a departure from the "Request and Offer" or "Formula" approach adopted by the GATT and the WTO in their many negotiation rounds, all other GATT and WTO principles were faithfully observed by ASEAN. The biggest variation ASEAN adopted was the Reciprocity Rule which differed from the full MFN principle in the WTO. Such interim non-compliance with the MFN principle was deemed a necessity to encourage voluntary phasing-in and was seen as a more acceptable approach to the ten ASEAN countries than the GATT/WTO's Request and Offer or Formula approaches. ASEAN also followed the GATT/WTO targets of completing their FTAs in goods within ten years and ensuring that its AFTA-CEPT covers in excess of 90% of all its tariff lines, even though the AFTA-CEPT was notified to the GATT/WTO under the Enabling Clause where ASEAN could have been excused from these two accelerating targets as a grouping of developing countries. ASEAN also continues to work progressively on the elimination of Non-Tariff Barriers (NTBs).

Conclusion

The process that the ASEAN Economic Ministers and the Senior Economic officials agreed upon and gradually implemented was indeed a unique pragmatic solution to what was initially seen as an impossible attempt to have the founding ASEAN countries and the four others that joined midway to achieve liberalisation in the most fundamental aspect of trade relations — the trade in goods across borders.

This essay is presented to show that indeed an impossible task can be achieved if all parties are willing to understand the difficulties that their partners face and be willing to constructively try to accommodate their needs so that all partners can together achieve their objectives in a reasonable and satisfactory way.

David CHIN Soon Siong is the Executive Director of the Singapore Maritime Foundation (SMF). He graduated with a Bachelor of Science degree (First Class Honours) in Engineering from Newcastle-Upon-Tyne Polytechnic, UK in 1971. In 1985, he joined the Trade Development Board (now known as International Enterprise Singapore) where he contributed in divisions including Export of Services, International Trading, Multilateral Trade Policy, Shipping and Logistics, and the Trade Facilitation and Administration. He became Deputy Chief Executive Officer in 1994 and was appointed Director-General (Trade) for the ASEAN Division in 2002. In January 2004, he was appointed as the Director-General (Trade) of the Ministry of Trade and Industry. He retired from the Singapore government service in 2007, and continued as a Consultant to the Ministry of Trade and Industry on trade issues until 2011. He was awarded the Public Administration Medal (Silver) on National Day in 1993 and the Public Administration Medal (Gold) on National Day in 2000 by the President of the Republic of Singapore.

ASEAN's Efforts to Combat Terrorism
in the Age of ISIS[1]

Kumar RAMAKRISHNA

৵ ট ৴

In April 2016, reports emerged of a "*wilayat*" or province of the Islamic State of Iraq and Syria (ISIS) being formed in Mindanao in the southern Philippines. As ISIS has come under severe Western-led coalition military pressure in its territorial base in Iraq and Syria, it has sought to retaliate by orchestrating or inspiring attacks within coalition territories by returning "foreign fighters" or self-radicalised "lone wolves". Southeast Asia, given its strategic location astride busy global sea-lanes as well as a quarter of the world's Muslim population, appears to have been targeted by ISIS planners in this regard. ISIS ideologues have expanded *Bahasa Indonesia* and Malay-language social media output in a bid to radicalise vulnerable communities in the region. Thus the alleged formation of the ISIS *wilayat* in Mindanao may signify the possibility of more ISIS-related attacks regionally.[2] In the face of such a looming threat, how equipped is ASEAN to cope? This essay shows that transnational terrorism of the ISIS variety is not new and since the Al-Qaeda assaults on New York and Washington DC on 11 September 2001, several counter-terrorism

---

[1] The author would like to thank Ms. Tang Ming Hui of RSIS for research assistance in the preparation of this essay.

[2] Bilveer Singh and Kumar Ramakrishna, "Islamic State's Wilayah Philippines: Implications for Southeast Asia", *RSIS Commentary*, July 21, 2017, https://www.rsis.edu.sg/rsis-publication/rsis/co16187-islamic-states-wilayah-philippines-implications-for-southeast-asia/#.WCgYfVfYr-Y

initiatives have been launched by ASEAN at regional, sub-regional and extra-regional levels. The challenge now is to ensure that ASEAN states keep pace with rapidly evolving trends in terrorism and in particular, the extremist ideologies that sustain terrorist networks.

Regional Level

On 11 October 2001, a month after the September 11 Al-Qaeda attacks in the United States, ASEAN Ministers at the Third ASEAN Ministerial Meeting on Transnational Crime (AMMTC) in Singapore, issued a joint communiqué affirming that they "recognised the growing need for the region to deal with many more forms of transnational crime, including terrorism…"[3] The communiqué "strongly condemned all acts of terrorism, in particular the terrorist attacks of 11 September 2001 on the US, which led to the loss of innocent lives of people of various nationalities and destruction of properties", and emphasised ASEAN's commitment to enhance "cooperation among our law enforcement agencies to combat terrorism".[4] The ministers also agreed to implement the ASEAN Plan of Action to Combat Transnational Crime with a particular focus on terrorism.[5]

In November 2001, ASEAN Member States (AMS) signed a very important document: the ASEAN Declaration on Joint Action to Counter Terrorism. They agreed to undertake several practical measures, including, in essence, the review and strengthening of national mechanisms to combat terrorism; calling for the early ratification of all relevant anti-terrorist conventions including the International Convention for the Suppression of the Financing of Terrorism; deepening counter-terrorism cooperation among front-line law enforcement agencies; studying relevant international conventions on terror-

---

[3] ASEAN, "Joint Communiqué of the Third ASEAN Ministerial Meeting on Transnational Crime", October 11, 2011, http://asean.org/?static_post=joint-communique-of-the-third-asean-ministerial-meeting-on-transnational-crime-ammtc-singapore-11-october-2001

[4] *Ibid.*

[5] *Ibid.*

ism with the view to integrating them with ASEAN counter-terrorism mechanisms; enhancing information/intelligence exchange on the modus operandi of transnational terrorist networks; strengthening existing counter-terrorism coordination between the AMMTC and other relevant ASEAN bodies; enhancing measures to combat terrorist organisations, support infrastructure and funding and bringing the perpetrators to justice; developing regional capacity building programmes to enhance existing capabilities of ASEAN member countries to investigate, detect, monitor and report on terrorist acts; exploring practical initiatives to increase ASEAN's counter-terrorism engagement with extra-regional partners within existing frameworks such as the ASEAN Plus Three (ASEAN+3), the ASEAN Dialogue Partners and the ASEAN Regional Forum (ARF); and finally, strengthening cooperation at bilateral, regional and international levels in combating terrorism in a comprehensive manner and affirming the major role of the United Nations at the international level.[6]

The ASEAN Declaration was in many ways a seminal document, shaping the overall approach taken by the AMS thereafter in tackling terrorism at all levels and sectors. In May 2002, moreover, ASEAN released a Work Program to Implement the October 2011 Plan of Action to Combat Transnational Crime, including strategies for addressing terrorism at a regional level. Strategies include the compilation of national laws pertaining to terrorism into a central repository, information sharing, exchanging information on the detection of weapons of mass destruction, and working toward ratification of international terrorism conventions.[7]

In January 2007, ASEAN signed a legally binding convention on counter-terrorism at the annual summit in the Philippines. The

---

[6] ASEAN, "2001 ASEAN Declaration on Joint Action to Counter Terrorism", November 5, 2001, http://asean.org/?static_post=2001-asean-declaration-on-joint-action-to-counter-terrorism

[7] ASEAN, "Work Programme to Implement the ASEAN Plan of Action to Combat Transnational Crime", 17 May 2002, http://asean.org/?static_post=work-programme-to-implement-the-asean-plan-of-action-to-combat-transnational-crime-kuala-lumpur-17-may-2002

ASEAN Convention on Counter-Terrorism (ACCT) stated that member states are required to adhere to the key international conventions and protocols designed to counter terrorism since the 1970s. Operationally, the convention requires the sharing of early-warning information on terrorist movements and requires member states to strengthen their capability and readiness in dealing with chemical, biological, radiological, and nuclear (CBRN) methods of terrorism. Also, the agreement calls for a regional counter-terrorism database to be set up.[8] The ACCT was ratified by all ten AMS and came into force on 27 May 2011.[9]

More recently, on 25 May 2016, the Tenth ASEAN Defence Ministers' Meeting (ADMM) issued a joint declaration on promoting defence cooperation for a dynamic ASEAN community. The ministers stated their commitment to work together to combat terrorism "in all its forms and manifestations, including through cooperation in areas such as the sharing of information and intelligence, conducting coordinated operations where feasible, and enhancing confidence and capability building mechanisms".[10]

At the regional level, much effort has been put into counter-terrorism capacity building of Member States. At the Annual Conference of ASEAN Chiefs of Police (ASEANAPOL) in Phnom Penh in May 2002, the members expressed their commitment to "effectively monitor, share information on and combat all forms of terrorist activities".[11] They also agreed to enhance cooperation among law enforcement agencies through the sharing of experiences on counter-terrorism and the

---

[8] ASEAN, "ASEAN Convention on Counter Terrorism", January 13, 2007, http://asean.org/?static_post=asean-convention-on-counter-terrorism

[9] ASEAN, "ASEAN Convention on Counter Terrorism Completes Ratification Process", January 13, 2013, http://asean.org/asean-convention-on-counter-terrorism-completes-ratification-process/

[10] ASEAN, "Joint Declaration of the ASEAN Defence Ministers on Promoting Defence Cooperation for a Dynamic ASEAN Community", May 25, 2016, http://asean.org/storage/2016/05/Joint-Declaration-10th-ADMM-25-May-2016-Promoting-Defence-Cooperation...pdf

[11] S.Pushpanathan, "ASEAN Efforts to Combat Terrorism", August 20, 2003, http://asean.org/?static_post=asean-efforts-to-combat-terrorism-by-spushpanathan

exchange of information on suspected terrorists, organizations and their modus operandi.[12] In July 2003, Malaysia launched the Southeast Asia Regional Centre for Counter-Terrorism (SEARCCCT), which is intended to serve as a regional centre to enhance the capacity of enforcement, security and government officials to tackle counter-terrorism challenges in collaboration with think tanks and international organisations.[13] SEARCCT continues to act as a key counter-terrorism capacity-building node within ASEAN.[14]

Sub-Regional Level

Within ASEAN, and in line with the November 2001 ASEAN Declaration, much work has been going on at sub-regional level to combat terrorism. For example, Indonesia and the Philippines in June 2005 committed to pooling their law enforcement capabilities to fight terrorism, including the coordination of the "apprehension as well as interrogation of apprehended suspected criminals and terrorists," and share "technical and operational expertise."[15] In April 2016, the Philippines and Vietnam agreed to draft a six-year action plan to enhance bilateral security ties from 2017 to 2022, including in the terrorism domain.[16] In May 2016, Singapore and Thailand reached an agreement on exchanging information on terrorism.[17]

Sub-regional cooperation also exists trilaterally. Malaysia, Indonesia and Philippines — sharing a vast tri-border corridor in the Sulu-Sulawesi

---

[12] *Ibid.*

[13] SEARCCT, "About SEARCCT — Introduction", http://www.searcct.gov.my/about-searcct/introduction

[14] http://www.searcct.gov.my

[15] "RP, Indonesia agree to pool anti-terror resources", *The Philippine Star*, June 22, 2005, http://www.philstar.com/headlines/282997/rp-indonesia-agree-pool-anti-terrorresources.

[16] Raul Dancel, "Philippines, Vietnam agree on six-year action plan to deepen security ties", *The Straits Times*, April 12, 2016, http://www.straitstimes.com/asia/se-asia/philippines-vietnam-agree-on-six-year-action-plan-to-deepen-security-ties.

[17] "Singapore, Thailand agree on exchanging intelligence", *Organisation of Asia-Pacific News Agencies*, May 31, 2016.

Sea — have tried to foster collaboration and interoperability. In May 2002, these three States formally agreed to improve border controls and allow the signatories to share airline passenger lists. They also called for joint training exercises, the establishment of hotlines, standard procedures for search and rescue, and the sharing of intelligence.[18] In May 2016, the three States agreed to launch joint patrols in the Sulu and Celebes seas, following a spike in kidnappings by a radical Islamist group based in the southern Philippines. In addition to the joint patrols, they affirmed the need for a communication hotline to facilitate coordination and sharing of information and intelligence.[19] Three months later — given the increasing ISIS threat — at the International Meeting on Counter-Terrorism in Bali, Singapore, Malaysia and Indonesia agreed to the systematic exchange of biometric information such as fingerprints on known militants and terror convicts.[20]

Extra-Regional Level

Following the November 2001 ASEAN Declaration, the association adopted a range of joint declarations with extra-regional States to counter terrorism. Such partners have included, *inter alia*, the United States (1 August 2002)[21]; China (4 November 2002)[22]; the European Union

---

[18] "RP, Indonesia, Malaysia Sign Pact vs International Terrorism", *The Philippine Star*, May 8, 2002, http://www.philstar.com/headlines/160075/rp-indonesia-malaysia-sign-pact-vsinternational-terrorism

[19] "Indonesia, Neighbours Agree to Launch Joint Sea Patrols to Thwart Kidnappings", *Today Online*, May 6, 2016, http://www.todayonline.com/world/asia/indonesianeighboursagree-launch-joint-sea-patrols-thwart-kidnappings

[20] Wahyudi Soeriaatmadja and Lim Yan Liang, "Move to Swop Biometric Info on Militants Across Borders", *The Straits Times*, August 11, 2016, http://www.strait-stimes.com/asia/se-asia/move-to-swop-biometric-info-on-militants-across-borders

[21] ASEAN, "ASEAN-United States of America Joint Declaration for Cooperation to Combat International Terrorism", August 1, 2002, http://asean.org/?static_post=asean-united-states-of-america-joint-declaration-for-cooperation-to-combat-international-terrorism-bandar-seri-begawan-l-august-2002

[22] ASEAN, "Joint Declaration of ASEAN and China on Cooperation in the Field of Non-Traditional Security Issues", 6th ASEAN-China Summit, November 4, 2002,

(27 January 2003[23]); India (8 October 2003)[24]; Russia (2 July 2004)[25]; Australia (2 July 2004)[26]; (29 July 2005)[27] and Pakistan (29 July 2005).[28]

On 30 July 2002, at the Ninth ministerial meeting of the ARF in Bandar Seri Begawan, member states adopted the ARF Statement on Measures Against Terrorist Financing, which included the freezing of terrorist assets, implementation of international standards, cooperation on exchange of information and outreach, and technical assistance.[29] In July 2012, ASEAN worked with Japan to establish a joint terrorism database, where each country translates terrorism-related information from their languages into English for sharing purposes.[30] In May 2016,

http://asean.org/?static_post=joint-declaration-of-asean-and-china-on-cooperationin-the-field-of-non-traditional-security-issues-6th-asean-china-summit-phnompenh-4-november- 2002-2

[23] ASEAN, "Joint Declaration on Cooperation to Combat Terrorism, 14th ASEAN-EU Ministerial Meeting, Brussels", July 27, 2003, http://asean.org/joint-declaration-on-co-operation-to-combat-terrorism-14th-asean-eu-ministerial-meeting-brussels/

[24] ASEAN, "ASEAN-India Joint Declaration for Cooperation to Combat International Terrorism", October 8, 2003, http://asean.org/?static_post=asean-india-joint-declaration-for-cooperation-to-combat-international-terrorism-2

[25] ASEAN, "ASEAN-Russia Joint Declaration for Cooperation to Combat International Terrorism", July 2, 2004, http://asean.org/?static_post=asean-russia-joint-declaration-for-cooperation-to-combat-international-terrorism-2

[26] ASEAN, "ASEAN-Australia Joint Declaration for Cooperation to Combat International Terrorism", July 2, 2004, http://asean.org/?static_post=asean-australia-joint-declaration-for-cooperation-to-combat-international-terrorism-2

[27] ASEAN, "ASEAN-New Zealand Joint Declaration for Cooperation to Combat International Terrorism", July 29, 2005, http://asean.org/?static_post=asean-new-zealand-joint-declaration-for-cooperation-to-combat-international-terrorism-vientiane-29-july-2005-2

[28] ASEAN, "ASEAN-Pakistan Joint Declaration for Cooperation to Combat International Terrorism", July 29, 2005, http://asean.org/?static_post=asean-pakistan-joint-declaration-for-cooperation-to-combat-terrorism-vientiane-29-july-2005-2

[29] ASEAN Regional Forum, "ARF Statement on Strengthening Transport Security Against International Terrorism", January 10, 2004, http://aseanregionalforum.asean.org/library/arf-chairmans-statements-and-reports.html?id=178

[30] "Japan, Southeast Asian Nations Share Terrorism Info on Internet", *Kyodo News*, July 19, 2012.

moreover, Brunei hosted the opening ceremony of the ADMM Plus Exercise on Maritime Security and Counter Terrorism, which involved ASEAN countries as well as Australia, China, Japan, India, ROK, New Zealand, Russia and the United States. The exercise aimed to strengthen the capability and interoperability of the ADMM-Plus militaries to more effectively address terrorism and maritime threats as they are put through "realistic sea- and land-based scenarios".[31]

Moving Forward: Coping with the Threat of ISIS Extremism

Michael Chertoff, a former Secretary of Homeland Security under President George W. Bush, opined that it is equally crucial to combat the violent extremist ideology — widely propagated on social media plat-forms — that drive the likes of ISIS and its affiliates.[32] AMS are increas-ingly cognizant of this issue as well, judging from several recent initiatives. In July 2016, for example, an ASEAN Regional Digital Counter-Messaging Communications Centre (RDC3) to combat ISIS propaganda online was set up.[33] Four months later, ASEAN worked with the United Nations to bring together international and regional specialists to discuss the issue of preventing violent extremism.[34] The same month SEARCCT organised a regional workshop on countering ISIS ideology.[35] In sum, as this survey — which by no means is exhaustive — has shown, ASEAN has over the past 15 years been very actively engaged in countering the physical and now the ideological threat posed by transnational terrorism, through a

---

[31] MINDEF, "ADMM-Plus Countries Ready to Counter Maritime and Terrorism Threats", May 3, 2016, https://www.mindef.gov.sg/imindef/press_room/official_releases/nr/2016/may/03may16_nr.html#.V8ZjD5N95fQ

[32] Michael Chertoff, "The Ideology of Terrorism: Radicalism Revisited", *Brown Journal of International Affairs* 15, Issue 1 (Fall/Winter 2008): 11–20.

[33] Kamles Kumar, "Malaysia Launches Regional Centre to Counter IS Messaging", *Malay Mail Online*, July 26, 2016, http://www.themalaymailonline.com/malaysia/article/malaysia-launches-regional-centre-to-counter-is-messaging

[34] 5th ASEAN-UN Regional Diaologue on the Prevention of Violent Extremism, Jakarta, 7–9 November, 2016.

[35] Kuala Lumpur, 28 November to 1 December 2016.

plethora of measures at regional, sub-regional and extra-regional levels. As a supra-national regional association, there is always scope for greater coordination in the counter-terrorism domain, as in other arenas such as economic integration and climate change for instance. As Daljit Singh observed some time ago, in the final analysis, "ASEAN countries have to demonstrate the political will to fight terrorism and undertake all the necessary measures to do so", quite simply because it is "in the region's own vital interest".[36] Fortunately, the signs are that — given the rising ISIS regional threat — this recognition appears to have taken root.

Kumar RAMAKRISHNA is Associate Professor, Head of Policy Studies and Coordinator, National Security Studies Programme, in the Office of the Executive Deputy Chairman, S. Rajaratnam School of International Studies (RSIS), in Nanyang Technological University, Singapore. He was previously the Head of the Centre of Excellence for National Security (CENS) at RSIS from 2006 to 2015.

A historian by background, he has been a frequent speaker on counter-terrorism before local and international audiences, a regular media commentator on counter-terrorism, and an established author in numerous internationally refereed journals. His first single-authored book, *Emergency Propaganda: The Winning of Malayan Hearts and Minds 1948–1958* (2002) was described by the International History Review as "required reading for historians of Malaya, and for those whose task is to counter insurgents, guerrillas, and terrorists". His most recent single-authored book on transnational terrorism is *Islamist Terrorism and Militancy in Indonesia: The Power of the Manichean Mindset* (2015).

---

[36] Daljit Singh, "ASEAN Counter-Terror Strategies and Cooperation: How Effective?", in *After Bali: The Threat of Terrorism in Southeast Asia*, eds. Kumar Ramakrishna and See Seng Tan (Singapore: Institute of Defence Studies/World Scientific, 2003), 217.

Some Observations on the Regional Architecture in Southeast Asia

Peter HO

~ ~ ~

What Is *Regional Architecture*?

A concise definition of regional architecture describes it as a "reasonably coherent network of regional organisations, institutions, bilateral and multilateral arrangements, dialogue forums and other relevant mechanisms that work collectively for regional prosperity, peace, and stability."

Regional architecture, thus defined, could describe a large chunk of the work of our diplomats, and more. But it is only when the various efforts in bilateral and multilateral diplomacy are stitched together within a coherent strategic framework that they could be considered as contributing to the regional architecture. In the absence of strategic logic, and when these efforts are uncoordinated, then any impression of a coherent regional architecture emerging must be purely coincidental.

Thinking about the regional architecture is a vital strategic exercise, and ought to be the pre-occupation of all diplomats.

Why Is Regional Architecture Important to Singapore?

We are often reminded that Singapore is a small country, too small to set the agenda regionally, let alone globally. We are also told that Singapore is a price-taker in international affairs.

I believe that this characterisation of Singapore is somewhat overstated. While we are not a superpower, or even a middle power, we can influence the regional and global agenda, even if we cannot set it.

Influence is exercised by having a network of like-minded friends — especially the large and powerful ones — and through regional and international groupings and institutions, which help amplify and provide platforms for Singapore's interests to be expressed. If skilful diplomacy helps to get our interests aligned, then we have a fighting chance to influence the agenda.

Regional Architecture in Southeast Asia

It is unlikely, given the diversity of the region that we live in — Southeast Asia — that we can, or should even try to, achieve a treaty-based framework centred on institutions like the EU and NATO, such as in Europe.

The reality of our region is a diversity of nations at various levels of economic development, different histories, languages, politics and cultures. This does not point to a tidy regional architecture. Instead, it suggests a formless collection of overlapping groupings and networks. This may appear messy, but there is a resilience inherent in such an untidy regional architecture. There is considerable redundancy, and the utility of each component grouping or network will depend on the issue and the situation. That is both the strength and the weakness of a loose regional architecture. There is no single point of failure, which makes it more robust and resilient. But it is cumbersome to mobilise, in the absence of common strategic outlooks, clear processes and legal infrastructure. But under the circumstances, it is what is realistically achievable in Southeast Asia.

The Southeast Asian regional architecture, characterised by its loose and sometimes duplicative and contradictory features, can seem tedious with innumerable and often long meetings. But it has one powerful redeeming feature. These regular meetings promote predictability in relations among countries in the region, and between the region and the extra-regional powers, creating over time, the habits of dialogue, and of consultation and consensus-building. Over the longer term, these habits build familiarity and trust, and create conditions for broadening and deepening cooperation.

Regional Architecture Is Not the Sole Province of Diplomats

But building the regional architecture is not the exclusive preserve of diplomats. Efforts outside the diplomatic arena are as important.

The concept of regional architecture is sprawling, covering a broad spectrum of areas like defence and security, trade and finance, society and culture, health and technology. Diplomats do not have the competence, let alone the bandwidth, to drive all these efforts. It is also most unlikely that their political leaders will give them a free hand anyway. Building the regional architecture requires a comprehension of the larger national interests, of which foreign policy considerations form only part.

Whole-of-Government Effort

In Singapore, we use a term "Whole-of-Government" to describe how ministries and agencies come together, setting aside narrow departmental interests, in order to work together to achieve common outcomes for national strategic interests.

Designing the shape and essential features of the regional architecture is a Whole-of-Government effort. In 2006, this consideration led to the formation of the inter-agency ASEAN National Committee.

Although the Permanent Secretary of the Ministry of Foreign Affairs (MFA) chairs the Committee, it was clear from the outset that MFA could not undertake this effort alone. At best MFA can help to conceptualise the regional architecture, and to coordinate the efforts to build it. But a large part of the resources, experience and knowledge that are required to build elements of the regional architecture reside in other agencies. So the Ministry of Trade and Industry (MTI) must be the prime mover of the trade and economic aspects of the regional architecture. The Ministry of Defence (MINDEF) takes the lead on defence matters. Organising the ministries and agencies to produce a coherent strategy for regional architecture is a Whole-of-Government effort.

Regional Architecture Beyond Diplomacy

So regional architecture is not just about building diplomatic institutions. The institutions also need not be centred on ASEAN. From Singapore's viewpoint, the Five Power Defence Arrangements (FPDA) is part of the regional architecture. The Asia-Pacific Economic Cooperation (APEC) is also part of the regional architecture. Although most ASEAN countries are members, through a lack of vision and political will, ASEAN lost its central position in APEC.

But APEC was the progenitor grouping to promote economic cooperation and free trade in the larger Asia-Pacific region, something that is vital to Singapore's economic interests. That is why Singapore campaigned — successfully — to host the APEC Secretariat.

ASEAN at the Core of the Regional Architecture

ASEAN is at the core of Singapore's strategy to build and develop the regional architecture. This is because our membership of ASEAN provides us with a platform to influence and shape the regional agenda. On our own, it would be extremely difficult.

At its formation, ASEAN was described as a socio-cultural grouping. In fact, that was a fig leaf because the more critical but unstated function was to help organise the political relations in a region that had been beset by conflict and strife. It is important that diplomats are able to sift through the rhetoric and grasp the reality.

So arguably, ASEAN is the foundation, because out of it grew what we now recognise as today's regional architecture. The regional architecture, at least as Singapore sees it, is largely ASEAN-centred. It includes ASEAN's relations with its ten Dialogue Partners (such as ASEAN-US, ASEAN-China, ASEAN-Japan, ASEAN-EU, ASEAN-India, and so on), the ASEAN Regional Forum (ARF), ASEAN Plus Three (ASEAN+3) and leaders-led meetings like the ASEAN Summit and more recently the East Asia Summit (EAS). Subordinate meetings like the ASEAN Ministerial Meeting (AMM), ASEAN Economic Ministers Meeting (AEMM), ASEAN Defence Ministers Meeting

(ADMM), the Post-Ministerial Conferences, and so on, are also integral to the regional architecture in Southeast Asia.

It needs to be recognised that ASEAN as a grouping is not in and of itself powerful, despite a respectable population size of 630 million, and a GDP of about US$2.6 trillion. Its influence arises because it threatens no one. The ARF was actually a Japanese idea. It was only when it was adopted (and adapted by ASEAN) that it became acceptable to potential members such as the ROK.

Importance of Extra-Regional Powers

It is not in our interest to have any one country dominate the region. In this respect, ASEAN helps, although it does not ensure, that all countries in Southeast Asia have a voice in influencing regional cooperation and development.

Likewise, it is not in our interest to have one large external power dominate the region. All countries in Southeast Asia, including Singapore, have an interest in the extra-regional powers having stakes in the region that promote trade and commerce, air and sea links, and so on. But if one power gains too much influence, then the danger for us is that it will dictate the regional agenda, to the detriment of all the regional nations, and in particular of smaller states like Singapore.

The United States and the Regional Architecture

In this regard, the United States has always been considered by Singapore as a critical element in maintaining regional peace and stability, by balancing other extra-regional powers, and creating the political and economic space for the Southeast Asian countries to develop. This is because the US' military presence and its foreign policy have been largely benign, and its economic policies strongly favouring free and open trade that is vital for Singapore's survival.

The biggest risk to our interests is a United States that is disengaged from the region, preferring to conduct its business with countries in the region directly on a bilateral basis, and from Washington. If this happens, then our influence, and our ability to influence the United States, would diminish.

In the 1990s, the United States conduct of foreign policy was essentially bilateral, focused on a hub-and-spoke arrangement centred in Washington. It eschewed multilateral platforms outside Europe. For Singapore, as for the other ASEAN members (it was just six members then), it was important to more firmly anchor the United States in the region. One way was to draw it into the emerging regional architecture, centred on ASEAN. It became a major reason why the ASEAN Regional Forum (ARF) was conceived. There were two arguments that were employed (ultimately successfully) to persuade the United States to join the ARF. First, that its involvement would not be at the expense of its bilateral ties. Second, that it would provide another channel for the United States to engage an emerging China.

Engaging China

Within ASEAN, China has been viewed with suspicion by some, and as a patron by others. Nevertheless in the early 1990s, when China was still in the proverbial international "doghouse" after the Tiananmen Square incident, it was becoming apparent that China would inexorably rise to be a major global power. The choice then, as now, was a simple one: whether to keep China at an arm's length, or to engage China. But engaging such a large country requires an ability to manage relations with it. Given China's size and growing clout, the key would be to engage China not just bilaterally, but also through the regional architecture.

The strategic engagement of China made a lot of sense then, as it still does today, because it would always be better to have China inside the international system, where it would be subject to norms and rules, and to the sanction of its peers, rather than have China on the outside.

Furthermore, it would be easier for ASEAN as a group to deal with a rising China, than just for each country to deal with China bilaterally. So China became a full Dialogue Partner of ASEAN in 1996, which was rapidly followed by the establishment of ASEAN+3.

By the turn of the new century, it was evident that China was moving beyond its phase of smiling diplomacy and peaceful rise, into a more assertive phase of its foreign policy that paralleled China's rise as an economic powerhouse, and as a global engine of economic growth.

The Regional Comprehensive Economic Partnership (RCEP) is a proposed FTA among the ASEAN Member States, and the six states with which ASEAN has existing FTAs (Australia, China, India, Japan, ROK and New Zealand). It is championed by China, and seen by some as an economic grouping that China will dominate, and a counterweight to the Trans-Pacific Partnership (TPP).

China of course is no longer playing just a regional game. It is now at the top of the big league, and its stage is global. It has now become a most important strategic issue for Singapore — and indeed for ASEAN — to find ways to engage a more confident and assertive China. Astute and firm diplomacy is clearly needed.

Size Is Important

Yet, even as the regional architecture evolves, an important judgement must be how big it should be allowed to grow, beyond which it is impossible to manage.

I recall a study, done some years ago that concluded that when a multilateral organisation grew beyond a certain size (I think it was 18 members), it would become dysfunctional because too many interests were brought to the table, resulting in decisions by consensus being almost impossible to achieve. And when decisions are made, they would invariably be based on the lowest common denominator, rather than in the larger strategic interest of the grouping.

When ASEAN was just five, then six, largely like-minded members, a lot of things were achieved, such as the ARF. With ten members, often with divergent interests on issues, political and economic, decision-making by consensus is getting harder to achieve. These challenges of unconstrained growth are overlooked in the enthusiastic but not very well-conceived pursuit of the enlargement of some ASEAN-based groupings.

In this regard, the ARF is an object lesson of how narrow interests of individual members take precedence of the larger interests of ASEAN. The ARF started in 1994 with 18 members. Today, its ranks have swelled to 27. Even as it is now becoming apparent that the sheer size of the ARF makes it a real challenge for any kind of serious decision-making, ASEAN members still find it hard to resist the appeals of other countries that have no connection at all to the region to join the grouping.

This is one of the reasons why Singapore continues to caution against admitting *willy-nilly* new members into ASEAN. For the sake of ASEAN effectiveness, we need to ensure that new members are able to take on the responsibilities of membership, just as they rightly expect to enjoy its benefits.

"ASEAN in the Driver's Seat"

"ASEAN in the driver's seat" is a phrase used in ASEAN circles to mean that ASEAN is at the centre of the regional architecture, and that it is setting the pace and leading the shaping of the regional agenda.

But the reality is often quite the opposite. The ASEAN members sometimes lack the energy, political will, and the vision to lead, content to accept the symbolism of being in the driver's seat, while in reality letting others, namely, the extra-regional partners set the tone and agenda. Indeed, many of the more substantive initiatives came from the non-ASEAN members.

Observations and Lessons from Building the Southeast Asian Regional Architecture

It is inevitable that the regional architecture will evolve over time, as the geo-political and geo-economic environment changes. Over time, it will move in new directions, not all of which will be aligned with our interests. For the foreseeable future, Singapore's vital interests are served by keeping ASEAN at the core of the regional architecture. The principle of keeping the United States and China engaged is also unchanging.

It is in Singapore's strategic interest to continue to speak up and play a role in shaping the regional architecture. It requires an ability to see through the rhetoric, and to deal with the reality. And when Singapore's strategic interests are at stake, we must be prepared to fight for our interests on our own.

Peter HO is the Senior Advisor to the Centre for Strategic Futures, and a Senior Fellow in the Civil Service College. He is also the Chairman of the Urban Redevelopment Authority of Singapore, Chairman of the Social Science Research Council, Chairman of the Singapore Centre on Environmental Life Sciences Engineering, Chairman of the National Supercomputing Centre, and Chairman of the Governing Council of the Campus for Research Excellence and Technological Enterprise. When he retired in 2010 after 34 years of public service, he was Head, Civil Service, concurrent with his other appointments of Permanent Secretary (Foreign Affairs), Permanent Secretary (National Security and Intelligence Coordination), and Permanent Secretary (Special Duties) in the Prime Minister's Office. Before that, he was Permanent Secretary (Defence). He was also the founding Chairman of the Maritime and Port Authority of Singapore.

Importance of Maintaining ASEAN Unity and Its Centrality in the Regional Architecture

TAN Seng Chye

∽ ✿ ∾

Review of ASEAN's Development and Achievements, and Success as a Regional Grouping

As ASEAN approaches its 50th anniversary, it is relevant to review its development and achievements since its establishment on 8 August 1967. ASEAN has established principles on the bilateral and at the ASEAN-level relations, consensus, the "ASEAN Way" and the Treaty of Amity and Cooperation in Southeast Asia (TAC) as well as building trust and confidence and the habit of cooperation that enabled ASEAN to achieve a peaceful and economically prosperous region.

Over the years, ASEAN has faced a number of challenges as it progressed. First, it was the accession of Vietnam (1995), Laos and Myanmar (1997), and Cambodia (1999) that brought greater diversity to ASEAN in terms of its members' different ideologies, economic systems and levels of economic development and regional outlooks. Second, it was the ASEAN dialogue partnerships for economic, social and functional cooperation, and in particular the ASEAN-China Free Trade Agreement (ACFTA) which brought rapid economic prosperity for ASEAN countries with the remarkable economic rise of China. Third, it was the US pivot to Asia in 2009 in response to China's growing political and economic influence in Southeast Asia and its military modernisation. This development resulted in US-China rivalry for influence in the region that included rising tensions in the South China

Sea (SCS) over territorial disputes among the claimant states, the US'
assertion of its "national interest" in the SCS and "Freedom of
Navigation", and China's declaration of the SCS as a core interest. In the
face of the new political and security dynamics in the region, individual
ASEAN countries became more assertive of their national interests and
more preoccupied with their domestic developments. As a result,
ASEAN's unity was affected. ASEAN faces the serious challenge of
maintaining ASEAN unity and its centrality in the region architecture
so that it can continue to play an important regional role of promoting
a peaceful and prosperous region.

ASEAN's Establishment and Its Principles

Since ASEAN's establishment in August 1967, the founding Member
States (Indonesia, Malaysia, Philippines, Thailand and Singapore) wanted
to build a peaceful and stable region away from the Cold War and major
power rivalry, and to promote closer economic and socio-cultural cooperation among its members. The ASEAN members promoted trust and
confidence and conflict prevention in order to foster peace and stability.
It was an important historical development. Prior to that, the founding
members were engaged in bilateral conflicts. One principle was that
to promote peace and stability in the region, cooperation among the
ASEAN Member States (AMS) must not be affected by their respective
bilateral issues and cooperation with external powers. This principle
coupled with the "ASEAN Way" and the principle of consensus in
decision-making, have helped to facilitate cooperation in ASEAN and
build better relations among its members. The agreements on Zone of
Peace, Freedom and Neutrality (ZOPFAN) in 1971 and on the Southeast
Asian Nuclear-Weapon-Free Zone Treaty (SEANWFZ) in 1995 were part
of ASEAN's efforts to build regional peace and stability.

Since ASEAN's establishment, there has been no threat of war or
open conflict among the ASEAN countries as the militaries of the
ASEAN countries were engaged in ensuring domestic stability and
State security. Political and defence diplomacies have been conducted
at the bilateral level and they focussed on building trust and confidence and improving bilateral relations among the AMS. ASEAN-level

military cooperation remains sensitive due to issues of sovereignty, equality and diversity of their national outlooks. In the late 1980s and 1990s, ASEAN was not comfortable to have formal defence cooperation at the ASEAN level, as various proposals for defence cooperation like multilateral exercises, defence ministers/officials meeting or ASEAN peacekeeping force, were not accepted. It was only in 2006 that the ASEAN Defence Ministers' Meeting (ADMM), a platform for defence and security discussions, was established.

It has taken almost ten years for the ASEAN countries which are so diverse in ethnicities, cultures, religions, and historical pasts, to build confidence and trust among themselves and to enable them to get along and become familiar with each other. The informality and close personal relations nurtured among the AMS have helped ASEAN to develop as a regional organisation.

These developments had enabled the convening of the 1976 Bali Summit which adopted the Bali Concord to promote economic cooperation, and the TAC which codifies relations between and among the ASEAN countries and ASEAN's relations with the dialogue partners. The TAC, inter alia, emphasised these principles, namely, (a) "mutual respect for the independence, sovereignty, equality, territorial integrity and national identity of all nations", (b) "the right of every State to lead its national existence free from external interference, subversion or coercion", and (c) "non-interference in the internal affairs of another". Regional countries wishing to join ASEAN have to accede to the TAC before being accepted as an ASEAN member. Similarly, external non-ASEAN countries have to accede to the TAC before they could become dialogue partners. These agreements reflected the conduct of political and economic diplomacies to promote cooperation among ASEAN countries, and peace and stability in the region, as well as cooperation with the dialogue partners.

Expanded ASEAN Membership and the Challenges

After the end of the war in Indochina in 1975, Vietnam, Cambodia and Laos, were not keen to join ASEAN. Vietnam was pursuing its interest to bring "genuine independence" to Southeast Asia and to fulfil

Ho Chi Minh's dream of "An Indochina Federation" which is "a great union of Vietnam-Laos-Cambodia" under Vietnam's leadership. These countries were preoccupied with domestic issues and consolidating their governments.

When Vietnam invaded and occupied Cambodia which was not yet an ASEAN member in December 1978, ASEAN opposed it strongly on the basis of the principles of respect for a State's sovereignty, and non-intervention in the domestic affairs of another country through force of arms or military invasion and occupation of a country by a larger and militarily more powerful neighbour. ASEAN mounted a successful diplomatic campaign at the UN and international fora as well as conducted a regional political and defence diplomacy campaign which eventually rolled back the Vietnamese invasion and occupation of Cambodia in 1991.

All these developments caused anxiety in ASEAN. It was a region divided by two groups of countries with different ideologies and systems of government and economy. In February 1984, Brunei became independent and joined ASEAN and it adapted well in the grouping.

Laos and Cambodia were worried about the Indochina Federation as they did not want to be dominated by Vietnam and wanted to remain independent. The Vietnamese invasion and occupation of Cambodia in December 1978 was of great concern to Laos. As a result of ASEAN's campaign in the UN and international fora, Vietnam became quite isolated and faced pressures from the West and China. After the Vietnamese occupation of Cambodia was rolled backed and a settlement achieved in 1991, Vietnam showed interest in ASEAN membership for geostrategic reasons and to engage in trade and economic cooperation with the ASEAN countries. Vietnam joined ASEAN in 1991.

Traditionally, Laos and Cambodia faced security threats from their neighbours and thus they were keen on ASEAN membership for reasons of ensuring their sovereignty, territorial integrity and non-interference in their internal affairs, through their accession to the TAC. Like Vietnam, they also wanted to improve trade and economic cooperation with the ASEAN countries. While Laos joined ASEAN in 1997, Cambodia could only join in 1999, after the UN supervised general election under UNTAC was held. Myanmar joined ASEAN at the 30th ASEAN Foreign Ministers Meeting in Kuala Lumpur in July 1997 as some ASEAN countries wanted to realise a "One Southeast Asia" goal. ASEAN wanted to engage Myanmar in regional activities through ASEAN membership. But Myanmar was preoccupied with its internal affairs and held the ASEAN Chairmanship only in 2014.

A few ASEAN countries supported Timor-Leste's bid to become a member of ASEAN while the others felt that Timor-Leste could only be admitted when it had the human resource capabilities to participate fully in all ASEAN meetings and activities. In the meantime, ASEAN is considering the possibility for Timor-Leste to participate in certain sectorial activities for capacity-building purposes.

Recent Developments and the Importance of Maintaining ASEAN Unity and Its Centrality in Regional Architecture

The United States pivot to Asia announced in 2009 was a response to China's remarkable rise and its growing political and economic influence and military strength. The US President's announcement of a web of Treaty allies and strategic partners in November 2011, which was viewed by China as countering its rise, had resulted in new regional dynamics including the emergence of major power rivalry. These tensions have affected ASEAN unity and pose challenges to ASEAN's centrality in the regional architecture.

In recent years, China's efforts to assert its territorial claims within the nine-dash-line coupled with reclamation of islands in the South China Sea and stationing of military assets and radars there, have caused unease in the region and attracted US' Freedom of Navigation (FON) operations by its military aircraft and naval vessels, which the Chinese strongly opposed. The change of Philippine leadership from President Benigno Aquino to President Rodrigo Duterte in May 2016, resulted in a significant shift in the Philippines' foreign policy to set aside the Arbitral Tribunal ruling and its confrontational posture on territorial claims in the SCS, and its distancing from the United States, so as to improve relations with China during Duterte's visit to China in

October 2016. This development was significant and it has calmed the waters on the SCS disputes. Another significant development was the election of President Donald Trump whose foreign and defence policies differ from that of President Obama. While it is still too early yet to assess President's Trump's policies towards Asia, Chinese academics have recently assessed that US-China rivalry in the SCS will remain.

During the last few years, ASEAN has worked hard to maintain ASEAN unity over the SCS disputes at the ASEAN Foreign Ministers' Meetings and ASEAN Leaders' Meetings. The ASEAN Leaders at their Summit in Vientiane, Laos, in September 2016, stressed the importance of maintaining ASEAN Centrality and unity in the evolving regional architecture and in their engagement with external parties. Thus, maintaining ASEAN unity and its centrality in the regional architecture is important for ASEAN to remain a peaceful and prosperous region.

References

The Bangkok Declaration, 8 August 1967.

1976 Declaration of ASEAN Concord, 24 February 1976 (http//www.aseansec. org/5049htm).

The ASEAN Treaty of Amity and Cooperation in Southeast Asia, Bali, Indonesia, February 1976.

http://www.aseansec.org/asean/about-asean/history, including declarations of admission to ASEAN memberships of Brunei Darussalam (1984), Vietnam (1995), Laos and Myanmar (1997), and Cambodia (1999).

The concept paper for the establishment of ASEAN Defence Ministers' Meeting (ADMM), October 2006.

President Obama's speech to Australian Federal Parliament on "America is here to stay in the Pacific" on 17 November 2011.

US Congressional Research Report for US Congress on Pivot to the Pacific? The Obama Administration's "rebalancing towards Asia".

UN Transitional Authority in Cambodia (UNTAC) — Summary background report.

Satu Limaye's article in PacNet #73 — September 2016 on "Why ASEAN Is Here to Stay and What That Means for the US".

"ASEAN and rising China looking for win-win solution" by Ambassador Ong Keng Yong, *Jakarta Post*, 10 October 2016.

Chairman's Statement of the 28th and 29th ASEAN Summits, Vientiane, 6–7
   September 2016.
Joint Communiqué of the 49th ASEAN Foreign Ministers' Meeting, Vientiane,
   24 July 2016.
"Trump Wants Absolute Control of S. China Sea: Chinese Academics", *Today*,
   26 November 2016.

TAN Seng Chye was a career Foreign Service Officer (1967–2005) and he had
served as Singapore Ambassador/High Commissioner to Thailand, Myanmar,
Australia, Fiji, Philippines, Laos and Vietnam. At the Ministry of Foreign
Affairs, he had served as Deputy Director of Political Division (1982–84) and
then as Director of Policy and Analysis (Southeast Asia) (1984–1987), Director,
Technical Cooperation Directorate and Director, Consular Directorate. He had
attended many ASEAN, regional and international meetings. After his retire-
ment in end 2005 from the Foreign Service in November 2005, he has been a
Senior Fellow at the Rajaratnam School of International Studies till now.

ASEAN's
External Relations

Australian Engagement with ASEAN:
A Southeast Asian Perspective

Joseph K. H. KOH

✢ ✢ ✢

> "Let's face it. ASEAN does not feature too prominently in Australia's priorities."

This is a common refrain whenever Australian engagement with ASEAN is discussed in ASEAN capitals. Even Gareth Evans, widely acknowledged as an Australian Foreign Minister (from 1988 to 1996) who had gone out of his way to develop closer personal relations with his ASEAN counterparts, including chasing golf balls,[1] has admitted that:

> "ASEAN doesn't feature as large in our collective consciousness as it should, … we just haven't given it the policy attention we should; our politicians don't go out of the way to forge personal relationships with regional counterparts as they should …."[2]

In a 15 March 2017 talk on how Australia was perceived by its diplomatic partners, Frances Adamson, the Secretary of the Australian Department of Foreign Affairs and Trade, merely gave her take of the views of six countries, viz., the United States, United Kingdom, Japan, India, China and Indonesia — in that order. She did not characterise

---

[1] Lee Kuan Yew, *From Third World to First: The Singapore Story: 1965–2000* (Singapore: Singapore Press Holdings and Times Editions, 2000), 432.
[2] Gareth Evans, (speech, *The Australia-ASEAN Dialogue: Tracing Forty Years of Partnership*, December 3, 2014).

ASEAN's perception of Australia. But acknowledging the strategic weight of Indonesia, she said:

> "We loom large for one another … we want Indonesia to look to Australia as a reliable source of acute judgement and sensitive advice."[3]

ASEAN's Relevance

To be fair to Adamson, ASEAN should not begrudge her silence on ASEAN in a speech that was intended to focus on the perceptions of individual countries considered important to Australia. In any case, ASEAN does not have an inflated sense of self-importance to be troubled by its ranking in Canberra's foreign policy agenda. It is quietly confident of its own economic and geostrategic relevance to Australia. As an economic community (with a small "c"), ASEAN has become Australia's second largest trading partner, second only to China, and well ahead of Japan, the European Union and the United States.[4] In geostrategic terms, the Australian 2016 Defence White Paper declares categorically that:

> "Australia has deep strategic security and economic interests in South East Asia. The geography of the archipelago to Australia's immediate north will always have particular significance to our security. Any conventional military threat to Australia is likely to approach through the archipelago as are other threats involving transnational crime including people smuggling and drug trafficking. The strong cooperation we have, and continue to build, with our close northern neighbours is crucial to guard against such threats."[5]

---

[3] Frances Adamson, "Australia in the world: How our diplomatic partners see us" (speech, the annual dinner of the ACT branch of the Australia Institute of International Affairs, March 15, 2017).

[4] Department of Foreign Affairs and Trade, Canberra, http://dfat.gov.au/pages/default.aspx

[5] Department of Defense, 2016 Defense White Paper (Commonwealth of Australia, Canberra), 39.

Improved Perception

Such economic and security imperatives have driven Australia to engage ASEAN and become its first Dialogue Partner in 1974. These calculations underpin Australia's enthusiasm in building an extensive web of substantive bilateral and multilateral collaboration with the region. Through such interactions, leaders and citizens in ASEAN became more aware of Australia's re-orientation towards Southeast Asia since the 1970s. Prior to that, Australia had suffered a serious image problem: there was a prevalent impression of a "happy-go-lucky" people living in an economically unproductive and protectionistic "White Australia" that risked becoming the "poor white trash" of Asia.[6] Australia's intimate engagement with ASEAN turned ASEAN's attitude from one of contempt to respect. Nowadays, Australia projects three new images in ASEAN eyes:

First, Australia is widely acknowledged in ASEAN as an advanced and innovative economy with a highly skilled workforce. It is seen to have become more inclusive and multiracial. Through various bilateral and multilateral free trade agreements it has signed with ASEAN Member States, Australia has demonstrated that it is now more confident of its own competitiveness and has become less protectionistic. It also sends a clear signal of its seriousness in building an economic partnership with ASEAN.

Second, Australia is appreciated as a steadfast supporter of ASEAN. Australia has not only been generous in its development assistance and capacity-building programmes for ASEAN, it has also been actively cooperating with ASEAN in promoting regional integration, and in jointly evolving modalities in confidence-building, conflict prevention, conflict resolution and management. While some Australians would like to believe that they have asserted "intellectual leadership" in regional community-building, it must be acknowledged that the Australians have indeed contributed many concepts and expended considerable energy in building that "multiplex" of regional architecture that prevails today.

---

[6]Jonathan Pearlman, "'White Trash' Warning Spurred Australia to be Better: Abbott", *The Strait Times*, March 26, 2015.

Third, while some in ASEAN have sneered at the self-image held by certain senior Australians as a "deputy sheriff" or a "middle power", generally speaking, Australia is respected as a significant and benign regional player. Many in ASEAN have witnessed Australia's instrumental role in negotiating and keeping peace in Cambodia, and in leading the peacekeeping operations in East Timor. They have developed a healthy respect of Australia's willingness and ability to contribute to regional security.

Australia is seen as a benign player because it advocates a rule-based international system. Its forceful renunciation of the "might is right" mentality resonates resoundingly in Southeast Asia. When differences erupted between Australia and individual ASEAN countries, or ASEAN as a group, Australia did not try to impose its will like a regional hegemon. Bilateral relations with some ASEAN countries have gone through rough patches, particularly in cases involving refugees, travel advisories and execution of Australian drug traffickers. But such problems have always been handled civilly and responsibly, in keeping with international norm of behaviour — no threats, trade boycott, megaphone diplomacy or state-orchestrated media frenzy. The problems soon blew over, and both sides moved on.

Australia also projects its soft power better than many other countries. Its educational institutions have been a powerful magnet to thousands of youngsters in Southeast Asia. Many Australian alumni now hold senior positions in ASEAN governments; others become local opinion leaders or captains of industry. Australia's vast landscape, wildlife, natural attractions, plus its elegant and vibrant culinary culture, attract countless tourists from ASEAN countries. They are confident that they can travel comfortably and safely, and be served in shops and restaurants attentively and courteously, and received by the locals with warm hospitality. Despite the cultural gap between Australia and Southeast Asia, most Australian tourists in Southeast Asia are well-mannered. They rarely attract complaints about obnoxious behaviour. As a government, Australia has been generous in technical assistance and disaster relief operations in ASEAN countries. It has earned admiration region-wide for the considerable resources it poured in to help in the search for the MH370, the Malaysian aircraft that went missing en route to Beijing.

Paradoxes

In theory, such improved ASEAN perception of Australia should synergise with Canberra's geostrategic and economic imperatives and propel the relationship to greater heights. However, an undercurrent of disenchantment if not mutual scepticism still lingers on, leading an Australian academic to characterise Australia's engagement with ASEAN as a "marriage of convenience".[7] Another likened Australia as a "mother-in-law trying to tag along in a honeymoon."[8] Yet another depicts Australia as an "awkward partner", noting the "liminality of being neither here nor there."[9] When he was Malaysian Prime Minister, the easily provoked Dr. Mahathir Mohamad dismissed Australia outright as "an outsider, which would never be accepted by ASEAN".[10] Some Australians were pained by this. One lamented that:

> "Australians feel that their country is expected to do both the giving and the taking: giving the aid and taking the insults; having to give in and take the blame as well ... Australian leaders are criticised for interference and impertinence if they take a close interest in Asian affairs, and for ignorance and indifference if they don't."[11]

Such problems may have their origin in the paradoxes that have continued to plague Australia's approach to Southeast Asia. These

---

[7] Susan Percival Wood, "Australia and ASEAN: A Marriage of Convenience?" in *The Australia-ASEAN Dialogue: Tracing 40 Years of Partnership*, eds. S. Wood, B. He and M. Leifer (Palgrave Macmillan, 2014).

[8] Alison Broinowski, *About Face: Asian Accounts of Australia* (Melbourne: Scribe Publications, 2003), 3.

[9] Baogang He, "The Awkwardness of Australian Engagement with Asia: The Dilemmas of Australian Idea of Regionalism", *Japanese Journal of Political Science*, 12, no. 2 (2011): 267–285.

[10] Alison Broinowski, p. 2.

[11] Alison Broinowski, p. 7.

paradoxes will be further accentuated with recent transformation in the strategic landscape — a more assertive China and a more unpredictable leader in the Oval Office. Australia will need to find a sweet spot by reconciling its dilemmas against the backdrop of a more uncertain world. This will not be easy, but these paradoxes are easy to define:

First, while realising the need to consolidate and strengthen relationship with ASEAN at the personal and institutional level, the time and resources directed at such an effort will be at the expense of other priorities: maintaining and expanding relationships with the United States, China, Japan, South Korea, and India.[12]

Second, Australia wants to remain a worthy partner in the United States alliance, but cannot ignore China's growing strategic weight and economic opportunities. How such a paradox is settled will define how far Australia can go to fulfil its commitment to uphold a rule-based international order and its insistence on the freedom of navigation in international waters.

Third, Australia's activism in constructing multilateral regional architecture is driven by an overriding need to engage the bigger powers, particularly at the summit level. Engaging ASEAN is secondary. But such a fundamental interest is more easily achieved if Australia works *through* and *with* ASEAN. An Australia that is seen to be working amicably and closely with ASEAN will have stronger credentials to be listened to in Washington and Beijing. But working closely with ASEAN would necessitate embracing the "ASEAN way", and enduring the pace and style of the ASEAN decision-making process. Not all Australian leaders will have an appetite for this. To ASEAN, its centrality in any regional architecture is non-negotiable, but to Australian policy-makers who are frustrated by ASEAN's purported "inability to cohere",[13] Australia's interests will be better served in new regional institutions

---

[12] Gareth Evans, speech, in *The Australia-ASEAN Dialogue: Tracing 40 Years of Partnership*, December 3, 2014.

[13] See Seng Tan, "Hobnobbing with Giants: Australia's Approach to Asian Regionalism". in *The Australia-ASEAN Dialogue: Tracing 40 Years of Partnership*, eds. S. Wood, B. He and M. Leifer (Palgrave Macmillan, 2014), 34.

where Australia can "walk among the giants"[14] and play big-power multilateralism games with the participation of only selected ASEAN members. Prime Minister Kevin Rudd's venture in 2009 to "consult" ASEAN on his bid for an "Asia-Pacific community" is a case in point. It was widely seen by ASEAN (and by many astute Australians) as a poorly conceived and thinly disguised attempt to supplant ASEAN. While ASEAN's reactions were predictable, ASEAN was surprised that Canberra had come out with a notion that was completely "out of touch with Asian sentiments and realities".[15]

Fourth, by instinct, Australia will want to champion western democratic norms and a degree of freedom of expression that can give licence to politically-motivated fake news and incendiary rhetoric that can destabilise multiracial societies. The situation is aggravated when the government is pressurised by that part of Australia's rumbustious media fixated with a crusading agenda. This can work against some of the fundamental tenets in ASEAN's concept of regionalism — respect for sovereignty, the rule of law, and non-interference in the domestic affairs of others. Worse, it can also reveal Australian double-standards in ASEAN eyes, e.g., condoning the execution of the Bali bombers while objecting to capital punishment on Australian drug traffickers.

Fifth, while most Australian leaders can understand the logic of free trade, there is a propensity to appease labour and shield industries (especially airlines) from Asian competition. While ASEAN countries are not ungrateful for the concessions Australia have given in various bilateral and multilateral free trade agreements so far, ASEAN can see the paradox: Australia's vocal advocacy of free trade is out of sync with a limited political courage to open the market further.

Going Forward

Depending how such dilemmas are resolved, Australia's engagement with ASEAN can either take off, or just muddle through into their fifth decade

---

[14] R. Babbage, "Learning to Walk among Giants: The New Defence White Paper", *Security Challenges*, 8, no. 3 (2008): 13–30.

[15] Tommy Koh, "Australia Must Respect ASEAN's Role", *Think Tank*, June 24, 2009.

of partnership. It is easy to speculate on the many potential triggers that can impede Australia's engagement with ASEAN. These can include an ascendency of politicians in Australia obsessed with trade imbalances and clamouring for job protection and narrow-minded mercantilism. Another would be a resurgence of the notion that ASEAN's internal division and preoccupation with consensus will hamper Australia's goals in multilateral big-power diplomacy, leading to renewed attempts at pushing for alternative regional institutions that will torpedo ASEAN centrality.

Such pessimistic scenarios should not be allowed to distract Australian and ASEAN from the more rigorous intellectual challenge: to come up with more positive and imaginative visions of ASEAN-Australia engagement. For instance, policy-makers may imagine an ASEAN-pivoted "coalition" — with Australia, Japan, ROK and New Zealand standing shoulder-to-shoulder with ASEAN collectively as a third pillar, alongside the United States and China, in the existing regional architecture. This should not become yet another forum, or worse, a new formally structured community entailing incessant "talk shops". It should remain just a mental framework or "virtual" platform to grow new ideas among coalition partners to work jointly to promote capacity-building, infrastructure and other development projects within ASEAN.

"Jointly" can be loosely interpreted: a "joint" project may just involve anything more than three parties, e.g., Australian and Singapore scientists can team up with counterparts of the three "Heart of Borneo" signatories to work on transboundary biodiversity surveys as an ASEAN-supported project. Others are free to join if they wish. In the same vein, Australian agencies can work with selected coalition partners to improve air connectivity within ASEAN through feasibility studies and consultancy services for the construction or enhancement of minor airports serving rural communities in ASEAN.

Such a loose coalition cannot be misinterpreted as a counterweight, a United States side-kick, or a bloc to contain China. By focussing our minds in conceiving multilateral projects in such an ASEAN-pivoted coalition framework, we will open new possibilities for cost-sharing, and pooling of resources, and getting a job done by a multinational and multi-disciplinary team of experts or specialists who can complement one another. We open up new demands for our products and services. We further entrench our habits of working together as a community. We increase our stake in one another. We raise the quality of life of our people collectively. We deepen Australia's engagement with ASEAN.

The coalition can also contribute to projects involving the intangible, such as deepening people-to-people understanding through a more ambitious version of the New Colombo Plan or the Australian-ASEAN Emerging Leaders Programme. Australia can also share such experiences with other coalition partners and inspire them to do likewise, or to establish a network to push these programmes jointly. Cross-posting teachers between ASEAN and Australia plus other developed coalition partners may be another idea worth exploring.

Immersion of Australian youths and educators in Southeast Asia will go a long way in upgrading the quality of Australian engagement with ASEAN. If nothing else, such exchanges will help at least some of the younger Australians see through the falsehoods peddled by those in the intellectual elite habitually hectoring at Southeast Asian governments through outmoded stereotyped lenses. It will help expose the intellectual puerility of opinion-makers who mindlessly inbred such distortions without any critical analysis, ironically with an outback version of the very Confucianist conformism they accuse the Asians of.

The coalition can also serve as a launch pad to promote Australian values and those of the other more developed partners such as Japan and New Zealand. ASEAN leaders will resent Australians for lecturing them on the need to conform to western notions of democracy and human rights, but there are other values in Australia, Japan and other coalition partners that can be shared more widely in ASEAN, e.g., the rule of law, the habit of "safety first", the consciousness of raising productivity, the primacy of quality control, and care of the environment and ecosystems.

Conclusion

There seems to be a tendency among Australian academics to agonise over issues such as whether Australia belongs to Asia or should or should not join ASEAN. There are others who lament that Australia has ventured into Asia with a brash and culturally insensitive approach that does much to undermine prospective relations.[16] Such self-flagellation is unnecessary: ASEAN countries are used to more muscular treatment from other diplomatic partners, sometimes even from those who ought to know better culturally. So long as we can look at the bigger picture, we will move on.

There is also no need for quibble over whether Australia needs ASEAN more than ASEAN needs Australia. Many enlightened thinkers in Australia and ASEAN can see that we live in an interdependent world. In any case, needs may change with circumstances, and table can turn.

Instead, Australian and ASEAN thinkers and policy-makers should refocus on the commonalities of aspirations between Australia and ASEAN. They should not over-philosophise over "form", "face", or ranking in each other's profile or priorities, but think more positively, boldly and imaginatively and work aggressively towards achieving concrete outcomes.

Australian informality and directness is not a sin, but a virtue. Frank dialogue often delivers better results than diplomatic niceties and empty talk. Frankly, ASEAN offers Australia the best ticket into the big-power multilateral diplomacy game. Frankly, it will serve ASEAN's interest if a benign partner can articulate or reinforce ASEAN's hopes and fears as Australia "walks with the giants". Frankly, the best "forward defence" for a wealthy Australia is to help build a secure, confident, prosperous, and integrated ASEAN!

---

[16] J. Blaxland, "The Australian Mindset in Asia", *The Interpreter*, October 30, 2012.

Joseph K. H. KOH was Singapore's High Commissioner in Canberra from 2002 to 2005, an appointment he had taken after a stint as a Deputy Secretary at the Ministry of Foreign Affairs in 1995 and Singapore's Trade Representative in Taipei from 1996 to 2002. After his tenure in Canberra, he was posted to Brunei Darussalam as Singapore's High Commissioner, before retiring in 2012. Before joining MFA, he worked at the Ministry of Home Affairs from 1983 to 1986 and the Ministry of Defence (from 1972 to 1983 and 1986 to 1995). He was trained as a zoologist with a First Class Honours in Science from the former University of Singapore. The author of several scientific books on Southeast Asian spiders, he currently chairs the Nature Reserves Scientific Advisory Committee of the Singapore National Parks Board.

ASEAN-New Zealand Relations

TAN Keng Jin

✿

Pre-ASEAN Relations

Relations between New Zealand and countries of Southeast Asia can be said to exist even in the 1800s. One such example was the career of John Turnbull Thomson from Northumberland, United Kingdom. He started his working career in Malaya and Singapore and concluded it in New Zealand. Employed by the East India Company, Turnbull arrived in Penang in 1837 to survey the large British estates in Penang and Johore.

In 1841, he was appointed the company's Surveyor of Singapore and later as Superintendent of Roads and Public Works. In Singapore, he designed and constructed numerous notable engineering works including bridges, roads, and hospitals. He conducted surveys of the neighbouring islands as well as marine surveys of the Straits of Singapore.

He returned to England in 1853 due to ill health and on recovery immigrated to New Zealand, where he worked as Chief Surveyor of the Otago Province then as Surveyor-General of New Zealand. He was also the original surveyor of the city of Invercargill.

In Southeast Asia, his outstanding achievement was the design and construction of the Horsburgh Lighthouse on Pedra Branca — a lighthouse which is still operating in current times.[1]

---

[1] John Hall Jones, *Mr. Surveyor Thomson* (New Zealand: 1971), 105–106.

During the 1940 to 1960 period, New Zealand's armed forces were engaged in conflicts in Southeast Asia participating in the Vietnam War; the Malayan Emergency; and during Indonesia's "Konfrontasi" and as a member of the Southeast Asia Treaty Organization.

There were two events in the 1970s that had a profound impact on New Zealand. The first was the British policy in 1971 of withdrawing its armed forces "East of Suez" and "East of Aden"; the second occurred in 1973 when Britain joined the European Economic Community (as it was then) which resulted in New Zealand losing its guaranteed favoured market access to Britain.

The ASEAN-New Zealand Dialogues

New Zealand's upgrading of its relations with Asia and the Southeast Asian states could be perceived as its response to the two events. It established diplomatic relations with China in 1972, (this later resulted in New Zealand becoming the first developed country to sign a Free Trade Agreement with China) and in 1975 became one of the first two countries to be an ASEAN Dialogue Partner (the other being Australia), this later led to New Zealand's participation in the various annual ASEAN dialogue fora.

In 1975, the first and second ASEAN-New Zealand dialogues were held in Singapore and Wellington respectively. Discussions on development projects, such as animal husbandry, trade expansion, dental health, reforestation and pine forest development, resulted in New Zealand undertaking to make contributions of $500,000 in 1975/76 ($4.8 million in 2015 equivalent value); $1 million in 1976/77 ($10 million) and over $2 million in 1977/78 ($20 million)[2] — contributions that were over and above New Zealand's bilateral aid.

New Zealand-ASEAN dialogue was started as a way of changing the nature of New Zealand's involvement at the time of the Vietnam conflict. It was a tangible expression of its support for regionalism, and

---

[2] Archives NZ, KL 203/2/1 part 6, 28 Feb. to 2 Mar. 1975, heads of mission: regional cooperation.

economic cooperation with ASEAN. New Zealand's then Foreign Minister Russell Marshall's statement of 1988 disclosed its rationale, when he said "New Zealand has a direct stake in the stability, security and prosperity of the ASEAN countries",[3] because they "occupy a strategically important position along one rim of the Pacific. They straddle vital communications routes for [New Zealand's] trade with North Asia, the Middle East and points beyond, and for inflows of technology, tourists and skilled people."[4]

In 1977, New Zealand held its third dialogue with ASEAN, and like the preceding two Dialogues in 1975, it dealt with development but in addition, paid more attention to trade. However, the more significant event in 1977 was then New Zealand PM Robert Muldoon's attendance (along with the Prime Ministers of Australia and Japan) at the ASEAN Heads of Government meeting in Kuala Lumpur, the second ASEAN summit, thus making them the first Dialogue Partners to hold Summits with ASEAN. The New Zealand-ASEAN Dialogues proceeded with biannual regularity with the fourth being held in 1979, the fifth in 1981, and the sixth in 1983, and most recently the 22nd in 2015.[5]

A Comprehensive and Strategic Partner

The ASEAN-New Zealand partnership reached a significant milestone in 2010, with the adoption of the Joint Declaration on Comprehensive Partnership for 2010–2015 and the Plan of Action to Implement the Joint Declaration at the PMC+1 Session in Hanoi, Vietnam. The aim of the Comprehensive Partnership was to broaden and deepen the ASEAN-New Zealand partnership in political and security, economic, and socio-cultural cooperation that is pro-active and responsive to future developments.

---

[3] Russell Marshall, "New Zealand and ASEAN", in *New Zealand and the ASEAN Countries: The Papers of the Twenty-Third Foreign Policy School*, ed. Ralph H.C. Hayburn (Dunedin: University of Otago, 1988), 10.

[4] *Ibid.*, 9.

[5] Malcolm McKinnon, *New Zealand and ASEAN: A History* (New Zealand: Asia New Zealand Foundation, 2006), 13–14.

ASEAN-New Zealand Dialogue Relations were "elevated" to the "Strategic" level in 2015 during the ASEAN-New Zealand Commemorative Summit that was held back-to-back with the 27th ASEAN Summit in Malaysia, marking the 40th anniversary of ASEAN-New Zealand relations.

Under the Plan of Action to implement the Joint Statement for ASEAN-NZ Strategic Partnership 2016–2020 (POA), the parties have committed to:

(i) Support ASEAN integration as well as ASEAN's efforts in realising the ASEAN Community Vision 2025;

(ii) Enhance New Zealand's engagement with ASEAN in various existing fora and mechanisms; and

(iii) Increase cooperation through two key strategies, namely, the People Strategy (which focuses on building stronger people-to-people connections) and the Prosperity Strategy (which focuses on expanding trade and economic cooperation).

However, some authorities consider the distinction in these tiers of Dialogue Relations to be largely symbolic. This is because each is considered on a case-by-case basis and there appears no consistent modalities for engagement with each strategic partner. For instance, ASEAN agreed to:

(i) have annual summits with strategic partners, China, ROK and Japan;

(ii) have biennial summits with Australia;

(iii) hold summits with the United States even before they became strategic partners,

(iv) have strategic relations with New Zealand [although they have not yet agreed (as of 2016) to regularise this Summit].

ASEAN's View of Its Relations with New Zealand

Today, ASEAN and New Zealand share a strong legacy, built on continuous cooperation shared over the past 41 years across a wide range of areas, including political, security, trade and economic, people-to-people and development cooperation. The past six years have been marked by stronger and more regular political engagement, increased two-way trade under the ASEAN-Australia-New Zealand Free Trade Agreement (AANZFTA), and the expansion of education, tourism and migration links.

Economic cooperation is the primary driving force of ASEAN-New Zealand relations today. ASEAN was New Zealand's fourth largest trading partner in 2014. The AANZFTA remains the most progressive FTA amongst the ASEAN+1 FTAs to date. Over the past five years, NZ's trade with ASEAN has grown at a rate higher than with any of its major trading partners with the exception of China. Work on the general review of the AANZFTA is currently underway, with completion targeted for 2017.

Aside from a common outlook premised on mutual economic benefit, New Zealand shares ASEAN's perspectives on political-security cooperation and regional architecture. Under the Points on Agreement (POA), ASEAN and New Zealand have agreed to continue dialogue and cooperation to address global and regional challenges, in the areas of terrorism, cyber-security, drug-trafficking, and maritime security. New Zealand has also committed to strengthening the East Asia Summit (EAS), as it recognises the strategic imperative of developing the EAS as a counterweight to the ASEAN Plus-Three. Importantly, New Zealand stands in solidarity with ASEAN as a staunch supporter of the peaceful resolution of disputes in accordance with international law including the 1982 UN Convention on the Law of Sea.

The ASEAN-New Zealand relationship has also been characterised by all rounded social-cultural cooperation. For instance, cooperation in disaster risk management has been undertaken through the "Disaster Risk Management Flagship Programme", focusing on New Zealand's support for the implementation of the ASEAN Agreement on Disaster Management and Emergency Response (AADMER) and operationalisation of the ASEAN Coordinating Centre for Humanitarian Assistance on disaster management (AHA Centre). In the area of education, the English Language Training for Officials (ELTO) programme has greatly contributed to improving English language skills of officials from ASEAN participating countries as part of the implementation of the Initiative for ASEAN Integration (IAI). New Zealand and ASEAN also cooperate on the environmental track in areas of mutual interest such as biodiversity cooperation, environmental governance, sustainable development, and climate change.

New Zealand's aid programme is focused on its expertise in agriculture, knowledge and skills, as well as disaster risk management. Aid to ASEAN is made up of programme funding for country-specific activities, including scholarships, regional initiatives, activities supported through the Partnerships Fund, and humanitarian response. New Zealand's ASEAN aid programme is currently focused mainly on six ASEAN countries — Cambodia, Laos, Indonesia, Myanmar, the Philippines and Vietnam. However, some have voiced concern that "we get the impression that in terms of our [ASEAN] dealings with the New Zealand Government that for them Singapore is No. 1 and Malaysia No. 2. We all come afterwards."[6]

Conclusion

New Zealand may not be the most substantial Dialogue Partner of ASEAN and its aid programme may not be the most extravagant but it is one of the oldest and a special friend to ASEAN. New Zealand has demonstrated that it is prepared to listen to ASEAN's views and prepared to accommodate them.

This was demonstrated in 1984 when New Zealand had initially removed Singapore and Brunei from their Generalized System of Preferences (GSP). [Note: The GSP, established in 1971 by the General Agreement on Tariffs and Trade, the forerunner of the World Trade Organization, exempted developing nations from the Most-Favoured Nation (MFN) principle. A principle that obliges nations to treat the imports from all nations no worse than they treat the imports of their "most favoured trading partners". The GSP is an accepted deviation to this principle which permits exports from less developed countries into the receiving country at lower, preferential importation tax rate.]

---

[6] Raj Vasil, *New Zealand and ASEAN: A Critical Review of the Relationship* (New Zealand: Institute of Policy Studies, 1995), 50.

Mr. Lee Kuan Yew wrote in his memoirs:

"In December 1984 (PM) Lange announced, without any prior consultation, the cancellation of Singapore's General System of Preference (GSP) status for our exports. In doing so. New Zealand had moved sooner than America or European Community. When our foreign minister explained to him that while our loss through the cancellation of GSP in New Zealand would be marginal, we would suffer grievously if the Americans or Europeans followed them and did the same, Lange accepted the argument and restored our GSP status."[7]

In my experience, the New Zealanders can be depended on to honour their undertakings.[8]

[7] Lee Kuan Yew, *From Third World to First: The Singapore Story: 1965–2000* (Singapore: Singapore Press Holdings and Times Editions, 2000), 448.
[8] *Ibid.*

TAN Keng Jin's thirty-three year career in the Ministry of Foreign Affairs of Singapore included three Ambassadorships, and two Chief of Protocol positions — when he served Singapore's First and Second Prime Ministers as well as the Second to the Sixth Presidents of Singapore. He was the Ambassador of Singapore to the Arab Republic of Egypt from 1986 to 1990 and concurrently accredited as Ambassador to the Hashemite Kingdom of Jordan, the Islamic Republic of Pakistan and the Socialist Federal Republic of Yugoslavia. He later served as Singapore's High Commissioner to Brunei Darussalam from 1990 to 1994 and to New Zealand from 2000 to 2004. He was Head of Public Affairs of the Institute of Southeast Asian Studies (ISEAS) from 2004 to 2015, and organized the Institute's lectures (including the Singapore Lecture series), conferences, seminars, dialogues, and other activities such as — book launches, golf tournaments and fund raising events. In 2015, he incorporated a private protocol consultancy firm — the Sg Protocol Pte. Ltd.

ASEAN-EU Dialogue: Moving Towards Strategic Relevance

YEO Lay Hwee

∙⃝ ◐ ⃨

Introduction

2017 is not only ASEAN's Jubilee, but it also marks 40 years of formal dialogue partnership between the European Union (EU) and ASEAN. This longstanding partnership has its trials and tribulations, but it is now entering a new phase as the EU acknowledges the role that ASEAN can play in the peace and development of the Asia-Pacific region. In May 2015, the EU issued a Joint Communication calling for an EU-ASEAN partnership with a strategic purpose. How much impact would this Joint Communication have on the further development of EU-ASEAN dialogue, and what are the challenges and opportunities? This essay will provide a broad overview of the 40 years of EU-ASEAN partnership and conclude with a prognosis into the future trajectory of their engagement.

Overview of 40 Years of EU-ASEAN Partnership

Relations between the ASEAN and the EU (then the European Community) which dates back to 1972 constitutes one of the oldest group to group relationships. Informal dialogue took place in 1972 aimed exclusively at achieving greater market access for ASEAN's exports and a price stabilization scheme for ASEAN's primary commodities. This was initiated by ASEAN concerned about the implications of the United Kingdom joining the European Community (common market) since the UK was a key trading partner for several of the ASEAN members.

After some informal and Joint Study Committee meetings, in 1977, the EU officially became one of the dialogue partners of ASEAN. This dialogue partnership was given a boost and a greater political significance with the signing of the ASEAN-EC Cooperation Agreement in 1980 at the second ASEAN-EC Ministerial Meeting held in Kuala Lumpur. The Cooperation Agreement provided the legal and institutional framework to further develop the inter-regional ties. The main emphasis of the Agreement was on economic cooperation and development, extending the Most-Favoured Nation (MFN) treatment to the contracting parties.

However, despite these positive developments in general, until the 1980s, ASEAN remained at the bottom of the EC's hierarchy of relations. In the area of development cooperation in particular, more attention was on the African, Caribbean and the Pacific (ACP) countries which also received more favourable trade benefits covered by the Lomé Convention. The ASEAN-EC relationship was also seen very much as a donor-recipient relationship, an unequal relationship in which the ASEAN countries were inevitably in a weaker bargaining position.

In contrast to this unequal economic relationship, political cooperation between ASEAN and the EC in the 1980s was boosted by their common concerns over the expansion of Soviet influence. Specifically, Vietnam's invasion of Cambodia (then known as Kampuchea) in December 1978, and the Soviet Union's invasion of Afghanistan in 1979 provided the impetus for the two regions to work to coordinate their positions and support each other on these two issues in international fora such as the United Nations. These two issues remained on the agenda for political discussions in successive AEMMs until their resolution in the late 1980s with the pullout of the Soviet forces from Afghanistan and the Vietnamese forces from Cambodia.

The end of the Cold War unfortunately ushered in a much more "contentious" phase of relationship as differences over democracy and human rights bubbled to the surface. Without the competition to keep ASEAN on the capitalist Western camp vis-à-vis the communist Soviet bloc, the EU, which witnessed the democratic transition of Central and Eastern European countries, was euphoric about the march of history towards democracy. The emphasis on democracy promotion and focus on human rights agenda began to dominate the discourse. ASEAN, recognised for the diplomatic role that it played in bringing about the end of the Kampuchean crisis, was brimming with confidence, and was not about to be pushed by the Europeans into quietly accepting the latter's agenda.

In 1994, following the publication of the EU's New Asia Strategy, a more pragmatic turn to capitalize on the EU-ASEAN partnership for broader economic gains in Asia was reflected in the 11th ASEAN-EU Ministerial Meeting in Karlsruhe in September. The issue over unrest and human rights abuses in East Timor was sidestepped and an EU-ASEAN Eminent Persons Group (EPG) was commissioned to develop a comprehensive EU-ASEAN partnership towards the year 2000 and beyond.

Unfortunately, the recommendations in both the 1996 EPG Report on "A Strategy for a New Partnership" and the Commission's own Communication on "Creating a New Dynamic in EU-ASEAN Relations" did not have a chance to be translated into concrete measures. A series of events and a number of factors, notably the Asian financial crisis, and the enlargement of ASEAN to include Cambodia, Laos and Myanmar, changed the dynamics and further impacted the dialogue between EU and ASEAN. In particular, Myanmar's entry into ASEAN in 1997 brought new tensions and strains in EU-ASEAN relations. Myanmar, with what was seen as an appalling human rights record by the Europeans, became a millstone around ASEAN's neck.

9/11 and development in international terrorism, the dramatic rise of China and the "re-invention" of ASEAN in the aftermath of the Asian financial crisis led the EU to adopt a more pragmatic and differentiated approach towards ASEAN and its member states. The Commission's policy paper in 2003 entitled "A New Partnership with Southeast Asia" acknowledged that EU-ASEAN partnership should not be held hostage by Myanmar as there are strong reasons for the EU to enhance its engagement with ASEAN, including first and foremost, the fight against international terrorism, as well as underlying economic imperatives. These must also be seen in the context of ASEAN then in the process of rethinking its regional cooperation model and seeking greater institutionalisation as it contemplated building an ASEAN Community by 2015.

From 2003, the EU scaled up efforts to engage ASEAN, in particular in the area of providing support for capacity building towards integration through programmes such as the ASEAN-EU Programme for Regional Integration Support (APRIS) from 2004 to 2010 and the current ASEAN Regional Integration Support from the EU (ARISE) 2011 to 2017. The EU also stepped up cooperation in counter-terrorism with several ASEAN Member States such as Indonesia and Philippines.

However, despite such efforts, EU-ASEAN dialogue continued to be plagued by disagreement on how to engage Myanmar, with ASEAN preferring constructive engagement over the EU's imposition of sanctions. It was not until Myanmar's election in 2011 that set in motion a credible reform process and a number of other factors that finally led the EU to truly re-evaluate its relations with ASEAN. What are some of these factors?

First and foremost, the United States pivot (or rebalancing) to Asia in 2011 changed the geopolitical undercurrents in the Asia-Pacific region. For the first time, the EU paid serious attention to the political and security dialogues platforms in the region, several of them being "driven" by ASEAN. Second, ASEAN's efforts to build an ASEAN Economic Community (AEC) with a market of over 600 million consumers were making some progress. Despite the low ambitions of the AEC with the key objectives of creating a single market and production base, and transforming ASEAN into an attractive investment destination, Southeast Asia remains an attractive region with a growing middle class, and good growth potential. The EU's needs to search for new growth areas to pick itself out of economic doldrums, makes ASEAN an increasingly attractive economic partner. Taken as a single entity, ASEAN is the EU's third largest trading partner outside of Europe, after US and China. ASEAN is also the fifth most important location for the EU's foreign direct investments.

In May 2015, the EU issued a Joint Communication on its relations with ASEAN entitled "The EU and ASEAN: A Partnership with a Strategic Purpose". In this Communication, the EU acknowledged that "it has a strategic interest in strengthening its relations with ASEAN because ASEAN "combines high rates of economic growth as well as economic dynamism" and that it is also "at the heart of the efforts to build a more robust regional security order in the wider Asia-Pacific". It added that the EU has a huge stake in the success of ASEAN, and that a united and self-confident ASEAN is not only in the direct interest of the citizens of the region, but also of the EU.

With such unequivocal acknowledgement of the importance of ASEAN, where and how should the dialogue partnership between the EU and ASEAN develop in the future?

Towards a Strategic Partnership?

Both ASEAN and the EU are actually facing tremendous challenges in their respective neighbourhoods and regional coherence of ASEAN and integration in the EU are under threat. The EU has been hit by wave after wave of crises from the sovereign debt crisis, to the Ukraine crisis in the East, and the migrant/refugees crisis emanating as a result of war and poverty in the Middle East and North Africa. The latest Brexit dealt a heavy blow to the EU, questioning the very essence of its model of integration. Similarly, ASEAN faces increasing pressure from an assertive China ready to claim its place in the sun in the Asia-Pacific. The strategic competition between China and the United States, and the rising tensions in the South China Sea has led to uncertainties in the region.

Despite the challenges that both the EU and ASEAN face, they remain the two regional entities that have made themselves relevant to their respective regions. The EU has been a beacon of hope and anchored peace and stability in Europe for more than 60 years. ASEAN has also played an important role in confidence building amongst its founding members, and provide these countries some space for manoeuvre in their foreign policy vis-à-vis the big powers in the Asia-Pacific region.

The "health" and development of the EU and ASEAN are vital for their respective regional orders. The risks of them turning inwards, or being "divided" and disintegrating as they face strong centrifugal forces in an increasingly volatile, uncertain and ambiguous world made it all the more important for them to work closely and support each other in their future developments. By deepening their engagement, they can reap the benefits of mutual policy learning, and ward off the inward-looking tendencies and beggar-thy-neighbour policies by strengthening multilateral forums such as the ASEAN Regional Forum (ARF) and the Asia-Europe Meeting (ASEM). They need to strengthen their partnership to reaffirm regionalism and a rules-based order to temper the tide of populism and regressive nationalism. They need to work together to champion international dialogue and cooperation to find win-win solutions to common problems instead of retreating to a zero-sum world. Only by working closely together also in other regional forums and supporting each other's development can they hope to help change the current tide of discontents and emerge stronger and more future-ready to face the challenges of our complex world.

YEO Lay Hwee is Director of the European Union Centre in Singapore. She is also Council Secretary and Senior Research Fellow at the Singapore Institute of International Affairs (SIIA), and Adjunct Fellow at the S. Rajaratnam School of International Studies (RSIS). Since 2011, she is the Co-Editor-in-Chief for the Asia Europe Journal.

Lay Hwee sits on several Academic Advisory Boards — Centre for European Studies at the Australian National University (ANUCES), the KU Leuven's Master in European Studies (MAES) Programme; the Centre for Asia-Pacific Studies, Tallinn University of Technology, and most recently as an International Advisory Council member of the Leiden Asia Centre in Leiden University.

An international relations expert, her research interests revolve around comparative regionalism, principles of multilateralism and governance networks. She has written extensively on issues pertaining to Asia-Europe relations in general, and in particular, the ASEM process and relations between the European Union and ASEAN.

ASEAN-Japan Relations since 1977

LIM Tai Wei

Japan's engagement with ASEAN can be divided into three main historical phases. The first phase began with an economic relationship that centred on resources. From 1977, with the inauguration of the ASEAN-Japan dialogue on synthetic rubber to the end of the Cold War in 1989, Japan's engagement in the Southeast Asian region was mainly economic and resource-based. This was the phase of a resource-based relationship and early gradual institutionalisation of a bilateral relationship. The second historical period in the bilateral relationship can be characterised by the post-Cold War period when Japan contributed to the stabilisation of some ASEAN economies affected by the 1997 Asian Financial Crisis (AFC) and helped former socialist economies in Southeast Asia to catch up with their ASEAN-5 counterparts. Institutionalisation of the bilateral relationship strengthened during this period. The final period covered in this essay is contextualised against changing geopolitical developments in the 21st century with the rise of China, greater parity and maturity in ASEAN-Japan relations.

The roots of Japan's engagement with ASEAN can be traced back to 1977. Historically, according to Japan's Ministry of Foreign Affairs, Japan's engagement with ASEAN formally began in 1973 with the inauguration of the ASEAN-Japan dialogue on a forum for discussing synthetic rubber.[1] The Forum came into being in March 1977. When ASEAN-Japan's relationship began, it was mainly based on a unilateral importation of Southeast Asian resources to supply raw materials needed for Japan's manufacturing activities. For most of the 20th century, Malaysia and Indonesia were the major producers of rubber in the world and so this platform became useful for linking up ASEAN with Japan bilaterally on an informal basis. This relationship with humble roots eventually saw Japan evolve to be one of the largest investors and traders with ASEAN. Initially a raw materials supplier, ASEAN countries later became an important market for Japan's machinery, ferrous/non-ferrous metals, chemicals and iron.[2]

In the 1970s, Japan was re-emerging as the largest economic power in East Asia and its labour costs were increasing after a double-digit income growth at a time of a post-war economic boom in the 1960s. Japanese companies needed to relocate its manpower-intensive, lower value-added industries that were no longer competitive with the labour market's rising labour costs and the costs of importing raw materials to more affordable locations. Against this context, with China under Western countries' embargo and Southeast Asia as the nearest and richest source of raw materials, Japan's engagement with Southeast Asian countries was mainly economic in the 1970s as it set up its production network chain in Southeast Asia during that decade. Thailand is probably one of the most important showcases of Japanese production networking as it emerged in the 1980s and 1990s as the "Detroit of the East" with numerous Japanese car manufacturing investments flowing into that country.

Economic investments paralleled Japanese attempts to smoothen political relations in the late 1970s when former Japanese Prime Minister, Fukuda Takeo inked what was later known as the "Fukuda Doctrine" to encourage a mutual win-win situation and cooperation with ASEAN countries in 1977. Japan won ASEAN people's trust and affection after

[1] Ministry of Foreign Affairs (MOFA), "40th Year of ASEAN-Japan Friendship and Cooperation", *MOFA Japan*, May 7, 2014, http://www.mofa.go.jp/region/asiapaci/asean/relation/ja40/index.html
[2] Kawai, Masahiro and Moe Thuzar, "ASEAN's Regional Role and Relations with Japan", *Chatham House*, February 18, 2016, https://www.chathamhouse.org/

declaring equal partnership and turning back on its turbulent pre-war history and geopolitical orientation. Through the "Fukuda Doctrine", cultural, academic, touristic, people-to-people and other Track II exchanges with ASEAN countries intensified as the two entities sought to understand each other better against the climate of the Cold War. Japan was a factor for geopolitical stabilisation of the East Asian region through its security partnership with the United States. After the US-Japan Alliance was signed in the 1960s, Japan played a major role as the pacifist partner of the security fulcrum in the free world during the bipolar Cold War climate. Through the "Fukuda Doctrine" and an earlier "Yoshida Doctrine" which envisioned a post-war Japan placed under a US security umbrella while Japan focused its resources on economic development, Japan became an economic power while maintaining a defensive and pacifist posture. That set the tone subsequently for ASEAN-Japan relations to take off politically.

In the post-Cold War years, Japan continued its important economic role in stabilising the region economically when it offered financial help and resources to economies embattled by the 1997 Asian Financial Crisis (AFC) and the currency crisis that started it. The ASEAN economies of Thailand and Indonesia were severely affected by the currency crisis. Although its mooted idea of an Asian Monetary Fund did not take off, Japan's loans, aids and promises of maintaining employment in Japanese companies at a time of crisis helped to stabilise the ASEAN economies. Arguably, an even more important institution emerged in the immediate aftermath of the 1997 AFC. Up to this point of time, institutionally, Japan and ASEAN communicated with each other through a number of institutions that encompassed Summit meetings, Ministerial-level meetings, gathering of experts including wise men and pioneering leaders of post-war independent Southeast Asian countries and meetings amongst senior officials.

But in 1997, partly out of the need for coordination to tackle the AFC, the platform of ASEAN Plus Three (APT) which allowed ASEAN member states (AMS) to discuss issues with their Northeast Asian partners (including Japan) was born. APT has far wider implications than ASEAN-Japan relations. Because of the geopolitical competition between major players in Northeast Asia and lingering historical memories that cyclically affected relations between major Northeast Asian powers, APT effectively placed a perceptively neutral ASEAN at the centre of any attempts (the so-called "driver's seat") to push forward with East Asian regionalism. APT helped ASEAN to play the role of a peacemaker for the region, contributing to a smoothening out of Sino-Japanese relations at times. At one ASEAN meeting in 2005 at a time of tense Sino-Japanese relations, ASEAN Leaders cajoled former Chinese Premier Wen Jiabao and former Japanese Prime Minister Junichiro Koizumi to exchange pens and handshakes while signing a document during an APT meeting!

The post-Cold War years also saw Japan contributing to ASEAN integration in a significant way. After the Cold War, Japan rendered crucial help when ASEAN needed to integrate former socialist econo-mies into the original ASEAN-5 (Indonesia, Malaysia, Philippines, Singapore and Thailand) market economies. Japan's loans, aids, invest-ments, transfers of technological know-how that were crucial for the industrialisation of the original ASEAN-5 economies could now extend to the CLMV (Cambodia, Laos, Myanmar, Vietnam) economies that aspired to join ASEAN. Japan subsequently became an important infra-structure builder and source of transfers of technological know-how to the new AMS to build up their economic capabilities and bring them on par with the ASEAN-5.

In the 21st century, another important geopolitical change happened in East Asia with the rise of China as a global economic superpower and an aspiring geopolitical power. Originally, during the Cold War, Indonesia was the largest recipient of Overseas Development Assistance (ODA) but the situation changed from 1979 onwards when China started its economic reforms and became the largest recipient of Japanese investments, loans and aids. However, Northeast Asian rela-tions between major powers like Japan and China remained rocky at times, cyclically turbulent and unpredictable. Japan's so-called "China Plus One" strategy initially began with economic diversification exer-cise to shift investments into Vietnam (the "little dragon" of East Asia) to hedge against political risks in rocky Sino-Japanese ties during the Koizumi administration. After the Chinese economy took off in the 21st century, Japanese investments is once again focused on Southeast

Asia, partly due to the "China Plus One" strategy where Japanese investments are flowing into Southeast Asia exceeding the amount heading to China and Hong Kong. According to the *Japan External Trade Organization* (JETRO) data republished by Bloomberg, the total flow of investments into ASEAN was approximately US$20 billion and into China, about US$10 billion, a trend in place since 2012.[3] Rising costs in China as well as other geopolitical concerns have resulted in the greater flow of Japanese investments to Southeast Asia. Japan's own aging domestic population and workforce was another domestic factor that contributed to this development.

Japan's security posture also came of age in the 21st century. In 1993, Japan sent eight peacekeepers to contribute to the United Nations-sanctioned Cambodian peace process. It has since upgraded its defence agency into a full-fledged Ministry of Defence. Japan's democratic legislative process has also approved the concept of collective self-defence, allowing Japan to come to the aid of its allies in case of conflicts, subjected to strict conditions for engagement. By the second decade of the 21st century, ASEAN-Japan cooperation began to extend into non-traditional security (NTS) cooperation in areas such as transnational crime. Japan is also upgrading bilateral relations with selected ASEAN countries. At the point of writing, Japan is in the midst of a constitutional debate with a strong Shinzo Abe administration in control of both houses of parliament (securing majority in the lower house in the 2015 elections and absolute majority in the upper house in the 2016 elections). Japan, along with the United States, is upgrading its military relations with Vietnam and the Philippines, providing the latter two ASEAN countries with coastguard patrol boats, equipment and funding. Japanese destroyers and submarines are also visiting the two countries. All signs point to more robust exchanges between some AMS and Japan and a growing ASEAN-Japan relationship.

---

[3] Ujikane, Keiko, "Japan Shifts Investment from China to Southeast Asia", Bloomberg, May 31, 2016, https://www.bloomberg.com/news/articles/2016-05-30/southeast-asia-is-winning-more-japanese-investment-than-china>

Beyond the traditional forms of cooperation, there are signs of converging interests between ASEAN and Japan in cooperation on new emerging issues. Three examples are discussed here briefly, though it is not a comprehensive list of growing common interests between the two. The first example of ASEAN-Japan convergence is the intensification of people-to-people exchanges to foster greater integration but with greater compatibility serving the interests between those involved, for instance, ASEAN university students getting quality training from ranking Japanese tertiary institutions that are affected by an aging population and low birth replacement rates. Another example of likely intensification is cooperation on disaster management through resilient infrastructure development. Japan is a leading supplier of technologies in the area of earthquake-proof infrastructure and tsunami prevention structures. Japan benefits from coordinating with ASEAN in these areas as well. Finally, the enhanced cooperation between ASEAN and Japan against cybercrime in Japan is likely to ramp up in the years leading up to the 2020 Tokyo Olympics as Japan copes with the opening up of its credit card and financial networks to incoming foreign visitors. ASEAN can learn from this unique experience in preventing hacking and identity thefts within the banking system.

What started as a politically equal but economically unequal relationship has transformed through the decades into a bilateral relationship that is equal both economically and politically. ASEAN as an economic region is slowly catching up with the overall size of the Japanese economy which faced growth maturity in the post-bubble years after 1989 and the effects of an aging population. Japanese firms and companies are adjusting well to the equalisation of this relationship as Japan continues to offer higher-value added items like environmentally-friendly technologies to ASEAN economies. The historically economics-weighted relationship may also see greater equalisation of a security relationship as Japan upgrades its security and military exchanges with some ASEAN countries in coastal and maritime defence within the context of a US-Japan security alliance and, with ASEAN as a whole, particularly in the non-traditional security field. The separation of economics and politics in the past few decades may eventually converge into a more comprehensive and integrated relationship with converging interests on new and emerging issues between ASEAN and Japan in the coming decades.

LIM Tai Wei is a Senior Lecturer at SIM University (UniSIM) and Research Fellow adjunct at the East Asian Institute of the National University of Singapore (NUS). His research can be found in the areas of Asian studies, contemporary area studies of East Asia, Sino-Japanese relations, East Asian/world histories and energy relations.

ASEAN-US Relations: Finding the Right Balance

CHAN Heng Chee

ASEAN was established in 1967 when the regional and international contexts were both unstable and fraught with Cold War tensions. During this period, three of the ASEAN Member States (AMS) were dealing with serious internal issues — Malaysia with game-changing race riots, Indonesia with a major internal Gestapu coup, while Singapore was working out its future with its abrupt independence.

On the external front, US President Richard Nixon, elected in 1968, announced in 1969 that he would expect Asian allies to be shouldering their own military defence. The United States would provide assistance but its military presence in Southeast Asia would be drawn down. To add further to the uncertainty, the Labour government of Britain, following economic problems and the devaluation of the pound, was determined to cut their forces East of Suez by 1971. In China, Chairman Mao launched the Great Proletarian Cultural Revolution, which was targeted domestically but threatened to spill across its borders. The Soviet Union, sensing a vacuum in the making, proposed a new security system for Asia.

Globally, the United States was seen to be the only power that could hold the line against communism. Nixon's bold opening to China opened new possibilities for the region in the Cold War atmosphere. Japan followed by establishing diplomatic relations with China in 1972, and Malaysia established relations with China in 1974.

This backdrop explains why it was only in the early 1970s that ASEAN as a regional grouping turned to its external relations. The five member states saw the need for external partners for investment and technical assistance for industrialisation. Thus ASEAN formalised links with its Dialogue Partners. Japan, Australia, New Zealand and the European Union were among the first in rapid succession.

The ASEAN-US relationship formally began when the United States became a Dialogue Partner in 1977. This did not mean that the United States did not have bilateral relations with the AMS. Thailand and the Philippines were and are treaty allies and American troops in Vietnam came to Singapore for rest and recreation. Indonesia under Suharto was seen by the United States as an anti-communist bulwark during the Cold War although the two countries did not sign any security or defence treaties. In the sixties, American investments were moving overseas to Asia, and the AMS were the beneficiaries. The United States began a dual track engagement of ASEAN even as ASEAN expanded. The US worked with ASEAN countries bilaterally and ASEAN multilaterally as a regional grouping. As a superpower, the United States has been more comfortable dealing with bilateralism than multilateralism. This was especially true when the military regime of Myanmar became an issue in American domestic politics with Congress and human rights groups. ASEAN became a hostage in the US-Myanmar relationship. In the nineties and during the Bush 43 Administration, the United States was unable to provide assistance to ASEAN if part of the grant went to Myanmar as it had placed broad sanctions on the country.

In the early post-Vietnam war years, ASEAN and the United States found themselves working quite closely together over the Indochina refugee crisis when boatloads of Vietnamese people, estimated to be in the hundreds of thousands, either expelled by or escaped from the communist regime, braving the treacherous seas, landed on ASEAN shores, a precursor of the thousands of migrant boat people in the 21st century. Most of the refugees were resettled to Western countries with the United States taking in more than one half of the total numbers of refugees, and the rest going to other Western countries. But it was the Vietnamese invasion of Cambodia on Christmas day in 1978 that seriously strengthened the cooperation between ASEAN and the United States. The Vietnamese occupation of Cambodia triggered another significant strategic outcome. The United States and China with little hesitation came together to work with ASEAN to counter the Soviet-backed Vietnamese occupation of Cambodia providing a clear and classic case of a proxy war.

The United States quickly saw a Soviet Union in its new phase of expansionism and aggression in the Cold War after it marched into Afghanistan. Soviet support for the Vietnamese occupation of Cambodia was seen as part of a larger strategic plan to spread its influence. Hence the United States was resolved to roll this back. China was determined to teach Vietnam a lesson for deposing its ally Cambodia, and Soviet backing for Vietnam whipped up Sino-Soviet rivalry. ASEAN wanted to stop any prospect of a Vietnamese attempt to spread communism beyond its borders into neighbouring ASEAN states.

From 1979 to 1991, ASEAN, the United States and China forged a close relationship working on the Cambodian issue at the UN. ASEAN mounted a resolution at the UN to mobilise the world community to put pressure on Vietnam to withdraw its troops from Cambodia, dismantle the Vietnamese-installed Hun Sen government and accept a UN comprehensive political settlement which included UN supervised elections.

In Washington, Singapore worked hard to secure the support of Congressman Stephen Solarz (D-NY), Chair of the House Foreign Affairs Sub-Committee on the Asia and Pacific for the Cambodian issue. Singapore managed to persuade the United States government to provide an aid package of US$5 million non-lethal assistance for the Coalition Government of Democratic Kampuchea or CGDK. This was an achievement as it was a sensitive matter for the Reagan officials because the Khmer Rouge was part of the coalition.

The end of the Cold War brought new concerns in ASEAN and East Asia that the United States may be less engaged with the Asia-Pacific. But the new international environment was fluid and new powers were emerging on the scene. Australia and ASEAN thought of new ways to ensure that all the major powers would be engaged in the region. The Asia-Pacific Economic Cooperation was established to bring both sides of the Pacific together and the ASEAN Regional Forum was conceived to allow the major powers especially the United States and China to come together to discuss important security issues.

Mindful that platforms for engagement must be effective and relevant, ASEAN in 2005 developed the East Asia Summit (EAS) to elevate security issues and cooperation to the highest level. The United States did not signal its wish to be part of EAS at the beginning. So EAS was formed of ASEAN plus China, Japan, the ROK plus Australia, New Zealand and India. It was the Obama Administration that realised the United States had to join the most important strategic forum in the Asia-Pacific which included the other major powers of the region. The United States formally became a member in 2011 at the same time as Russia. This was seen by many as an early signal of President Obama's "pivot to Asia", the "re-engagement with Asia" or the "rebalance to Asia".

The truth is the United States never disengaged itself from Asia. It could not possibly. It was a matter of greater or lesser high level attention and at what moment.

Even after the Cold War, regional and international crises ensured that the United States would keep firmly engaged with ASEAN. In 1997, in the second term of President Bill Clinton, the Asian Financial Crisis unravelled, starting in Thailand, followed by Malaysia and spread to Indonesia and South Korea. The impact was deep and wide across East Asia. The United States fearing a collapse of the Asian markets and the contagion acted to shore up the problem when the crisis hit South Korea. The IMF bailout package was severely criticised by the affected countries as too tough and austere and was believed to be advocated by the Clinton Administration. They felt let down by the United States. In Indonesia, it triggered the collapse of the Suharto government and a tumultuous transition. The Asian Financial Crisis kept the United States, especially the US Treasury heavily involved in Southeast Asia putting ASEAN on the radar screen. The fall of the Suharto government which had been in power for decades in the largest country in ASEAN had the Administration focused fully on the transition and its outcome especially since it came in tandem with the East Timor independence issue.

The terrorist attacks of 9/11 ensured that President George W. Bush could not ignore ASEAN and Southeast Asia. It is a region of 250 million Muslims. The Bush 43 Administration sought to demonstrate they could work with Muslim countries, supported moderate Muslim democracies and worked with countries that were also vigilant against the global war on terrorism. The Bush 43 Administration negotiated and concluded the US-Singapore FTA initiated during the Clinton Administration and towards the end of President Bush's second term took the decision that the United States should join the P4 project that is New Zealand, Chile, Singapore and Brunei to become P5 which was then renamed the Trans-Pacific Partnership (TPP) and bringing other countries into the trade agreement. With these two trade initiatives, President George W. Bush took two significant strategic steps for the United States in the Asia-Pacific.

In reality, ASEAN has to compete with other regions to get the attention of the world's superpower as the Asia-Pacific region is considered less volatile except for the Korean peninsula, than the Middle East, Eastern Europe and terrorism. As the millennium was ushered in, so did the world discover jihadist terrorism which later metamorphosed into ISIS and other off-shoots of jihadist terrorism.

But President Obama has made it a mark of his foreign policy and would like his legacy to be his engagement with Asia. It has been earlier argued that the United States never stopped engaging with Asia. A rising China has been on the minds of every American President since the end of the Cold War. It was a matter of time before China and the United States would confront each other in a tussle for influence and the reshaping of the regional order in the Asia-Pacific. Obama's "pivot to Asia" is in reality more about the new emphasis on Southeast Asia or ASEAN. As the only American President to grow up in the Hawaii and having spent three years of his childhood in Indonesia, Obama is disposed to put emphasis on Asia and Southeast Asia. In 2009, the United States became a party to the Treaty of Amity and Cooperation in Southeast Asia paving the way for their membership in the EAS. In 2010, the United States became the first non-ASEAN country to establish a diplomatic mission at the ASEAN Secretariat and appointed a resident Ambassador to ASEAN.

The South China Sea has emerged as the theatre of rivalry between the United States and China with ASEAN countries caught in the middle. Chinese assertiveness in the South China Sea following the tabling of the nine-dash lines claim at the UN led to strained relations between ASEAN and China. Many of the countries in ASEAN have strengthened their relationship with the United States in light of these developments.

The rapid Chinese build-up and militarisation of the islands and atolls of the South China Sea, in a clear attempt to change the facts on the ground provoked a robust United States response concerned with the freedom of navigation of the sea-lanes and airspace. Though only four AMS are claimants in the territorial disputes, ASEAN as a grouping has been trying to forge a common position on the dispute as it relates critically to the freedom of navigation, the peaceful resolution of disputes and the peace and stability of the region. It should be noted that the disputes are not just between the AMS and China, they also exist between the AMS with each other. Increasingly, ASEAN countries feel they are pressured to choose sides. This is something most member states do not want to do. ASEAN wants to be friends of both powers.

For the first time since ASEAN has engaged with the United States, President Obama in 2009 initiated the ASEAN-US Leaders' Summit to be held annually. In November 2015, at the KL ASEAN Summit meeting, ASEAN and the United States elevated its relationship to a Strategic Partnership. In February 2016, the US President hosted ASEAN Leaders and the ASEAN Secretary-General to a two-day US-ASEAN Special Leaders' Summit in Sunnylands, California. This Summit, the first ever to be held in the United States, was important for its symbolism and demonstrated the high importance the United States put on cooperation with the regional grouping, meeting them in the same location President Obama met Chinese President Xi Jinping in 2013. The Sunnylands Declaration, a much negotiated document, contained 17 points, which included respect and support for "ASEAN centrality and ASEAN-led mechanisms in the evolving architecture of the Asian Pacific" and a reference "to the shared commitment to peaceful resolution of disputes including full respect for legal and diplomatic processes in accordance with the universally recognised principles of International Law and the 1982 UN Convention of the Law of the Sea." This formulation was the only allusion to the South

China Sea and the International Tribunal process, highly sensitive matters for China, that was acceptable to all present and included in the Declaration. The Strategic Partnership and the Sunnylands Summit marked the high point of the ASEAN-US relationship.

But US engagement with ASEAN would be incompletely understood if cast only in security terms. The United States has a long economic relationship with ASEAN. In 2014, US total trade with ASEAN stood at US$226 billion. ASEAN is the United States' fourth largest trading partner. US foreign direct investment (FDI) stock today in ASEAN totals US$226 billion. It is doubled that of 2008. The US invests more in ASEAN than any other market in Asia. In fact, more than one third of its investments in Asia go to ASEAN, more than US investments in China, India, South Korea, Hong Kong and Taiwan. The TPP is the single most important trade initiative for the United States in the Asia-Pacific. So far four of the ten AMS are members of the TPP — Singapore, Brunei, Vietnam and Malaysia. For the ASEAN countries not in the TPP, the United States has been working at Trade and Investment Framework Agreements and at formal trade dialogues with them. But the domestic politics of the United States has gone highly anti-trade and the passage of TPP at the end of 2016 is in jeopardy. The pivot or rebalance to Asia would lose much of its substance if the United States fails to pass and ratify the completed trade agreement.

At the time of writing in 2016, the United States is about to elect a new President. There is concern about the continuity of foreign and trade policy and the role the United States will play in Asia. The question of whether the United States will stay in the region is one that irks all American officials who cannot understand why they have to constantly reassure their allies and friends in the region of their commitment. Perhaps ASEAN is too aware of the distractions that take away a superpower's attention. There is no question ASEAN would like to see a continuation of the substantial relationship that has been historically in place for the last 50 years.

During the Cold War, ASEAN, a grouping of anti-communist, pro-market economy countries, was a natural partner for the United States. In the post-Cold War, era new powers have arrived on the scene and ASEAN has had to adjust to the new environment. Going forward, it must find the right balance to live peacefully with the great powers and at the same time, protect its interests and ensure a secure and peaceful regional environment.

CHAN Heng Chee is Ambassador-at-Large with the Singapore Foreign Ministry and concurrently, Singapore's Representative to the ASEAN Intergovernmental Commission on Human Rights (AICHR). She is Chairman of the Lee Kuan Yew Centre for Innovative Cities in the Singapore University of Technology and Design (SUTD), and Chairman of the National Arts Council (NAC). Heng Chee was appointed Member of the Presidential Council for Minority Rights in July 2012. She is a Trustee of the National University of Singapore and member of the Yale-NUS Governing Board. She sits on the Board of Governors of the S. Rajaratnam School of International Studies, Nanyang Technological University. Heng Chee is a Founding Director on the Board of the S. Rajaratnam Endowment CLG Limited. She is a Trustee of the Asia Society, New York. She is a Member of the Board of Lowy Institute for International Policy, Australia. Heng Chee served as Singapore's Ambassador to the United States from July 1996 to 14 July 2012. She was Singapore's Permanent Representative to the United Nations from 1989 to 1991 and was concurrently High Commissioner to Canada and Ambassador to Mexico.

ASEAN-ROK Relations

Peter TAN

In the past decade or so, Korean dramas and the *Hallyu* (Korean wave) have emerged as one of Korea's top cultural exports. These movies, dramas and music have travelled far and wide, captivating the hearts and minds of many all over the world. ASEAN is no exception. It is one of the top consumers of K-pop music and Korean television dramas.

As ASEAN celebrates its 50th Anniversary in 2017, it is noteworthy that 2017 has also been designated as the ASEAN-ROK Year of Cultural Exchange. This Korean success story goes beyond the cultural sphere. Many of the ROK's top brand-names in electronics, automobiles and household goods have found a ready market of more than 620 million people in ASEAN.

ASEAN-ROK Partnership

The ASEAN-ROK relationship has evolved rapidly since the establishment of dialogue relations in 1989. This relationship was elevated to a Strategic Partnership at the 13th ASEAN-ROK Summit in October 2010.

As a signal of its continuing commitment to the region, the ROK established the ASEAN-Korea Centre in 2009 and a dedicated ROK Mission to ASEAN in Jakarta in 2012. The ROK is in the process of establishing a dedicated team of officers based in Jakarta to oversee the implementation of ASEAN-ROK cooperation projects, and will inaugurate an ASEAN Culture House in Busan in 2017. Both sides also adopted the ASEAN-ROK Plan of Action to implement the Joint Declaration on Strategic Partnership for Peace and Prosperity (2016–2020) in August 2015 as a guide for future cooperation.

This points to the fact that ROK is one of ASEAN's most important and dynamic partners. The relationship encompasses cooperation in various key sectors, including the political and economic spheres, as well as people-to-people exchanges and infrastructure development. In fact, ASEAN has become ROK's second most important trading partner, after China. Building a strong ASEAN-ROK relationship will continue to be vital in strengthening regional peace, stability and prosperity.

ASEAN's founding anniversary is a timely opportunity for us to take stock of our journey and look ahead. ASEAN's future lies in its continued ability to build mutually reinforcing and beneficial partnerships with key regional countries such as the ROK. ASEAN and the ROK have gained from our strategic partnership, which has allowed us to enjoy a more peaceful, stable and prosperous region. As we look ahead to the future, we must continue to look for further avenues of cooperation and not rest on our laurels.

A Relationship of Opportunities

ASEAN and the ROK are strong economic partners. With a young and dynamic population of over 620 million people, ASEAN offers a promising market for Korean businesses looking for new growth areas, and the ROK government has encouraged its companies to take advantage of the newly established ASEAN Economic Community.

The ASEAN-ROK Free Trade Agreement (AKFTA) signed in 2009 has facilitated ROK's rise to become ASEAN's fifth largest trade and investment partner, while ASEAN is the ROK's second largest trade and investment partner. The ASEAN market will continue to grow as it reaps the benefits of its demographic dividend with more than half its population currently below the age of 30. According to the Asian Development Bank, the size of the middle class in the region is projected to rise from 24 percent to 65 percent of the population by 2030.

How can both sides capitalise on these opportunities?

The AKFTA has benefitted exporters by easing the administrative burden on traders and reducing the time taken to bring a product to market. This has streamlined the production process and allowed consumers to enjoy high-quality products more quickly and at cheaper rates. Going forward, further liberalisation of the AKFTA would serve to create opportunities for the more than 620 million people living in ASEAN and the ROK and boost our current combined GDP of US$2.6 trillion through a more liberal market access and investment regime.

Increasing regional connectivity will also boost people-to-people links and allow us to realise the full potential of our partnership. In this regard, we welcome the ROK's support for the new Master Plan on ASEAN Connectivity 2025, a key part of which is in improving air connectivity. The ASEAN-ROK Air Services Agreement (AKASA), which is currently being negotiated, offers significant mutually beneficial opportunities in terms of tourism and trade. Over five million ROK nationals visited the ASEAN region in 2015, making it the most popular travel destination for Koreans. Similarly, 1.8 million people visited the ROK from ASEAN, representing the third largest number of foreign visitors to Korea. There are also 370,000 ASEAN nationals residing in the ROK, and 300,000 Korean nationals living in ASEAN. These people-to-people ties act as a bridge connecting our two regions. The liberalisation of traffic rights through the AKASA would allow us to strengthen these connective threads and further enhance the flow of goods, people and ideas between our two regions.

These aside, what more can we do together to create more economic opportunities?

One, the launch of the ASEAN-Korea Business Council (AKBC) in December 2014 is a step in the right direction. The AKBC will facilitate the expansion of private sector cooperation between ASEAN and the ROK. For instance, several Singaporean food-manufacturing companies have signed MOUs with the Foodpolis development in North Jeolla Province as Korea aims to become the food-manufacturing hub of Northeast Asia. These partnerships play a meaningful role in the economic ecosystem of the region. They create quality employment and allow ASEAN and the ROK to share productivity-enhancing know-how.

Two, the changing innovation landscape also offers opportunities for collaboration. With the advent of disruptive technologies, society at large is at an inflexion point. People are constantly imagining new ways of doing things. One example is Grab, a ride-hailing company based in Southeast Asia which has changed the way people commute. Given the ROK's expertise at the cutting edge of technology, ASEAN and the ROK can cooperate on the development of systems and infrastructure to build digital-centred "Smart Nations" throughout Southeast Asia. One example is the ongoing collaboration between Singapore's Economic Development Board/Infocomm Development Authority and the Pangyo Techno Valley — the "Silicon Valley of Korea" — located 30-minutes outside of Seoul. Both sides are collaborating on a Launchpad for start-ups seeking to establish themselves in the Korean and Singapore technology ecosystems.

Three, the ASEAN-ROK partnership allows us to collectively address issues of global concern. ASEAN and ROK have increased cooperation on non-traditional global security issues such as climate change, forestry issues and the environment. The ROK's commitment of US$100 million towards promoting low-carbon green growth has been channelled through initiatives under its "East Asia Climate Partnership." The Asian Forest Cooperation Organisation (AFOCO) was also established in 2015 with the objective of strengthening cooperation in forestry issues and enhancing the region's capacity to deal with climate change. These initiatives are especially timely given the entry into force of the Paris Climate Agreement on 4 November 2016. They are a tangible signal of the ROK's commitment to tackling the key global and regional challenges.

Looking Ahead

As ASEAN approaches its 50th anniversary, the ASEAN-ROK partnership has a bright future. We must continue to seize every opportunity to enhance our shared peace by strengthening cooperation in politics and security, shared prosperity by bolstering economic cooperation, and shared progress by enhancing collaboration in society and culture. There is a saying in Korean — 백지장도 맞들면 낫다 (paek-ji-jangdo

maj-deul-myeon nat-da) — that is similar to the English proverb that
"two heads are better than one". The ASEAN-ROK partnership has
shown that we are stronger and more effective when we work together.
As we celebrate our achievements thus far and look to the future, my
hope is that this partnership will continue to grow from strength to
greater strength for many years to come.

Peter TAN Hai Chuan is Deputy Secretary/Southeast Asia & ASEAN in the
Ministry of Foreign Affairs. He graduated with a BA (Hons) from the National
University of Singapore in 1992. He was awarded the Fulbright Scholarship and
obtained his MA (East Asian Studies) from Columbia University, United States
in 2000. Since joining the Ministry of Foreign Affairs in 1992, he has served in
various capacities in the Southeast Asia, Northeast Asia, Europe, and Australia,
New Zealand and the Pacific Directorates. He also served in the Singapore
Embassy in Tokyo as First Secretary from 1995 to 1998 and in the Singapore
High Commission in Kuala Lumpur as Counsellor from 2000 to 2002. He also
served in the Singapore Embassy in Tokyo from 2002 to 2005 as Deputy Chief
of Mission. He was Director of the Southeast Asia Directorate from 2006 to
2010, before serving as the Singapore Ambassador to the Republic of Korea
from 2011 to 2015.

ASEAN-China Relations: Progressing from Antagonism to Cooperation

LYE Liang Fook

China's assertiveness in the South China Sea and ASEAN's apparent disarray or disunity over the same issue have gripped media headlines and unwittingly created the impression that all is not well with ASEAN-China relations. Such a perception overlooks the broad and deep relationship that ASEAN shares with China today.

At the time of writing this essay when ASEAN-China ties are going through a rough patch, it is timely and useful to review how far this relationship has progressed over the years. It is worthwhile to look back at the circumstances leading to ASEAN's establishment of full dialogue relations with China in 1996. Essentially, ASEAN-China ties have shifted from outright antagonism to one where the two parties cooperate in many fields and at many levels. By adopting a broader perspective, one may be better able to appraise the current differences between ASEAN and China and not blow them out of proportion.

Initial Antagonism

China was bitter and antagonistic towards ASEAN when the latter was formed on 8 August 1967. An article in *Beijing Review* (a mouthpiece of the Chinese government) on 18 August 1967 referred to the initial five founding members of Indonesia, Thailand, the Philippines, Singapore and Malaysia as "reactionaries", "US stooges", "US lackeys" and even "US imperialism's running dogs in Southeast Asia". China saw ASEAN as an outright "counter-revolutionary alliance" and even "military alliance directed specifically against China". It saw ASEAN as a puppet of "US imperialism" and "Soviet revisionism" in an anti-China front.

Beijing also did not expect ASEAN to last long. In its view, this anti-China front was a "tattered and tottering alliance, no stronger than a twist of straw". The article concluded that ASEAN would eventually falter and fail, similar to the fate of previous US-led initiatives such as the Baghdad Treaty Organization which had collapsed and was replaced by the Central Treaty Organization that was "now split at the seams", and the Southeast Asia Treaty Organization which "today exists in name only".[1] Other media platforms like the *People's Daily* and *Xinhua News Bulletin* (of the Xinhua News Agency) also carried similar views denouncing ASEAN.

Improvements in Ties

China's outright antagonistic view gradually gave way to a more positive appraisal of ASEAN in the mid-1970s. It began to see ASEAN as a body distinct from the United States and Russia, and accorded greater recognition to ASEAN's claim that its primary purpose was to promote economic growth, social progress and cultural development. For instance, at a banquet that Chinese Premier Hua Guofeng hosted for visiting Singapore Prime Minister Lee Kuan Yew to Beijing in May 1976, Hua reportedly gave China's endorsement of the first ASEAN summit held in Bali in February 1976 which had "reaffirmed its positive proposals for the establishment of a zone of peace and neutrality in Southeast Asia, and achieved significant results in strengthening regional economic cooperation".[2]

To be sure, China's decision to improve ties with ASEAN was shaped by changes in the broader strategic environment such as its worsening relationship with the Soviet Union which saw the two countries clashing

---

[1] "Meeting in Bangkok: Puny Counter-Revolutionary Alliance", *Peking Review*, vol. 10, no. 34 (1967), accessed November 14, 2016, https://www .marxists.org/subject/china/peking-review/1967/PR1967-34 .pdf

[2] "Hua: We Back ASEAN's Objectives…", *The Straits Times*, May 12, 1976.

in a border skirmish in 1969. In addition, there was the China-US détente after US President Nixon's visit to China in 1972. With this improvement in ties, ASEAN was no longer seen as being in cahoots with the United States against China but more as an association in its own right. China moved to establish diplomatic relations first with Malaysia (in May 1974), followed by the Philippines (in June 1975) and Thailand (in July 1975). Although Singapore was not ready for formal ties with Beijing due to the concerns of its bigger Malay neighbours, it saw the importance of improving relations with China.[3] This was demonstrated by the visits of Mr. S. Rajaratnam and Mr. Lee Kuan Yew to China in 1975 and 1976 respectively, the first ever by a Singapore foreign minister and prime minister.

After Deng Xiaoping enunciated China's open door and reform policy in 1978, it became more important for China to have better relations with Southeast Asia so that it could focus its energy on growing its economy. An equally, if not more important factor, from the perspective of ASEAN-China relations was Vietnam's invasion of Cambodia in that same year which fortuitously aligned the interests of China and ASEAN, driving them to work together on a common cause of stopping Vietnamese aggression and Soviet expansionism.

More specifically, China recognised and supported ASEAN's role at the annual sessions of the UN General Assembly beginning in 1979 to canvass international support against Vietnam's invasion of Cambodia and promote a political settlement to the Cambodian issue. On its part, China launched a military offensive against Vietnam in 1979 to "teach Hanoi a lesson" and keep up the military pressure on the Sino-Vietnamese border. It further extended military and financial aid to the Cambodian coalition forces arrayed against the Vietnamese-backed regime in Phnom Penh. From 1979 till the 1991 Paris Peace Accords that sanctioned a transitional authority in Cambodia, China largely collaborated with

---

[3] Singapore made it clear in the 1970s that it would be the last ASEAN member to establish formal ties with China. When Indonesia established diplomatic relations with China in August 1990, Singapore followed suit shortly after in October 1990.

ASEAN to prevent Vietnam's occupation of Cambodia from becoming a *fait accompli* and force Vietnam's eventual withdrawal from Cambodia.

Beyond the Cambodian issue, China-ASEAN relations generally continued their upward trajectory with key milestones such as China being invited as a guest to the opening session of the 24th ASEAN Ministerial Meeting in Kuala Lumpur in 1991; China's admission as ASEAN's full dialogue partner in 1996; China's offer to establish a free trade area (FTA) with ASEAN in 2000 to allay ASEAN's concern with the competition that would be posed by China's WTO entry (which occurred in 2001); China and ASEAN signing the Framework Agreement on Comprehensive Economic Cooperation in November 2002 to establish the ASEAN-China Free Trade Area (ACFTA); China's accession to ASEAN's Treaty of Amity and Cooperation (TAC) in 2003; China-ASEAN upgrade of their relationship to a strategic partnership in 2003; China's Guangxi province hosting of the annual China-ASEAN Expo (since 2004) to promote trade and investment linkages; and China expressing its intention to accede to ASEAN's Southeast Asia Nuclear Weapon-Free Zone Treaty (SEANWFZ).

Among the above developments or initiatives, China was the first among ASEAN's dialogue partners to accede to TAC, to propose a FTA with ASEAN, and to express its intention to accede to the Protocol to the SEANWFZ. China's pro-activeness generated a positive momentum for other ASEAN dialogue partners to follow up with similar commitments. Over the years, China also announced a number of financial initiatives to support ASEAN-China cooperation such as the setting up of the ASEAN-China Cooperation Fund (with an initial capital of US$5 million) in 1996 to sponsor various priority projects; the China-ASEAN Investment Cooperation Fund (of US$10 billion) in 2009 to support infrastructure, energy and natural resources projects; the China-ASEAN Maritime Cooperation Fund (US$500 million) in 2011 to promote cooperation in areas like marine research and environmental protection, navigation safety, and search and rescue; and the Silk Road Fund (of US$40 billion) in 2014 and the Asian Infrastructure Investment Bank (of US$100 billion) launched in 2016 to support projects related to China's "One Belt, One Road" initiative.

Final Remarks

ASEAN-China ties have come a long way from the initial acrimonious, tense and suspicious relationship. When ASEAN was formed in 1967, China viewed ASEAN in extremely negative terms and was opposed to its very existence. Today, there is a strong interdependence between ASEAN and China and the two sides collaborate in eleven priority areas of cooperation, namely agriculture, information and communication technology, human resource development, Mekong Basin Development, investment, energy, transport, culture, public health, tourism and environment. China has also scored a number of firsts in its relationship with ASEAN such as being ASEAN's first dialogue partner to accede to TAC, to propose a FTA with ASEAN, and to express its intention to accede to the Protocol to the SEANWFZ.

There was then a prevailing view in ASEAN that China was ASEAN's most active dialogue partner as well as a "good neighbour, good friend and good partner" of ASEAN.[4] This term "good neighbour, good friend and good partner" seemed to gain greater traction after China refrained from devaluing the *Yuan* following the 1997 Asian financial crisis and contributed about US$4 billion in aid to the Operational Budget of the IMF to help Thailand and Indonesia, two ASEAN Member States (AMS) most affected by the crisis. As mentioned above, there were also a slew of cooperative measures and initiatives that Chinese leaders brought to the table when they met their ASEAN counterparts for meetings. In this light, China was perceived as a reliable and responsible partner of ASEAN and one that was willing to share "weal and woe" with ASEAN.

In other words, up till 2009 China successfully portrayed itself as being very skilful at striking the right resonance with ASEAN to grow their relationship. Its "charm offensive" was working well, buttressed by growing economic ties and progress in various other fields with the

---

[4] Jiang Zemin, "Towards a Good-Neighborly Partnership of Mutual Trust Oriented to the 21st Century", MFA China, December 16, 1997, accessed November 16, 2016, http://www.fmprc.gov.cn/mfa_eng/topics_665678/zgcydyhz_665920/dyczgdm_665922/t25994.shtml

AMS. Relatively, the other ASEAN dialogue partners were apparently found wanting in their relations with ASEAN. China managed to create an image where it could do no wrong or make no mistakes. However, this virtual infallible image of China has taken a beating over the past few years with the geostrategic shift in the balance of power between the United States and China, and China's more assertive foreign policy posture especially in the region. The ASEAN-China relationship is in a high state of flux in light of these broader developments.

LYE Liang Fook is Research Fellow and Assistant Director at the East Asian Institute, National University of Singapore. His research interests cover China's foreign policy, China's One Road, One Belt initiative, China-ASEAN relations and China-Singapore relations. He was part of a government-sanctioned team that completed a review of the Suzhou Industrial Park, the first flagship project between China and Singapore. His research extends into other government-to-government projects between the two countries such as the Sino-Singapore Tianjin Eco-city and the China-Singapore (Chongqing) Demonstration Initiative on Strategic Connectivity. His publications have appeared in *Routledge, International Relations of the Asia Pacific, Journal of Chinese Political Science, Copenhagen Journal of Asian Studies, Eastern Universities Press, Institute of Southeast Asian Studies (ISEAS) Publishing, Konrad Adenauer Stiftung Publishing, World Scientific Publishing,* and *China: An International Journal.* He also manages the Singapore Secretariat of the *Network of East Asian Think Tanks* (NEAT) and the *Network of ASEAN-China Think Tanks* (NACT), two Track II bodies that aims to promote regional cooperation.

ASEAN-Russia Relations: The Way Forward*

Bilahari KAUSIKAN

In 2016, ASEAN and Russia held their first high-level Summit in Sochi, Russia. This meeting underscored the reality that Russia is a geopolitical fact that ASEAN cannot ignore, and that ASEAN will pursue its own interests with Russia, irrespective of the attitudes of its Western dialogue partners.

ASEAN's Interests in Russia

ASEAN was reluctant to describe its relationship with Russia as "strategic" even though this is an adjective that ASEAN has used promiscuously or at least attached to other dialogue relationships without much concern for consistency of meaning.

This is perhaps understandable since the relationship with Russia is the least developed of ASEAN's dialogue relationships.

The Sochi Declaration only said that ASEAN and Russia would "Further strengthen the Dialogue Partnership … with a view to working towards a strategic partnership." The doubly qualified condition for strategic partnership does not suggest that either side regards this goal as a matter of great urgency.

---

*A version of this article was first published in the June/July 2016 issue of *ASEANFocus*, a publication of the ASEAN Studies Centre at ISEAS-Yusof Ishak Institute, Singapore.

Nor is there a realistic plan to move the relationship in this direction. The Sochi Declaration and the Comprehensive Plan of Action (CPA) are laundry lists of aspirations, when they do not merely record existing projects. Both documents were primarily intended to give a semblance of substance to an event whose significance was mainly symbolic.

The Russians wanted a Summit largely for reasons of *amour propre*; ASEAN's other dialogue partners have had summits, so why not Russia? ASEAN agreed largely because there was no reason not to agree; other dialogue partners have had summits, so why not Russia?

What ASEAN and Russia seem to have most in common at this stage of their relationship, is a penchant for privileging form over substance.

Realising ASEAN-Russian Aspirations

I would be pleasantly surprised if more than a few of the aspirations expressed in the Declaration and the CPA were to be substantially realised. I would be a little shocked if the report of the ASEAN-Russia Eminent Persons Group (AREPG) were taken as a serious guide to the future of the relationship.

Many of the areas these documents identified for future cooperation seem better suited for bilateral follow-up by individual member states than ASEAN-wide projects. But there is no harm in attaching the term 'ASEAN' to them even if this is not strictly accurate. I do not mean to suggest that there will be no movement forward in ASEAN-Russia relations.

Some ASEAN members, Singapore among them, are interested in developing links with the Eurasian Economic Union (EAEU) in which Russia is the largest and most developed economy.

Russia wants to expand economic and other ties with ASEAN. It is interested in, among other things, promoting arms and energy exports to Southeast Asia, attracting investments to the Russian Far East, cooperating in scientific research and anti-terrorism linkages. Some ASEAN members will see it in their interests to respond positively in some of these areas.

The essential obstacle to moving ASEAN-Russia relations towards a strategic partnership is thus not the lack of scope or intention. What both sides must confront is the more fundamental and complex challenge of conceptualising how each fits into each other's visions of their roles in the region.

Neither side has ever seriously tried to do so, and the Sochi Summit contributed nothing in this respect. The Summit only improved the atmospherics of ASEAN-Russia relations but this is already dissipating.

The lack of such a conceptual framework is what most starkly distinguishes ASEAN-Russia relations from ASEAN's other dialogue relationships. The United States, China, Japan, Australia, New Zealand, the ROK and India all have defined ideas of their roles in East Asia. ASEAN has its own ideas of how these countries ought to fit into its own notion of regional order.

These ideas may well vary in scope and sophistication and the ideas of ASEAN and these countries are not always aligned. But these complications are beside the point: the point being that they exist as frameworks within which specific projects are instrumentalities and hence gives focus and strategic significance to these dialogue relationships.

Without such a broader conceptual framework, no matter how many items "ASEAN" — as individual states or collectively — ticks off on the Sochi laundry lists, these projects will remain discrete and ad hoc and will not cohere into anything which has a strategic meaning that is larger than the sum of its parts; the number of such parts in any case is unlikely to be very large.

In this respect, the ASEAN-Russia relationship resembles ASEAN's relationships with the EU and Canada. Neither Brussels nor Ottawa has a coherent or consistent concept of their role in East Asia. Consequently these are the least strategically significant of ASEAN's dialogue relationships.

ASEAN brought Russia into the East Asia Summit and other ASEAN-led forums almost casually, as if its size, geography and status as a nuclear weapon state and Permanent Member of the UN Security Council needed no further elaboration or deeper justification.

But these are generic factors which in themselves prescribe nothing very useful in the way of any specific concept of an East Asian role for Russia. Having admitted Russia, ASEAN has been content to let the situation drift. There is no consensus within ASEAN on what Russia's role should be, no interest in reaching a consensus on a role for Russia, or even awareness that a consensus on this matter is required.

On its part, Moscow still most naturally looks westward and defines and validates itself primarily in relation to Europe and the US, not Asia. Its approach towards Asia has usually been tactical. Since the time of Peter the Great, Moscow has turned eastwards usually only after Western rebuffs or to gain Western approbation. Post-Soviet Russia's Asia policy fits into this historical pattern.

The souring of Russia's relations with the West over Ukraine was the proximate cause of the latest phase of Russia's turn to the East. But it was taken, I believe, reflexively under pressure and without a holistic assessment of overall Russian interests. It therefore risks locking Russia into a subordinate relationship with China and an essentially passive regional role.

Some signs of this are already discernible. China recently appropriated Russia's position on the South China Sea. Russia's stance on this issue is in fact more nuanced than China made it out to be, but Moscow had to bite its tongue and did not clarify its position. The Russian Navy has conducted exercises with the PLA Navy (PLAN) in disputed areas in the South China Sea. There is of course no reason why the Russian Navy should not exercise with PLAN. But the oceans are vast and was it really in Russia's interests to do so in a disputed area? But fortunately the situation is not yet irreversible.

Let me conclude by declaring my interest. I was Ambassador to Russia and must plead guilty to having been a member of the AREPG. I take no joy in the current state of ASEAN-Russia relations. I believe that ASEAN-Russia relations do have strategic potential and that it would be a great pity if that potential went unrealised.

Three Conditions

To realise the potential, three conditions must be fulfilled.

First, ASEAN must reach consensus on what strategic role we want Russia to play in our region. This need not be difficult. ASEAN's basic and enduring purpose is to help its members preserve some modicum of autonomy in the midst of great power competition. Russia as an active and autonomous participant in regional diplomacy will widen our scope for manoeuvre, particularly when, as I think will occur sooner or later, the United States and China reach a new *modus vivendi* over Southeast Asia.

Second, to play an autonomous role, Russia must more clearly and clinically distinguish its interests on its western border from its interests on its eastern border. Moscow has legitimate grievances in the west where the United States and Europe made a fundamental strategic error in the immediate post-Soviet period by treating Russia as a defeated country. The West broke promises, explicit or implied, about the expansion of its security system in Europe as if Russian interests could forever be ignored. The crisis in Ukraine was the denouement of this mistake.

But the Western security system in East Asia is no longer directed against Russia unless Moscow makes it so by its positions on the maritime disputes in the East and South China Seas. Moscow should not let anger with the West drive its policy in East Asia.

Third, the West and in particular the United States, must encourage Moscow to make this differentiation in its interests by itself differentiating its approach to Russia in Europe from its approach to Russia in East Asia. The current blanket system of sanctions against Russia only promotes Moscow's dependence on China by depriving it of alternatives.

At the Shangri-La Dialogue in Singapore in 2016, Defence Secretary Ashton Carter hinted at United States willingness to see Russia playing a security role in East Asia. It is not entirely clear what the United States meant. But it is in Moscow's interest to put United States intentions to the test. This could be by a new articulation of Russia's position on the South China Sea and clear support for the UNCLOS decision on the legal issues that the Philippines brought before the Arbitral Tribunal.

Will these conditions be met? Only one is within ASEAN's control. The most important decisions are clearly going to be made in Moscow.

Bilahari KAUSIKAN is currently Ambassador-at-Large in the Ministry of Foreign Affairs of Singapore.

From 2001 to May 2013, Mr. Kausikan was the second Permanent Secretary and subsequently Permanent Secretary of the Ministry of Foreign Affairs.

He had previously served in a variety of appointments in the Ministry and abroad, including as the Permanent Representative to the United Nations in New York and as Ambassador to the Russian Federation.

He has been awarded the Public Administration Medal (Gold) and the *Pingat Jasa Gemilang* (Meritorious Service Medal) by the Singapore Government.

Raffles Institution, the University of Singapore and Columbia University in New York all attempted to educate Mr. Kausikan.

ASEAN-India@25

Jonathan TOW

⌒ ⅊ ⌒

Coinciding with Singapore's "India Fever" of the 1990s, India's "Look East" policy similarly helped ignite Indian interest in our region. Looking back in 2006, India's Prime Minister Manmohan Singh noted that the "Look East" policy was not "merely an external economic policy" but a "strategic shift in India's vision of the world and India's place in the evolving global economy". PM Singh added that "India's destiny [was] interlinked with that of Asia, and more so Southeast Asia". As we mark the 25th anniversary of ASEAN-India relations, PM Singh's words proved prescient with India since deepening its engagement from that of "Look East" to "Act East".

The early roots for India's turn to Asia, and ASEAN in particular, were economic. Thrust into the premiership in 1991, Narasimha Rao inherited an economy burdened with a balance of payment crisis. Faced with the prospect of default, Rao and his reform-minded Finance Minister Manmohan Singh moved decisively to dismantle India's Socialist-era market controls with sweeping economic reforms. At the same time, India sought partners that could provide the trade and investment necessary to fulfil their vision of a "New India". In 1992, India became a Sectoral Dialogue Partner and from the first ASEAN-India Joint Sectoral Cooperation Committee, the ASEAN-India Business Council was formed to help nurture budding commercial links.

Convinced of India's economic and strategic potential, Singapore sought India's deeper engagement in the regional architecture which was then starting to take shape. As a small country, Singapore envisioned a region that is open, stable and one where major powers had a stake in. We actively played our part by pushing for India's elevation to full Dialogue Partner status. At an informal meeting of the 1994 ASEAN Summit, Singapore's Prime Minister Goh Chok Tong proposed granting India full Dialogue Partner status. Despite initial reservations at the ASEAN senior officials' level, a consensus soon emerged among the leaders, and India became ASEAN's fifth Dialogue Partner the following year. India's Foreign Secretary Krishnan Srinivasan acknowledged Singapore's role saying that "Singapore was the first and, at the time, the only ASEAN country to take India seriously."

Since then, ASEAN-India relations have grown from strength to strength. India became a Summit-level Partner in 2002, and a Strategic Partner ten years later. Trade between both sides rose from US$2 billion in the early 1990s to US$58 billion to 2015. The ASEAN-India FTA (AIFTA), which was fully concluded in 2015, is expected to catalyse further economic flows. There are 30 ASEAN-India Dialogue Mechanisms across a variety of sectors, including trade, tourism, agriculture and energy. In 2013, India established the ASEAN-India Centre and appointed its first resident Ambassador to ASEAN in 2015. India also participates constructively in ASEAN-led regional forums, such as ASEAN Regional Forum (ARF), ASEAN Defence Ministers' Meeting-Plus and East Asia Summit (where Singapore also strongly supported India's membership).

This active interaction demonstrates that the economic and strategic imperatives for ASEAN-India engagement remain strong. Economically, ASEAN and India both enjoy good growth prospects despite a weakening global outlook. India is projected to become one of the world's fastest growing economies, with expected growth of about seven percent. ASEAN has grown at about six per cent over the past decade and is expected to maintain this rate. There are strong economic complementarities between both regions. The ASEAN Community comprises a market of 630 million people and a combined GDP of US$2.5 trillion, which India can use to boost its services and manufacturing sector. At the same time, ASEAN can ride on India's growth to diversify its economic networks. That said, given the proximity of both regions, the fact that ASEAN-India trade only made up 2.6 percent of ASEAN's total trade in 2015 shows that we can do a lot more together; in comparison, ASEAN-China and ASEAN-Japan trade comprised 15.2 percent and 10.5 percent respectively.

The strategic rationale for India's deepening of engagement with ASEAN is perhaps stronger today as we enter a period of geopolitical uncertainties. Questions of how the US, China, India and other major powers will engage the region and impact the broader dynamics with ASEAN are yet to be answered. Like others, India will have to consider how to best position itself in this evolving landscape. As a major power, it is in India's interest to stay engaged in the region, and in particular to actively support ASEAN centrality and for the region to remain open and inclusive.

Looking back over the past 25 years, we applaud India for "Looking East". It has also helped ASEAN "Go West". As we enter the next phase of our partnership, India may wish to consider three areas of cooperation as part of "Acting East".

First, ASEAN and India should redouble efforts to promote trade and investment as engines of growth. Trade is not insignificant to the Indian economy. It accounted for 42 percent of India's GDP in 2015, a higher proportion than China, Japan and the US. Roughly 15 percent of all jobs in India are related to its exports sector. To achieve greater economic flows, ASEAN and India will need to work together to ensure that AIFTA remains useful. Beyond the AIFTA, the Regional Comprehensive Economic Partnership (RCEP) would significantly help transform East Asia into a single integrated market containing roughly 45 percent of the world's population and a combined GDP of nearly US$21 trillion. For India, RCEP should be more than mere numbers, but also a way to anchor its strategic presence in Asia-Pacific. For Singapore, we will be happy to act as a business hub for Indian companies investing in ASEAN and Asia.

Second, in terms of infrastructure, India should pursue connectivity projects more vigorously. As infrastructure helps shape economic geography, there will be strategic implications for India over the longer term. While ASEAN and India have made progress developing overland linkages such as the trilateral India-Myanmar-Thailand Highway, these are largely limited to Northeast India and continental Southeast Asia. An obvious area demanding immediate attention is air connectivity, especially since numerous airports and airlines are already available to operate between ASEAN and India. Air connectivity act as "invisible roads" that can quickly spur greater trade, investment and tourism flows. While this benefits ASEAN, there are also strong economic arguments in favour of India. A study commissioned for IATA found that a small ten percent increase in air connectivity can boost India's economy by approximately 40 billion rupees (about US$600 million). All it takes is the boldness to further liberalise the Air Services Agreement between India and ASEAN Member States.

Third, while historical and cultural links between ASEAN and India are key to our close ties, it cannot be taken for granted that future generations will continue this trend. ASEAN and India have young populations that should interact more closely to write tomorrow's story. Apart from encouraging regular educational, cultural and leadership exchanges, the introduction of digital connectivity could be an area that India uses to help shape connections for the future. With high rates of internet penetration in ASEAN and India, there would be more opportunities to develop digital platforms to link the next generation and forge meaningful connections. If we succeed, it will help us add to the foundation of a long lasting friendship.

Jonathan TOW is Director-General of the South Asia and Sub-Saharan Africa Directorate in the Ministry of Foreign Affairs. Prior to this appointment, he was Deputy High Commissioner at the Singapore High Commission in New Delhi from 2011 to 2014.

He graduated from the National University of Singapore with a BA (Hons) in History in 1996. In 2005, he obtained an MA (with honours) in Security Studies from Georgetown University on a Fulbright Scholarship and attended the Beijing Language and Culture University in 2006.

He joined the Singapore Civil Service in 1996 and has held various research and management appointments in the Ministry of Defence and Ministry of Foreign Affairs. From 2007 to 2010, he served as First Secretary (Political) at the Singapore Permanent Mission to the United Nations in New York.

ASEAN-UN Relations: A Regional Family Within the Global Family of States

TAN York Chor

On 8 August 1967, the foreign ministers of Indonesia, Malaysia, the Philippines, Singapore and Thailand signed the Bangkok Declaration establishing ASEAN. Born amidst reconciliation, mediated by Thailand, between Indonesia and Malaysia,[1] ASEAN aimed "to establish a firm foundation for common action to promote regional cooperation… and thereby contribute towards peace, progress and prosperity in the region". Not far away, war in Vietnam was spreading to neighbouring Laos and Cambodia, but the ASEAN founding members were concerned too about communist insurgency within their own borders.

ASEAN's stated purposes had a strong socio-economic focus on collaboration, joint endeavours and mutual assistance in the economic, social, cultural, educational, professional, technical, scientific and administrative fields, in training and research, greater utilisation of agriculture and industries, trade expansion, improving communications and transport facilities, and raising the living standards of their peoples. ASEAN also committed "to promote regional peace and stability through abiding respect for justice and the rule of law in the relationship among countries of the region and adherence to the principles of the United Nations Charter". The underlying premises for a virtuous circle in the region, between progress and prosperity, and peace and stability,

---

[1] Malaysia had borne the brunt of the 1963–1966 *"Konfrontasi"* pursued by Indonesia under its previous President Soekarno, which also targeted Singapore.

were thus laid, and ASEAN's economic development turned out to be a good antidote to communism. Since what ASEAN seeks to achieve corresponds to the UN's goals, UN agencies in diverse fields have found opportunities to contribute their relevant expertise, starting in 1972 with the UN Development Programme (UNDP).[2]

Beyond its economic success, ASEAN has the value of fostering habits of consultation and consensus to advance common interests, not only among its members but its external partners as well. This "ASEAN spirit" of prizing dialogue over confrontation has served the region well, facilitating the easing of tensions to prevent conflicts. ASEAN members have also helped in conflict mediation (e.g., Malaysia helped broker a peace deal in Mindanao, while Indonesia, as the ASEAN Chair in 2011, attempted to ease Thai-Cambodian tensions over a strip of land near the Preah Vihear temple). Even though the European Union (EU) — where war between its members is now unthinkable — remains an inspiration, ASEAN can be said to have contributed, in its own region, to fulfilling the UN's ends of "(practising) tolerance and living in peace with one another as good neighbours", "international peace and security, non-resort to armed force", and the "promotion of eco-nomic and social advancement of all peoples".

ASEAN came to international prominence when it led opposition against Vietnam's 1978 invasion, followed by its occupation (until 1991), of Cambodia, which violated the UN Charter.[3] ASEAN's instinct was to turn to the UN, requesting the Security Council to consider the situation and to demand Vietnam's withdrawal from Cambodia. However, ASEAN's draft resolution, which garnered 11 votes in the Council, was vetoed by Vietnam's ally, the Soviet Union. Still, ASEAN pressed on for years until the Permanent Five (P5) Security Council members, following the failure of the 1989 Paris Conference on Cambodia, resolved to work out a plan. This rare display of P5 cooperation, as the Cold War ended,

---

[2] Some recent agreements are with the UN University in 2004, UN Fund for Women in 2006, UN Office on Drugs and Crime as well as UN Education, Scientific and Cultural Organization in 2012, and UN Children's Fund in 2014.

[3] E.g., Articles 2.3 on settling international disputes by peaceful means, and 2.4 on refraining from "threat or use of force against the territorial integrity or political independence of any State".

enabled the UN to successfully usher a political settlement. Interestingly, thereafter, Vietnam lost no time in seeking to join ASEAN, and was welcomed into ASEAN in July 1995. Laos and Myanmar followed suit in July 1997, and Cambodia in April 1999. The UNDP helpfully funded, in 1997, a month-long attachment for 12–15 diplomats from Cambodia, Laos and Myanmar to learn ASEAN procedures at the ASEAN Secretariat.

In the developing world, ASEAN stands out for its achievements. Successive UN Secretaries-General (UNSGs) since at least Boutros Boutros-Ghali have held ASEAN in high regard and tried every fall to meet ASEAN Foreign Ministers in New York. The end of the Cold War lifted inhibitions to UN-ASEAN relations. Since the first ASEAN-UN Summit in Bangkok in 2000, the UNSG and heads of UN bodies have met ASEAN Leaders at seven further Summits: 2005 (New York), 2010 (Hanoi), 2011 (Bali), 2013 (Bandar Seri Begawan), 2014 (Nay Pyi Taw), 2015 (Kuala Lumpur) and 2016 (Vientiane). Since 2010, an ASEAN-UN Ministerial Meeting takes place yearly in New York where the General Assembly President, UNSG and ASEAN Foreign Ministers exchange views on matters of mutual interest.

Although ASEAN-UN relations are sited within the global context of the UN's work, they are focused on producing results in the region and proceed along ASEAN's tested step-by-step approach of first addressing basic needs, then going further in scope as capacities develop. This was the case of the periodic series of ASEAN-UN Workshops (held in 1993–1994, ahead of the establishment of the ASEAN Regional Forum) or Conferences (held annually from 2001–2001) on Peace or Conflict Resolution and Preventive Diplomacy. That the latest in this series of seminars, held in 2012 and 2013, were on "Lessons Learnt and Best Practices" is broadly indicative of the progress made.

As ASEAN matures, the value for the ASEAN and UN Secretariats to share experiences and expertise has become more pertinent. The UNSG and ASEAN Secretary-General signed a MOU between ESCAP (UN Economic and Social Commission for Asia and the Pacific) and the ASEC in 2002, followed by an ASEAN-UN MOU in 2007. The latter was upgraded to a Comprehensive Partnership in 2011, and a five-year Plan of Action was adopted in 2016 to synergise the ASEAN Vision 2025 and the Global 2030 Agenda for Sustainable Development. In 2006, ASEAN formally received UN Observer status, but rather than sending an observer to New York, ASEAN has pragmatically decided to continue to cover the UN through ASEAN Member States and especially the ASEAN Chair. Since 2014, however, the UN has deployed liaison officers to work with the ASEC.

The strengths of ASEAN as a regional family of States, and of its relations with the UN, the wider family supported by the UN Secretary-General, came through clearly in times of adversity. The 2004 Indian Ocean tsunami hit Indonesia most badly, killing an estimated 167,800. The UN and ASEAN immediately mobilised help for Indonesia, Thailand and other affected States. In early May 2008, Cyclone Nargis unleashed comparable devastation, killing nearly 140,000 in Myanmar, flattening 700,000 homes and 75% of the medical facilities in the Irrawaddy Delta, and raising the spectre of an epidemic crisis that could kill over a million more people. It did not help that the then military junta, ever distrustful of the outside world and hesitant to let the UN in to mount much-needed disaster recovery humanitarian work, was rattled by pronouncements of certain European leaders who suggested invoking the "responsibility to protect" to forcibly intervene to aid the Myanmar people. Fortunately, the ASEAN Foreign Ministers, meeting in Singapore on 19 May 2008, negotiated a breakthrough. Acting as Myanmar's trusted intermediary, ASEAN established with Myanmar and the UN, a Tripartite Core Group, paving the way for the UN to assist Myanmar. That was only possible because in the face of Western criticisms and to the detriment of ASEAN dialogue partnerships with the EU and Canada, ASEAN had, over the years, stood by Myanmar while it strived to change — although ASEAN knew when and how to be firm with Myanmar such as when monks were shot in September 2007.

Incidentally, Singapore was the Chair of ASEAN when both Myanmar incidents occurred. It was the tactful way that the ASEAN Chair and Member States dealt with Myanmar on both occasions — as a family member that had erred and needed help — that persuaded Myanmar to accept ASEAN playing its rightful role. When the monks were shot, the ASEAN Foreign Ministers, who were at the UN in New York, held an emergency meeting and issued a statement *that Myanmar accepted*, expressing revulsion at the shooting. In the aftermath of Cyclone Nargis, when Myanmar did not allow the international community to deliver critical aid and assistance, Singapore acted again, as Mr. George Yeo, who was then Singapore's Foreign Minister, recounted later (in 2011, in response to a question in Parliament about the role of the ASEAN Chair): "We… still in the Chair, convened an emergency meeting, got everybody together, persuaded the Myanmar Foreign Minister that ASEAN had to be involved… He said, "Let me call back my headquarters". An hour later he came back and said "Yes." He agreed to ASEAN's involvement. And so a tripartite arrangement was established and that prevented a second wave of deaths in the Irrawaddy Delta."

In June 2009, then UNSG Ban Ki-moon wrote:

"The United Nations and ASEAN have long shared the goal of building a more stable and prosperous world. Our organisations have worked together on many important economic and social development programmes across Southeast Asia, including efforts to control disease, improve disaster preparedness and response, and deepen regional integration. In May 2008, by joining forces to respond quickly and effectively to the devastation left by Cyclone Nargis in Myanmar, we demonstrated how successfully we can work together at a time of crisis to save lives in a complex and difficult environment."

In his statement at the 61st Session of the UN General Assembly in 2006, then Foreign Minister Mr. Yeo noted our now "messier world which presents new challenges to global governance". Mr. Yeo recognised that "(T)he UN is already stretched and can only do so much. Instead, let us in each of our regions do our part and work with the UN … in a complementary way." and that "(I)f every region of the world, working with the UN, can help to stabilise its own immediate environment and promote favourable economic conditions, the prospects for global peace and development will be enhanced." In essence, that encapsulates ASEAN's contribution to the UN.

TAN York Chor is currently appointed as Group Director/ International Relations in the Agri-Food & Veterinary Authority (AVA) of Singapore. He joined the Singapore Civil Service in 1985 and had worked in various capacities in the Ministry of Defence and the Ministry of Foreign Affairs. He served as First Secretary in the Singapore Embassy in Paris (1991 to 1993), Counsellor in Bangkok (1993 to 1994) and in Canberra (1997 to 1999), and Minister-Counsellor and Deputy Permanent Representative in the Singapore Permanent Mission to the United Nations in New York and concurrently Deputy High Commissioner in the Singapore High Commission to Canada (2002 to 2005). He was Deputy Director/Europe (1995–1997), Deputy Director/Other Southeast Asia (2000 to 2002), Senior Deputy Director/Policy, Planning & Analysis Directorate II covering North America and Europe (2002), Director/Europe (2006 to 2007) and concurrently Director/International Economics (March to October 2006) and Director/International Organisations (April to November 2007). He was the Permanent Representative of Singapore to the United Nations in Geneva (November 2007 to November 2010) and was concurrently accredited as the Permanent Representative of Singapore to the International Atomic Energy Agency in Vienna. He was Singapore's Ambassador to the French Republic and to the Portuguese Republic from 1 January 2011 to 11 July 2015. From 1 September 2015 to 28 February 2017, he was Director/Special Duties in the Ministry of Foreign Affairs. He was awarded the Long Service Medal in 2008. He is married to Mdm Lim Boon Siang and they have three daughters.

The Evolution of the ASEAN Plus Three Process

K. KESAVAPANY

~ ~ ~

Introduction

ASEAN, a grouping of ten states in Southeast Asia was set up in August 1967 with the aim of fostering intra-regional cooperation in the political, security and economic fields. The Vietnamese Occupation of Cambodia galvanised the-then-six member states into joining the rest of the international community in resisting Vietnam's aggression against its neighbour. This early diplomatic victory helped to profile ASEAN as a regional entity, which could be relied upon to uphold international law and help maintain peace in the region.

Following this early harvest in regional cooperation, ASEAN turned its attention to the fostering of intra-regional economic cooperation. Despite several initiatives, economic cooperation did not take off. This was primarily because most of the economies were complementary in nature and there was little scope for intra-regional trade and investment. Also, nationalism held sway and member countries were inclined to keep what was available for themselves rather than share and share alike. A case in point was the slow pace in implementing the ASEAN Industrial Projects and the ASEAN Joint Venture Schemes. Except for one or two, none of the projects took off.

It was against this impasse of "painfully slow" economic growth that ASEAN began the process of looking outside the region. Giving the rationale for such a move, Singapore's Foreign Minister Mr. S. Rajaratnam said in April 1973 "Economic realities suggest that regional economic cooperation must be wedded to external economic participation if

ASEAN is to achieve its objectives. It is not intra-regional trade and investments but extra regional trade and outside investments which will accelerate ASEAN's economic growth."

Starting with the "informal dialogue" with the European Community, ASEAN embarked on a plethora of Dialogue relationships with its major trading partners, including Australia, New Zealand, Japan, ROK, the United States and India. One such Dialogue relationship was the ASEAN Plus Three (ASEAN+3) involving ASEAN, China, Japan and the ROK.

East Asian Economic Grouping (EAEG)

The genesis for this particular relationship had its origin in a proposal put forward by the then Malaysian Prime Minister, Dr. Mahathir Mohammad in December 1990. Speaking at a dinner on the occasion of China's Premier Li Peng's visit to Malaysia, Dr. Mahathir noted the "unhealthy trend" towards establishing economic blocs. He castigated many countries, including Singapore, for entering into Free Trade Agreements (FTAs) citing the reason that the economic blocs formed through such agreements were "obstructing fair and free trade".

However, recognising that FTAs were becoming a fact of life, Dr. Mahathir said "Malaysia has re-examined her stand and is of the view that for the world to achieve balanced economic development, the countries of the Asia-Pacific region should strengthen further economic and market ties so that eventually an economic bloc would be formed to countervail the other economic blocs." He called for the establishment of an EAEG.

As Rodolfo C. Severino notes in his authoritative book *Southeast Asia in Search of an ASEAN Community*, Dr. Mahathir, ten months later, elaborated on his idea as follows:

"If ASEAN is to have a bigger say in trade negotiations internationally, then it must work together with the East Asian countries. The East Asia Economic Group or EAEG will be sufficiently strong to gain the respect of both the EC and the NAFTA."

Dr. Mahathir warned that "Unless we have this group, ASEAN and everyone else will be at the mercy of the trade blocs of Europe and America… We will all remain developing countries forever."

Due to a lack of consultations, on the part of Malaysia, Dr. Mahathir's idea did not find resonance with the other ASEAN Member States. Some were also uncomfortable with the anti-Western tone of the proposal. The proposal was subsequently re-named "East Asia Economic Caucus". In yet another mutation, at the December 1997 ASEAN Summit in Kuala Lumpur, Malaysia, as host, invited the leaders of China, Japan and ROK to meet with ASEAN Leaders. Over time, this meeting came to be called the ASEAN+3 forum.

The impetus for the formation of the ASEAN+3 forum came from the fear on ASEAN's part, that with the rapid integration of the economies of China, Japan and ROK, "ASEAN was in danger of being left out". However, in political terms, the Northeast Asian countries, could not achieve cohesion on account of negative World War II memories, strategic rivalry between China and Japan and territorial disputes. ASEAN seized the opportunity to be the "middle man" and offered a platform for the thirteen countries to come together and promote in the words of Severino, "political goodwill, economic integration, and regional cooperation".

Pursuant to this and, at the 1998 ASEAN+3 Summit, the following specific proposals were made:

- the formation of an East Asia Free Trade Area;
- the establishment of an East Asian Investment Information Network;
- the extension of the ASEAN Investment Area to cover all of East Asia;
- the consideration of a regional financing facility;
- a regional mechanism for the coordination of exchange rates; and
- the "evolution" of the ASEAN+3 summits into the East Asia Summit (EAS)

The ASEAN+3 forum was subsequently expanded to include other countries in the region provided they fulfilled three conditions: Substantive relations with ASEAN; full Dialogue Partner status; and access to the Treaty of Amity and Cooperation. At the ASEAN Foreign

Ministers' meeting in Vientiane on 26 July 2005, India, Australia and New Zealand became eligible to participate in the EAS process. Russia participated in the EAS as a "guest" as it was deemed not to have met the conditions stated above.

Impact of the Asian Financial Crisis of 1997/1998 on the Enhancement of Regional Economic Integration

Yet another impetus for the formation of the regional grouping was the role played by the Asian Financial Crisis in 1997/1998. As Ambassador Tommy Koh has noted, "The crisis started in Thailand and ricocheted northwards to affect South Korea. The lesson learnt was that North-East Asia and South-East Asia were inter-linked. This is the logic behind ASEAN+3."

In a recently published report, the ADB has also described the 1997/1998 economic crisis as a "landmark event" for ASEAN+3.

Chiang Mai Initiative (CMI)

Arising out of the efforts to cope with this regional financial crisis, ASEAN Finance Ministers met frequently among themselves, with their ASEAN+3 counterparts and with representatives of the IMF / World Bank and ADB. One positive outcome of these meetings was the decision to "devise a collective decision making mechanism for the activation of the swap and repurchase agreements". Another decision taken was to substantially increase amounts involved in the swaps, which now stands at US$2 billion.

The CMI can be hailed as the "finest hour" for ASEAN+3. However, the IMF conditionalities that were attached to the "draw down" arrangements were not to the liking of some participating members. They preferred to go directly to the money markets in New York and London.

According to an ADB Initiative Working Paper dated January 2013, "another fundamental issue that still needs to be addressed upon is CMIM's role and how it fits in among existing regional and global financing facilities".

The ASEAN+3 Macroeconomic Office (AMRO) established in May 2011 was tasked with suggesting possible areas in which the effectiveness of CMIM and AMRO "may increase, despite constraints and limitations". One outcome of AMRO (located in its Singapore Office), has been a regular study of each ASEAN+3 economy's budget and fiscal policy and carry out cross country analyses within the ASEAN+3 economies. This is aimed at serving as a surveillance mechanism and prevent unexpected shocks like the 1997 financial crisis.

ASEAN+3 Cooperation Work Plan 2013–2017

The CMI aside, steady work is being undertaken under the rubric of the above work plan. Among the areas covered are: Political and Security Cooperation, Strengthening Peace and Stability in the region; Combating Transnational Crimes and addressing other non-traditional security issues.

In the field of Economic and Financial Cooperation, the focus is on promoting trade and investment. Enhancing energy cooperation, promoting small and medium enterprises (SMEs) and enhancing cooperation in food, agriculture, fisheries and forestry are also areas where work is being undertaken.

In the field of socio-cultural and development cooperation, attention is being paid to, inter alia, developing cooperative activities towards realizing the UN Millennium Development Goals, forging closer cooperation in poverty alleviation and supporting the efforts to protect and promote labor rights.

Conclusion

While the various projects outlined in the ASEAN+3 Work Plan 2013–2017 to promote East Asia Cooperation are laudable, certain developments have to be taken into account in assessing the prospects of the ASEAN+3 forum becoming an entrenched institution.

The gravitational pull of a rising China affecting ASEAN Centrality; China's own projects like the "One Belt, One Road" and the rise of nationalism among countries in the region are factors which might impede the ASEAN+3 process. The South China Sea dispute has in particular become a divisive issue for ASEAN and other countries.

On the other hand, the United States' withdrawal from the Trans-Pacific Partnership has galvanised the countries in the region to step up on the efforts to promote regional stability and security and enhance efforts to bring about the East Asian Community, with ASEAN+3 as the core pillar.

At the ASEAN Summit held in Manila from 29 to 30 April 2017, ASEAN Leaders reaffirmed their determination to help conclude the 16-nation Regional Comprehensive Economic Partnership (RCEP) by the end of 2017. Such an outcome would add to the many accomplishments of ASEAN and enhance its reputation, as described by Kishore Mahbubani and Jeffery Sng, as a "living and breathing modern miracle".[1]

K. KESAVAPANY was the Director of the Institute of Southeast Asian Studies, Singapore from October 2002 until February 2012. Prior to this, he was Singapore's High Commissioner to Malaysia from 1997 to 2002. He served as Singapore's Non-Resident Ambassador to Jordan from 2003 to 2015. He also served as Singapore's Permanent Representative to the United Nations in Geneva and concurrently accredited as Ambassador to Italy and Turkey from 1991 to 1997. He was elected as the first Chairman of the General Council of the WTO when it was established in January 1995. He graduated from the University of Malaya with a Bachelor of Arts (Honours) degree and obtained a Master of Arts (Area Studies) degree from the School of Oriental and African Studies, University of London. He is an Adjunct Professor, Lee Kuan Yew School of Public Policy, NUS. Among other civic positions, he is a Governor on the Board of the Singapore International Foundation.

---

[1] Kishore Mahbubani and Jeffery Sng, *The ASEAN Miracle A Catalyst for Peace* (Singapore: NUS Press, 2017).

Making of the
ASEAN Charter

Drafting the ASEAN Charter: Some Lessons Learnt

Tommy KOH

✦

Introduction

In 2005, the ASEAN Summit had appointed an Eminent Persons Group to make recommendations on the drafting of an ASEAN Charter. The EPG submitted its report to the ASEAN Summit, in January 2007, in Cebu, The Philippines. The next step was to appoint the High-Level Task Force, consisting of the representatives from each ASEAN country, to draft the Charter. Our then Foreign Minister, George Yeo, appointed me to represent Singapore, with Professor Walter Woon, as my deputy.

The Singapore Delegation

The Singapore delegation consisted of myself, Walter Woon, Andrew Tan, Chan Sze-Wei and Deena Bajrai. Three of us were from the Ministry of Foreign Affairs and two, Walter and Deena, were from the Attorney-General's Chambers. The five of us worked very well together and there was never a clash between an MFA view and an AGC view.

First Chairman of HLTF

By alphabetical rotation, Philippines occupied the chair from January to July when Singapore took over the chair. The Filipina veteran diplomat, Rosario Manalo, was our first Chairman. She was intelligent, charismatic, eloquent and experienced. She did, however, encounter one problem — the problem was the contradiction between her role as her country's representative and as a neutral chairman. This was especially difficult on the issue of human rights. The Philippines was a strong champion of human rights and of the need for an ASEAN Human Rights Commission. She had difficulty in convincing the advocates of the opposite view that she was willing to accommodate their views.

Lesson No. 1: Be a Neutral Chairman

Learning from the difficulties of my predecessor, I decided to be a neutral chairman. I requested my colleague, Walter Woon, to speak for Singapore. In this way, I was able to focus exclusively on securing compromises that would lead to a consensus. This division of labour between Walter and me worked well.

Lesson No. 2: Work with the Secretariat

The ASEAN Secretariat served the HLTF with ability and dedication. The Secretariat team consisted of the Secretary-General, Ong Keng Yong, Dr. Termsak Chalermpalanupap, Teh Lip Li, Carla Budiarto and Serena Wong. Ong Keng Yong was a fountain of wisdom and he helped to solve some difficult issues with his combination of candour and humour. Termsak was a walking encyclopaedia on ASEAN and a prodigious worker. Our policy of working closely with the Secretariat was the right thing to do.

Lesson No. 3: Managing Strong Personalities

The HLTF consisted of very senior officials from the ASEAN countries. Apart from Rosario Manalo, Dr. Kao Kim Hourn from Cambodia, Pak Dian Triansyan Djani of Indonesia, Mr. Bounkeut Sangsomsak of Laos and Nguyen Tung Thanh (Tommy) from Vietnam, were colleagues with strong personalities. One of my challenges, as Chairman, was to manage the clashes between the different personalities and keep the family harmonious. I remember taking time to sit down with Pak Djani to listen to his concerns on an important issue. I was then able to propose a compromise which he accepted. We were then able to submit the compromise on both our behalves to the HLTF. In any negotiations, maintaining good inter-personal relations between and among the principal negotiators is an imperative. As Chairman, I considered it my responsibility to settle differences that arose and to maintain collegiality and goodwill.

Lesson No. 4: Different Work Ethics

The different members at ASEAN do not have the same work ethic. Some did not mind working long hours. Others preferred that we adjourned promptly at 5 pm every day. However, I succeeded in making every one work very long hours on the 20th of October, at our meeting in Vientiane. I was determined to conclude our work on that day. After a brief recess for dinner, I managed to persuade all my colleagues to return to work. We succeeded in wrapping all our work by midnight. The lesson is that there is a time for firmness in the process of negotiations. When the time is ripe, you must seize the opportunity and press on till you conclude the negotiations successfully.

Lesson No. 5: Focus on the Substance

In ASEAN, we work in English. Some of our colleagues are not as proficient in the use of the English language as others. This created a problem in our work as we were drafting a Charter. I decided to put content first and to clean up the language later. Thus, when some ASEAN colleagues put forward proposals which were good in substance but were not well formulated. I accepted their proposals. This strategy worked out well because in the second stage of our work, our legal experts managed to clean up the language into proper charter language. It was important to level the playing field and not allow the mastery of the English language to be a decisive factor.

Lesson No. 6: ASEAN Culture of Mutual Accommodation

On some issues, such as human rights, the positions of the delegates were far apart. In the discussions of the issue, sometimes, strong words were exchanged and tempers got out of control. I tried, as the neutral Chairman, to keep peace in the family and to bring about reconciliations between colleagues. The ASEAN culture of seeking mutual accommodation, compromise and consensus, usually worked. When the battles were over, colleagues remained friends and they were very proud of what had been achieved.

Decision-Making in the ASEAN Charter Process

CHAN Sze Wei

If there is an emblematic characteristic of ASEAN as an organisation, it is the emphasis on consultation and consensus. These two words are ubiquitous in depictions of the organisation being bound, over 50 years of history, to an "ASEAN Way" that prefers informal procedures and peer influence over binding commitments.[1] The consensus decision-making rule comes under continuing fire from quarters inside and outside Southeast Asia for blocking ASEAN from being an effective actor in controversial and urgent matters, within the region as well as in wider international interactions.[2] When ASEAN Leaders initiated the process to establish an ASEAN Charter in 2005, it proved to be a timely occasion to address this criticism. The 2007 Report of the Eminent Persons' Group on the ASEAN Charter (EPG Report) proposed mechanisms for

---

[1] C. Rodolfo Severino, *Southeast Asia in Search of an ASEAN Community: Insights from the former ASEAN Secretary-General* (Singapore: ISEAS, 2006), 11. The "ASEAN Way" itself has never been officially defined. These terms are also now the title of the ASEAN Anthem, which was adopted in 2008 after a public competition. The Anthem does not mention the words "consultation" or "consensus".

[2] Examples range from the inability to quickly mobilise regional responses to political and humanitarian crises within ASEAN countries (2008 Cyclone Nargis, 2012–present riots in Rakhine state, 2014 political coup in Thailand), disputes between member states (2008–2011 Cambodia-Thailand tensions regarding Preah Vihear temple dispute) to the lack of a common ASEAN position on international tensions such as maritime boundary disputes in the South China Sea.

voting as an alternative to consensus. However, the ASEAN Charter that emerged a year later as the outcome of the 2007 drafting process did not incorporate these proposals.

Did ASEAN miss a crucial opportunity to transform itself into a more effective and relevant organisation? Looking in greater detail at the final text of the Charter and the processes surrounding its negotiations, the answer is both yes and no. It also begs another question: Is consensus itself the problem with ASEAN?

At the heart of the discussions and negotiations on ASEAN's decision-making mechanisms is a debate regarding the organisation's very nature and objectives. The ASEAN Charter established ASEAN's legal personality but did not change the intergovernmental nature of ASEAN — in fact, it codified it. "As a basic principle, decision-making in ASEAN shall be based on consultation and consensus." (ASEAN Charter Article 20.1) In ASEAN, this means that all decisions, agreements and statements of the organisation remain the outcome of consultation and negotiation between sovereign and equal member states. The intricacy of consultation and consensus, based on the Indonesian ideas of *mushawarrah* and *mufakat*, is explained by former Secretary-General Rodolfo Severino:

> "... consensus in ASEAN does not necessarily require genuine unanimity, although many ASEAN decisions are arrived at on the strength of genuine unanimity. Consensus on a proposal is reached when enough members support it — six, seven, eight or nine, no document specifies how many — even when one or more have misgivings about it, but do not feel strongly enough about the issue to block action on it. Not all need to agree explicitly. A consensus is blocked only when one or more members perceive the proposal to be sufficiently injurious to their national interests for them to oppose it outright." (34)

The above description encapsulates the fact that in the day-to-day functioning of ASEAN, consensus generally does not prove to be a problem. But because decision by consensus gives every member a veto, the search for consensus tends to drive ASEAN decisions to a lowest common denominator. Even when a majority of member states might be in favour of a more ambitious approach, the ASEAN outcome must remain that which is acceptable to the most conservative or constrained position.

On decision-making and other controversial questions, the stakes are perhaps clearer if we substitute "ASEAN" with "ASEAN governments". For the sake of the effectiveness of the organisation, would ASEAN governments be ready to relinquish a part of their sovereignty? Would they accept a sacrifice of national interests when overruled by a majority? These questions were addressed head-on during the process of both the Eminent Persons' Group on the ASEAN Charter (EPG, January–December 2006) and the High Level Task Force on the ASEAN Charter (HLTF, January–November 2007).

It is important to note that both the EPG and HLTF processes, as well as those of the ASEAN Foreign Ministers and ASEAN Heads of State/Government who mandated, guided and adopted their outcomes, *were all themselves products of consensus.*[3] It might be considered that the Charter process was itself an exercise in decision-making at the most fundamental, sensitive and high-profile level.

The mandate for the ASEAN Charter was in some ways a contradictory one. The ASEAN Summit's 2005 Kuala Lumpur Declaration on the Establishment of the ASEAN Charter officially started off the Charter process and established the EPG.[4] The text of the Kuala Lumpur Declaration reveals the awareness of the need for reform of ASEAN's institutional framework to support the realisation of the ASEAN Community and serve future goals, while calling for the codification of past norms, rules and values. "Decision making on the basis of equality, mutual respect and consensus" was listed as one of the elements to be codified. At the same time, the senior statesmen of the EPG were enjoined to come up with "bold and visionary" recommendations.[5]

---

[3] See the Terms of Reference of the Eminent Persons Group on the ASEAN Charter, and Terms of Reference of the High Level Task Force on the ASEAN Charter.
[4] The EPG and HLTF processes were preceded by the mention of an ASEAN Charter in the 2004–2010 Vientiane Action Programme, and several years of senior officials' meetings to review ASEAN's institutions and grant legal personality to ASEAN.
[5] Report of the Eminent Persons Group on the ASEAN Charter, 12.

The EPG report was endorsed by the ASEAN Summit in January 2007. The Leaders' instructions were to draft the Charter on the basis of "our directions given at the 11ᵗʰ and 12ᵗʰ ASEAN Summits, the relevant ASEAN documents, together with the EPG recommendations." The majority of representatives appointed for the drafting process were senior foreign ministry officials who had worked directly with the day-to-day planning and implementation of ASEAN initiatives in the Senior Officials Meeting or as Directors-General in the ASEAN Standing Committee (precursor to the Committee of Permanent Representatives). They were understood to be in the best position to negotiate a Charter that would be practical and implementable.

Eminent Persons' Group

My strongest impression of the EPG is of the collegial trust among a particular generation of ASEAN figures, most of whom had been colleagues as Foreign Ministers in the ASEAN Ministerial Meeting. There was a sense that they understood the constraints of each other's positions and shared a trust that allowed them to speak frankly. This was particularly evident among then-Deputy Prime Minister S. Jayakumar (Singapore), Tun Musa Hitam (Malaysia), the late Pak Ali Alatas (Indonesia), Kasemsamosorn Kasemsri (Thailand), Nguyen Manh Cam (Viet Nam), Pehin Dato Lim Jock Seng (Brunei), and President Fidel V. Ramos (Philippines). They were advised by then-Secretary-General Ong Keng Yong and Dr. Termsak Charlermpalanupap.

"Bold and visionary" were words that the EPG took to heart. Not feeling bound by practical implementation, the EPG aimed for visions more ambitious than those articulated in ASEAN Vision 2020 (1997) and the Bali Concord II (2003). The EPG considered that ASEAN cooperation had expanded far beyond its conception in 1967. They sought how ASEAN could address a perceived lack of effectiveness, low implementation of its commitments, and lack of legitimacy among the citizens of ASEAN Member States. Discussions went as far as an ASEAN Union, ASEAN Parliament, ASEAN Court and a Human Rights Mechanism — ideas that challenged some members' positions on what ASEAN could be. Eventually, the proposals of the EPG report were those that all delegations could accept. While each member was a senior figure in his own right, they also remained aware that they held a degree of accountability to their countries' core priorities. Interestingly, the proposal for a Human Rights Body was one that did not find consensus in the EPG and was thus mentioned only in Part II of the report but not in the draft articles of Part III.

The EPG began its work from a draft based on earlier discussions by the Senior Officials Meeting. In response, several delegations circulated draft papers with provisions on areas including objectives and principles, organisation, resource mobilisation, dispute settlement and legal personality. The most influential turned out to be the "Alatas paper" — Pak Ali's article-by-article draft charter that became the basis for Part III of the EPG Report.

On decision-making, Pak Ali drew inspiration from other regional organisations including the European Union, African Union, and Organisation of American States. His answer to the problem of ASEAN deadlock over controversial issues was to differentiate issues by their level of importance and sensitivity, and to calibrate where consensus or voting could be applied. The hierarchy of issues ranged from procedural decisions such as the adoption of a meeting agenda, to sanctions and expulsion of membership.

The High Level Task Force on the ASEAN Charter

An account of how the EPG recommendations were adapted in the Charter has been succinctly described by Ambassador Tommy Koh[6] and Professor Walter Woon[7]. What I would like to highlight is that the HLTF process was closely supervised by the ASEAN Foreign Ministers Meeting (AMM), and that negotiations on the decision making mechanisms of ASEAN were conducted primarily by the Foreign Ministers themselves.

---

[6]Tommy Koh, "The Negotiating Process", in *The Making of the ASEAN Charter*, eds. Tommy Koh, Rosario G. Manalo and Walter Woon (Singapore: World Scientific, 2009), 47–68.

[7]Walter Woon, *The ASEAN Charter: A Commentary* (Singapore: NUS Press, 2015).

The EPG proposals on voting and sanctions were recognised immediately as highly controversial for many delegations. Aware of their tight
11-month timeline, the HLTF sought guidance from the AMM, following the HLTF's second meeting and subsequently its eighth meeting.
The Ministers' instructions were clear: maintain consensus, no voting,
and the ASEAN-X formula to be applied only for implementation of
economic commitments.

The HLTF attempted to outline more flexible options for procedural matters under Article 21, but could not find consensus. In the
course of HLTF negotiations themselves, it became clear that even the
adoption of an agenda could be of great sensitivity.[8]

Hierarchy weighed heavily on the HLTF's negotiating process.
It seemed difficult to escape the consciousness that the HLTF were draft-
ing provisions that would define the roles of Ministers and Heads of
State/Government. I recall one delegation leader exclaiming, "Who am
I to tell the Leaders what to do?" With this approbation, it was difficult
for the drafters to introduce innovative proposals for these sections.

Side by Side

In the ASEAN Charter, Chapter VII on Decision-Making comprises
only two articles; "Consultation and Consensus" and "Implementation
and Procedure". In particular, Articles 20.2 ("Where consensus cannot
be achieved, the ASEAN Summit may decide how a specific decision can be made") and 20.4 ("In the case of a serious breach of the
Charter or non-compliance, the matter shall be referred to the ASEAN
Summit for decision") have been most criticised for being vague and
circular. I do not contradict those assertions. These two provisions in
particular are opaque in a plain reading. However, it may be useful to
compare the recommendations of the EPG with the eventual Charter
provisions adopted.

---

[8] Tommy Koh, "The Negotiating Process", in *The Making of the ASEAN Charter*,
eds. Tommy Koh, Rosario G. Manalo and Walter Woon (Singapore: World Scientific, 2009), 62–63.

EPG Report	ASEAN Charter
Executive Summary Para 8:	Article 20: Consultation and Consensus
ASEAN's consensus style of decision making has served ASEAN well and should be preserved as the guiding principle. Consensus should aid, but not impede, ASEAN's cohesion and effectiveness. As the range of activities within ASEAN increases, ASEAN should consider alternative and flexible decision-making mechanisms…"	1. As a basic principle, decision-making in ASEAN shall be based on consultation and consensus. 2. Where consensus cannot be achieved, the ASEAN Summit may decide how a specific decision can be made. 3. Nothing in paragraphs 1 and 2 of this Article shall affect the modes of decision-making as contained in the relevant ASEAN legal instruments.
Chapter V: Decision-Making Process (45) 63. The ASEAN Charter should institutionalise a more effective decision making process.	4. In the case of a serious breach of the Charter or non-compliance, the matter shall be referred to the ASEAN Summit for decision.
• The decision making process in ASEAN shall, as a general rule, be based on consultation and consensus, especially on decisions in more sensitive areas of security and foreign policy.	Article 21: Implementation and Procedure
• On other areas, if consensus cannot be achieved, decisions may be taken through voting, either on the basis of a simple majority, or on the basis of a 2/3rd or 3/4th majority.	1. Each ASEAN Community Council shall prescribe its own rules of procedure. 2. In the implementation of economic commitments, a formula for flexible participation, including the ASEAN Minus X formula, may be applied where there is a consensus to do so.
• The ASEAN Council (*Author's note: equivalent to the ASEAN Summit*) shall prescribe rules of procedure governing situations when there may be voting by a simple majority, a 2/3rd majority or a 3/4th majority.	
• On certain ASEAN cooperation issues or projects, the formula for flexible participation of "ASEAN minus X" or "2 plus X" may be applied, to be decided upon by the relevant Councils (*Author's note: equivalent of the current Community Councils*) of the ASEAN Community.	
• Decisions on temporary suspension of rights and privileges of membership shall be taken by unanimity, without participation of the Member State or Member States to which the decision shall be applied.	

Consensus and sovereignty

What springs to mind when the two texts are placed side by side is that while they differ substantively, they are not in fact very different in their motivations. Foremost, they are both concerned with the preservation of the principles of consultation and consensus; an acknowledgement of how this practice has served ASEAN well in uniting countries of diverse circumstances and priorities. The foregrounding of this tenet at all stages in the Charter process leaves no doubt about member states' continuing concern with issues of sovereignty. Whereas consultation and consensus had been largely an unwritten understanding in 40 years of ASEAN's functioning,[9] it was now codified in the Charter. Some analysts deride ASEAN states' protectiveness of their sovereignty as a postcolonial obsession with nation-building and a shortsighted position that undermines ASEAN's credibility. However, witness the past 20 years in Southeast Asia and there is no doubt that the wounds of history are still raw. It is astounding that the Charter was even concluded between 2006–2007 against a backdrop of political unrest in Thailand, regime transformation in Myanmar, and natural disasters in Indonesia. In this context, it is difficult to imagine that the Charter could have been concluded without enshrining this central principle.

Hierarchy and disparity

The EPG proposals and Charter provisions reflect both the hierarchical and disparate nature of ASEAN institutions at its 40th anniversary. First, the ASEAN Summit remains the ultimate decision-making body of ASEAN, to which unresolved issues are referred. This pre-existing practice was codified in the ASEAN Charter. It is for this reason that the EPG suggests that the application of voting in sectoral bodies should only occur with the authorisation of the ASEAN Council (their proposed title for the ASEAN Summit). The Charter provisions accordingly point

---

[9] The consensus principle is mentioned in several pre-Charter instruments, including the 1993 Declaration on the Conduct of Parties in the South China Sea, 1995 ASEAN Regional Forum Concept Paper, 1998 Ha Noi Declaration, and the 2001 Rules of Procedure for the High Council of the Treaty of Amity and Cooperation.

to the ASEAN Summit when consensus cannot be reached or there is a serious breach or non-compliance in any subordinate bodies. A similar procedure applies at lower levels, where senior officials may refer to their equivalent ministerial body for direction. Such a structure does, however, imply that notwithstanding references to a rule-based organisation, all issues in ASEAN are ultimately decided by a political process.

Second, that ASEAN by its 40th anniversary had grown into a sprawling web of sectoral entities with differing practices and sensitivities. Both texts evince an aspiration for differentiated decision-making procedures that could maintain consensus in sensitive issues but offer flexibility and efficiency for decisions in other areas. The EPG recommendations distinguish security and foreign policy issues as examples of sensitive areas in which consensus decision-making should be maintained. In other areas, voting might be applied based on a simple majority, ⅔ or ¾ majority. The Charter provisions do not go so far, but the inclusion of Article 21.2 giving the three Community Councils the prerogative to determine their own rules of procedure (potentially including decision-making procedure) suggests that the issues addressed by the Political-Security, Economic, and Socio-Cultural communities may not require similar procedures. A proposal during the HLTF meetings to attempt to define "sensitive" and "non-sensitive" subject matters was met with the response that "It would be too sensitive to define the sensitive areas."[10] This was met with good humoured laughter but there seemed to be a clear understanding that this discussion could go no further.

Both texts mention the "ASEAN Minus X" formula that was already being used in the Economic Community at the time of drafting.[11] The EPG's proposal was to extend this, along with the less commonly used "2 Plus X" formula, for "flexible participation" in all sectors of ASEAN where approved by the Community Councils.[12] The report did not elaborate how "flexible participation" might differ from the existing practice where an economic initiative or agreement was adopted by

---

[10] Walter Woon, *The ASEAN Charter: A Commentary* (Singapore: NUS Press, 2015), 158.

[11] Report of the High Level Task Force on ASEAN Economic Integration, adopted via the 2003 Declaration of ASEAN Concord II.

[12] EPG Report, 21 and 45.

consensus of all ten member states, while it was accepted that some states would proceed with implementation sooner than others. The AMM instructed the HLTF that ASEAN-X should be limited to the implementation of economic agreements. In doing so, the flexibility in implementation was codified, but constrained at a status quo level.

Breaking the impasse

Both texts acknowledge that consensus decision-making had led the organisation to deadlocked situations. "Where consensus cannot be achieved" (Article 20.2) could describe occasions when the organisa-tion is split or when one or more member states vetoes the intent of the majority.[13] I believe that there was a keen awareness at all levels — EPG, HLTF, Foreign Ministers, Summit — that the resulting organisational paralysis had repeatedly damaged ASEAN's international credibility. The difficulty was to balance ASEAN's international credibility against fracturing the organisation's unity and by implication, its very existence. The text of Article 20.2 on where consensus could not be reached was the result of protracted discussions during the Ministers' retreat (a special session of the Foreign Ministers meeting where sensitive issues are addressed in a small group comprising only the Ministers, one assistant each, and the Secretary-General as note-taker). I understand that there was no consensus until Secretary-General Ong Keng Yong proposed the wording "Where consensus cannot be achieved, the ASEAN Summit may decide how a specific decision can be made". The Ministers' language was transplanted directly into the Charter text. The understanding was that the Summit could enable a decision in a ministerial or senior offi-cials' level by voting or other means. However as Prof. Woon points out, this measure is circular if it applies to an impasse in the Summit itself.

---

[13] Following the organisation's enlargement in the 1990s, it is assumed that this split often takes the form of a divide between the older (Brunei Darussalam, Indonesia, Malaysia, the Philippines, Singapore and Thailand) and the newer members (Viet Nam, Laos, Myanmar and Cambodia). As the current South China Sea disputes demonstrate, however, the geometries vary according to international and domestic issues.

Non-compliance and breach of the Charter

Early in the HLTF process, the Foreign Ministers instructed decisively that suspension, withdrawal and expulsion were not to be mentioned in the Charter. Article 20.4 envisions the scenario of a "serious breach of the Charter or non-compliance" but does not specify measures to be taken. The decision-making aspect of such measures is impracticable if the consensus rule is maintained; a state facing expulsion or sanctions would presumably withhold agreement. On this point, the EPG proposed that such decisions should be taken by unanimity without the participation of the state to whom the sanctions were to be applied.[14]

The HLTF was not able to agree on the decision-making procedure of the Summit in such situations. The resulting Article 20.4 reads "In the case of a serious breach of the Charter or non-compliance, the matter shall be referred to the ASEAN Summit for decision." The referral to the Summit could be understood to point back to Article 20.2; a proposal for sanctions, suspension or expulsion would be unlikely to find consensus. The arrangement may presume to be further subject to another layer of consensus under the Rules of Procedure for the referral of unresolved disputes and non-compliance to the Summit, adopted in 2010 and 2012 respectively. It is conceivable that a member state could block consensus on recommendations to be submitted to the Summit, as well as its inclusion in the agenda of the Summit (usually agreed by consensus).

Conclusion

Many criticisms of ASEAN decision-making suggest that consensus itself is the biggest stumbling block. It should follow that if ASEAN states were to reach a consensus to make certain sacrifices of sovereignty and apply some form of voting system, then it would become a much more effective organisation with greater international influence.

I contend that such optimism mistakes the very nature of the organisation. At the time that the ASEAN Charter was drafted, there

---

[14] EPG Report, 45.

was simply too great a trust deficit among the member states to shift away from the consensus decision-making rule, even on procedural issues. Looking at the unpredictable international and domestic political climate for ASEAN countries in 2017, it is clear that the trust gap continues to exist, while nationalist and protectionist rhetoric is on the rise. The reluctance to make sacrifices of sovereignty to enhance the influence of ASEAN can be read either as a continuing sense of fragility on the part of its member states, or more ominously, the sense that the member states do not see ASEAN as central to their foreign policy.[15]

Were voting mechanisms to be hypothetically imposed overnight, I predict that the decision-making mechanisms of ASEAN would suffer the same fate as its various dispute settlement mechanisms: carefully constructed, but never used. Even where consensus might not be required, another rule of procedure such as a quorum requirement could similarly be used to block a decision. Unlike neglected dispute settlement mechanisms, however, the paralysis of decision-making machinery could well spell the end of ASEAN.

Framing this issue as a dilemma between consensus and voting, or a trade-off between effectiveness and sovereignty appears to be an unproductive path. Successive proposals raised at the EPG and HLTF levels as well as recommendations by academia and policy think tanks have pointed to a common direction: to assure consensus decision-making for sensitive policy areas while adapting decision-making processes in limited areas beginning with procedural or project implementation decisions. One can hope that with time the repeated proposals will become more tangible and less threatening, and follow the examples in other areas of years of persistence culminating in gradual compromise.[16]

---

[15]Shaun Narine. "ASEAN in the Twenty-First Century: A Sceptical Review", in *The 3rd ASEAN Reader* (Singapore: ISEAS, 2015), 175.
[16]For example on the principle of non-interference to allow for greater flexibility allowing for mutual disaster assistance, defence cooperation, and the increasing inclusion of urgent domestic developments on the agenda of the ASEAN Foreign Ministers Meeting and ASEAN Summit. Repeated proposals and negotiations over time also allowed for the unexpected breakthrough in the establishment of an ASEAN human rights mechanism.

We might take a leaf from the development of the language on non-interference, and emphasise the need for *flexibility* in adapting decision-making mechanisms. With this perspective, political will can enable as well as impede. It is not unimaginable that voting could be agreed on in future, should geopolitical developments shift dramatically such as to make ASEAN unity the only option for member states' survival. In terms of flexibility, the vagueness of the Charter provisions on decision-making may eventually prove to be useful, allowing for an ad hoc decision at the Summit level to introduce alternative and possibly hybrid decision-making mechanisms without requiring a laborious amendment of the Charter.

Critics may well contend that such an approach would not conform with the principle of rule-based organisation. Yet the reality of ASEAN at 50 is that the EPG's point about political will remains fundamental. The Charter and its decision-making provisions are only as useful as the members of the organisation are prepared to allow it to be.

CHAN Sze Wei is a Research Associate at the Centre for International Law at the National University of Singapore. Her research is focused on ASEAN Law and Policy, in a continuation of her work for the Singapore Ministry of Foreign Affairs on the ASEAN Charter process as an assistant to then-Deputy Prime Minister S. Jayakumar in the Eminent Persons' Group and Ambassador Tommy Koh as chairman of the High Level Task Force on the ASEAN Charter. She was an editorial assistant for the publication *The Making of the ASEAN Charter*, eds. Tommy Koh, Rosario G. Manalo and Walter Woon (2009) and *The ASEAN Charter: A Commentary* by Prof. Walter Woon (2016).

Practical Implementation of the ASEAN Charter

Jeffrey CHAN Wah Teck

❧ ❦ ☙

Introduction

The ASEAN Charter was signed on 20 November 2007 by the Leaders of the ten ASEAN Member States (AMS) at the 13th ASEAN Summit in Singapore. 2007 marked the 40th Anniversary of the establishment of ASEAN. The Charter came into force on 15 November 2008 when Thailand delivered the tenth and final instrument of ratification of the Charter.

In the Singapore Declaration on the ASEAN Charter made at the time when the Charter was signed, the ten ASEAN Leaders reaffirmed their conviction "…*that the Charter shall serve as a legal and institutional framework as well as an inspiration for ASEAN in the years ahead;…*" and reiterated their full resolve to advance ASEAN integration through the creation of an ASEAN Community.

Basis for the ASEAN Charter

The ASEAN Charter was based to a large extent on the Report of the Eminent Persons Group on the ASEAN Charter ("the EPG"). This was a group of outstanding ASEAN public figures who were mandated by the ASEAN Leaders to consider bold and visionary ideas to strengthen ASEAN.

Significant among the EPG's recommendations in its Report of December 2006 were that there must be a strengthening of democratic values, good governance, rejection of unconstitutional changes of government, the rule of law, including international humanitarian law, and respect for human rights and fundamental freedoms. They called for ASEAN to take obligations seriously and noted that one problem ASEAN had was ensuring compliance and effective implementation of agreements entered into. They strongly recommended that Dispute Settlement Mechanisms (DSM), including compliance, monitoring, advisory, consultation as well as enforcement mechanisms be established in all fields of ASEAN cooperation.

The EPG postulated that ASEAN should have the power to take measures to redress breaches of ASEAN objectives, major principles and commitments. Failure to comply should be referred to the ASEAN Summit. Sanctions can include suspension of rights and privileges of membership. The EPG also recommended that while decision-making by consultation and consensus should be retained for all sensitive important decisions, if consensus cannot be achieved, then decisions can be taken by voting. The Rules for voting are to be determined by the ASEAN Council.

These recommendations departed from existing ASEAN practices and have often, and usually, been referred to as moving ASEAN towards a "*rules-based*" organisation.

Drafting of the ASEAN Charter

The ASEAN Charter itself was drafted by a High Level Task Force (HLTF). Unlike the EPG, the HLTF comprised representatives of the ten Member States of ASEAN. Their positions in the negotiating process for the Charter were thus those of their respective states, not their own personally.

Nearly all the recommendations of the EPG were accepted by the HLTF and found expression in the ASEAN Charter. The recommendation that ASEAN should adopt measures to move it to a "rules-based" organisation was never in doubt and was reflected in a number of important provisions in the Charter. These provisions require legally binding rules in order for them to have effect. To state just a few:

Article 3 of the ASEAN Charter stated that: "*ASEAN, as an inter-governmental organisation, is hereby conferred legal personality*." This sets out a principle which has to be given legal effect through implementing rules. In the absence of legal rules that implements this principle, the declaration that ASEAN is conferred with legal personality would merely be a statement without any effect. Likewise, Article 25 of the ASEAN Charter mandates the establishment of "*appropriate dispute settlement mechanisms, including arbitration for disputes which … concern the interpretation or application of [the] Charter and other ASEAN instruments*". This clearly contemplates rules being subsequently formulated to implement this provision. Likewise, Article 26, which is entitled "*UNRESOLVED DISPUTES*" mandates that disputes which remain unresolved despite the application of the dispute settlement mechanisms of the Charter are to be referred to the ASEAN Summit. However, the Charter itself is silent as to how such disputes are to be placed before the ASEAN Summit. There is thus a need for clarity here.

Apart from the above, there are other matters where implementing instruments needed to be formulated if the lofty ideals of the ASEAN Charter are to be given effect. To give an example, Article 41 paragraph 7 of the Charter empowers ASEAN to conclude agreements with countries in sub-regional, regional and international organisations and institutions. It is provided in this paragraph that the procedures for concluding such agreements shall be prescribed by the ASEAN Coordinating Council (ACC) in consultation with the ASEAN Community Councils. Before the ACC can undertake such consultations, it must first be provided with a draft of these procedural rules. Draft rules thus must be formulated for this provision.

Additionally, it was noted that as ASEAN is to have legal personality, the attributes of that legal personality should be identical in all states. At the very least the attributes of ASEAN as a legal person should be identical under the laws of all ten AMS. This can be achieved only through an Agreement with these states which would then be given effect to in domestic laws. Flowing from this would be the issue of the Privileges and Immunities to be accorded to ASEAN and its officers.

These all are governed by the respective domestic laws of states. The ideal would be for ASEAN and its officers to be accorded identical Privileges and Immunities (Ps & Is) in all states. At the very least, they should be accorded identical Privileges and Immunities in all the ten AMS. Again, this would require the formulation of an Agreement to be entered into by states to confer Ps & Is to ASEAN and its officers.

The High Level Legal Experts Group (HLEG)

The task of formulating the legal instruments to implement the principles underlying the ASEAN Charter fell onto the ASEAN High Level Legal Experts Group or HLEG. HLEG was established in July 2007 by the ASEAN Foreign Ministers. In its Statement on the ASEAN Charter made in Singapore on 21 July 2008, the ASEAN Foreign Ministers agreed, among other things, to establish a "High-Level Legal Experts Group on Follow-up to the ASEAN Charter".

The HLEG comprised a Legal Expert from each of the ten AMS and the ASEAN Secretariat (ASEC). Every HLEG Member would be assisted by one or more assistants, most of whom are legally qualified and who together comprise the Group of HLEG Assistants. HLEG and the Group of HLEG Assistants were supported by officers and staff of the ASEC who provided resource and administrative support.

The terms of reference provided to HLEG by the ASEAN Foreign Ministers required the HLEG to address the following:

- Legal Personality of ASEAN
- Dispute Settlement Mechanisms
- Other legal issues under the ASEAN Charter

The HLEG thus had very broad Terms of Reference (TORs) to address any legal issue arising from the provision of ASEAN Charter which the Group deemed necessary. However, there were constraints on the HLEG.

Firstly, the HLEG was given timelines to pace its work. It was, for example, required to report its progress on Legal Personality and

Dispute Settlement Mechanisms by December 2008. There was an initial understanding that the HLEG would complete its work within a year, after which its term would lapse. Secondly, during their briefings to HLEG, a number of ASEAN Foreign Ministers stated very clearly that ASEAN is not and should not be a supra-national organisation. In other words, whatever instruments the HLEG may formulate or recommendations that it may make, these should respect the sovereign status of all ten AMS. They should not be subject to obligations that they are not willing to undertake. To put the issue differently, the HLEG should not look to the processes as well as the Directives and Regulations of the European Union as models for ASEAN.

Commencing the Work of HLEG

The first meeting of HLEG was held in Singapore on 21 July 2008. The HLEG's TOR stipulated that the chair of the HLEG is to be aligned with the ASEAN Chair. As Singapore held the ASEAN Chair in July 2008, Singapore chaired this first meeting of the HLEG. The HLEG's first meeting started off on a very positive note with a free-wheeling discussion which threw up a number of ideas on what can be done to legally operationalise various aspects of the ASEAN Charter. It also agreed to present a report with recommendations on ASEAN legal personality and dispute settlement mechanisms (DSMs) to the ASEAN Foreign Ministers in December 2008. Then, subject to the guidance and directions of the ASEAN Foreign Ministers, the HLEG would draft the necessary legal rules and model legal instruments.

At this first meeting, there was a preliminary exchange of views on ASEAN legal personality as well as DSMs. It was apparent at this early stage that the HLEG would have to address a number of difficult issues. Foremost would be what was intended by the various provisions of the ASEAN Charter. There were different understandings of what the wordings meant. There were also different expectations as to what can be achieved. Some members preferred to be very precise about certain process and outcomes whereas other members preferred greater flexibility and more consensual outcomes. It was apparent that drawing up legally binding instruments to implement the provisions of the ASEAN Charter was not going to be an easy exercise.

After the meeting in Singapore, the ASEAN Chair passed from Singapore to Thailand. From thenceforth, the distinguished Khun Vasin Teeravechyan, chaired the proceedings of HLEG. Almost all of HLEG's work was done in 19 meetings from mid-2008 till end-2009. These were hosted in turn by all ten AMS and the ASEC.

Legal Personality of ASEAN

The first major issue addressed by HLEG was that of legal personality. Article 5 of the ASEAN Charter required all AMS to effectively implement the provisions of the Charter and obligations of membership. This includes enacting the required domestic legislation. In HLEG's view, this includes legislation recognising the legal personality of ASEAN. This would translate into empowering ASEAN to enter into legal relationships and to enjoy Ps & Is.

The discussion here gave rise to numerous issues. One rather perplexing issue was whether persons engaged by ASEAN Dialogue Partners who are stationed at the ASEC are entitled to Ps & Is. There was no difficulty with public officials employed by the Dialogue Partners. But the issue was whether these same Ps & Is should be accorded to the employees of private contractors engaged by the Dialogue Partners to provide services to ASEC and AMS. Although ASEC and some AMS voiced support for this request, others were not so enamoured.

Another thoroughly debated issue concerned who can bind ASEAN to a legal transaction, i.e. who can incur legal liabilities for ASEAN. Some HLEG members thought that this was not an issue since ASEAN would enjoy diplomatic immunity. But in today's world, absolute immunity is rarely found so the issue of legal liability cannot be ignored. Eventually it was agreed that for commercial transactions, the Secretary-General of ASEAN, his Deputies and officers authorised by the Secretary-General are the only ones authorised to legally bind ASEAN.

After prolonged discussion which ran over many meetings, the HLEG settled on the principles which are to govern the exercise of ASEAN's legal personality. These resulted in the Agreement on the Privileges and Immunities of the Association of South East Asian Nations signed by the ASEAN Foreign Ministers on 25 October 2009 in Cha-Am, Thailand. But given the limited time available, the HLEG was unable to finalise details such as the rules for ASEAN to conclude agreements under the domestic laws of the states where it is present, and also for ASEAN to conclude agreements with other states and actors in international law.

ASEAN Dispute Settlement Mechanisms

The most challenging aspect of HLEG's work was with regard to Chapter VIII of the ASEAN Charter — Dispute Settlement Mechanisms (DSM). This was mainly because these provisions in the Charter were very sparse and can be subject to different interpretations. Partly this was because ASEAN had in November 2014 entered into the ASEAN Protocol on Enhanced Dispute Settlement Mechanisms (the "Vientiane Protocol"). The scope of the Vientiane Protocol was very extensive. Questions were raised as to what then would fall within the DSM provisions of the ASEAN Charter.

It was said that the DSM provisions under the ASEAN Charter can arguably apply to disputes arising from socio-cultural agreements entered into by ASEAN. But these disputes are not likely to be numerous or politically significant. Also, while Article 25 of the ASEAN Charter states specifically that the DSM would be established for disputes concerning the interpretation or application, of the Charter, Article 51 of the Charter prescribes that the interpretation of the Charter shall be undertaken by the ASEC at the request of a Member State. It was queried whether this meant that in the event of a dispute over the interpretation of a provision of the Charter, the contending parties are in fact the ASEC on one hand, and the Member State that disagreed with its interpretation on the other hand.

Compounding the difficulty here was the fact that the DSM provisions of the Charter lacked precision and clarity. At the suggestion of the ASEC, HLEG decided to seek clarification from Prof Walter Woon, then Solicitor-General of Singapore, when the HLEG held its session in Singapore. Prof. Woon was a member of the HLTF and a leading contributor to the DSM provisions of the ASEAN Charter.

During the meeting with the HLEG in Singapore, Prof. Woon provided insights into the drafting of the DSM provisions of the ASEAN Charter. The lack of precision and details as regards the process was deliberate as it was intended all along that the process should be flexible and able to meet the needs and expectations of all AMS. It was understood then that the HLEG has a free hand to formulate these DSM processes such that the eventual outcome would be acceptable to all AMS.

Following from this, the HLEG then sought to operationalise the DSM provisions of the ASEAN Charter by formulating what it regarded as the minimum legal rules and processes necessary to give effect to these provisions. It was agreed that these would comprise the following:

(a) A Protocol to the ASEAN Charter on Dispute Settlement Mechanisms ("the DSM Protocol")
(b) Annexes to the DSM Protocol consisting of:

    i. Rules of Good Offices
    ii. Rules of Mediation
    iii. Rules of Conciliation
    iv. Rules of Arbitration

The Rules of Mediation, Good Offices and Conciliation and Arbitration were mandated by Article 25 read with Article 23 of the ASEAN Charter.

The HLEG took considerable time to formulate these instruments. The DSM Protocol and its four Annexes were adopted in Hanoi, Vietnam on 8 April 2010. These marked a departure from the previous ASEAN paradigm of resolving disputes through consultation and consensus. It provided for the AMS an institutional framework with clear processes for disputes to be resolved. Yet it preserved aspects of

ASEAN practices that has worked well for ASEAN, such as diplomatic and non-adjudicative means of dispute resolution. These include consultations, good offices, mediation and conciliation. At the same time it provided for a determinative means of dispute resolution, i.e. arbitration.

Differing Views

The discussions on the DSM Protocol and its Annexes revealed a gulf between states who favoured speedy and certain outcomes in the event of disputes with the outcomes determined by the application of legal rules, and states which preferred disputes to be resolved through "the ASEAN Way". This meant having outcomes being determined through dialogue and, to an extent, through the application of political considerations. In between these two differing viewpoints were a range of views.

There were also details in the implementing Rules set out in the Annexes which proved troublesome. For example, in the discussions on the Rules on Arbitration, there were severe disagreements on time-lines. Those in favour of the most efficient processes argued for shorter and strictly enforced time-lines for various actions required under these Rules, e.g. the filing of Defences. Others argued for much longer time-lines and also generous provisions for extensions of time-lines.

There were also differing views over appointment of arbitrators. At one end it was argued that any person who is suitably qualified, regardless of nationality, can be appointed as an arbitrator as this would assure the quality of the decision rendered. Other members insisted that only ASEAN nationals can be appointed as arbitrators. An argument made several times in this regard was that this would provide for their nationals the opportunity to be appointed as arbitrators.

One aspect related to DSM which took up much time was the reference of Unresolved Disputes to the ASEAN Summit. The HLEG took some time to reach a consensus on what the term "Unresolved Dispute" meant. Another contentious issue discussed was the role of the ASEAN Coordinating Council (ACC) in such references. Should the ACC merely place the issue on the agenda of the ASEAN Summit or can it take some action to resolve the dispute before referring it to the ASEAN Leaders. Here, it was eventually agreed that the ACC may suggest to the contending parties to use another DSM instead of immediately referring the dispute to the ASEAN Summit. A view expressed that the ACC should refer the unresolved dispute to arbitration did not achieve consensus.

These and numerous other issues took up much of the HLEG's time. As it finally turned out, the HLEG could not resolve all the issues it identified. So by end-2009 when the HLEG's term ended, there were still a number of instruments that were identified as needing to be drafted which the HLEG had either not fully completed, or had not yet begun to draft.

Finalisation of HLEG's Work

The above notwithstanding, the HLEG had largely resolved all the legal issues necessary to implement the ASEAN Charter and had laid the foundations for the drafting of the remaining instruments. These were reported by the HLEG and accepted by the ASEAN Foreign Ministers.

The ASEAN Agreement on Privileges and Immunities as well as the DSM Protocol and the four Rules in the Annex were adopted by the ASEAN Foreign Ministers in Hanoi on 8 April 2010 and now forms part of the constitutional documents of ASEAN.

The issues identified by the HLEG were subsequently examined by a Working Group of the ASEAN Senior Officials Meeting ("the SOM WG"). These comprise diplomatic officers from each AMS assisted by one or more legal officers from that state. Many of these assistants were also the HLEG assistants. The SOM WG held fifteen meetings from 2010 to 2011 and, building on the work and conclusions arrived at by the HLEG, formulated a number of instruments to give legal effect to various provisions of the ASEAN Charter.

Foremost among the instruments formulated by the SOM WG were the Rules for the Reference of Unresolved Disputes to the ASEAN Summit. This built on the directions which the HLEG had set in its discussions on this subject. The WG also formulated the Rules for the Reference of Non-Compliance to the ASEAN Summit. Under these Rules, the ACC will refer the Non-compliance to the ASEAN Summit with a report that can include reports filed by the Secretary-General under Article 27 of the Charter. There is no prescription as to what the ASEAN Summit can or should do when such reference is made. It can only be assumed that the ASEAN Leaders will apply their collective wisdom to determine how the non-compliance is to be dealt with.

To give effect to the two new instruments, the SOM WG crafted Instruments of Incorporation to link them to the DSM Protocol. With this, the DSM under Chapter VIII of the ASEAN Charter now comprise the DSM Protocol and 6 Rules set out in the Annexes to the Protocol.

The SOM WG also drafted a number of what can be termed as "administrative rules" viz:

(a) Rules of Authorisation for Legal Transactions Under Domestic Laws
(b) Rules of Procedure for the Conclusion of International Agreements by ASEAN
(c) Rules of Procedure for the Interpretation of the ASEAN Charter

Conclusion

The HLEG process was to a large extent a microcosm of the ASEAN experience. The ASEAN Charter sought to introduce fundamental changes in the paradigms applied by ASEAN and move ASEAN from a somewhat informal collegiate body of regional states to a "rules-based" and effective regional inter-governmental organisation. In line with this, the Singapore Delegation pressed for the establishment of precise and effective rules and legal processes to implement the provisions of the ASEAN Charter. What was clear very quickly into the HLEG process was that not all our fellow AMS shared our view, even if they echoed the same sentiments that we did.

It was inevitable that in order to complete its Terms of Reference, the HLEG Members had to make compromises. Numerous compromises were made by all HLEG Members, although to different degrees. That was also the case in the SOM WG. These compromises were perhaps the only means whereby the objectives of the HLEG as well as the SOM WG could be achieved within the given time frame. Nonetheless the eventual outcomes of HLEG's and the SOM WG's efforts are all significant steps in

ASEAN's progress towards an Integrated ASEAN and a Rules-based ASEAN Community.

Jeffrey CHAN Wah Teck, Principal Senior Consultant, Attorney-General's Chambers, Singapore read law at the University of Singapore and Harvard Law School, USA. He joined the Singapore Legal Service in 1973. He retired in 2005 after holding a variety of appointments including Deputy Solicitor-General, Chief of Staff and Director, Legal Services, MINDEF. His legal practice covered a wide range of subjects. Among other things, he was Chairman of the United Nations Commission on International Trade Law and also chaired its Working Group on Electronic Commerce as well as its Working Group on Online Dispute Resolution. He was Singapore's Chief Negotiator for the Treaty on Mutual Assistance in Criminal Matters Among Like-Minded States as well as the Singapore-Indonesia Extradition Treaty. He has wide experience in ASEAN matters and was Singapore's Representative in the ASEAN High-Level Legal Experts Group on the ASEAN Charter. He is presently the Singapore Focal Point for the ASEAN Senior Law Officials Meeting (ASLOM).

ASEAN and Civil Society

A People-Oriented ASEAN and Singapore

Simon TAY

The ASEAN Community was inaugurated by its Leaders at end 2015 and more now call for it to become more "people-oriented". To do so will be a considerable challenge and reorientation for the regional group. From its beginnings in 1967, ASEAN has been focused on inter-governmental relationships and, indeed, can be even more narrowly centered on foreign affairs ministers and leaders. To a large extent, it remains so today.

When we consider the lack of trust among the founding governments in the 1960s, this has been a key contribution by ASEAN. A similar trust-building exercise has been necessary when the group enlarged in the late 1990s, following the end of the Cold War, to represent all ten of the countries of the sub-region. Trust and cooperation have developed and, today, ASEAN serves as a useful unit of analysis.

Analysis of each state's national interest, rather that of the region's, however predominates; notwithstanding that many of the states are recent, multiracial, multilingual and multireligious constructions of nation-building. Moreover, when we look at ASEAN and its members, diversity remains a critical component. Almost in every measure of politics, economics, society, culture and environment, there is a diversity that is rich, even bewildering, and that must be managed, if there is to be a regional community.

These factors set the context for ASEAN's relationships with the people and civil society of the region.[1] Can and should ASEAN shift from its state- and government-centric focus to better involve civil society? If so, how?

The first part of this brief essay summarises ways in which ASEAN government-civil society relations have developed in recent years. A second part will consider particular areas of engagement in which functional or issue-based civil society organisations have had dealings with ASEAN. In concluding, the essay considers how to move ahead on ASEAN government-civil society ties.

A Brief History of ASEAN and Civil Society

The ambition to involve the people within ASEAN arose some thirty years after the founding of the group. In 1997, it was proposed that ASEAN create "a concert of Southeast Asian nations, outward looking, living in peace, stability and prosperity, bonded together in partnership in dynamic development and *in a community of caring societies*". This was affirmed in the ASEAN Vision 2020 statement and, in the 2003 Bali Concord II, which proposed the creation of an ASEAN Community by 2015, including an ASEAN Socio-Cultural Community (ASCC).

The ASCC Blueprint furthers the agenda in six areas that are often on the agenda for civil society groups, including social justice and rights, environmental sustainability and building the ASEAN identity. To develop an ASEAN identity, the governments envisage efforts to promote "greater awareness and common values in the spirit of unity in diversity at all levels of society", and saw the need to, "build a people-oriented ASEAN where people are at the centre of community building, through the participation of all sectors of society." Concrete implementation plans listed include the engagement of ASEAN-affiliated NGOs on an annual basis. The ASEAN Charter of 2007 went

---

[1] I adopt a definition of civil society that also includes non-governmental organisations, but excludes Parliamentarians — who are part of an organ of the State — and business chambers, who are profit seeking.

on to enshrine the idea of a "people-oriented ASEAN" as one of the group's goals.[2]

As the documents of ASEAN recognised this goal, practice changed. In the early decades of ASEAN, few civil society organisations (CSOs) and NGOs had engaged the group. Perhaps the first, starting from 1983, was the think tank network known as the ASEAN Institutes of Strategic and International Studies (ASEAN-ISIS). This think-tank network, including the one which the author chairs, engages with governments on a regular basis on what has been called "track II" diplomacy.[3]

Others viewed ASEAN as an "elitist organisation comprising exclusively diplomats and government officials,"[4] and preferred instead to focus their lobby efforts on their local governments or else, bypassed ASEAN altogether and engaged international and multilateral organisations. This has changed in tandem with ASEAN's avowed wish to be

---

[2] Article 1.13 states that one of the purposes of ASEAN is "to promote *a people-oriented ASEAN* in which all sectors of society are encouraged to participate in, and benefit from, the process of ASEAN integration and community building".

[3] The collective work of these think tanks has informally and formally provided analyses and suggestions for governments to consider in moving ahead with cooperation for ASEAN and the wider region. The track-II work of the ASEAN-ISIS has resulted in many memoranda of recommendations and analyses sent directly to governments and policy-makers. For example, the first effort taken by the ASEAN-ISIS (AI) Institutes to engage ASEAN leaders with official recommendations derived from AI meetings occurred in 1990. The ASEAN-ISIS submitted a Chairman's Report on the "Superpower Military Presence and the Security of Southeast Asia: Problems, Prospects and Policy Recommendations" to ASEAN governments. In 1991, the ASEAN-ISIS meeting in Jakarta submitted a Memorandum, A Time for Initiative — Proposals for the Consideration of the Fourth Summit "became the basis for movements and initiatives not only by ASEAN governments, but … also had its echo with some ASEAN Dialogue Partners." These memoranda from the ASEAN-ISIS have had an influence in creating a significant official process — the ASEAN Regional Forum that now annually gathers foreign ministers from 21 countries. The success of these submissions is due to the credibility of the organisational process of producing them, and can be seen by their acceptance by ASEAN governments.

[4] ASEAN Secretariat, "Report of the Eminent Persons Group on the ASEAN Charter", accessed November 5, 2009, http://www.aseansec.org/19247.pdf

more people-centric. Indeed, at times, there has been a profusion and some confusion over processes to include CSOs in ASEAN.

From 2000 to 2009, the ASEAN People's Assembly (APA) was organised by the ASEAN-ISIS think tank network to help CSOs, NGOs and other Track III actors to bridge the ASEAN official decision-making process.[5] While the series has ended after a decade, APA can be said to have triggered changes in thinking. Today, there are many more networks of CSOs that seek input into ASEAN.[6] For governments, a number of ASEAN Summit hosts initiate their own events to relate to CSOs[7] and will grant CSO representatives with direct access to ASEAN process and even to briefly meet with ASEAN Leaders.[8]

---

[5] At the opening of the first APA, the then chairman of the ASEAN ISIS characterised APA as a "bridge" created by track II (ASEAN-ISIS) for track I officials and track III CSOs. A short memoranda from the first APA was prepared and sent to governments, as well as a larger publication of views from APA. This good feedback process arrives from the existing personal and professional relationships that have formed between ASEAN ISIS and ASEAN officials. The APA continued to be convened by ASEAN ISIS until its Seventh Assembly at Manila, Philippines in March 2009.

[6] Other regional networks of NGOs have developed, such as the Solidarity for Asian People's Advocacy (SAPA), Forum-Asia, the Southeast Asian Committee for Advocacy (SEACA), the Third World Network (TWN) and the Asian Partnership for the Development of Human Resources in Rural Asia (AsiaDHRRA). At times, each of these has also sought to interact with ASEAN and to meet with ministers and leaders formally, whether directly or through the consultations organised by the host governments.

[7] The first was the ASEAN Civil Society Conference (ACSC), organised in 2005 by the Malaysian government as host of the ASEAN Summit. It was attended by more than 120 participants from ASEAN NGOs. In 2006, the Philippines government adopted the APA effort by ASEAN-ISIS. In 2007, the Singapore government as Summit Host supported the SIIA think tank to organise the 2007 ASEAN Civil Society conference in October. This involved the direct participation of representatives from the ASEAN Secretariat for two full days of discussion, including the ASEAN Secretary-General HE Ong Keng Yong, who then brought the chairman's statement from the conference to the attention of the ASEAN Summit.

[8] The statement from this first ACSC was presented to the Heads of State during the 11th ASEAN Summit in Kuala Lumpur. See "Preface", in *ASEAN Civil Society: Building a Common Future Together*, eds. Salleh, Umminajah, Ainul Rusmin Ghazali,

Questions and controversies, however, arise about the legitimacy and quality of this process. In 2008, Thailand as Summit host convened the ASEAN Civil Society conference together with the ASEAN People's Forum (APF). However, one government protested the inclusion of a particular CSO representative, leading to the original meeting being postponed. When the meeting was reconvened, the effort was marred by a walkout by CSOs, who claimed that certain representatives were barred, and five of the ten elected representatives had been replaced by government-approved nominees.[9] This has left a lingering doubt about how CSO representatives engage with the ASEAN Summit and its Leaders.

The proliferation, overlap and intersections of the above events and pathways shows that civil society engagement is still an emerging and evolving concept in ASEAN. The functionality of these efforts can also be questioned. The meetings mentioned above covered the broadest range of diverse interests[10]. Viewpoints presented to ASEAN are often extremely broad and without specific policy recommendations, without impact.

Engagement by Sectors

Another different thread in ASEAN-civil society engagement has developed within specific sectors. Two bear special mention, in human rights, and concerning the haze. These examples relate to what sometimes are called "global affairs", relating not only to matters between states but what

---

Masturah Alias, and Mohammad Rizal Abidin (Kuala Lumpur, Malaysia: Ampang Press, 2006), xiii.

[9] "Civil Rights Activists Walk Out of Meeting with ASEAN Leaders in Protest", *Xinhua*, October 23, 2009, accessed November 19, 2009, http://www.philstar.com/Article.aspx?articleId=516928&publicationSubCategoryId=200

[10] Topics at the meetings surveyed above included art, ASEAN processes, corporate social responsibility and governance, democracy (Myanmar/East Timor), education, environment and resource sustainability, human rights and migration, rural development and agriculture, poverty, human security, media and communication, peace, conflict and development, traditional security concerns, religion, rule of law, the role of civil society and women and empowerment of children and youth.

each state does *within* its own borders. This brings these concerns often into conflict with a long established tenet of ASEAN — the principle of non-intervention.

The creation of the ASEAN Intergovernmental Commission on Human Rights (AICHR) in October 2009 is generally viewed as one of the more successful partnerships between ASEAN and civil society. The initial idea for an ASEAN human rights mechanism came from governments in a 1993 Declaration as governments were preparing for the 1993 Vienna World Conference on human rights, amidst the rhetoric of the time about Asian values. Thereafter, the ASEAN governments did not pursue the idea further. However, regional think-tanks and CSOs did.

The longest standing of these was the effort of the ASEAN-ISIS network of think tanks to hold an annual Colloquium on Human Rights (AICHOR). Experts and think tanks at AICHOR considered ways for ASEAN to take incremental steps forward on a broad remit of human rights.[11] AICHOR also helped bring together another group that focused particularly on the need for an ASEAN human rights body, known as the Working Group for an ASEAN Human Rights Mechanism ("Working Group").

The Working Group worked consistently in partnership with various ASEAN governments to hold workshops to create recommendations, timelines, and terms of references for the ASEAN Human Rights Body, setting out ambitious proposals they felt would be of "international standard". In 2008, when the draft ASEAN Charter promised to create a human rights body, the Working Group held its Seventh Workshop on Human Rights Mechanism in Singapore in partnership with the Singapore Institute of International Affairs (SIIA). This workshop attracted the participation of officials from all ASEAN member countries as well as the ASEAN Secretary-General. Its recommendations were made directly to Secretary-General Surin Pitsuwan and to all ASEAN governments.[12]

---

[11] Including measures for the protection of women and children; trafficking in peoples and the protection of migrant workers; and promotional work for human rights education.

[12] The discussions were marked by a division between the Working Group's core recommendations for a Commission as noted above, and less ambitious

An ASEAN Human intergovernmental Rights Commission was subsequently created by the ASEAN governments at the 2009 Summit. While the terms of reference for the Commission are far from the principles of design propounded by the Working Group, this is an example of ASEAN-civil society engagement having shown progress and outcome.

Another sector that has seen ASEAN-civil society engagement is in respect of the environment and the transboundary haze caused by land and forest fires in Indonesia.[13] Beginning soon after the fires of 1997–1998, the SIIA working with think tanks, NGOs and others in the region, has endeavoured to bring attention and recommend actions to be taken to address the problem.[14] These efforts led by the SIIA and other CSOs in the region continue until today.[15]

---

proposals that others including this author felt were more realistic for ASEAN to begin with. Singapore Institue of International Affairs, "7th Workshop on ASEAN Human Rights Mechanism", accessed on November 19, 2009, http://www.siiaonline.org/?q=events/7th-workshop-human-rights-mechanism-asean

[13] This section includes an area where the SIIA and the author have been directly involved. As such, much of this has been drawn from an independent and scholarly source: Francesch-Huidobro, Maria, "The Power of Circumvention: Fighting the Southeast Asian Forest Fires and Haze," in *Governance, Politics and the Environment* (Singapore: Institute of Southeast Asian Studies, 2008), 245–81.

[14] The first major regional dialogue by CSOs on the haze was held in 1998, organised by the SIIA and the Singapore Environment Council. Following this dialogue, this author, representing the CSOs at the dialogue, was the first non-government representative invited to present the recommendations to ASEAN Senior Officials at the Regional Taskforce Meeting, which was held in Singapore that year. *Ibid.*, p. 249.

[15] Three more haze dialogues were held in 2006, 2007 and 2009 by the SIIA with each attended not only by CSOs and think tanks but also by the relevant ASEAN officials. In subsequent years, the SIIA has organised a colloquium in Brunei for ASEAN governments on the issue and related environmental issues, such as climate change. From 2014, the SIIA has organised the annual, high profile Singapore Dialogue on Sustainable World Resources, focusing on the agro forestry sector that is the source of most of the fires and haze, drawing the leading CSOs as well as key policy makers. Workshops on the haze and related issues have also been held, with the latest being in Jakarta with a focus on peatland restoration to allow sustainable development without fires.

In this period, the ASEAN officials have moved from a non-binding plan of action to having more regular and focused meetings to deal with the haze. A treaty has been concluded on this issue, with Indonesia's ratification coming in 2015. Within Indonesia too, the issue has gained more support in recent years and especially under the administration of President Joko Widodo, who has recognized that his country and people are the first victims of this problem, especially in terms of public health and economic damage.

While the haze persists, policies and actions have been ratcheted up over the years, often aligned to CSO recommendations generated by the dialogues. The dialogues have also brought in media attention to encourage ASEAN and Indonesia to move forward on this concern. No doubt that governments remain the focal point, and yet the efforts of CSOs in this sector have supplemented and encouraged action.

Concluding Observations

From the turn of the century, ASEAN has begun to move on its ambition to become more "people-oriented". As with most new initiatives, there are tentative efforts and even missteps. The proliferation of platforms for CSOs has not necessarily assisted, in terms of either functionality or of legitimacy. ASEAN is still struggling to arrive at a successful mechanism by which to structure modes of inclusive dialogue with CSOs. Notwithstanding this, the examples discussed — of ASEAN-ISIS and on the specific issues of the ASEAN human intergovernmental rights commission and on the transboundary haze — have shown that CSO inputs can have influence. ASEAN and civil society both have a better knowledge base from which to draw upon if this relationship is to grow in the coming years.

But the question of effectiveness depends not only on ASEAN but also how different ASEAN governments deal with civil society relations at the national level. The diversity in ASEAN is evident here. In some cases, member governments have long established democratic and decentralised processes to engage their CSOs at the national level. Others are newer to the phenomenon. For Singapore, the efforts of government to engage and govern civil society have evolved at the national level. While there has been some engagement at the ASEAN level — notably in relation to the issue of transboundary haze discussed above — there may need to give further thought on how best to represent Singapore civil society in ASEAN.

Ideally, the engagement of governments with civil society in ASEAN will not only be about a process for show. The process cannot be straight-jacketed by the most conservative governments, citing the principle of non-intervention. Nor should it be hijacked by any government to opportunistically raise issues to embarrass another government. Civil society engagement can instead be structured to become a more consistent and meaningful process that takes in and considers ideas and wider perspectives from society, as well as the specialised expert knowledge and epistemic communities. Government-civil society ties will also do better when it is realised that there are policy goals that require the cooperation of people (and corporations) beyond what can be commanded by national laws and executive directions.

Much of this can and should be done by national governments, which remain the engine room of the ASEAN process. A supplementary process can however be developed with the ASEAN Secretariat, especially as these relate to cross border and ASEAN-wide issues. As these processes are put in place, the question that has arisen of how CSO representatives engage with the ASEAN Summit and Leaders should be a non-issue. Beyond symbolism, the ASEAN government-civil society engagement needs to be fuller and more functional, and only that can enhance the ASEAN process in reality and in its legitimacy.

The ASEAN Charter is now nearly ending its first decade and there are calls for its review. One of the questions for review will be how much more ASEAN will move towards becoming "more people-oriented", and the ways in which this be done. It is timely to consider how to better structure the methods and processes of engagement, making it more legitimate and effective as well as more inclusive.

Selected Bibliography

Collins, Alan. "A People-Oriented ASEAN: A Door Ajar or Closed for Civil Society Organisations?" *Contemporary Southeast Asia* 30, no. 2 (2008): 313–331.

Francesch-Huidobro, Maria. "The Power of Circumvention: Fighting the Southeast Asian Forest Fires and Haze", in *Governance, Politics and the Environment* (Singapore: Institute of Southeast Asian Studies, 2008), 245–281.

Hernandez, C. "Track Two and Regional Policy: The ASEAN ISIS in ASEAN Decision Making", in *Twenty-Two Years of ASEAN ISIS: Origin, Evolution and Challenges of Track Two Diplomacy*, eds. H. Soesastro *et al.* (Jakarta, Indonesia: Centre for Strategic and International Studies, 2006), 19.

"ASEAN 'must listen more' to grassroots", *Jakarta Post*, December 9, 2006, http://pseudonymity.wordpress.com/2006/12/09/asean-must-listen-more-to-grass-roots

Mely Caballero-Anthony. "ASEAN ISIS and the ASEAN People's Assembly (APA): Paving a Multi-Track Approach in Regional Community Building", in *Twenty Two Years of ASEAN ISIS: Origin, Evolution and Challenges of Track Two Diplomacy*. eds. H. Soesastro *et al.* (Jakarta, Indonesia: Centre for Strategic and International Studies, 2006), 56.

"Preface", in *ASEAN Civil Society: Building a Common Future Together*, eds. Salleh, Umminajah, Ainul Rusmin Ghazali, Masturah Alias, and Mohammad Rizal Abidin (Kuala Lumpur, Malaysia: Ampang Press, 2006), xiii.

Soesastro Hadi, "Introduction", in *Twenty-Two Years of ASEAN ISIS: Origin, Evolution and Challenges of Track Two Diplomacy*, eds. H. Soesastro, *et al.* (Jakarta, Indonesia: Centre for Strategic and International Studies, 2006), 19.

Soesastro, Hadi. "Foreword", in *Report of the Fifth ASEAN People's Assembly: The Role of the People in Building an ASEAN Community of Caring and Sharing Societies* (Philippines: Institute for Strategic and Development Studies, 2007), vii.

1977 & 2006 — ASEAN Inter-Parliamentary Organisation/Assembly, http://www.aipasecretariat.org

2000–2009 — ASEAN People's Assembly, website: http://siiaonline.org/?q=node/2607

Simon TAY is an associate professor at the Faculty of Law, National University of Singapore specialising in international and regional law and policy. He is concurrently chairman of the Singapore Institute of International Affairs (SIIA) that represents Singapore in the ASEAN Track II network of think tanks and the SIIA has advised a number of governments in the region on regional integration and relations with the major powers.

Human Rights and ASEAN: Perspectives from MARUAH[1]

Braema MATHI and LEE Sze Yong

૮ ৮ ৴

This essay will focus on ASEAN's human rights as part of ASEAN's 50th anniversary celebrations. It is a difficult story to write on how we, in Singapore, wanted a commitment from the people sector to pursue work in the area of human rights. But it gets better when we narrate how we contributed to the processes of the ASEAN Human Rights Mechanism. And it gets stronger as we look at the strengths and challenges of working on human rights in ASEAN. We conclude with our hopes, aspirations and inspiration for human rights in ASEAN.

Advocacy for ASEAN's Human Rights — The Beginning

Human rights became an interesting arena when Braema was a Visiting Research Fellow[2] in the then Institute of Southeast Asian

---

[1] The authors are founding members of MARUAH (Working Group for ASEAN Human Rights Mechanism, Singapore) which is a Singapore human rights NGO. MARUAH means Dignity in Malay, Singapore's national language. Human rights is about maintaining, restoring and reclaiming one's dignity at the individual, regional and international level. MARUAH is the Singapore focal point for the Working Group for an ASEAN Human Rights Mechanism. www.maruah.org

[2] Braema Mathi was a Visiting Research Fellow at the then Institute of Southeast Asian Studies and also the institution's Gender Studies Coordinator, from 2005 to 2008. In these capacities as well as the additional knowledge from her volunteer work with gender- and migrant worker- focused non-governmental organisations, she researched and presented discussion papers at forums in ASEAN.

Studies (ISEAS). She was involved in ASEAN-related discussions that primarily took place in the Philippines and Thailand. These were organised by the ASEAN-Institutes of Strategic and International Studies (ASEAN-ISIS) network. The meetings were held at the ASEAN People's Assembly (APA)[3] and the Working Group for an ASEAN Human Rights Mechanism (WGAHRM)[4]. They co-hosted consultations with ASEAN governments on human rights. The Vienna Declaration of 1993[5] became a clarion call for dedicated academics, lawyers and activists to work on human rights in ASEAN. Their quiet diplomatic advocacy and consultations with governments and Ministers from ASEAN Member States (AMS) also led to established Civil Society Organisations (CSOs) being invited, from mid-2000s, to participate in the forums and consultations on human rights in ASEAN.

As a researcher and as a CSO advocate in Singapore, Braema was one of the many leaders who was raising awareness in ASEAN on

---

[3] That primary responsibility from 2000 to 2009, when APA functioned, was through the think tanks of the ASEAN-Institutes of Strategic and International Studies (ASEAN-ISIS) network, whose secretariat was then the Centre for Strategic and International Studies (CSIS Indonesia) and was led by a committed, passionate group of ISIS representatives from ASEAN countries.

[4] The Working Group for an ASEAN Human Rights Mechanism (WGAHRM) was created in 1995 by the Human Rights Committee of LAWASIA to push for the creation of an inter-governmental human rights body after 1993's Vienna Declaration on Human Rights when ASEAN "agree[d] that ASEAN should also consider the establishment of an appropriate regional mechanism on human rights". http://www.aseanhrmech.org/aboutus.html. The WGAHRM is a group of well-respected individuals who have contributed to the discussions on human rights internationally and regionally. Some amongst them were/are also Special Rapporteurs on specific human rights topics for the United Nations.

[5] In 1993, the Vienna Declaration and Program of Action emphasised the need "*to consider the possibility of establishing regional and sub-regional arrangements for the promotion and protection of human rights where they do not already exist*". That same year, the ASEAN Inter-Parliamentary Organization (AIPO) stated that "*it is...the task and responsibility of member states to establish an appropriate regional mechanism on human rights*" in its Declaration on Human Rights. http://www.aseanhrmech.org/aboutus.html

human rights. As a Singaporean, her assessment was that advocacy for human rights mechanisms at the national level was hard work and that it could be better supported, if Singapore CSOs advocated concurrently at the regional level through for ASEAN to observe, promote, protect and fulfil human rights. She therefore worked to establish human rights at the national level through regional efforts.

The Shaping of MARUAH as a Singapore CSO Involved in Human Rights

Braema presented papers at forums organised by APA and WGAHRM. As Singapore was going to host the ASEAN Summit in 2007, WGAHRM was keen to see a stronger Singapore CSO engagement, though it had the Think Centre[6] as its representative, which had taken over from the Singapore Institute of International Affairs (SIIA)[7]. There were discussions to re-constitute stakeholder representation[8] for the ASEAN Summit. A wide spectrum of activists and some opposition party members attended a meeting in August 2007 that saw Braema offering to be an interim coordinator to work on the reconstitution and use the Vientiane Action Programme (VAP)[9] as a platform for advocacy work that AMS would work to the agreed deadline of 2010. Braema enthused many CSO representatives, some former Nominated Members of Parliament (NMPs), some former Law Society Presidents, some

---

[6] Think Centre, Singapore, http://www.thinkcentre.org/about-us/

[7] Singapore Institute of International Affairs, Singapore, http://www.siiaonline. org/our-history/

[8] Indonesia, the Philippines, and Thailand had National Working Groups on ASEAN Human Rights Mechanisms that had/have a wide spectrum of individuals and organisations to discuss human rights in ASEAN. Members included National Human Rights Institutions (NHRIs), CSOs working on human rights as a cause on specific issues and members of the academia. Myanmar has formed an NHRI recently and CSOs there are involved in both regional, national and international human rights mechanisms for their causes.

[9] In 2004, ASEAN adopted the Vientiane Action Program (VAP) which listed human rights action points with a 2010 deadline.

academics, pioneering individuals[10] and the Think Centre to attend a discussion to look at structural models that could lead to a network of multi-stakeholder partnerships focused on a common engagement on human rights.

However this was not to be. There were objections from the Think Centre regarding the interim committee's inclusion of former Nominated Members of Parliament (NMPs). The ex-NMPs were deemed to be "government representatives", "elitist" and "deceitful", and would not represent human rights issues adequately. These unfounded objections did not delay the interim committee's work, which stayed focused on setting up MARUAH, outlining objectives and working on an action plan. It also remained committed to observing the principle of freedom of expression which meant leaving these allegations alone for CSOs to observe and make their own conclusions.

However, these differences dried up efforts to garner a multi-stakeholder network support focused on human rights for Singapore and for ASEAN. The people who were gentlemanly about the then interim committee which became MARUAH later, were the opposition party representatives and their young members whom we met and told them that the decision was not to have political party members — ruling party or opposition — as members in the human rights committee/organisation. But we assured them that we will represent causes that were crucial to building up democracy in Singapore. We also informed WGAHRM on the interim committee/then MARUAH, and stayed focused on the work

---

[10] There was interest but many declined with one saying openly that human rights will be problematic work in Singapore. Those who agreed were former NMPs Mr. Siew Kum Hong, Ms. Braema Mathi, and Mr. Peter Low, a former Law Society President. CSOs that agreed to be part of the multi-stakeholder set up were Transient Workers Count Too and Humanitarian Organisation for Migration Economics. Others declined though one was a very active advocacy-oriented organisation as they did not see, ironically, their work as inclined towards human rights. Founder members of the Interim Committee are Ms. Braema Mathi, Mr. Siew Kum Hong, Mr. Thomas Koshy, Mr. Alex Au, Mr. Leong Sze Hian and Mr. Lee Sze Yong. More details on the early history can be found here — Maruah, Singapore, https://maruahsg.files.wordpress.com/2017/06/swc4ahrm-factsheet.pdf

ahead. As an example, there were two co-chairs — MARUAH[11] and Think Centre — that were appointed to complement the Chair's work in organising the CSO consultations for the ASEAN Summit in 2007.

As a national conclusion on CSOs' work on human rights, we still find this a sad state of affairs brought upon ourselves by CSOs that work on human rights. The years of formation (from 2007 to 2009) were tough years on all of us, not because of the work we were doing as volunteers but because of the unnecessary animosity.

There were already enough challenges working on human rights in Singapore. One example is when MARUAH finally registered itself as a society in 2010, it was immediately gazetted as a Political Association[12] by the Singapore Government, to which we sent an appeal to no effect[13]. The present legislation pose limitations on the range of advocacy work, e.g. events featuring foreign speakers require special permit applications. Since 2007, those in the interim committee and in MARUAH have carried on as volunteers, with pooled money from our own pockets and small donations, and using personal leave to attend regional or local weekday events. On representing views to the ASEAN regional bodies on human rights, as registered members of the WGAHRM, we do get sponsorship support from WGAHRM. We failed in our funding appeals to well-to-do Singaporeans and Foundations except for one donation of S$3,000 from an individual.

Human rights is seen by many as potentially dangerous to their public reputation and personal advancement, which is untrue. But with the advent of social media, the scene here is changing. The Alliance of

[11] This is an act of solidarity for CSOs working on human rights to come together for such preparatory work and so we expressed that MARUAH cannot be the sole co-chair with Mr. Simon Tay, Chairman of SIIA, and asked that Think Centre be a co-chair too.
[12] Singapore Elections Department, "Gazetting of Singapore Working Group for an ASEAN Human Rights Mechanism (MARUAH) as a Political Association under the Political Donations Act", http://www.eld.gov.sg/pressrelease%5CRPD2010%5CPR%202010-09-09%20-%20Gazetting%20of%20Singapore%20Working%20Group%20for%20an%20Asean%20Human%20Rights%20Mechanism%20(MARUAH).pdf
[13] Singapore Management University, https:??www.smu.edu.sg/sites/default/files/smu/news_room/

Like-Minded CSOs in Singapore (ALMOS)[14] and the Community Action Network (CAN)[15] are some examples of human rights social media groups. This is the good news at the national level as much of the impetus to discuss human rights, which went into a hiatus after the early detentions without trial, began again through ASEAN's human rights discussions. Today we see AMS committed to Conventions to promote and protect the rights of children, women and people with disabilities[16]. The other factor that is getting more CSOs and individuals committed to human rights work is the work on the Universal Periodic Review (UPR)[17] as the process requires the AMS governments to be accountable for their human rights records.

These are good developments for human rights in Singapore. Thanks to ASEAN and international discussions, the advocacy work has gone on in spite of some recent legislation.[18]

MARUAH's Contributions to AHRM and to National Human Rights Discussions

MARUAH has been the Singapore CSO representative at consultations, forums with WGAHRM that was engaged with the Eminent Person Group (EPG) on the ASEAN Charter that was set up in 2005, the

---

[14] Alliance of Like-Minded CSOs in Singapore, https://www.facebook.com/ALMOS. human.rights/; MARUAH was not invited to the discussions because of objections. Think Centre is a member. MARUAH is also not a member of Forum-Asia, a regional CSO, which has multiple members from individual countries. From Singapore the sole representative member is Think Centre. However, MARUAH has support from many member organisations in other countries.

[15] Community Action Network — CAN Singapore, https://www.facebook.com/ Community-Action-Network-CAN-Singapore-581508831988816/

[16] Convention on the Rights of the Child, Convention on the Elimination of All Forms of Discrimination against Women, Convention on the Rights of Persons with Disabilities.

[17] Office of the UN High Commisioner for Human Rights, http://www.ohchr.org/ EN/HRBodies/UPR/Pages/BasicFacts.aspx.

[18] Laws including the Administration of Justice (Protection) Act, Public Order Act, Public Order (Unrestricted Area) Order.

High-Level Panel[19] on an ASEAN Human Rights Body, the ASEAN Intergovernmental Commission on Human Rights (AICHR)[20] and the ASEAN Commission on the Promotion and Protection of the Rights Women and Children (ACWC).[21]

The 2006 EPG report reflected views shared by many stakeholders, including that of MARUAH's. The EPG asked for ASEAN to become "more people-centred",[22] and to have a greater respect for human rights and fundamental freedoms. MARUAH also documented the public consultations held, developed position papers on the ASEAN Charter[23], ASEAN Human Rights Declaration (AHRD)[24]

---

[19] ASEAN, http://www.asean.org/wp-content/uploads/images/archive/documents/AICHR/HLP-Members.pdf

[20] ASEAN Intergovernmental Commission on Human Rights, http://aichr.org/documents/

[21] ASEAN, "ASEAN Ministerial Meeting on Social Welfare and Development (AMMSWD)", http://asean.org/asean-socio-cultural/asean-ministerial-meeting-on-social-welfare-and-development-ammswd/acwc-php/

[22] The EPG supports the "promotion of ASEAN's peace and stability through the active strengthening of democratic values, good governance, rejection of unconstitutional and undemocratic changes of government, the rule of law including international humanitarian law, and respect for human rights and fundamental freedoms" as one of the recommendations of the several fundamental principles and objectives of its report. ASEAN, "Report of the Eminent Persons Group on the ASEAN Charter: December 2006", http://www.asean.org/storage/images/archive/19247.pdf.

[23] MARUAH, "Position statement on the ASEAN Charter", https://maruah.org/2007/11/21/position-statement-on-the-asean-charter

[24] MARUAH, "MARUAH presents Position Paper on ASEAN Human Rights Body to High Level-Panel", https://maruah.org/2008/09/13/maruah-submits-position-paper-on-asean-human-rights-body/ Report on public consultation on ASEAN Human Rights Body https://maruah.org/2009/04/04/report-on-public-consultation-on-asean-human-rights-body; MARUAH, "Public consultation on the ASEAN Human Rights Declaration, "https://maruah.org/2011/10/06/public-consultation-on-the-asean-human-rights-declaration-15-oct-2011 https://maruah.org/2011/10/17/event-report-public-consultation-on-the-asean-human-rights-declaration

and the processes of engagement in selecting the AMS' AICHR representatives.[25]

We share a summary of our key positions on some of these matters:

- We commended ASEAN for keeping to the 2010 VAP deadline and the setting up of the ACWC.
- We also complimented the work of the EPG and the High-Level Panel,[26] and that ASEAN Secretariat had improved its organisational structure to give support to Human Rights.
- We lauded the ASEAN Charter and liked the clearly expressed principles as embedded in the Charter's Preamble. We also liked Article 14 of the Charter on the need to set up a human rights body, as this was a contentious area among those who drafted the ASEAN Charter.
- We were critical of the Charter's non-compliance provisions since the Charter also endorsed "non-interference in the internal affairs" of the AMS. We remain perturbed on how human rights of the people can be overturned by this provision. On the AHRD we asked for more clarifications on the "rights and responsibilities" phrasing and limitations on human rights based on "public morality". We also asked for more Articles to deal with protection of human rights and for greater alignment with Article 1(7) of the ASEAN Charter as well as the Universal Declaration on Human Rights (1948).

---

[25] MARUAH, "Adopt NMP Process to Pick Rep for ASEAN Rights Body", https://maruah.org/2009/08/25/adopt-nmp-process-to-pick-rep-for-asean-rights-body; MARUAH, "MARUAH's recommendations on ASEAN Intergovernmental Commission on Human Rights (AICHR)", https://maruah.org/2009/09/04/maruahs-recommendations-on-asean-intergovernmental-commission-on-human-rights-aichr; MARUAH, "Registration for Consultation Workshop on ASEAN Inter-governmental Commission on Human Rights, " https://maruah.org/2009/08/07/registration-for-consultation-workshop-on-asean-intergovernmental-commission-on-human-rights

[26] The Singapore representatives on this High Level Panel on an ASEAN Human Rights Body were MFA's former Permanent Secretary, Mr. Bilahari Kausikan and the assistant, Mr. Harry Goh, Foreign Service Officer. Both were open in consultations and views were shared, even if we did not agree all the time. Respect between CSO and government representatives, we would like to think, was mutual.

- On the selection of AICHR candidates, we asked, a few times, at consultations and in a paper too, for greater consultations with CSOs and other stakeholders on choices of final representatives, as is done in Thailand and Indonesia.
- We also stated that AMS cannot just direct CSO consultations with AMS' approved organisations.[27] CSOs are multi-faceted and have multi-interests and may not always have diplomacy as their calling card, for which they can be told off. But if CSOs work hard on human rights, then AMS need to develop higher threshold levels to deal with that diversity.
- We also asked for transparency, accountability and a sharing of timelines as to when the ASEAN Charter will be reviewed, along with the AHRD, and when a regional human rights court can be set up.

We have asked for enhancement of power for the ASEAN Secretary-General rather than the current model of administrating to the ten AMS Leaders, especially when he/she needs to deal with immediate and pertinent issues relating to human rights violations.

At the national level as part of a human rights mandate, MARUAH has also made submissions to the Singapore Government that include observations on various issues relating to democracy and human rights in the country. We have also responded with press statements on incidents relating to violation of persons' rights. At the national level, we have conducted capacity-building for CSOs on the Universal Periodic Review (UPR) and submitted a consolidated report[28] in 2011 and 2015. MARUAH remains concerned[29] that Singapore representatives to the Universal Periodic Review (UPR) are not elected officials, e.g. cabinet ministers. To date, Singapore has been represented by civil service officers who are accounting for the government's track record on human rights.

---

[27] One instance that did not spell well for the CSO belt is when AMS(s) refused to meet the representatives of the ACSC/APF at ASEAN Summit interfaces. This happened again recently at the ASEAN Summit in the Philippines when Cambodia, Laos and Singapore had no government representative during a meeting of the ASEAN Chair with ACSC/APF representatives.

[28] MARUAH, "Universal Periodic Review", https://maruah.org/=upr/

[29] MARUAH, "MARUAH's Forum Letter on Singapore's Participation in UPR Process", https://maruah.org/2016/02/04/maruahs-forum-letter-on-singapores-participation-in-upr-process/

The Challenges and Aspirations as ASEAN Celebrates Being 50

The current challenges facing ASEAN could be said to be: unaccountability in business practices; corruption; power structures interplay for General Elections; multiple South China Sea claims on ownership; the North Korea-United States confrontation that can lead to conflict; the newly elected US President and his unclear approach on international relations, peace and harmony; the changes in global immigration policies; the rise in refugees and the dominant threats of terrorism.

ASEAN's slow response to the plight of Rohingyas goes against the principles cited in the ASEAN Charter. As conflicts can rise in the region, there is every reason to review the Treaty of Amity and Cooperation. This is crucial as religion is being politicised internationally and ASEAN must retain and maintain its peace and order whilst protecting women, children, indigenous communities and minority groups, ensuring that their rights are not violated.

There needs to be a stronger commitment to ensuring that ASEAN's Declarations are aligned to universal norms and not particularised to regional and national concerns.

Is the "ASEAN Way" still reliable? The "ASEAN Way" of flexibility and non-interference is cited as an advantageous way of working. Yet there was delayed action on the plight of the Rohingyas. Indonesia's President Jokowi was vivid in his description of the migrant workers' plights when he asked for AMS' Leaders to show a greater commitment to protect migrant workers. But this discussion on migrant workers goes around in circles, as countries cannot agree, despite the Charter, the AHRD and the AICHR. We also talk about poverty and the empowerment of women but access to education and training remain a challenge in this regional bloc.

When it comes to the human rights of the people in ASEAN, basic provisions are yet to be mainstreamed, despite statements made by AMS governments, in the much touted 'ASEAN Way'.

We have come a long way since 1967 and 1993. But over the next 20 years, an adherence to a human rights approach, to the principles of the ASEAN Charter and the independence of AICHR Representatives have to become a norm. The work for groups like us, MARUAH and all

CSOs, will also have to focus on these demands that we are making. And we hope for more open consultations between governments and CSOs as we need to work together to ensure that people's rights are promoted, protected and fulfilled.

Braema MATHI was a Nominated Member of Parliament (2001–2004) in Singapore, President of the Association of Women for Action and Research (AWARE) (2002–2004), and Vice-President of Action for AIDS (2005–2008). She founded and led Transient Workers Count Too (2002–2007), is a founding member and was President of MARUAH (Singapore Working Group for an ASEAN Human Rights Mechanism; (2007–2016)) and was also the Regional President of the International Council of Social Welfare (Southeast Asia and Pacific; 2008–2013). Braema previously worked as a teacher, a journalist, in senior management, as a co-ordinator and researcher and was a consultant on corporate communication, structural and management practices in the non-profit sector, researcher on social policies. Today, she is a Director at ASEAN CSR Network. Braema has published articles, tries to live by human rights values and has worked on instruments such as Convention on the Elimination of all Forms of Discrimination Against Women (CEDAW), Convention on the Rights of Persons with Disabilities (CRPD) and the Universal Periodic Review (UPR) as advocacy tools that help to protect people and fulfil their rights.

LEE Sze Yong is currently an exco member in MARUAH. Sze Yong graduated with a degree from the NUS Department of Building, but ended up with working stints in three non-governmental organisations (NGOs), in the construction, consumer protection, and medical fields respectively. A fan of the Convention on the Elimination of all Forms of Discrimination Against Women (CEDAW), concept of substantive equality and the Universal Declaration of Human Rights (UDHR) Article 29, he hopes to encourage more people to look at issues through a human rights lens, and to mainstream human rights into all areas.

Singaporeans in ASEAN

An Accidental Diplomat: Reflections from Singapore's First ASEAN Secretary-General

CHAN Kai Yau

I was born in Hong Kong and educated in Penang, Malaysia before and after the Second World War. I was educated in Chinese schools before joining the University of Malaya in 1950. Upon graduation, I was posted to Beatty Secondary School as a teacher and later transferred to the then Teachers' Training College (now the National Institute of Education) in 1956. In the course of time, I became a citizen of Singapore and moved to the Ministry of Education in 1964. Years later I served as the Director of Education. I was never a diplomat to begin with.

In 1982, one fine day, I was asked to go to the Ministry of Foreign Affairs for a briefing, to learn about ASEAN and thereafter, to be posted to the ASEAN Secretariat in Jakarta, Indonesia. It all came as a surprise to me but I went to MFA dutifully. The briefing was not very long. I was given files to read in MFA for about three weeks before I was sent on my way on 18 July 1982 as Singapore's first official appointed as ASEAN's Secretary-General. There was little time to make arrangements to bring my family with me so in the end, we decided that my wife and young children would remain in Singapore, while she could join me now and then in Jakarta.

My first impression was that the Indonesian Government was very generous to ASEAN. A large house had been set aside for the Secretary-General. It had a sentry, a gardener and a housekeeper who was the gardener's wife. There was also an official car with a driver. All the

ASEAN staff were friendly and took good care of me and my wife when she joined me.

I remember the first event I had to officiate was the ASEAN Day reception on 8 August 1982. I had only arrived in July. This was a grand affair as the ASEAN Foreign Ministers would fly to Jakarta to attend the reception. Our Foreign Minister at that time was Mr S Dhanabalan. I was told that we were to invite no less than 800 guests and to offer a spread of many types of food and specialties from the ASEAN countries. There used to be much food wastage as the staff tended to cater exactly for the number of guests. So after discussing and analysing a typical invitation with my staff, we catered for 500 guests. There was no food wastage and some financial savings and all the staff enjoyed themselves.

It was a very good experience for me to learn what went on within ASEAN for the first time, living and working inside the Secretariat as it was a very different experience from being a civil servant working in Singapore. It was a tremendous change for me at that time. From the heavy schedule I had as the Director of Education in MOE, I found that the Secretariat's work was comparatively less heavy. There were many meetings but ASEAN at that time comprised only five founding members with newcomer Brunei joining near the end of my term in 1984. There were six Member Countries. We were focused primarily on deepening our economic linkages so the work at the Secretariat was very much on facilitating trade and investment. The member countries were familiar with each other and should there be any teething issues, the relevant Directors in charge of ASEAN in the Member States and the Secretary-General would pick up the phone and discuss. As a result, the formal meetings were usually quite technical in nature. For example, we would be working on coordinating the taxation within ASEAN. Country A might be charging 5% and Country B 15%, so when we had to facilitate business within ASEAN, we needed to harmonise the taxation to make ASEAN attractive. In this instance, representatives from the relevant tax departments from the six countries would meet to discuss and whenever possible reach a solution.

On another occasion, when we had police matters to coordinate, the Police Chiefs from each country would gather to deal with the matter. We would have a coordinating meeting whenever ASEAN was going to meet its Dialogue Partners, countries like Australia, Japan and the United States and a group of countries like the European Union. As ASEAN worked on the basis of consensus, it was important that all six countries went prepared to meet our Dialogue Partners with a consensus position. In those days, we were supposed to organise an ASEAN Summit annually but as different countries had to deal with some challenging issues, we did not even have a Summit one year. Today, ASEAN has evolved to having two Summits in a year.

During my two-year term, I learnt about the different cultures within ASEAN. I had a team of less than ten professional staff who were sent by different member countries on a rotational basis to work at the Secretariat. In addition to the officers in charge of administration and finance, there were three coordinators, one was in charge of science, and one was in charge of commerce and industry and trade, and one in charge of culture. All of us at the ASEAN Secretariat were posted from different member countries but we had a common interest which was to grow trade and investment in the ASEAN region and to reduce internal conflicts.

Food, in particular, durian, played an important part in cultivating ASEAN diplomacy. I recall the durian parties in Jakarta, Malaysia and Thailand, when the officials working on ASEAN would get together over a basket of durians! Some preferred the highly aromatic Malaysian durians while some others preferred to enjoy the Thai durians, eaten before they are fully ripened. The camaraderie we enjoyed within ASEAN helped us to talk through issues, not that we had very many tricky political issues in those days, but compared with today, those were simpler days.

Before I left my post, the Secretariat had completed a project to review the role of the ASEAN Secretary-General, to upgrade the functional post from just being in charge of the Secretariat, to overseeing overall ASEAN work processes. The Foreign Ministers had proposed it and a committee was formed, chaired by the then Permanent Secretary of the Thai Foreign Ministry, Mr. Anand Panyarachun, who would later become a Prime Minister of Thailand. We had a number of meetings and came up with a plan. However, this was only implemented much later. Today, there are four Deputy Secretaries-General assisting the ASEAN Secretary-General. How much the work of coordination within ASEAN has grown!

In retrospect, the strategic background that ASEAN worked within was quite different. Great power relations were also different. We had just come out of a bruising war and serious confrontations and struggles in the region, and the urgent goals were to rebuild and also to reconcile. Everyone was trying to recover from them, and to move on. So our work was focused on facilitating intra-regional peace and trade and encouraging our Dialogue Partners to invest in our region, so that each of the ASEAN economies could gradually come into its own. Even in our discussions with the ASEAN Dialogue Partners, it was mainly about trade and industry, to persuade them to invest in the region. I would say that the contribution of ASEAN in the early years was building the foundation of peace and mutual respect among member countries and economic cooperation in and outside the region, to allow better flow of trade into the region and thereby improving the lives of the people of ASEAN.

CHAN Kai Yau was born in Hong Kong and educated in Penang, Malaysia. He entered the University of Malaya in 1950 and was posted to Beatty Secondary School as a teacher after graduation. He was the Director of Education from 1975 to 1982 and took on the position of Singapore's first ASEAN Secretary-General from July 1982 to 1984. Mr. Chan retired from the Singapore Education Service in 1984. He has one daughter, two sons and five grandchildren.

ASEAN: Managing Egos and National Interests

ONG Keng Yong

∾ ᵇ ᴖ

I served as the 11th Secretary-General of ASEAN from 1 January 2003 to 31 December 2007: five years as stated in the rules. I handed over my duties to Surin Pitsuwan of Thailand on 7 January 2008 as the convention then was for the Indonesian Foreign Minister to preside over the handing and taking over ceremony at the ASEAN Secretariat in Jakarta (ASEC). The baton could not be passed to Surin earlier as then Indonesian Foreign Minister Hassan Wirajuda was away from the Indonesian capital. The ceremony was an open event covered by the mass media with the Diplomatic Corps in Jakarta and other local dignitaries invited to witness the proceedings.

Before my appointment, Mr. Chan Kai Yau was the only other Singaporean who served as Secretary-General of ASEAN (from July 1982 to July 1984). At that time, the job was more limited and the stint was for two to three years each term. ASEAN Leaders broadened the mandate of the Secretary-General in 1992 and accorded the office-holder full ministerial status with a fixed term of five years each time from January 1993 when Malaysian Ajit Singh took over the helm. He was succeeded by Rodolfo Severino of the Philippines in January 1998 and I took over from the latter in January 2003. The rotation was based on the alphabetical order of the English names of the ASEAN Member States (AMS).

Raising Expectations

I had asked Prime Minister Goh Chok Tong what was expected of me in the ASEAN job. He said that it was important to get Singaporeans more aware of the value of ASEAN to their country's interests. He noted that Singapore officials tended to be clinical and impatient with the antics of ASEAN — a lot of eating, golfing, singing and travelling. The fact was that the other Southeast Asians were watching the Singaporeans — to see if they were sincere and willing to do more for ASEAN. Mr. Goh pointed out that Singapore would always be different from the rest of Southeast Asia and I could help to explain that to the people in other AMS so that there could be a better understanding of Singapore and its policy. He added that it would be best that I speak up objectively on Singapore's stand on specific issues in ASEAN. The bottom-line was to treat all the AMS equally and fairly.

There were high expectations within the rank and file of ASEC with my appointment as Secretary-General of ASEAN. Firstly, Singapore was always regarded as a "no nonsense" member state which would speak out or act whenever there was an issue Singapore could not accept or agree with. Singapore's reputation as an efficient government would mean a Secretary-General who would make the Secretariat more professional and dynamic. Secondly, many ASEAN officials and ASEC staff believed that the Secretary-General from Singapore would have a plan to do something new and special to distinguish his term from that of his predecessors'. This feeling was fanned by talks in ASEAN circles that the Singapore Government would provide more resources for Initiative for ASEAN Integration (IAI) projects. The fact that I was Press Secretary to then PM Goh Chok Tong reinforced this view. Mr. Goh was widely regarded in ASEAN, especially in Cambodia, Laos, Myanmar and Viet Nam (CLMV), as the originator of IAI which focused on narrowing the development gap among the AMS. Thirdly, my youthfulness (49 years old then) and the youngest man to take the top job in ASEAN was regarded as a sea change. The sense of the ASEC staff was that as a younger serving diplomat, Ong Keng Yong would be pro-active and also, comfortable dealing with the mass media and speaking in public, to shape the narratives in the media outlets on what ASEAN was doing.

Not all these expectations were fulfilled though the Singapore contribution to IAI went up as it offered more technical assistance to the AMS. I introduced the International Standards Organisation (ISO) framework for administration, management practice and performance measurement at the ASEC. I did not wish to give the impression that I was imposing Singapore Civil Service rules on the systems in the Secretariat and the ISO rules seemed suitable instead. I increased the headcount of ASEC staff and ensured that nationals from all the AMS were represented in the manpower establishment in the Secretariat. I promoted several long-serving and competent staff members to higher grades and sent a handful of good staff members for tertiary scholarships overseas on condition that they would return to the ASEC for a specific period of employment after graduation.

Pushing the Priorities

ASEAN pushed the three "Cs" during my stint as Secretary-General of ASEAN: Community, Charter and Connectivity. At the working level in Singapore, there was initially some reluctance to go full steam on the Charter as the feeling was that the timing was not ideal. Fortunately, then Foreign Minister S. Jayakumar and his successor George Yeo were strategic in their thinking. They saw the potential benefits of a more formalised ASEAN. The ASEAN economic agenda also needed a bigger scale to stay competitive and to attract more foreign direct investments (FDI) into Southeast Asia. The AMS must convey a seriousness about ASEAN and its economic integration to convince investors to build factories across ASEAN to substantiate the ASEAN strategy of a single market and production base. Without the three "Cs", ASEAN could not plug into the global economy easily and the ASEAN Dialogue Partners would see fewer incentives to deepen relations with ASEAN as a regional grouping. The geopolitical environment at the regional and international levels was changing rapidly as well and a new gloss for ASEAN would enable ASEAN to remain in the driver's seat of regional architecture.

Furthermore, the idea of ASEAN centrality required a different formality to root down. This notion of centrality was important on two fronts: using ASEAN to push for domestic reform in the AMS to make the region a bigger market; and upholding ASEAN interests in transacting with the external powers which wanted to secure their respective interests in Southeast Asia. Basically, it was a case of the national ego versus the regional ego. An ASEAN with a legal personality after the adoption of the Charter would facilitate the change of domestic laws and rules to bring them in line with ASEAN community-building plans and institutionalise more sectoral cooperation within ASEAN such as in defence and finance. ASEAN priorities ought to be internalised into the national policies of the AMS. Doing so would encourage the ASEAN Dialogue Partners to take the ASEAN role in regional architecture more seriously as ASEAN would be organisationally prepared and capable of delivering what was expected for political and security goals.

I seized the opportunity during the period to promote ASEAN as a regional body capable of managing power relationships impinging on Southeast Asia, particularly to balance the major powers (United States, China and Russia) which wanted to get more from the strategic and geopolitical significance of the region to advance their respective interests. The more public speeches I made to this effect, the more interested the major powers and other countries such as Australia, Japan and New Zealand became on "the promise of ASEAN", as former Australian Foreign Minister Alexander Downer described it. Luckily for me, none of the AMS kicked up any fuss with my media "over exposure".

Delivering the Charter

In drafting the ASEAN Charter, the CLMV countries were focused on not being cornered about their respective political systems. They persuaded me to help ensure there were no embarrassing situations highlighting their countries. I often arranged for the ASEC team to prepare early drafts for the CLMV officials to mull over. ASEC staff also pursued the concerns of these AMS before they were raised at the formal discussions. In his role as Chair of the Charter drafting committee, Tommy Koh innovated with the Assistants Group wherein the junior officers accompanying each delegation head were allowed to knock around with permutations of wordings for the different articles of the Charter beforehand. I facilitated this process by assigning seasoned ASEC staff members to help the Assistants. The senior officials from Cambodia and Laos were the front men in getting democracy, human rights and "people-oriented ASEAN" couched in acceptable terms.

The most astute move in drafting the Charter was played by Viet Nam: openly constructive but overly cautious behind the scenes. Hanoi wanted the Charter as it would strengthen ASEAN; hence relieving the pressure from China and providing more time for Viet Nam to further normalise ties with the United States. A number of Thai officials told me they also saw Vietnamese officials using the drafting process to exert "brotherly care" on Cambodia and Laos, and getting to know Myanmar better. At the same time, Hanoi worked on limiting the democratising nature of the Charter by warning ASEAN counterparts of the portents of a "people-centred ASEAN" leading eventually to the adoption of the more benign "people-oriented ASEAN".

During the drafting of the ASEAN Charter, the trust deficit among the AMS was obvious. There was unwillingness to let another member state dictate the future development of ASEAN. There was a lack of the big-picture consideration except that ASEAN would remain an inter-governmental organisation and not a supranational body. Indonesia and the Philippines went about their democratic song and dance as well as pro non-governmental organisation (NGO) stance unabash-edly. Even the middle-of-the-road Malaysian and Thai delegations were overwhelmed by the unrestrained ways of the Indonesian and Filipino negotiators. Fortunately, Tommy Koh and his opposite numbers from Malaysia and Thailand were able to persuade the competing interests on a compromise text.

Seeking Cohesion

My takeaway from the Charter, Community and Connectivity initiatives was an acceptance that ASEAN solidarity and unity remained elusive. It appeared that most of the AMS simply wished ASEAN could give each of them more benefit from time to time to justify their membership. They were happy with "live and let live". Few policy incumbents outside the CLMV countries remembered the Cold War situation in Southeast Asia and the geopolitical imperatives of that time which led to the founding of ASEAN. There was limited effort made by most officials to build on the achievements of ASEAN: shaping and sharing norms of inter-state behaviour; balancing the strategic interests and influences of states having an impact on the security and prosperity of the region; and seizing opportunities which preserved peace and stability for Southeast Asia. The AMS would likely stay together but it would be an imperfect association. Only common external threats such as the occupation of Cambodia by Viet Nam with the toppling of the Khmer Rouge and the 1997–1998 "tom-yam" financial crisis rallied the AMS into concerted actions. However, external challenges could no longer guarantee a cohesive ASEAN response as competing territorial claims in the South China Sea have demonstrated so far.

Nevertheless, the ASEAN show must go on. ASEAN had weathered difficult times in the past. The coming together of the AMS to establish the East Asia Summit as another ASEAN-led mechanism to manage power relations in Southeast Asia affirmed the capability of ASEAN to act strategically. Some experts claimed that the top-down nature of ASEAN decision-making, based on consensus and consultation, created an insurmountable obstacle going forward. Yet, ASEAN supporters argued that ASEAN is not unique in this respect. The problem is the belief among individual AMS that they need not change their national systems and operational ways to be in ASEAN. Some of the AMS point to ASEAN agreement on specific issues when the AMS could give and take on the lowest common denominator. However, the question should be: "is this enough?" Imagine the possibilities open to ASEAN acting in unison and tackling the challenges confronting them. There is a sense that the AMS tend to make decisions on short-term political expediency instead of the long-term well-being of ASEAN as a whole. It will probably be like this always, but ASEAN is the only one of its kind and the AMS will manage somehow.

ONG Keng Yong is Executive Deputy Chairman of the S. Rajaratnam School of International Studies at the Nanyang Technological University in Singapore. Concurrently, he is Ambassador-at-Large at the Singapore Ministry of Foreign Affairs, non-resident High Commissioner to Pakistan and non-resident Ambassador to Iran. Mr. Ong also serves as Chairman of the Singapore International Foundation (SIF).

Mr. Ong was High Commissioner of Singapore to Malaysia from 2011 to 2014. He served as Secretary-General of ASEAN, based in Jakarta, Indonesia from January 2003 to January 2008.

Mr. Ong started his diplomatic career in 1979 and was posted to the Singapore Embassies in Saudi Arabia, Malaysia and the United States of America. He was Singapore's High Commissioner to India and concurrently Ambassador to Nepal from 1996 to 1998. From September 1998 to December 2002, he was Press Secretary to the then Prime Minister of Singapore, Mr. Goh Chok Tong. At the same time, Mr. Ong held senior appointments in the Ministry of Information, Communications and the Arts, and the People's Association in Singapore. From 2008 to 2011, he served as Director of the Institute of Policy Studies (IPS) in the Lee Kuan Yew School of Public Policy at the National University of Singapore.

Mr. Ong graduated from the then University of Singapore with a LLB (Hons) and the Georgetown University (Washington DC, USA) with a MA in Arab Studies.

Role of the ASEAN Committee of Permanent Representatives

LIM Thuan Kuan

❧ ❦ ❧

Denigrated by many as "No Action, Talk Only" (NATO), ASEAN continues to bedevil and confuse its critics by its frustratingly slow but yet ever forward movement in its development as a regional organisation. In the earlier years, I would have classified myself as an adherent to the NATO school of thought, with the survival of the organisation itself being seen as a sign of success. Lest my views are misunderstood, ASEAN has been, and even to this day, continues to be a very useful organisation for the region. It managed to bring together a diverse set of countries, fostering a habit of consultation and close personal interactions at all levels, which in turn fostered peace and stability in the region. My reservations rested on the way the organisation had organised itself and its path towards progress. It was an organisation built on informality, with a lack of credible institutions. It was messy in its approach. In some ways, those were the very elements of its success, but how will it develop as it matures, as all organisations must, if it is to keep moving forward, much less survive, in the longer term? It is true that ASEAN has had successes. It spawned off the likes of ASEAN Regional Forum (ARF), ASEAN Defence Ministers' Meeting Plus (ADMM Plus), ASEAN+3 and the East Asia Summit (EAS) over the years, and in a sense, that has kept the organisation relevant, regardless of what one thinks of these entities. In a sense, ASEAN has built additional wings to its building. However, the foundation is still suspect. These "successes", if one can refer to them as such, do not really speak to the core of ASEAN, of how, going forward, it will develop in order to at least maintain some relevance in the strategic evolution of our region, apart from providing the settings for others to do so. The alternative is to continue to do things as we have always done and hope for the best.

For me, a sliver of hope for the organisation came with the promulgation of the ASEAN Charter. To be sure, ASEAN has not flipped overnight in grade just because of it. ASEAN is still messy, though perhaps maybe a little less so. There is still a preponderance to talk, but some action is taking place. There is still confusion, but there is now more understanding of what the confusion is about. I believe that a lot of the clearing of ASEAN's messiness, and with it the establishment of some form of coordination and cohesion, has and will continue to happen as ASEAN slowly fleshes out the requirements of the Charter. The Charter brought in huge changes, one of the biggest being the creation of new institutions and an attempt to rationalise its existing institutions. This is not as simplistic as it sounds, especially with a half century old organisation already steeped in its way of doing things, and of institutions, even at the apex, whose mandates do not sit and sync with reality. I once sat through a fascinating discussion between Foreign Minister George Yeo and then EU's High Representative for Common Foreign and Security Policy (CFSP) Javier Solana, and they were discussing the two paths towards organisation development — institutional or gradual evolution. And of course, there was no final conclusion. With the promulgation of the Charter, we could well see an ASEAN experimenting with both approaches.

Lest I be accused of being overly optimistic, let me just say that I see an opportunity because a clear path has been laid by the Charter to, inter alia, establish an organised structure that would lend itself to greater coordination, coherence and efficiency. A well-built ASEAN machine, one where its gears mesh, is critical to ASEAN's future development. Getting this done, which is a huge challenge in itself, is but just one part of the exercise. The other critical element is whether the ASEAN collective will over time progress economically such that it can stand its own ground, politically as well as economically.

To me, the Committee of Permanent Representatives (CPR), of which I was once a part of, is one of those newly created institutions which has the potential, over time, to develop into a game changer for

ASEAN. It is never easy to start an institution from scratch, and so it proved with the CPR. The very first challenge came even before its birth. There were views circulating then that the representative should perhaps be at the Counsellor level. The decision by ASEAN member countries that it should be headed by a full-fledged Ambassadorial grade representative did much to give the nascent institution a boost and a status to effect some change or make some difference. The initial phase of its existence was challenging as it sought to clarify its mandate and put in place a mode of operations for the work it was tasked to do. The former — its mandate — was the more challenging of the two. ASEAN practices and the way things were done had by then ossified, and we are here talking only about the Foreign Ministry side of the fence. The CPR, as configured, was essentially MFA-centred. It was intended to take over much of the work that was previously done by the ASEAN MFA Directors-General (DGs), and perhaps some aspects of the work done by the ASEAN Senior Officials Meeting (SOM). This was further complicated as the SOM had also by then taken over some of the work of the DGs and there was some duplication. Changes are never easy when one becomes accustomed to a certain way of doing things, much less having to give up part of one's work, along with the perks, to another. Such was the challenge faced by the CPR and it took some time for the issue to be sorted out and for the capitals to adapt to the changes wrought by the new kid on the block.

At the same time, being based in Jakarta, the CPR was brought into closer association with the ASEAN Secretariat (ASEC), which it was mandated to oversee. This brought its own set of challenges. For ASEC, having the CPR in close proximity and breathing down its neck on a regular and continuing basis was never ever going to be a walk in the park. Expectations and workload increased as the CPR met regularly, to be briefed by ASEC officials across a whole host of issues, including the Administration of the organisation. For the CPR, ASEC was the primary core of all ASEAN activities, it needed to be well managed and effective. But there were a whole host of problems, including lack of resources with some ASEAN Member States being unwilling to increase the budget. This is understandable. However, you do get what you pay for, and in my time, ASEC, to be fair, was stretched.

As things settled, the CPR began to focus on its substantive work schedule, including meeting with the Dialogue Partners. Issues which the ASEAN MFA DGs used to handle were being taken up in the weekly CPR meetings. Having ten countries sitting around the table sorting out issues on a constant basis was always going to be more effective than the earlier practice of issues being settled only when periodic meetings of the ASEAN DGs take place, or through the correspondence route. Consider, for example, the decision to have the ASEAN flag flying alongside the national flags of the ASEAN countries in all our Embassies abroad. I would have thought this would take ages to be decided, but to my surprise, it was agreed to in only a couple of meetings. By comparison, the rules on the display of the flag took an inordinately longer time to address! Our Dialogue Partners became more sensitised to the role of the CPR as it related to their dealings with ASEAN, and from a situation of their bilateral Ambassador handling such ASEAN-related issues, we progressed to having our Dialogue Partners each beginning to send a separate Ambassador to ASEAN to Jakarta.

As time progressed, the CPR began to look towards issues which went beyond what the ASEAN MFA DGs were tasked to do. There was a realisation that the CPR was charged with all three pillars, and not just the political/security pillar which was the domain of the MFAs. Tentative attempts were made to get the focal points of the other two pillars to become more involved and to use the CPR as the channel to handle issues. Of the two pillars, the economic pillar was more structured having Senior Economic Officials Meeting (SEOM) as the focal point, while the socio-cultural pillar was more diffused. The underlying rationale was that while they could use the CPR as a channel, they needed to be represented within the CPR given the nature of the issues they handled which were outside the expertise of the MFA-centred CPR. The key was to have all ten member countries send their representatives to the CPR so that issues under their purview could be addressed and decisions taken in Jakarta. There was some bite from SEOM during my time as I understand that some discussions had taken place, even addressing issues such as the status of an economic representative within the CPR. However, efforts fell by the wayside with, I think, changes of personalities within SEOM. In life, timing is everything and I guess it was not meant to be, then. But I think that having the second and third pillars represented within the CPR is a question of "when", rather than "if". And when it happens, it will also signal a sea change for ASEAN in the way the other two pillars do their work and the speed in which issues are addressed and decisions taken, with attendant implications for our Dialogue Partners.

There are other aspects to the workings of the CPR that I have not addressed. For one, the collegiate atmosphere among the ten representatives played a large part in getting issues settled. There was more give and take. That said, I hope the above gives a flavour of how the CPR started and where I think it will be heading … eventually. It will mean a more efficient and coordinated ASEAN. We have to bear in mind however that this is but only one aspect of ASEAN. Important as it is, it is but one cog in the ASEAN engine. There are other facets and challenges which ASEAN faces in the immediate future which may well undermine the natural progression of the organisation. But that is an issue for another time.

LIM Thuan Kuan is Singapore's High Commissioner to the Republic of India. He joined the Ministry of Foreign Affairs in August 1984. Within the Ministry, he covered several portfolios including Malaysia, Indonesia and Brunei, the United States, Public Affairs and Regional Policy before taking charge of the South Asia, Africa, Middle East and Latin America Directorate (2000–2002); the Southeast Asia Directorate (2002–2004) and the ASEAN Directorate (2004–2005). He was the Singapore Ambassador to Vietnam (2005–2008) before becoming the first Singapore Permanent Representative to ASEAN (2009–2013). He was awarded the Public Administration Medal (Silver) and the Long Service Medal in 2007.

De-Mystifying the Committee of
Permanent Representatives to ASEAN (CPR)

TAN Hung Seng

✦ ✦ ✦

"Why does Singapore have two Ambassadors in Jakarta?"
"Do you work for the ASEAN Secretariat?"
"What is the purpose of the CPR?"
Since assuming my position in August 2013, as Singapore's second Permanent Representative to ASEAN (PR), I have encountered these questions on innumerable occasions, not just from Indonesians, but also from Singaporeans and even fellow diplomats. Seemingly easy questions, they actually touch on key issues relating to the origin of the CPR, its roles and functions, as well as the CPR's relations with other ASEAN organs. More importantly, these questions underscore the fact that the CPR continues to be a relatively unknown entity, whose existence and purpose remain a mystery to a great many ASEAN citizens. Hence, I hope that this short essay will, in a modest way, shed some light on how the CPR has evolved since its establishment in 2009.

Genesis of the CPR

Although the CPR was established in 2009, the idea for such a body had been bandied about since the 1980s. The idea was "first mooted in a report of the 1982-1983 Task Force for the Strengthening of the ASEAN Secretariat chaired by Mr. Anand Panyarachun of Thailand, and re-surfaced in the 1991–1992 report by the panel headed by Tan

Sri Ghazali Shafie of Malaysia."[1] The idea finally gained traction, when ASEAN Member States (AMS) accepted the recommendation of the Eminent Persons Group on the ASEAN Charter (EPG) to appoint Permanent Representatives (PRs) based in Jakarta to represent the AMS.[2] Consequently, the ASEAN Charter, which came into force in 2008, stipulated that "*Each ASEAN Member State (AMS) shall appoint a Permanent Representative to ASEAN with the rank of Ambassador based in Jakarta*". Hence, the establishment of the CPR took more than three decades, from the time the idea was first mooted in the 1980s, to its incorporation into the ASEAN Charter in 2008, and finally, the appointment of the first PRs in 2009.

Singapore enjoys the distinction of being the first AMS to appoint a PR to ASEAN.[3] This was followed in quick succession by other AMS and Dialogue Partners. Currently, all AMS, except Cambodia, have appointed dedicated PRs to ASEAN, while nine out of the ten Dialogue Partners (with the exception of Russia), have appointed dedicated Ambassadors to ASEAN.[4] Since 2009, the composition of the CPR has undergone significant changes. By the time I assumed post in 2013, most of the first-generation PRs had moved on. The current CPR, which comprises second- and third-generation PRs, is different in two key aspects. *First*, unlike the first-generation PRs, the current batch comprises mainly first-time Ambassadors. Only three of the ten PRs have had earlier stints as Heads of Mission. *Second*, the gender balance has improved markedly, with four AMS (Brunei, Malaysia, Philippines and Thailand), and four Dialogue Partners (Australia, Canada, New Zealand and the United States), being represented by female PRs/ Ambassadors to ASEAN. This reflects positively on the progress that ASEAN has made in terms of gender mainstreaming.

[1] Walter Woon, *The ASEAN Charter: A Commentary* (Singapore: NUS Press, 2015), 130.
[2] Report of the Eminent Persons Group on the ASEAN Charter (EPG), para 38.
[3] Ambassador Lim Thuan Kuan served as Singapore's first PR to ASEAN from 2009 to August 2013.
[4] There are indications that Cambodia and Russia are considering the appointment of a dedicated PR/Ambassador to ASEAN.

Evolution of the CPR

The role and functions of the CPR are defined by two documents, namely, the ASEAN Charter, and the Terms of Reference (TOR) of the CPR. Specifically, Article 12 of the ASEAN Charter serves as the cornerstone upon which the CPR's role and functions are constructed. However, since Article 12 only sets out the broad parameters of the CPR's role and functions,[5] the task fell on the first-generation PRs to draft the TOR, which was approved by the 41st ASEAN Ministerial Meeting (AMM) in July 2008. Since then, the CPR's role and functions have expanded significantly.

For a better sense of how the CPR's role and functions have evolved, it is instructive to compare the agenda of the CPR's inaugural meeting on 21 May 2009, with the agenda of a recent CPR meeting on 29 September 2016. At its inaugural meeting seven years ago, the CPR was preoccupied with issues such as the frequency of its meetings, the appropriate level of representation, and whether the ASEAN Secretary-General should be present. In contrast, the agenda of the CPR's meeting in 2016 covered a broad range of substantive issues that included follow-up on the outcomes of the 28th and 29th ASEAN Summits and Related Summits, matters related to ASEAN-China and ASEAN-EU Dialogue Relations, East Asia Summit (EAS), ASEAN Connectivity and a host of issues related to the operations of the ASEAN Secretariat (ASEC). Evidently, the CPR's role and functions have evolved since 2009, and three key trends are worth highlighting.

First, the CPR has consolidated its role as the focal point to *"facilitate ASEAN's cooperation with external partners"*. This function has

---

[5](a) Support the work of the ASEAN Community Councils and ASEAN Sectoral Ministerial Bodies.

(b) Coordinate with ASEAN National Secretariats and other ASEAN Sectoral Ministerial Bodies.

(c) Liaise with the Secretary-General of ASEAN and the ASEAN Secretariat on all subjects relevant to its work.

(d) Facilitate ASEAN cooperation with external partners.

(e) Perform such other functions as may be determined by the ASEAN Coordinating Council.

grown in tandem with the growing number of Dialogue Partners that have appointed dedicated Ambassadors to ASEAN. Although each AMS takes turn to act as the country co-ordinator for one Dialogue Partner, the CPR is collectively responsible for ensuring that the overall relationship and cooperation with the Dialogue Partners proceed smoothly across all the three ASEAN Community Pillars, namely, political-security, economic, and social-cultural. The CPR is also responsible for negotiating the five-year Plans of Action (POAs), which serve as the roadmaps for ASEAN's engagement with the Dialogue Partners. 2015 was a particularly busy year as the CPR negotiated and concluded seven POAs over a 12-month period. In addition to the annual Joint Coordination Committee (JCC) meeting between the CPR and Dialogue Partners, the CPR and Dialogue Partner Ambassadors interact frequently. A number of Dialogue Partner Ambassadors, such as Australia, Canada, New Zealand and the United States, make it a point to invite the CPR to meet their senior officials visiting Jakarta. Hence, I have had the pleasure of meeting a diverse spectrum of foreign interlocutors, ranging from admirals to scholars, social activists to politicians. The CPR attaches great importance to such engagements as they provide an excellent opportunity for the CPR to get a sense of how our important Dialogue Partners view ASEAN and to share with them our take on developments in our region. But the highlight for the CPR must surely be the annual photo opportunity with US President Barack Obama. It is President Obama's personal way of signalling the importance that he attaches to ASEAN.

Second, the CPR has been entrusted with more substantive responsibilities, particularly, in three specific areas. *One*, the CPR has assumed the responsibility of negotiating key outcome documents arising from Leaders-level meetings.[6] These time-consuming negotiations are led by the country co-ordinator and involve two steps; first, to secure ASEAN

---

[6] In 2016, for example, the negotiated the Sunnyland Principles with the United States, the Sochi Declaration with Russia, and the Joint Statement of the 19th ASEAN-China Summit to commemorate the 25th Anniversary of ASEAN-China Dialogue Relations with China was negotiates by the CPR.

consensus and once that has been achieved, the second step is to lead the negotiations with the concerned Dialogue Partner. In most cases, 90 to 95% of the draft outcome document can be finalised by the CPR in Jakarta, leaving only a few paragraphs dealing with contentious issues such as the South China Sea dispute necessitating negotiations at Senior Officials' Meeting (SOM) or Ministerial-level. The first-ever Leaders-level outcome document that the CPR succeeded in finalising, without escalating to a higher level, was the Joint Statement of the 19th ASEAN-China Summit to Commemorate the 25th Anniversary of ASEAN-China Dialogue Relations. *Two*, the CPR has been tasked with monitoring and implementing the recommendations made by the High Level Task Force on Strengthening the ASEAN Secretariat and Reviewing ASEAN Organs (HLTF). Since the HLTF's recommenda-tions were adopted by the 25th ASEAN Summit in Nay Pyi Taw at the end of 2014, the CPR has worked closely with ASEC to implement measures to strengthen ASEAN by streamlining and improving its processes, and coordination among various ASEAN organs, as well as strengthening ASEC. One of the most important measures that the CPR has successfully implemented was the enhancement of ASEC's system of remuneration, which has helped to retain talents. Although it is still unable to match other regional organisations such as the Asian Development Bank (ADB), the enhanced remuneration system has improved staff morale and made ASEC a more attractive employer. *Three*, the CPR was recently tasked to scope the exercise to update the ASEAN Charter, which is due for a review.[7] This important exercise process, which will have significant and long lasting impact on ASEAN, is being spearheaded by the Philippines during its 2017 ASEAN Chairmanship.

Third, the CPR has taken on additional roles since 2009. In tandem with the pace of ASEAN Community building, the CPR has been called upon to assume more responsibilities. Consequently, all the PRs wear multiple hats. At the minimum, all the ten PRs wear four additional "hats", as their national representatives on the ASEAN Connectivity

---

[7] Article 50 of the ASEAN Charter states that "*This Charter may be reviewed five years after its entry into force or as otherwise determined by the ASEAN Summit.*"

Coordinating Committee (ACCC), the Initiative for ASEAN Integration (IAI) Taskforce, the ASEAN Foundation's Board of Trustees (BOT), and the East Asia Summit (EAS) Ambassadors' Meeting in Jakarta. Several others, including myself, wear seven "hats". In addition to the CPR, ACCC, IAI Taskforce, ASEAN Foundation BOT and EAS Ambassadors' Meeting, we represent our countries on the ASEAN Institute of Peace and Reconciliation (AIPR) Governing Council and the ASEAN-China Centre Joint Council.

Challenges Facing the CPR — Empower, Equip, Entrust

Even as the role and functions of the CPR have expanded since 2009, we should remember that it is still a fairly young ASEAN organ. The CPR is still growing and trying to find its feet. Going forward, the CPR faces three key challenges. *First*, AMS must continue to empower the CPR. Essentially, AMS can be divided into two groups, namely, those that keep their PRs on a short leash; and those that want to empower the CPR so that it can fulfil this mandate as laid out in the ASEAN Charter. This dichotomy dates to the genesis of the CPR. Unfortunately, not all AMS were equally enthusiastic or convinced of the CPR's value and utility. The following observation, made by Brunei's representative on the HLTF to draft the ASEAN Charter, Pengiran Dato Paduka Osman Patra, is particularly revealing: "*Frankly, several members were not particularly convinced about how the potential of this Committee would be realised unless the capitals of ASEAN are ready to empower and entrust full responsibilities to their PRs in Jakarta.*"[8]

Second, AMS must equip their PR Missions with adequate manpower resources in two important areas. *One*, AMS should ensure that their PR Missions have enough officers to handle the growing range of issues and number of meetings. In order to keep pace, it has become fairly common for the CPR Working Group (CPRWG) to hold concurrent meetings, which is possible only if all the PR Missions have sufficient

---

[8]Pengiran Dato Paduka Osman Patra, "Heart Labour", in *Making of the ASEAN Charter*, eds. Tommy Koh, Rosario G. Manalo and Walter Woon (Singapore: World Scientific, 2009), 13–14.

officers.[9] *Two*, it is high time for AMS to second officers from the AEC and ASCC Pillars to their PR Missions. Although the secondment of officers from the other Pillars was a key recommendation of the HLTF on Strengthening the ASEAN Secretariat and Reviewing ASEAN Organs, which has also been endorsed by ASEAN Leaders, AMS have been reluctant to implement it. This has severely handicapped the CPR as it is unable to fulfil the role that the drafters of the ASEAN Charter have envisaged for it to be "*a coordinating body cutting across all three pillars*".[10] It has also diminished the ability of the CPR to fully engage the Dialogue Partners' Missions to ASEAN, many of which include officers from all the three ASEAN Community Pillars[11]. If this short-coming is not rectified in the near future, the Dialogue Partners' Missions may begin to question the credibility and utility of the CPR as an interlocutor.

Third, AMS should continue to entrust the CPR to take on more substantive roles and responsibilities. Expectedly, this will be a slow and continuous process as the ASEAN capitals adjust to the existence of the CPR. At the same time, the CPR must continue to earn the trust of their capitals by delivering concrete outcomes. Fundamentally, some ASEAN capitals continue to be wary of the possibility that the CPR could erode their roles. As ASEAN Charter drafter, Prof Walter Woon, had observed, some AMS were "*concerned that the role of the Senior Officials Meeting (SOM) and directors-general of ASEAN affairs in the foreign ministries would be weakened*". However, as the pace of ASEAN Community building accelerates, the CPR, being the only standing ASEAN body, is well placed to take on more responsibilities and build on its track record of being able to deliver.

---

[9] The number of CPR/CPRWG meetings have increased from 136 in 2010 to 281 in 2015.

[10] Walter Woon, *The ASEAN Charter: A Commentary* (Singapore: NUS Press, 2015), 133.

[11] The American, Australian, Chinese, Japanese and Korean Missions to ASEAN are well-resourced, with officers representing all the three ASEAN Community Pillars. These Dialogue Partners are using their Missions to ASEAN as a "one-stop center" for all ASEAN-related issues. A Japanese Ambassador to ASEAN had characterised his Mission as a "mini Kasumigaseki".

Conclusion

Hopefully, this short essay has helped to de-mystify the CPR and provide some insights into its role and functions, as well as the answers to the three questions that were posed at the beginning.

- Singapore has two Ambassadors in Jakarta because the Ambassador to Indonesia handles Singapore-Indonesia relations, while the PR to ASEAN represents Singapore's interests in ASEAN.
- No, the Singapore PR to ASEAN does not work for the ASEAN Secretariat; he is Singapore's representative to the CPR.
- The purpose of the CPR, in a nutshell, is to enhance ASEAN's efficiency and effectiveness.

TAN Hung Seng has been serving as Singapore's Permanent Representative to ASEAN since 9 August 2013. Prior to his current appointment, Mr. Tan served as Singapore's Ambassador to the Arab Republic of Egypt, with concurrent accreditation to Libya and the State of Kuwait. Mr. Tan studied at the National University of Singapore, and obtained a post-graduate degree from the School of Oriental and African Studies (SOAS), University of London. Mr. Tan has worked in various capacities in the Ministry of Foreign Affairs on issues related to International Organisations, ASEAN/ASEAN Regional Forum and the Middle East. His overseas postings included two earlier stints in Egypt as well as a posting in Bangkok. He was awarded the Public Administration Medal (Silver) in 2011 and the Long Service Medal in 2013. Mr. Tan is married to Madam Kayo Suzuki and they have two daughters.

Singapore and the ASEAN Secretariat: A Marriage Made in Heaven

Kishore MAHBUBANI

ASEAN is a living, breathing modern miracle.[1] It has brought peace and prosperity to one of the most difficult and diverse corners of planet earth, the Balkans of Asia. In the process, one of the biggest beneficiaries has been Singapore, a modern global city surrounded and protected by the ecosystem of peace crafted by ASEAN. My new book on ASEAN documents how this ecosystem was created.

Having benefitted so much from ASEAN, what is Singapore doing to repay ASEAN? The honest answer is that Singapore has done a lot. A lot of the political and intellectual leadership that has driven ASEAN's success has come from Singapore. However, even though Singapore has done a lot, it has not done enough. The time has therefore come for Singapore to reciprocate and present ASEAN with a big gift.

It will be very easy for Singapore to present ASEAN with a big gift. Singapore is very strong in one area where ASEAN is very weak. All Singapore has to do is to share its strengths with ASEAN. And what is this area? Singapore is very strong in building its institutional capacity. ASEAN is very weak in developing its institutional capacity. Indeed, various studies have shown that the weakness of the ASEAN Secretariat is crippling ASEAN's ability to grow and develop.

---

[1] Center for International Relations and Sustainable Development, "ASEAN as a Living, Breathing Modern Miracle CIRSD (2015)", http://www.cirsd.org/en/horizons/horizons-winter-2015--issue-no2/asean-as-a-living-breathing-modern-miracle

The ASEAN countries have long been aware of the need to develop and strengthen the ASEAN Secretariat. Deepak Nair has documented how the ASEAN countries accepted the recommendations of the United Nations Development Programme (UNDP)-funded five-member "Panel of Eminent Persons" on how to strengthen the ASEAN Secretariat at the ASEAN Summit in Singapore as far back as January 1992.[2]

Twelve years later, the ASEAN Leaders issued a special "Declaration on Strengthening the ASEAN Secretariat" on 12 November 2014. In it, they reaffirmed their "commitment" to strengthening ASEAN's institutional capacity and to "strengthening the ASEAN Secretariat". Yet, the ASEAN Secretariat remains miserably weak.

Many observers of ASEAN have commented on the weaknesses of the ASEAN Secretariat. Joshua Kurlantzick said in an article for the Council of Foreign Relations blog in September 2012, "Many leaders in Indonesia and Singapore, the two most important ASEAN members, have started to see the downside of a weak secretariat. For these nations, one option in the face of a weak secretariat would be simply to engage with other world powers bilaterally, or through other organisations like the G-20 or the Organization of Islamic Cooperation, a temptation both Indonesia and Singapore have indulged in."[3]

So what can Singapore do? Ambassador Tommy Koh, my guru, has always advised me to make three points. Let me therefore recommend three things Singapore can do. First, it can make a national commitment to strengthening the ASEAN Secretariat. Second, it can create a new means of financing the ASEAN Secretariat based on the well-accepted UN principle of "capacity to pay". Third, it can, through a process of osmosis, share its genius of developing strong institutions with the ASEAN Secretariat.

All this has to begin first with a strong national commitment. Why is this commitment important? The simple reason is that most Singapore policymakers believe that the goal of strengthening the

---

[2] Nair, D. "A Strong Secretariat, a Strong ASEAN? A Re-evaluation", *ISEAS Perspective*, Issue 2016, No. 8 (2016): 5.

[3] Joshua Kurlantzick, "Why ASEAN Will Stay Weak", *CFR*, http://blogs.cfr.org/asia/2012/09/04/why-asean-will-stay-weak/.

ASEAN Secretariat is "Mission Impossible". Since the Secretariat is owned by ten ASEAN countries, many in Singapore believe that it will be impossible for Singapore to single-handedly reform it. Indeed I can predict the reaction of Singapore policymakers when they read this suggestion. They will respond with a condescending sneer and say "there goes Kishore, with another one of his wild ideas".

Nevertheless, even with the sneer remaining on their faces, they should ask themselves how their contemporaries regarded some of the bold visions of our founding fathers. When Dr. Goh Keng Swee proposed an industrial estate in Jurong, he was greeted with a sneer. The estate was called Dr. Goh's folly. When the idea surfaced of creating a world class airline, it was also greeted with a sneer. How could a country with no airspace create a world-class airline? And why did our founding fathers succeed? Because they had stout hearts and bold visions.

The sad truth about Singapore policymakers is that these stout hearts have been replaced with faint hearts. We have created an ecosystem of risk-aversion which discourages bold and risky initiatives. Clearly, any effort to strengthen the ASEAN Secretariat is a bold and risky initiative. And it could fail. Since senior Singapore policymakers don't want to touch anything that might fail, we are not likely to get any champion today for such a risky venture.

This is why we need a strong national commitment. Since Singapore is clearly a huge beneficiary of ASEAN's success, it is a no-brainer that Singapore should try to strengthen the ASEAN Secretariat. This is a decision that must be made at the highest level and implemented with a clear recognition that the mission might fail. But what would Singapore lose by trying and failing? And what would Singapore gain by trying and succeeding? Isn't the decision obvious?

The second step is to acknowledge that one reason why the ASEAN Secretariat is weak is because it has been deprived of resources. The ASEAN Secretariat has to service the 630 million people of ASEAN. Yet, its total budget of US$17 million in 2015[4] is smaller than the

---

[4] David Pilling. "The Fiction of a Unified, Harmonised ASEAN", *Financial Times*, December 10, 2015, https://www.ft.com/content/cba00b70-9dcf-11e5-8ce1-f6219 b685d74.html

budget of People's Association[5] (S$900 million or about US$667 million in 2015) which only services four million people. The EU Secretariat budget is enormous at €145 billion in 2015.[6] ASEAN should not copy the EU but does its budget have to be 0.0103% of the EU budget? Why is the ASEAN budget so small? The reasons are complicated but one clear reason is that ASEAN insists on the principle of equal payment by all ten member states. In the year when the ASEAN Secretariat was established, 1976, ASEAN had only five members. Their national capabilities were quite similar. Hence, they agreed on the simple principle of equal payments to the ASEAN Secretariat to avoid squabbling over who should pay more and who should pay less. At that time, it was a generous gesture on the part of Singapore as it had agreed that despite its small population of 2.293 million, it would pay an equal share as Indonesia, which had a population of 132.4 million, 60 times the population of Singapore.

By 2014, ASEAN had ten member states. The disparity between the ten states had also grown enormously. Laos and Cambodia, for example, had GDPs of US$11.9 billion and US$16.7 billion in 2014, in contrast to Indonesia's GDP, which stood at US$888 billion or 74 times larger than the smallest ASEAN GDP. This immediately creates a structural problem which stunts the growth of the ASEAN Secretariat. By insisting on equal payments, we are condemning the ASEAN Secretariat to permanent stunted growth, because the annual payments for the Secretariat cannot exceed the capacity to pay of the *poorest* ASEAN Member State.

So can we adopt a different principle to determine payments to the UN? Since the ten ASEAN members have accepted this principle of "capacity to pay" for the UN, which is a far less important organisation to their national interests than ASEAN is, why not agree on the same principle of "capacity to pay" for the ASEAN Secretariat? Fortunately, the

---

[5] Rachel Au-Yong, "Parliament: People's Association Has to Cater to More Sophisticated Population", *The Straits Times*, April 14, 2016, http://www.straitstimes.com/singapore/parliament-peoples-association-has-to-cater-to-more-sophisticated-population

[6] "European Union: Budget", *European Union* 2015, http://europa.eu/pol/financ/index_en

ASEAN countries will not have to reinvent the wheel to determine how much each should pay to the ASEAN Secretariat. There is a very simple mathematical solution. The ten ASEAN countries should pool together the respective percentages they pay to the UN Secretariat. In 2014, the ten ASEAN countries paid the following percentages to the UN budget: Brunei — 0.026%; Cambodia — 0.004%; Indonesia — 0.346%; Laos — 0.002%; Malaysia — 0.281%; Myanmar — 0.010%; Singapore — 0.384%; Thailand — 0.239%; the Philippines — 0.154%; and Vietnam — 0.042%. If we were to adopt this principle of capacity to pay, we could significantly increase the budget of the ASEAN Secretariat without worrying whether the poorest ASEAN Member States could pay its portion.

An Asian Development Bank (ADB) report has also strongly recommended that ASEAN reconsider its principle of equal funding from all ten members. It says: "It is clear that the way contributions are currently collected does not allow meeting ASEAN's increased financing needs. Anchoring funding on equal shares not only hampers budget growth: it also makes the group intrinsically dependent on external funding from international donors. In practice, while funds are typically available, donor and ASEAN priorities do not always match. Thus, ASEAN is unable to independently accomplish its plans and realise its strategies as decisions are distorted by accommodating requests from the many external stakeholders contributing to the association's budget. If ASEAN is to become a mature and thriving institution, member countries should realise that the principle used in funding the budget is obsolete."[7] Since Singapore clearly has one of the most rational governments in the world, it should take the lead in accepting this advice from ADB and work on implementing the UN principle of capacity to pay for the ASEAN Secretariat. In the long term, Singapore's share would continue to diminish as our economy will never grow as fast as our neighbours'. Hence this formula is also in the long term interest of Singapore. Please see Table A. It shows that Singapore's share of ASEAN GDP is going to decline significantly from 12% in 2015 to 6.4% in 2030.

---

[7] "ASEAN 2030: Toward a Borderless Economic Community", *ADB*, http://www.adb.org/sites/default/files/publication/159312/adbi-asean-2030-borderless-economic-community.pdf

Table A[8]

ASEAN: The Next Horizon

	Population (million)		GDP (US$ billion)		GDP per capita (US$)	
	2015	2030	2015	2030	2015	2030
Brunei	0.42	0.5	13	26	30,942	49,958
Cambodia	15.4	17	18	54	1,198	3,132
Indonesia	255.5	280	858	2,105	3,357	7,528
Laos*	6.9	8	13	32	1,838	4,160
Malaysia	30.5	37	294	694	9,657	18,619
Myanmar	52.5	54	65	254	1,246	4,683
Philippines	101.6	126	290	772	2,850	6,114
Singapore	5.5	6	292	356	52,744	59,578
Thailand	69	73	396	814	5,737	11,109
Vietnam	91.7	101	193	436	2,109	4,292
Asean	628.9	704	2,432	5,531	3,867	7,857

Note: *Based on International Monetary Fund World Economic Outlook data as official country statistics are not yet available.

The third step that Singapore can take to strengthen the ASEAN Secretariat is the easiest step. It can try to influence the working culture of the ASEAN Secretariat through a process of osmosis. In short, all it has to do is to share the excellent working culture of its institutions with the ASEAN institutions.

How can this osmosis happen? There are many simple steps that can be taken. Firstly, Singapore has an unusually good supply of senior civil servants, including permanent secretaries, who have retired relatively early, in their early sixties. They still remain active and dynamic. The Singapore government can compensate them well and then offer their services on a voluntary basis to the ASEAN Secretariat. This is not new. Other organisations have done this. For example, retired American businessmen have set up SCORE (previously called the

---

[8]The graphic first appeared in a *Straits Times*' article "ASEAN — the New Growth Frontier", by Jacqueline Woo. The article can be accessed at http://www.straitstimes.com/business/asean-the-new-growth-frontier

Service Corps of Retired Executives) which was founded in 1964. They have provided their counselling services to more than 8.5 million clients. A study by SBA Entrepreneurship Education says that SCORE's work helps create an estimated 25,000 new jobs annually in America. It is also affiliated with the US Small Business Administration. In short, informal counselling can improve the performance of the ASEAN Secretariat.

Secondly, Singapore can also offer free training courses to ASEAN Secretariat officials in Singapore organisations. Singapore is blessed to have many excellent world-class training institutions including the Civil Service College, Lee Kuan Yew School of Public Policy, NUS and SMU Business schools, INSEAD to name a few. It is in Singapore's national interest to use its Singapore Cooperation Programme funds to provide training courses in Singapore for ASEAN civil servants. The benefits will not be felt overnight. However, over time, the osmosis will happen and the working culture and efficiency of the ASEAN Secretariat will improve.

Thirdly, Singapore can also fund a study to assess the organisational health of the ASEAN Secretariat. It is possible that some of the leading consulting firms like McKinsey, Bain, Accenture or Deloitte, may offer to do it pro bono. Such a study will provide a baseline of where the ASEAN Secretariat is. It could also offer pointers on the areas of priority that could be worked on.

In short, despite the current assumptions of many Singaporean policymakers, the goal of reforming the ASEAN Secretariat is not "Mission Impossible". It will be difficult. We will also have to be very sensitive to the political currents at play in the ASEAN Secretariat. Yet, Singapore has undertaken even more difficult assignments and succeeded when our policymakers had stout hearts. Let us therefore use this exercise of reforming the ASEAN Secretariat to demonstrate that our policymakers continue to have stout hearts.

Kishore MAHBUBANI is the Dean of the Lee Kuan Yew School of Public Policy, NUS. Concurrently, he serves in the Boards and Councils of institutions around the world. Before that, he served in the Singapore Foreign Service for 33 years (from 1971 to 2004) — notably as Singapore's Ambassador to the UN, President of the UN Security Council (in January 2001 and May 2002), and Permanent Secretary at the Foreign Ministry (from 1993 to 1998). He speaks and writes extensively on public policy issues, and has authored six books: *Can Asians Think, Beyond the Age of Innocence, The New Asian Hemisphere, The Great Convergence* (selected by *Financial Times* as one of the best books of 2013*), Can Singapore Survive,* and *The ASEAN Miracle.* He was selected as one of *Foreign Policy's* Top Global Thinkers in 2010 and 2011, as well as one of *Prospect* magazine's top 50 world thinkers for 2014.

Why Did I Join the ASEAN Secretariat?
A Singaporean's Perspective

LEE Yoong Yoong

✦ ✦ ✦

I grew up during the privileged 1980s and 1990s when ASEAN's original mission to maintain regional peace and neutrality amid communist threats and other external political manoeuvrings had largely disappeared. As far as I could recall, ASEAN was a heterogeneous grouping of Southeast Asian states with diverse levels of political, economic and social development. While ASEAN Member States respectfully minded their own businesses and developments, nothing substantive was ever achieved other than symbolic pictures of leaders doing the customary "ASEAN-Way" handshakes.

I had my first real dose of ASEAN and the work of the ASEAN Secretariat (ASEC) when I entered the Singapore Public Service, joining the Economic Development Board (EDB) of Singapore (from 1995 to 2002) — started as an Executive Officer (EO) of Resource Development, and subsequently, in Asia-Pacific Operations. The latter appointment was particularly relevant in laying the foundation of my regional knowledge. As the EO in Asia-Pacific Operations, I had to represent Singapore's interests in the ASEAN Working Group on Industrial Cooperation (WGIC), of which the mandate was to promote intra-ASEAN industrial collaboration beyond just equity participation, but rather, to have industrial projects integrated in a vertical manner for production units specialising in the manufacture of parts and components located in different

ASEAN Member States. Incidentally, it was during this time that I first visited the ASEC office in Jakarta. Little did I know then that I would join this important organisation one day.

My First Spell in the ASEAN Secretariat

I left EDB to pursue a Master's degree in International Relations in the Nanyang Technological University (NTU) from 2002 to 2003. My one-year study coincided with the endorsement of the Declaration of ASEAN Concord II, also known as Bali Concord II, during the Ninth ASEAN Summit in Indonesia. The signing of the Bali Concord II by the ASEAN Leaders was a historic step towards regional integration, and paved the way to forming the ASEAN Community we have today.

Feeling excited, I began to read up and undertake more academic analysis on ASEAN, including its history, its vision, its relevance, and perhaps more significantly, the role of the ASEC. Through research, I realised that ASEAN is almost everything I had imagined it not to be. Far from being a pomp and show organisation, efforts had gone into the formulation of concrete regional policies ranging from political security to economic development to socio-cultural issues that accom-modated the disparate interests of ASEAN Member States.

Just before graduation in mid-2003, I wrote to Ambassador Ong Keng Yong — who had already assumed the post of Secretary-General (SG) of ASEAN — and sought his approval for me to do a three-month internship in ASEC. I thought such an internship attachment would serve me well in terms of knowledge and awareness creation on the role of ASEC in the entire ASEAN value-chain. To my relief, Ambassador Ong agreed, and I was assigned to join the Bureau for Economic Integration (BEI), which was the predecessor of the ASEAN Economic Community Department (AECD) in ASEC today. I remembered being mentored by a fellow Singaporean who was the Assistant Director (ADR) in BEI. For the next three months, I carried out research and wrote two concept papers — one on the possible expansion of the ASEAN Plus Three platform, and another on the relevance of "2 Plus X" vis-à-vis "10-minus-X" — for SG's Ong's perusal.

Upon the completion of my internship in end-January 2004, I returned to Singapore and pondered what to do next. A month later, I received an email from the Human Resources Division in ASEC, informing me that there was an opening of Senior Officer (SO) position in various Divisions within ASEC, and that I should apply if I was interested. I went through the interview process, and on 12 April 2004, began my life-long affiliation with ASEC, started off as the SO BEI, handling the regional cooperation in trade, investment, industrial cooperation and free-trade area (FTA) agreement. In less than one and a half years, I was promoted to head the Infrastructure Unit, overseeing the regional integration of Transport (Land, Air, Sea, and Facilitation), Energy, and Minerals.

For the next few years, I travelled almost every week, making official mission-trips to different parts of ASEAN and to Dialogue Partners, including China, India, Japan, Republic of Korea, Australia, New Zealand, and the European Union (EU) HQ in Brussels. All of these trips were not just eye-opening experiences. More importantly, I felt I was part of the process in contributing to the growth and expansion of international spaces and ties for ASEAN with the rest of the world.

I left ASEC in August 2008, and returned to Singapore due to personal reasons. While it was unfortunate that I had to cut short my stay — especially with the new SG Surin Pitsuwan at the helm, I thought it was certainly an enriching four years as I looked back, because I got to witness the emergence of ASEAN as a geopolitical and economic bloc. I was extremely proud to know by this time, many scholars and academics began to consider ASEAN as the second most successful regional grouping project after the EU, given that I had played a role in advancing the ASEAN brand name globally.

In my next few career moves, I continued to work on ASEAN and kept a lookout on the happenings from the ASEC. I maintained my network of friends and colleagues through social media like Facebook and caught up with them whenever they travelled to Singapore for official missions. They were a source of reference and information to me, in particular, on the latest development in ASEAN. Deep down in me, I know I would be back in ASEC one day because I simply love this organisation too much not to be directly involved in its work.

Second Spell

That opportunity came in April 2015, when I re-joined ASEC as the Head of the Executive Support Division in the Office of the Secretary-General (OSG). My role was to provide the administrative, analytical and research support to the incumbent SG, including the drafting and vetting of speeches, talking points and briefing notes, and letters cum official correspondences. For the next one year, I was able to have a helicopter view of matters and issues which warranted the SG's attention. Being in OSG, it meant that, sometimes I would be required to work on cross-sectoral/cross-pillar issues, e.g. empowerment of women entrepreneurship (which involved AECD and the ASEAN Socio-Cultural Community Department, ASCCD).

Sometime in March 2016, I was — given my extrovert personality — encouraged to apply for the post of "Director for the Community Affairs Directorate", within the Community and Corporate Affairs Directorate (CCAD). This post, which was left vacant for a year since the departure of its last Director (incidentally, also another Singaporean), oversees two Divisions i.e. Community Relations (CRD) and Information Resource Management (IRMD). The former is all about bringing ASEAN closer to its 630 million people through the engagement of relevant stakeholders like media, youth, businesses, NGOs, and policymakers etc. The latter is, as the name implies, managing information resources through library, archives, knowledge management, publications, digitalisation of core treaties/documents/reports, and the storage of important agreements. I did apply and, in April 2016, began another chapter of my life in ASEC as the Director for the Community Affairs Directorate.

At the point of writing this essay, there are seven Singaporeans working in ASEC, including myself and the Deputy Secretary-General for the ASEAN Political-Security Community Department (DSG APSCD), a political appointee. With a total staff of 315, Singaporeans constitute only about 2.22 percent of the entire work-strength in ASEC.

In my humble opinion, ASEC can definitely do well with a few more Singaporean staff, because Singaporeans can communicate — write and speak — fairly well in English (ASEAN's official language), and we are products of the rule-of-law system. Yet, the fact remains that, for whatever reasons, ASEC has traditionally found it tough to recruit two nationalities to work in its office. One is Bruneians, and the other, Singaporeans. One can only hope that the new salary-scale structure, which has been put in place since 2015, will help to reverse this trend in time to come.

People — Heart of ASEAN's Community

On the whole, I enjoy my work in the ASEC because I believe I am making a difference in the lives of the ASEAN people. I hold the firm opinion that people are at the heart of ASEAN's efforts, and that ASEAN's success is ultimately measured by how the Community building efforts have benefited the lives of its citizens.

Right from the start, ASEAN was committed to peace, freedom and prosperity. Five decades since its formation, ASEAN is committed to establishing a people-oriented, people-centred and rules-based ASEAN Community, where all its people, stakeholders and sectors of society can contribute to and benefits from a more integrated and connected Community. The community will cooperate on the political-security, economic and socio-cultural fronts, for sustainable, equitable and inclusive development.

Indeed, over the years, ASEAN has been slowly reinventing itself to remain relevant to the region and the world. Today ASEAN is considered to be a successful regional experiment, and in that aspect, the ASEC has played a unique and critical role in supporting the work of ASEAN.

Reflections

As it approaches 50, ASEAN is still a work-in-progress, and there will always be debates regarding its usefulness and effectiveness. The future of ASEAN is not a given, as many in ASEAN remain doubtful about its long-term viability. Some have argued that in large parts of Southeast Asia, people hardly know of ASEAN's existence. Apart from the SG of ASEAN and ASEC, there are few region-wide institutions and mechanisms to stand up for ASEAN.

I was born a few years after the establishment of ASEAN. The organisation was not something which I needed to know or worry about for the first half of my life. The relative peace and prosperity in the region was a great blessing. ASEAN facilitated a positive development despite the ups and downs of the global economy. The inter-ASEAN Member States relations were generally progressive and ASEAN was regarded as important even though it was a slow-moving machine for regional cooperation and consultation. However, many things have changed as a result of the intensification of globalisation and advancement in technology. The Chinese and Indian economies are also growing rapidly. ASEAN responded quickly with a plan to integrate economically to obtain benefits from economies of scale. ASEAN also gambled on a free trade strategy. It decided to champion trade liberalisation and greater market access. To demonstrate commitment and seriousness, ASEAN drew up comprehensive blueprints including the ASEAN Charter. It was a question of survival. For me, the plans and actions for the ASEAN Community opened up more opportunities in Southeast Asia and it was necessary to get to know the region better for my own future.

There is a sense of excitement as ASEAN engages countries like China, India, Japan, ROK, Australia, New Zealand, EU, Russia, Canada and the United States. There is also a feeling that more and more Southeast Asians have become more educated and locked into the global grid. They wish to connect and be involved with the rest of the world in moving and transforming their respective nations. ASEAN is seen by those in and out of the region as the vehicle to realise their respective aspirations. At a minimum, ASEAN can help to improve their basic livelihood. If well-managed by its political leadership, ASEAN can secure the future of Southeast Asia.

As the activities intensify in the region, I am able to witness the evolution of this unique inter-governmental organisation. Increasingly,

I hold the view that ASEAN does matter to Southeast Asia, including citizens like myself and my children, and this is why, I am glad to have joined the ASEC, and to have made a difference in this region.

LEE Yoong Yoong is the Director for Community Affairs in the ASEAN Secretariat (ASEC), based in Jakarta. He manages the daily operation of the Community Relations and Information Resource Management Divisions, and has two decades of experience in international relations and public policy development. Prior to his current position, Yoong was the Head for Executive Support in the Office of Secretary-General (OSG) where he provided technical and administrative support to the ASEAN Secretary-General.

Yoong started his career with Singapore's Economic Development Board (EDB). He spent four years with the Institute of Policy Studies (IPS), an outfit within the Lee Kuan Yew School of Public Policy, handling public policy research and analysis for the Economic and Business cluster. His other international experience included a one-year stint in United Nations Economic and Social Commission for Asia and the Pacific (UNESCAP) in Bangkok in 2011. Yoong holds a Master of Science in International Relations from the Nanyang Technological University.

Post-Charter ASEAN

The ASEAN Community 2015

KWOK Fook Seng

2015 marked the attainment of the ASEAN Community. This was the first temporal target set by ASEAN Leaders to spur the holistic integration of this regional grouping, and the first of many incremental steps to build up the institutional character of ASEAN following the ASEAN Charter of 2008. Fast forward to 2017, ASEAN marks its 50th anniversary just months after the world experienced some of the most unexpected developments in geopolitics in 2016. With much of the global community still trying to make sense of what impact 2016 will bring, it will be a mistake not to acknowledge the quiet triumphs which this regional grouping has secured for Southeast Asia. It has laid foundations in norm-building for regional and international relations which will help its Member States cope precisely with such trying times.

The ASEAN Community can be understood via a quick recap of some attributes which the ASEAN Charter vests in the organisation that hitherto operated cooperatively in an informal but practice-defined manner: i) politically-backed enhancements to its legal personality (including legally-binding commitments and targets), ii) strengthened institutional capacities both within Member States and at the ASEAN Secretariat, and iii) the creation of three pillars through which community-building efforts will be pursued: the ASEAN Political-Security Community (APSC), the ASEAN Economic Community (AEC) and the ASEAN Socio-Cultural Community (ASCC).

For Singapore, this holistic exercise was a welcome opportunity to invest further in a maturing regional architecture which we helped seed and nurture through the years. ASEAN's gaining of institutional depth would not only benefit the grouping internally, it would serve the network of important regional meetings which the organisation anchors, like the ASEAN Regional Forum (ARF)[1], the ASEAN Defence Ministers Meeting (ADMM), and the East Asia Summit (EAS), to name but a few.

The APSC is often characterised by commentators as being "talk shop" meetings. Those on the outside easily miss the significance of an insider community forged through frequent and regular contact. It breeds familiarity to reduce friction. It helps enhance understanding of each other's operating imperatives — from leaders, to ministers, to senior and junior officials. Most importantly, this community forges a sense of the common cause in our region. Through the institutions of constant political engagement (even through periods of tension), ASEAN builds a beneficial regional commons which endures beyond the persistent irritants in the various relationships of its Member States. Whether it is disputes between Member States or with external parties, the common interests of peace and security in the region frame the pursuit of solutions. ASEAN Member States are guided by such regional imperatives to seek solutions to conflict which do not, in themselves, spur further strife and uncertainty. Such solutions necessarily take time to build, and cannot be measured with the impatient yardsticks of a world prone to instant gratification. ASEAN and its Dialogue Partners are engaged in a long-term project, the temporal horizon of which often escapes recognition by commentators.

The most tangible pillar of work, of course, is the AEC which today translates into an integrated regional market with the combined trading volume of US$2.5 trillion, and is poised to grow to US$4 trillion by 2030. The intertwined economies of ASEAN Member States is a large contributor to the notion of common cause. The mutual benefits generated are clearly greater than just the sum of its parts. This is a concept well understood and supported by ASEAN Leaders, such that when confronted with the Great Financial Crisis in 2008, ASEAN's economic response was to accelerate its collective targets for liberalisation and

---

[1] To date, still the only international meeting at which the Democratic People's Republic of Korea participates.

integration from 2025 to 2015. The collective wisdom, of accepting bitter medicine to double down on liberalisation when the global economy
was ailing, has resulted in unprecedented growth levels enjoyed by the
younger ASEAN economies even today, where tepid growth is common around the world.

The challenge today, in the face of nativist and anti-globalisation
sentiment, is to ensure the continued delivery of benefits from economic growth. The AEC allows Member States a full spectrum of
engagement, from capacity-building by fellow Members and Dialogue
Partners, to best practices which enhance trade and investment prospects, to the negotiation and review of ASEAN's various collective
free-trade agreements, just to name a few. Efforts exist to ensure that
Member States progress at all levels — domestic reforms, regional
cooperation and international obligations. That the AEC, through its
Scorecard system, helps Member States set targets and track achievement of sectoral measures is another under-appreciated fact. This systemic regional effort of peer assistance to achieve and deliver benefits
for the broader collective has long been the hallmark of regional economic cooperation, underpinned and facilitated by decades of peace
and stability.

The ASCC takes that sense of common cause a step further towards
building a stronger regional identity. A common cultural identity was a
luxury of the second order during those years when ASEAN governments were each struggling to secure their respective rice bowls. By
2008, there was sufficient development and regional momentum to
recognise the benefits of "branding" ASEAN as the dynamic region that
it is, and to inspire future generations to protect this brand for their
own benefit. As an ASEAN Anthem came into being, so did roadmaps
and plans for people-to-people links which would match the economic
and geographic connectivity that the other two communities
were pursuing. By 2017, we have a growing sense of affinity among our
citizenry. Not only do our peoples feel that we hail from the same
region, we know we have all overcome adversity to get where we are
today. Projects to promote exchanges span a broad spectrum of sectors
from the arts, sports and youth, to disaster management and trans-

boundary haze and civil service cooperation. Formation of the ASEAN Intergovernmental Commission on Human Rights (AICHR) was yet another demonstration that there is regional understanding of the need to build institutional capacity, to promote and protect values consistent with a mature and responsible global citizenship.

As ASEAN turns 50, the aspiration to build better institutions continues to be a work in progress. There will be, without doubt, future targets set for more milestones which will further deepen our regional integration. This journey may seem fraught to observers who are impatient for "big bang" outcomes at the end of each milestone. Inevitably they compare ASEAN to the European Union or other regional institutions with which they are more familiar, and this is to misunderstand the exercise. Institution-building in Southeast Asia is not about achieving supranational conformity to idealised principles. The spectrum of political systems and the differing levels of economic development never made this a worthwhile pursuit for ASEAN. Community-building for ASEAN is based on practical operational considerations, and the pragmatism of integrating what is an inherently diverse group of polities and economies such that they deliver benefits which are greater than the sum of their parts.

ASEAN was forged in a crucible of diversity and uncertainty in the 1960s, and its pioneers would remember predictions that Southeast Asia would be "balkanised". That we have managed a peaceful and cogent region which defies typified characterisations of political analysts is in itself a quiet triumph. ASEAN Member States value sure-footedness over haste, and two things remain critical to its community-building efforts: i) that the overall directionality is maintained for the greater good, and ii) it is recognised from the outset that individual Member States might move at different paces. To benefit the entire region and not individual Member States, it is more important that the collective vision and direction is clearly communicated to external partners. The region sets a series of goals which aim to bring investments and support which can help those lagging to make good on their commitments, and catch up with the leaders of the pack. Those who are able have the duty to forge ahead, so as to provide demonstration of the benefits and help build bottom-up community support for the necessary reforms across the region's economies and polities. In codifying its first 40 years of cooperative endeavours, the ASEAN Charter did not seek to completely replace past practices. It sought to introduce pathways for institutions across all three communities to be continually enhanced and improved upon. The cycle is to keep setting targets, keep building and enhancing institutional capacity, and to keep monitoring and evaluating progress. Whether it is the APSC, AEC or ASCC, it is this virtuous cycle which will prevent back-sliding, keep the region pointed in the correct direction, and compel ASEAN's partners to support our collective endeavours.

From the regional fragility of the 1960s, the governments of ASEAN Member States have created a safe space to cope with external challenges as partners and as equals. They have successfully journeyed in relative harmony with the avoidance of armed conflict for 50 years, while building political, economic and cultural links with nations which represent over 55% of global population and global Gross Domestic Product. Not many commentaries of the recent past readily associate ASEAN with strategic nous, but the ASEAN Community which has been and is being built, certainly carries more significance than it is recognised for.

KWOK Fook Seng is currently Singapore's High Commissioner to Australia. Previously, he was Ambassador for Climate Change, negotiating the Paris Agreement which was concluded at the 21st Conference of Parties of the United Nations Framework Convention on Climate Change (UNFCCC) in December 2015. As Singapore's Permanent Representative to the World Trade Organization (WTO) and the World Intellectual Property Organization (WIPO) in Geneva from 2011 to 2014, he chaired the Coordination Committee (Executive Board) of WIPO from 2012 to 2013, and the Special Session of the Committee on

Trade and Development at the WTO (a pillar of the trade negotiations under the Doha Round) from 2012 to 2014. Mr. Kwok was Director-General of the ASEAN Directorate at the Ministry of Foreign Affairs from 2008 to 2010. He has a Bachelor of Arts in Communications Studies (Honours) from Murdoch University, Western Australia, and a Master of Public Management (MPM) from the Lee Kuan Yew School of Public Policy at the National University of Singapore.

The ASEAN Community and the Principle of ASEAN Centrality

Dominic GOH

A foreign service officer has to be ever adaptable and resourceful. Upon my return from a posting in Berlin, I was assigned to the ASEAN Directorate of the Ministry of Foreign Affairs in 2008. The ASEAN Charter had recently been signed. ASEAN Member States were working on the establishment of the ASEAN Community, and were busily negotiating the three ASEAN Community Blueprints (Political/Security, Economic and Social/Cultural). I had no experience in the workings of ASEAN, and yet I had been thrust into the birth pangs of the ASEAN Community, and assigned the task of negotiating the ASEAN Political Security Community (APSC) Blueprint on behalf of Singapore.

The idea of an ASEAN Community has its origins in the Asian Financial Crisis of 1998. During the crisis, ASEAN Leaders had noticed a dramatic fall in foreign investments in ASEAN, and that those investments were heading for China or India, bypassing ASEAN. Growing regionalisation was increasing economic competition. In his Keynote Address at the opening of the 32nd ASEAN Ministerial Meeting in Singapore on 23 July 1999, Singapore's Prime Minister Goh Chok Tong said that "ASEAN must become more united to stand up to the rise of regionalism in North America, South America and Western Europe".

ASEAN's answer to global competition was to move towards greater unity and integration, through the formation of an ASEAN Community. In their Declaration of Bali Concord II dated 7 October 2003, ASEAN Leaders adopted a framework to achieve a "dynamic, cohesive, resilient and integrated ASEAN Community" comprising three pillars, namely, the ASEAN Security Community (later to become the ASEAN Political-Security Community); the ASEAN Economic Community; and the ASEAN Socio-Cultural Community. The ASEAN Community's founding document would be the ASEAN Charter, setting out ASEAN's basic principles, objectives, and the roles of its key institutions and bodies. Cooperation under each of the three pillars would be governed by its own Community Blueprint, setting out a range of activities and measures to enhance integration.

ASEAN Centrality

One key principle is that of ASEAN Centrality. Article 1(15) of the ASEAN Charter states that "one of the purposes of ASEAN is to maintain the centrality and proactive role of ASEAN as the primary driving force in its relations and cooperation with its external partners in a regional architecture that is open, transparent and inclusive". In addition, the ASEAN Chair is charged with ensuring the centrality of ASEAN [Article 32(b)]. The concept relates to ASEAN's central role in convening and setting the agenda for the main regional forums in Southeast Asia, such as the ASEAN Plus One dialogue relationships, the ASEAN Plus Three (ASEAN+3), the East Asia Summit (EAS) and the ASEAN Regional Forum (ARF).

The concept of ASEAN Centrality developed in the 1990s as ASEAN began to convene regional forums such as the ARF and the ASEAN+3[1]. In 2008, in a speech handing over the ASEAN Chairmanship to Thailand, Singapore's Foreign Minister, Mr. George Yeo, said:

> "With the rise of China and India changing the polarity of the world, we must make sure that the political, economic and security architecture of the region takes into account the interest of ASEAN. Over the years, ASEAN, in a peaceful non-threatening way, has helped to bring countries in the region together. We have been able to do this through enlightened diplomacy

---

[1] Walter Woon, *The ASEAN Charter: A Commentary* (Singapore: NUS Press, 2015).

and by offering our hand of friendship to all the major powers. We must never lose this position. We must take an active interest in regional and global affairs and play a role which is helpful to others. We ensure the centrality of ASEAN in the evolving regional architecture, not by force or assertion but by the openness and neutrality of our position and by our usefulness to others."

However, ASEAN's centrality in the regional architecture soon came under attack. Then Australian Prime Minister Mr. Kevin Rudd proposed an initiative in June 2008 to create an Asia-Pacific community (APc) by 2020 that would bring together countries "as disparate as the United States, China, Japan, India, Indonesia and Australia". According to Rudd, the community should be "able to engage the full spectrum of dialogue, cooperation and action on economic and political matters and future challenges related to security"[2]. Note that Rudd did not include mention of ASEAN participation in the APc in his initial announcement of the initiative. Later clarifications by the Australian Government showed that while ASEAN might participate in the forum, the APc would not necessarily be ASEAN-centred. Then Australian Foreign Minister Mr. Stephen Smith, said on 18 July 2008:

"The conversation doesn't diminish any of the existing regional bodies. On the contrary, they will continue to play their essential roles. *There could be a new piece of architecture,* (emphasis added) as ASEAN and APEC once were. Or it could emerge from and through the existing architecture, as the ARF and EAS have."

In other words, ASEAN would not necessarily be an integral part of the APc. ASEAN thus saw the APc as a direct challenge to its centrality as it threatened to provide a forum for regional powers to discuss regional issues, bypassing established ASEAN-centred forums. Singapore galva-

---

[2] Tim Colebatch, "Rudd's grand vision for Asia Pacific", *Sydney Morning Herald*, June 5, 2008.

nised ASEAN to oppose the APc on the basis that it would erode ASEAN's centrality and driving role in the regional architecture. ASEAN's unity in opposing the APc, and the United States' recognition of ASEAN's central role in the regional architecture eventually shifted the discussion away from the APc towards expanding the membership of the EAS to include the United States and Russia[3].

ASEAN centrality received a further boost when Singapore's Foreign Minister Mr. George Yeo proposed an ASEAN Connectivity Master Plan in 2009. The idea was to boost ASEAN integration and economic linkages through enhancing physical infrastructure, information technology and tourism linkages among ASEAN countries. The concept was immediately accepted by all ASEAN Member States and adopted by the ASEAN Summit in Cha-am/Hua Hin, Thailand on 24 October 2009. The Master Plan on ASEAN Connectivity (MPAC) continues to be a key priority of ASEAN. As the physical linkages among ASEAN countries develop, closer ASEAN integration will follow as a natural consequence.

At the time of writing this essay, ASEAN unity and centrality continues to be challenged by the South China Sea issue. While ASEAN Member States generally agree on the principles of peaceful resolution of disputes, primacy of international law, and the applicability of the United Nations Convention of the Law of the Sea (UNCLOS), some member states are wary about calling out infringements of these principles. ASEAN diplomats need to realise that as a grouping of small countries, it is in ASEAN's collective interests to show unity in standing up for the principles and application of international law. In so doing, we are not taking sides with one claimant or another, but we would be expressing our support for the principle of primacy of international law. This is important as we need to move the practice of international relations away from the law of the jungle where "might makes right", towards a more civilised paradigm where the conduct of international relations is governed by international law.

---

[3] The United States and Russia officially joined the EAS in 2011.

Lessons Learned

ASEAN will continue to face challenges to its centrality. As Singapore's and ASEAN's interests are tied to an economically vibrant ASEAN playing a key convenor role in the regional architecture, we will have to be ever alert to counter these challenges and defend ASEAN's centrality.

Although Singapore is a small country, we can exercise an influence exceeding our size through good ideas, rational thinking and a consistent defence of basic principles.

ASEAN's unity and centrality can be strengthened through closer political cooperation, economic integration, building physical linkages among member states, and fostering an ASEAN community mindset among our peoples. It is therefore important to continue ASEAN's Community-building efforts through the three pillars of the ASEAN Community.

The major powers will pressure ASEAN to support their positions. If they are unable to get ASEAN support, they could even try to split ASEAN. ASEAN Member States need to be aware of this. Instead of taking sides, we should take consistent positions and stand united in favour of principles that are in ASEAN's long-term interests.

The views expressed in this essay belong to the author and are not a reflection of the Singapore Government's position.

Dominic GOH is currently Singapore's Ambassador to the Lao People's Democratic Republic. He joined the Singapore Foreign Service in October 1994. Mr. Goh has served postings in Bonn and Berlin. He has also covered several portfolios including ASEAN where he served as Deputy Director-General for ASEAN Regional Policy and the ASEAN Political and Security Community. He was part of the team handling Singapore's ASEAN Chairmanship in 2008. He also served as Director-General for International Economics and Director-General of the Europe Directorate. In 2014, he was appointed an Honorary Companion of the Order of St Michael and St George by Her Majesty Queen Elizabeth II.

An Insight into the Regional Security Architecture

Sally ANG

 ᐧᴑ ᒪ ᴗᐧ

Established in 2006 and 2010 respectively, the ASEAN Defence Ministers' Meeting (ADMM) and ADMM-Plus were one of the last ministerial sectoral bodies to be added to the ASEAN framework. Today, the ADMM and ADMM-Plus are recognised as key cornerstones of multilateral defence diplomacy in the region, and have achieved remarkable results. Singapore, as one of the five founding members of ASEAN, played an instrumental role in shaping and strengthening the value proposition of the ADMM and ADMM-Plus.

Genesis of the ADMM and ADMM-Plus

Unlike the United Nations (UN) and the North Atlantic Treaty Organization (NATO) which were founded in the aftermath of World War Two, multilateralism only took root in Southeast Asia with the founding of ASEAN on 8 August 1967. However, even with the mushrooming of regional multilateral platforms on the economic, diplomatic and social fronts, there remained a deep-seated belief that formalised security and defence cooperation under the ASEAN ambit was too sensitive, and the region was not ready for it. Given such dynamics, we made some headway with the adoption of the Bali Concord which established the ASEAN Security Community in October 2003, and this paved the way for the inaugural ADMM on 9 May 2006.

Interestingly, the idea of developing a complementary security framework involving extra-regional countries quickly emerged during the inaugural ADMM. However, some ASEAN Member States were skeptical as they felt that the ADMM needed time and space to grow before creating another framework. From the onset, Singapore felt the importance of establishing an open and inclusive regional security architecture, especially since the security of the region was increasingly intertwined with the larger Asia-Pacific landscape. We also strongly believed that an ADMM with constructive relationships with major powers would enhance the region's capabilities in dealing with trans-boundary security challenges, and profile the strategic relevance of ASEAN beyond the region. With the belief that we needed to "start right", Singapore actively advocated the concept of "ADMM-Plus", and achieved a breakthrough when the second ADMM adopted the concept paper on the ADMM-Plus during our tenure as Chair in 2007.

The concept paper laid down strong foundations for the ADMM-Plus, but its inauguration remained a work-in-progress. Singapore worked closely with Thailand, the next ADMM Chair, to adopt a concept paper on the principles of membership for the ADMM-Plus.[1] Thailand also hosted an ADMM Retreat in November 2009 for ASEAN Defence Ministers to discuss the configuration and composition of the ADMM-Plus, two key issues which would form the DNA of the ADMM-Plus. Specifically, the Ministers considered the following configurations: (a) ADMM+1 where ADMM would engage individual Dialogue Partners; (b) ADMM+3 which brings together ADMM, China, Japan and the Republic of Korea (ROK); or (c) ADMM+X where "X" refers to the countries that were able to satisfy the principles of membership. Eventually, the Ministers agreed that an ADMM+X formulation would facilitate greater openness and transparency, and provide a balanced representation of views to effectively address

---

[1] The three principles are: (a) the Plus country shall be a full-fledged Dialogue Partner of ASEAN; (b) the Plus country shall have significant interactions and relations with ASEAN defence establishments; and (c) the Plus country shall be able to work with the ADMM to build capacity to enhance regional security in a substantive manner.

regional security challenges. This decision was eventually formalised into a concept paper which was adopted by the fourth ADMM in Hanoi in May 2010.

Throughout the process of establishing the ADMM-Plus, we also encouraged key extra-regional countries to actively engage the ASEAN defence track so that they would be regarded as natural partners for the ADMM-Plus. Singapore also sought to pique the major powers' interest in joining the ADMM-Plus, and leveraged informal engagements on the sidelines of multilateral meetings to socialise them to the idea. Notably, China was the most active extra-regional country to engage ASEAN having hosted several ASEAN-China security-related events such as breakfast on the sidelines of the annual ARF Security Policy Conference (ASPC). Australia and New Zealand also responded positively by hosting an ASEAN-Australia-New Zealand tea reception on the sidelines of ASPC in May 2008. Following this model, the United States initiated an informal tea reception in 2010, while Japan organised the inaugural ASEAN-Japan Defence Senior Officials' Meeting in 2009, an event which has now become a permanent fixture in the ASEAN calendar.

Singapore's efforts paid off as it became clear that the extra-regional countries were ready to come on board. The ASEAN Defence Ministers also unanimously decided that the ADMM-Plus should not suffer the same fate as the ARF which had an unwieldy membership of 27 countries. Hence, they agreed on an ADMM+8 modality which included Australia, China, India, Japan, New Zealand, ROK, Russia and the United States. The final touches were completed when the fourth ADMM agreed to inaugurate the ADMM-Plus in Hanoi in October 2010, and then-US Secretary of Defense Robert Gates announced that he would attend the inaugural ADMM-plus even before the invitations were sent out! This was a powerful signal from the United States, and set the tone for the other Plus countries. The inaugural ADMM-Plus saw a good turnout, and was attended by Defence Ministers from all ADMM-Plus countries except Russia.[2]

---

[2] Russia was represented by First Deputy Minister of Defence GEN Nikolai Makarov.

Achievements of the ADMM and ADMM-Plus

The ADMM commemorated its tenth anniversary in 2016, while the ADMM-Plus conducted its third meeting in 2015. Both platforms have done well in facilitating strategic dialogue between Defence Ministers. This has transpired into greater trust and confidence — the basis of effective defence diplomacy. Indeed, the early decision for the ADMM-Plus to meet biennially instead of triennially demonstrates member states' desire to exchange views on a more frequent basis.[3]

The ADMM and ADMM-Plus also effectively promoted practical cooperation amongst militaries, and implemented tangible measures to ensure regional peace and security. Notably, the ADMM had placed special emphasis on strengthening ASEAN's capacity for Humanitarian Assistance and Disaster Relief (HADR) operations given that Asia-Pacific is plagued with more than 70% of the world's natural disasters. This led to the establishment of entities such as the ASEAN Militaries Ready Group on HADR (AMRG) and the ASEAN Centre of Military Medicine (ACMM), amongst other things.[4] Singapore also co-organised the first ASEAN militaries HADR Exercise with Indonesia in July 2011, and the second Exercise with Brunei in June 2013 to promote tangible HADR cooperation amongst ASEAN militaries.

Today, practical cooperation is synonymous with the ADMM-Plus, and is institutionalised through seven Experts' Working Groups on Maritime Security, Counter-Terrorism, Military Medicine, HADR, Peacekeeping Operations, Humanitarian Mine Action and Cyber Security. In 2013, Singapore, Vietnam, China and Japan co-organised the first combined ADMM-Plus HADR and Military Medicine Exercise which saw the deployment of approximately 3,200 personnel, 15 helicopters and seven ships. It was noteworthy that China and Japan were both part

---

[3] In 2012, the ADMM agreed to convene the ADMM-Plus biennially instead of triennially.

[4] Malaysia and Thailand proposed the establishment of the AMRG and ACMM respectively. The concept papers and terms of references for both entities were adopted by the ninth ADMM in 2015 and tenth ADMM in 2016 respectively.

of the Exercise steering committee. This illustrated that the ADMM-Plus was a useful avenue for countries to put aside their bilateral political tensions for practical cooperation.

Singapore also co-organised the ADMM-Plus Maritime Security and Counter-Terrorism Exercise with Australia, Brunei and New Zealand in May 2016. This was the largest ADMM-Plus Exercise to date with some 3,500 personnel, 18 naval vessels, 25 aircraft and 40 Special Forces teams, and involved countries such as China and the United States coming together as part of a larger multinational force to counter the terrorist threat. Such Exercises are strategically valuable as they provide ADMM-Plus militaries with opportunities to forge a strong sense of camaraderie through living, learning and training together. They also institutionalise strong foundations for the ADMM-Plus to respond collectively in times of crises, and distinguish the ADMM-Plus from other platforms that have been labelled as "talk-shops".

Way Forward

As the geostrategic landscape continues to evolve, and the region becomes more integrated, it is crucial for the ADMM and ADMM-Plus to maintain their relevance. To do so, the ADMM must continually engage the Plus countries constructively, while persist in preserving ASEAN centrality so that it is not divided by the Sino-US rivalry for influence in the region. It is also important for the ADMM-Plus to maintain its positive momentum of practical cooperation so that any bilateral unhappiness between states do not spillover and upset multilateral cooperation. Furthermore, while there is general consensus that hot-button issues such as territorial disputes in the South China Sea would unlikely be resolved in the near future, the ADMM and ADMM-Plus can adopt risk mitigation measures and international rules of the road to guard against escalation of tensions, and strengthen a rules-based regional order. To this end, Singapore hopes to work with others to promulgate norms of behaviour such as the Code for Unplanned Encounters at Sea (CUES), and similar protocols for the air and underwater domains. This will institutionalise an overlapping network of international legal norms, and form the bedrock for continued peace, prosperity and security in our region.

Sally ANG is a Policy Officer at the Defence Policy Office in the Singapore Ministry of Defence. As part of her portfolio, she covers multilateral defence cooperation under the ADMM and ADMM-Plus. She is a recipient of the Defence Merit Scholarship, and graduated with a LLB from King's College London in 2014, and a LLM in International Legal Studies from the New York University School of Law in 2015. She enjoys travelling for good scenery and food, and hopes to visit all 18 ADMM-Plus countries one day!

The ASEAN Economic Community: Can It Deliver for the People of ASEAN?

Manu BHASKARAN

ASEAN has made important strides in bringing together into one cooperative venture 630 million people of diverse ethnic and religious identities living in ten nations with widely varying characteristics. This is no mean feat and the establishment of the ASEAN Economic Community (AEC) as one of the three pillars of the ASEAN Community takes ASEAN several steps further in achieving integration for the common good of all the peoples of ASEAN.

This article makes two assertions. First, the AEC can deliver important benefits to the region as a whole even if it might take some time before it is fully effective. Second, however, much more needs to be done if the AEC is to enable ASEAN to compete effectively given the changes in the world economy, including challenges to free trade and the increased competition from resurgent powers such as China and India.

The AEC Takes ASEAN Integration to a Higher Plane

Economic integration in ASEAN has progressed from separate and somewhat partial or incomplete initiatives such as the Common Effective Preferential Tariff (CEPT) which developed into the ASEAN Free Trade Area (AFTA), the ASEAN Comprehensive Investment Agreement (ACIA) and the ASEAN Agreement on Movement of Natural Persons into a more comprehensive integration framework. The AEC achieves this through several pillars:

- **A single market and production base** is being effected by facilitating the free flow of goods, services, skilled labour and investment. Trade in goods within ASEAN is now virtually tariff-free while non-tariff barriers are being tackled through initiatives such as the ASEAN Agreement on Customs and the harmonisation of standards. Services trade is also being enhanced through continuous efforts to expand the ASEAN Framework Agreement on Services. Mutual recognition arrangements are now in force in eight areas to facilitate the free flow of skilled labour. Already several hundred engineers and architects have been registered under this scheme giving them the right to work across ASEAN nations. And to ease the flow of capital within the region, the ASEAN Comprehensive Investment Agreement has established four pillars (investment liberalisation, protection, promotion and facilitation) to help promote investment flows within the region. An ASEAN Financial Integration Framework is being expanded to promote the integration of financial markets within the region.
- **The creation of a competitive, connected economic region**: The ASEAN open skies initiative has been a success with efforts underway to improve transport connectivity by addressing the missing links in the proposed ASEAN Highway Network. Initiatives are also underway to promote competition laws and consumer protection frameworks within the region.
- **Equitable economic development**: Recognising the wide differences in economic development across the region, the Initiative for ASEAN Integration (IAI) was launched in 2001 to narrow the divide through regional cooperation. This has been strengthened with the adoption of the ASEAN Framework for Equitable Economic Development in 2011.
- **Integration with the global economy**: ASEAN has emerged as a key player in the network of free trade agreements and economic partnership schemes linking major economic regions of the world. ASEAN has completed such agreements with China, the Republic of Korea (ROK), Japan, India, Australia and New Zealand. ASEAN is also a

critical piece of the Regional Comprehensive Economic Partnership (RCEP) currently being negotiated with China, ROK, Japan, India, Australia and New Zealand.

But Many Gaps Remain before the Region Is Truly Integrated

As the above discussion shows, the AEC has made progress but there is still some distance to go before there is the full flow of goods, services, people and capital that would make ASEAN one fully integrated economy. Substantial non-tariff barriers to the free flow of goods remain despite efforts to gradually remove them. Moreover, services trade is barely liberalised and the free flow of labour only applies to selected professions and does not touch unskilled or semi-skilled labour at all.

The absence of a strong set of legal systems across ASEAN is a particular challenge for companies doing business in the region. While countries such as Singapore and Malaysia have well-established systems, others do not. This can make enforcing agreements a tricky and uncertain process.

This is important because the critical determinant of the AEC's success is whether its various initiatives make a real difference to businesses operating at the ground level. Only if the practical obstacles they face in trading across ASEAN borders are resolved can the AEC be said to be complete and effective. Feedback from businesses suggests that non-tariff barriers prove insurmountable in too many cases. There are consistent complaints from companies with operations straddling several ASEAN countries of the difficulties faced in moving goods from one country to another, or in setting up branches or subsidiaries outside their home countries. Financial services have proven to be an especially difficult area. An ASEAN company with an inspiring new idea or business model would still struggle to gain scale by leveraging off the ASEAN market and so compete with Chinese and Indian companies.

The performance of corporate ASEAN shows this challenge clearly. ASEAN is the third largest economic region in the world in population terms. Yet, it has just 227 companies with revenues exceeding US$1 billion, behind countries such as France, the United Kingdom and Germany. It is instructive that average company revenue in ASEAN lags substantially behind in peer comparisons, clear evidence that ASEAN companies are facing difficulties scaling up to compete against larger and consequently more cost-efficient firms elsewhere. For example, Germany with one-seventh the population of ASEAN has 463 companies with revenues over US$1 billion while these companies have an average revenue of US$3.7 billion compared to the ASEAN average revenue of just US$1.1 billion.

As the World Changes, the Current Approach May Not Be Enough

There is little doubt that ASEAN's guiding lights are working hard to bring about the maximum integration possible given the immensely diverse political, economic and social characteristics of the region. However, the global environment is increasingly challenging for ASEAN. This means that much more is expected of the AEC if ASEAN is to prosper and thrive.

First, world trade is growing much more slowly, challenged by growing protectionism and structural changes such as the "reshoring" of production back to developed countries from developing ones such as ASEAN. The backlash against globalisation and free trade in the United States and Europe will have disturbing implications for the trade and investments that are so vital for ASEAN. Moreover, consumer preferences appear to be shifting away from the production of snazzy goods such as electrical and electronics items that ASEAN has excelled at producing to services and experiences that ASEAN is less adept at. And new technologies such as robotic and artificial intelligence raise doubts as to whether the competitive advantages ASEAN economies enjoyed in manufacturing and business process outsourcing can be maintained.

Second, ASEAN faces much more intense competition as it strives to defend its share of global exports and foreign direct investment. China and India have tremendous scale, which makes them much more attractive to foreign investors. This scale also enables companies based in those giant economies to rapidly gain scale economies and emerge as massive and cost-efficient competitors against anything that ASEAN can offer. Elsewhere, more and more developing economies are improving their fundamentals and so becoming substantially greater competitive threats to ASEAN's position. Countries such as Mexico, Peru and some in central Europe such as Poland come to mind.

Conclusion — The Way Forward

All in all, there are two reasons to remain optimistic.

First, ASEAN recognises these gaps and is determined to maintain the momentum built up with the launch of the AEC at the end of 2015. This was the reason for the AEC Blueprint 2025 which seeks to complete the process of economic integration through further initiatives.

And, second, despite concerns about the practical difficulties they face, more and more companies are developing ASEAN-based corporate strategies. Clearly, they believe that the AEC will eventually deliver for them, otherwise they would not be adjusting their corporate strategies to accommodate the AEC.

Nevertheless, ASEAN needs to refine its approach towards economic integration. First, it needs to give greater priority to achieving practical progress for companies that operate at the ground level, allowing these companies to scale up and become globally scaled competitors.

Second, given the divergent levels of economic development across ASEAN, it may make sense to expand the ASEAN-X approach of allowing some countries within ASEAN to pursue more rapid economic integration so that they are not held back by other ASEAN members. For example, Malaysia and Singapore as the most open economies in the region would have an interest in moving forward on integration initiatives ahead of other ASEAN members. Over time, these other ASEAN countries could join in the integration initiatives thus created.

Manu BHASKARAN is a Partner of the Centennial Group, a strategic advisory firm headquartered in Washington DC and, as Founding CEO of its Singapore subsidiary Centennial Asia Advisors, he coordinates the Asian business of the Group which provides in-depth analysis of Asian macro trends for investment institutions, government agencies and companies with interests in Asia, leveraging off his more than 30 years of studying Asia. Manu is also Adjunct Senior Research Fellow at the Institute of Policy Studies in Singapore where his main interests are in analysing macro-economic policy frameworks in Singapore. He is also a Member of the Regional Advisory Board for Asia of the International Monetary Fund.

ASEAN: Connectivity to Community[1]

ONG Keng Yong

In 2007, the Leaders of ASEAN formally launched the ASEAN Economic Community (AEC). The blueprint of the AEC listed the actions needed to integrate the ten economies in ASEAN. Collectively, the ASEAN market had a population of 630 million people with a regional GDP of over US$2 trillion. The Leaders were of the view that the AEC would generate the momentum for a greater inflow of foreign direct investments (FDI) into Southeast Asia and put ASEAN more substantially into the global supply chain. From Singapore's perspective, however, one key element must also be incorporated into the ASEAN agenda to make the AEC initiative more attractive for the investor community. This was intra-regional connectivity to make it more convenient to travel and do business across the entire territory of ASEAN.

The comparative advantage of ASEAN vis-à-vis the hyperactive Chinese economy and the emerging Indian market at that point in time centred around the urban areas of Singapore, Bangkok, Jakarta, Kuala Lumpur and Manila. At the same time, growing sub-regional economic areas of ASEAN, for example, Bangkok-Ho Chi Minh City with the Mekong Delta, and Medan-Penang with South Thailand and Myanmar

---

[1] The research for this paper was provided by Mr. Lim Chze Cheen of the ASEAN Secretariat (ASEC) and Mr. Phidel Marion Gonzales Vineles of the S. Rajaratnam School of International Studies (RSIS). The author also relied on ASEC publications for his analysis.

were not well connected with the rest of ASEAN. It would take several days to travel from these less connected parts of ASEAN to other locations within the region. Better infrastructure, seamless logistics and freer mobility of capital and manpower could lead to lower costs of cross-border transactions and enhanced competitiveness. This would open up additional localities in ASEAN to more investments, thereby generating stronger economic growth, creating jobs, spreading out urbanisation and reducing development pressure on existing cities.

Moreover, the ASEAN Leaders had also moved to put in place the other two pillars of the ASEAN Community, namely, ASEAN Political-Security Community and ASEAN Socio-Cultural Community. The foundation of the ASEAN Community would not be just economic integration alone. It needed physical connectivity and narrowing of the development gaps among ASEAN Member States. Inclusive regional development would also be well served. With a comprehensive development plan, the region would be equipped to play a bigger role on the international stage, thereby enhancing ASEAN centrality in the evolving regional architecture.

For Singapore, the strategic initiative to take ASEAN to the next level as a credible regional inter-governmental organisation involved the three "Cs", namely, Charter, Connectivity and Community. Then Foreign Minister of Singapore George Yeo persistently articulated the case for a Master Plan on ASEAN Connectivity (MPAC). There was resonance from Malaysia and Thailand as their respective economies would benefit from the improved linkages across ASEAN. Indonesia, on the other hand, was not very comfortable to move quickly as it felt vulnerable to more commercial penetration by foreign companies at the expense of domestic firms and industries. Yet, Indonesian officials realised they could not miss the opportunity of improving the country's connectivity. Therefore, they adopted a middle path: if resources were available for their own high-priority infrastructure projects, Indonesia would cooperate and move the MPAC. This compromise helped the ASEAN proponents of MPAC to proceed.

The MPAC was adopted on 28 October 2010 in Hanoi. MPAC 2010 culminated many months of negotiations during which senior officials argued intensively on how to settle the Plan. There were several meetings where international financial institutions like the World Bank and Asian Development Bank (ADB), and the private sector participated actively to assess their respective roles in funding infrastructure projects. UNESCAP and the ASEAN-China committee responsible for the Singapore Kunming Rail Link (SKRL) were also engaged. A great deal of time was spent on self-education of ASEAN officials on mobilising resources for projects, particularly on the modality of public-private partnerships (PPPs). ASEAN Dialogue Partners, principally Japan, were also engaged. Japanese aid agencies and Japanese financial institutions saw the MPAC as an impetus to complete existing technical assistance programmes for Cambodia, Laos, Myanmar and Viet Nam.

Progress

After six years, what is the achievement of MPAC 2010? Analysing progress on connectivity in the region is divided into three dimensions: physical connectivity, institutional connectivity, and people-to-people connectivity. The highlights are noted in the following.

Physical Connectivity

Progress has been achieved on physical connectivity in the region. According to the ASEAN Secretariat (2016), the ASEAN Highway Network (AHN) has established efficient, integrated, and sustainable land corridors linking ASEAN Member States and their neighbouring countries. Through AHN, the total length of roads below Class III (narrow two-lane roads with double bituminous treatment) was reduced to 2,454 km in 2015 from 5,311 km in 2010. The implementation of the SKRL sections that will link Singapore to Phnom Penh are on schedule. On the other hand, the SKRL sections from Cambodia to Viet Nam and also in Lao PDR are still awaiting funding provisions to start work.

The establishment of an ASEAN Roll-on/Roll-off (RoRo) Shipping Network and Short-sea Shipping was completed in March 2013. This will cover the following routes: Dumai-Malacca, Belawan-Penang-

Phuket and Davao/General Santos-Bitung. Sustainable electricity supply is also part of the ASEAN connectivity agenda and so far, the region has nine power interconnection projects and 13 bilateral gas pipelines under ASEAN Power Grid (APG) and Trans-ASEAN Gas Pipeline (TAGP), respectively. To improve the region's internet connectivity, the ASEAN Broadband Corridor was established and completed in March 2013. This resulted in the start of several projects like ASEAN Internet Exchange Network (AIX) and ASEAN Single Telecommunications Market, which encouraged the private sector to establish more internet connections across the region.

Overall, however, the results are patchy. Projects have been initiated but actual implementation is slow. One shortcoming is the limited publicity on work done and the benefits derived. Consequently, public awareness and support is low.

Institutional Connectivity

ASEAN is undertaking several measures and agreements to facilitate trade in goods and services across the region. For example, there is the ASEAN Framework Agreement on the Facilitation on Inter-State Transport (AFAFIST), ASEAN Framework Agreement on Multimodal Transport (AFAMT), and ASEAN Framework Agreement on the Facilitation of Goods in Transit (AFAFGIT). The problem is full ratification of these agreements and their protocols remain pending. By April 2016, Indonesia and Singapore began using the ASEAN Single Window (ASW) to exchange information in specified domains with regard to ASEAN Trade in Goods Agreement (ATIGA) Certificate of Origin Form D. In 2015, the ASEAN Policy Guidelines on Accreditation and Conformity Assessment and ASEAN Policy Guidelines on Standards, Technical Regulations and Conformity Assessment Procedures were adopted.

The agreements and the protocols to develop the ASEAN Single Aviation Market, namely, the Multilateral Agreement on the Full Liberalisation of Air Freight Services (MAFLAFS), Multilateral Agreement on Air Services (MAAS) and Multilateral Agreement on the

Full Liberalisation of Passenger Air Services (MAFLPAS) have been ratified by all ASEAN Member States. The implementation frameworks of the ASEAN Single Aviation Market and of the ASEAN Single Shipping Market are adopted and endorsed, respectively. Since the soft launch of ASEAN Solutions for Investments, Services and Trade (ASSIST)/ASEAN Trade Repository (ATR) / National Trade Repositories (NTRs) which took place at the ASEAN Business and Investment Summit 2015, all ASEAN Member States have established their NTRs as a precursor for the full implementation of the ATR.

The progress is not a bad record. Yet, the key is implementation and not signing numerous agreements. The business sector is expecting speedy activation of agreed facilitation measures.

People-to-People Connectivity

ASEAN's people mobility agenda encompasses education, tourism, and labour. At the regional education level, ASEAN aims to promote intra-social and cultural understanding and development. Improving the educational curricula and standards are realised through the adoption of several agreements. For example, the ASEAN Curriculum Sourcebook was developed in 2012 to promote supplementary materials that improve ASEAN studies in schools. In addition, the ASEAN University Network (AUN) has made progress in building a cooperative framework for the 30 universities in the Network. More information is shared through the AUN and there is an increase in the exchange of students and scholars, as well as more internship schemes and scholarship awards.

There are also significant steps undertaken to encourage intra-ASEAN tourism. Easing visa requirements for ASEAN nationals has helped to facilitate people mobility in the region, considering intra-ASEAN tourism represents 43 per cent of total tourist arrivals in ASEAN. In addition, ASEAN has Mutual Recognition Arrangements (MRAs) for six sectors and framework agreements for two more: engineering, nursing, architecture, medicine, dentistry, tourism, surveying (framework) and accountancy (framework). However, these MRAs represent only 1.5 per cent of the region's workforce because 87 per cent of intra-ASEAN migrant workers are unskilled and, therefore, not governed by formal agreements.

The potential and benefits of people-to-people connectivity are huge. In this context, the implementation of the facilitation measures is not up to public expectation even though it is acknowledged that this dimension of MPAC 2010 is broad and multi-faceted.

Conclusion

There are 125 measures in MPAC 2010. These comprised of 55 physical, 50 institutional and 20 people-to-people connectivity measures. As of October 2016, 39 measures have been completed, 63 measures are expected to be completed from 2015 onwards with implementation plans in place and 16 measures are unlikely to be completed because no implementation plan is in place or no financing has been secured. Four measures have yet to start because there is no ASEAN sectoral body to lead the necessary action. Another three measures will not be pursued as they are not viable economically or because the ASEAN sectoral body in charge decided not to proceed.

According to various analysts, three issues affected the implementation of measures in MPAC 2010: lack of resources; cumbersome ownership and coordination processes; and insufficient regulations. ASEAN Member States have engaged ASEAN Dialogue Partners, the World Bank and ADB to mobilise more resources for the uncompleted measures. PPPs and other emerging funding vehicles to support infrastructure development will continue to be explored by the ASEAN Member States. The lack of clear coordination and ownership is being addressed by the ASEAN Connectivity Coordinating Committee (ACCC). As for regulations, the main problem is aligning and amending domestic rules and legislations to establish the necessary infrastructure and institutions to support the implementation of the ASEAN commitments.

Infrastructure development remains a huge challenge in ASEAN. It is estimated by ASEAN Investment Report (2015) that the region's annual infrastructure needs exceed US$110 billion a year. Although funding may be available from vehicles such as the Asian Bond Market

Initiative (ABMI), Asia Bond Fund (ABF), ASEAN Infrastructure Fund (AIF), Asian Infrastructure Investment Bank (AIIB), New Development Bank (NDB), and the PPP frameworks, it is time consuming to settle on inter-agency coordination and cooperation. MPAC 2010 has provided the frameworks to deliver ASEAN Connectivity. The progress made and lessons learned have resulted in a better planning and design of the successor MPAC 2025. The key to success is what Indonesian officials had anticipated in 2010: more funding and prioritisation of projects to be implemented.

ONG Keng Yong is Executive Deputy Chairman of the S. Rajaratnam School of International Studies at the Nanyang Technological University in Singapore. Concurrently, he is Ambassador-at-Large at the Singapore Ministry of Foreign Affairs, non-resident High Commissioner to Pakistan and non-resident Ambassador to Iran. Mr. Ong also serves as Chairman of the Singapore International Foundation (SIF).

Mr. Ong was High Commissioner of Singapore to Malaysia from 2011 to 2014. He served as Secretary-General of ASEAN, based in Jakarta, Indonesia from January 2003 to January 2008.

Mr. Ong started his diplomatic career in 1979 and was posted to the Singapore Embassies in Saudi Arabia, Malaysia and the United States of America. He was Singapore's High Commissioner to India and concurrently Ambassador to Nepal from 1996 to 1998. From September 1998 to December 2002, he was Press Secretary to the then Prime Minister of Singapore, Mr. Goh Chok Tong. At the same time, Mr. Ong held senior appointments in the Ministry of Information, Communications and the Arts, and the People's Association in Singapore. From 2008 to 2011, he served as Director of the Institute of Policy Studies (IPS) in the Lee Kuan Yew School of Public Policy at the National University of Singapore.

Mr. Ong graduated from the then University of Singapore with a LLB (Hons) and the Georgetown University (Washington DC, USA) with a MA in Arab Studies.

ASEAN: A Colourful Tapestry of Diverse Cultures

YEO Whee Jim

✧ ❧ ✧

More than 50 years ago — predating ASEAN's establishment — a historic cultural event took place in the heart of Southeast Asia.

From 8 to 15 August 1963, Singapore played host to the first South-East Asia Cultural Festival, which was mooted by Singapore's first Culture Minister, the late Mr. S. Rajaratnam. The week-long festivities coincided with the official opening of Singapore's National Theatre. The Festival featured some 1,500 artistes from eleven countries and territories[1] including Hong Kong, India and Pakistan as well as several others that have since become ASEAN Member States.[2] The audiences that packed the seats numbered more than 45,000 strong. Among them were Yang di-Pertuan Negara Yusof Ishak, and royalty and dignitaries from around the region.

One might be forgiven to think that the Festival was light-years ahead of its time, given that the concept of *Southeast Asian arts and culture* was evolving. Indeed, the idea of *Southeast Asia* as a geographical

---

[1] These were: the Kingdom of Cambodia, the Colony of Hong Kong, the Kingdom of Laos, the Federation of Malaya, the Republic of Pakistan, the State of Singapore, the Kingdom of Thailand, the Republic of Vietnam, the Republic of India, the State of North Borneo and the Republic of the Philippines.

[2] Jennifer Lindsay, "Festival Politics: Singapore's 1963 South-East Asia Cultural Festival", in *Cultures at War: The Cold War and Cultural Expression in Southeast Asia*, eds. Tony Day and Maya H.T. Liem (New York: Southeast Asia Program Publications, 2010), 235.

Performance by a cultural dance troupe from Laos at the South-East Asia Cultural Festival at Singapore's National Theatre, August 1963. (Ministry of Information and the Arts collection, courtesy of National Archives of Singapore.)

region in itself was still rather new — D.G.E. Hall's *History of Southeast Asia* published in 1955 was perhaps one of the very first books to link Southeast Asian experiences in a single historical volume.[3] And it was only in 1957 in Manila that one could trace the grouping of Southeast Asian art in a single exhibition, a result of the *First Southeast Asia Art Conference and Competition.*[4] As a Singaporean, I am extremely proud to say the Festival supports the view that Singapore was one of the earliest proponents of the idea of a *Southeast Asian culture.* It is not difficult to understand why.

As a multiracial and multicultural society, Singapore always understood and appreciated the need to embrace different cultures, as the

[3] Mary Somers Heidhues, *Southeast Asia: A Concise History* (London: Thames & Hudson, 2000), 13.

[4] Kathleen Ditzig, "An Exceptional Inclusion: on MoMA's Exhibition Recent American Prints in Color and the First Exhibition of Southeast Asian Art", *Southeast of Now: Directions in Contemporary and Modern Art in Asia*, Vol. 1, No. 1 (March 2017).

Image of the First Southeast Asia Art Competition Exhibition, Manila, May 12, 1957. (Courtesy of Vanessa Ban. Original source can be found in the Museum of Modern Art (MoMA) Archives, New York IC/IP I.A.408.)

way life should be. The starting point is that each community in Singapore has always had the space to express its unique artistic and cultural practices and traditions. Beyond that, Singapore sees it as important that our different communities understand one another, appreciate one another's cultures, and build meaningful relationships across different communities for the common good[5]. The Festival was merely an extension of this belief that the arts and culture could bring the peoples of our region closer together.

More than fifty years later, we still believe in this intrinsic power of the arts and culture. We remain committed to the vision of a collective Southeast Asian culture and identity — a key building block to ASEAN solidarity. We have put our minds to making this vision a reality, starting right here in Singapore.

---

[5] Yeo Whee Jim, "ASEAN Plus China Cultural Cooperation" (keynote speech, Senior Director, Ministry of Culture Community and Youth, 10th ASEAN-China Cultural Forum, September 16, 2015).

Children from different communities on a heritage trail visiting a traditional provision shop in Singapore's Kampong Glam area, organised by the Malay Heritage Centre. (Image courtesy of the National Heritage Board.)

In some ways, it is a shame that the National Theatre, where so many Southeast Asian artistes once shared a stage, no longer exists. But this has spurred us to explore newer ways to share and celebrate Southeast Asian culture with our friends from the region, and indeed the world. A case in point is the Asian Civilisations Museum, which explores our region's historical cultural interconnectedness. In the words of the Museum's Director Mr. Kennie Ting, these linkages have perhaps been somewhat "forgotten", as best exemplified by the humble (or not so humble) betel box.

A more recent example is the National Gallery Singapore, which boasts the world's largest public display of modern Southeast Asian art. I should also highlight the STPI (Singapore Tyler Print Institute) and the Singapore Art Museum, lest I leave you with the impression that Southeast Asian arts and culture is always about looking back.

Boasting contemporary works created from residency projects (some of which have even found their way to New York's MoMA), the STPI regularly flies Southeast Asia's flag aboard. As STPI Director Ms.

The origins of betel chewing was widespread in Southeast Asia and beyond, as a pastime by 1500. It was fashionable among Asians, Europeans and Eurasians. The assortment of ingredients required several utensils, which led to the creation of elaborate boxes with many small containers. The betel or sirih box drew from a wide variety of cultural influences. Until the early twentieth century, it was also the ultimate luxury object, made of the costliest materials. (From the collection of the Asian Civilisations Museum, courtesy of the National Heritage Board.)

Emi Eu puts it, the STPI is the only gallery from the region currently that is accepted to participate in all three Art Basel fairs. On the other hand, the Singapore Art Museum focuses on contemporary art in Southeast Asia, and it has astutely drawn on the incredible diversity of Southeast Asian cultures to present the Singapore Biennales, which was already into its fifth edition in 2016. Many of the works presented at the Singapore Biennale, such as Eddy Susanto's *The Journey of Panji* speak to Southeast Asia's shared histories and the ongoing discourse on Southeast Asian identity.

This brings me to the point about the challenge that Southeast Asia's cultural diversity poses. Collectively, Southeast Asia has nearly twice the population of the United States.[6] The countries in the region

---

[6] ASEAN Secretariat, ASEAN Statistical Yearbook 2014; and "United States Census Bureau", http://www.census.gov/popclock/, accessed November 8, 2016.

Eddy Susanto, *The Journey of Panji*, 2016. Ink on canvas, acrylic and wood. 300 × 500 × 300 cm. (Collection of the Artist. Singapore Biennale 2016 commission.)

The images in this artwork are taken from reliefs illustrating episodes from the Panji cycle, a collection of stories revolvng around the legendary Prince Panji, which originated in Java around the fourteenth century and spread to what is now modern-day Malaysia, Cambodia, Myanmar, the Philippines and Thailand. Their outlines are rendered in scripts, starting first with the Javanese script, then flowing out into scripts reflecting the various regions and localities that this narrative has travelled to: a calligraphic cartography charting the movement of the Panji cycle throughout Southeast Asia. Even as the work reminds us of Southeast Asia's shared cultural histories, the letters spilling out from the compendium of Panji stories suggest the impossibility of 'containing' Southeast Asia and the limits of any attempt to unify its histories or to conceive of the region as a singular entity. (Image courtesy of Singapore Art Museum.)

span different systems of government, development trajectories, religious beliefs and hundreds of languages and ethnicities. In Indonesia alone, there are over 300 languages and dialects that are spoken[7]. If Southeast Asia were one single country, our land area would be larger

---

[7] Albert Vincent Y. Yu Chang and Andrew Thorson, *A Legal Guide to Doing Business in the Asia-Pacific*, 2010.

than the EU[8]. There does not appear to be a singular way of life or culture in Southeast Asia.

Incidentally, "Southeast Asia" and "ASEAN" are by no means completely identical. Established in 1967, ASEAN is an alliance of regional interests, whose membership has and will probably continue to change over time. We must keep this in mind, as we speak of building a shared ASEAN culture and identity premised on Southeast Asian solidarity.

Fortunately, ASEAN has never shied away from our diversity. Instead, we have embraced our cultural diversity as a strength, while slowly but steadily reinforcing our shared purpose and common ground. This approach is in line with ASEAN's emphasis on mutual respect and consensus-building, and is enshrined in documents like the ASEAN Socio-Cultural Community Blueprint 2025 and the 2011 Bali Declaration on ASEAN Unity in Cultural Diversity.

As we embrace and explore our diversity, we cherish even more closely the common threads that *do* weave throughout the tapestries of our diverse cultures. The lands of Southeast Asia are connected by the sea, and the trade routes that brought us faraway religions, philosophies and other influences over the years, especially from South Asia and East Asia. Most countries in the region have also undergone colonial rule and hardships in World War Two, and emerged stronger from these experiences. To some extent, such crucibles have enlarged the space for us to explore our shared experiences and common reference points. Shows like the National Gallery Singapore's *Artist and Empire: (En)countering Colonial Legacies* exhibition[9] explore the

---

[8] ASEAN Secretariat, ASEAN Statistical Yearbook 2014; European Union, "Living in the EU", https://europa.eu/european-union/about-eu/figures/living_en, accessed November 8, 2016

[9] Organised in association with Tate Britain, this exhibition ran in the National Gallery Singapore from October 2016 to March 2017, exploring the different ways in which the British Empire has been represented and contested through art. It critically examines art produced for the British Empire from a contemporary perspective, and features viewpoints from Southeast Asia.

Lee Wen, [Untitled](*Raffles*), Artists Investigating Monuments series, 2000. Video of 4:41 duration. (Collection of National Gallery Singapore (Resource Centre). Image courtesy of Ken Cheong.)

George Francis Joseph, *Sir Thomas Stamford Bingley Raffles*, 1817. (Collection of National Portrait Gallery, London. © National Portrait Gallery, London)

relationship between our region's colonial history and the development of modern art.

Sceptics might observe that awareness of Southeast Asian arts and culture internationally and indeed, within Southeast Asia itself, leaves much to be desired. For instance, in Singapore, I have observed the tendency among our youths to look towards the West or perhaps closer to home, Chinese, Japanese or more recently Korean culture. However, this is gradually changing with Singapore's cultural institutions regularly showcasing to Singaporeans the best of what Southeast Asia has to offer, and with budget airlines making travelling within the region more affordable than ever before.

Internationally, we are seeing more attention on Southeast Asia culture. For instance, Dr. Eugene Tan, Director of the National Gallery Singapore has been invited to join the Bizot Group, a prestigious alliance of directors of some of the world's most prominent museums.

Exploring the historic city of Hoi An. (Image by Yeo Whee Jim.)

On a more personal note, memories of exploring ancient temple ruins in Siem Reap with my late wife, cycling from Chiang Mai to Luang Prabang to raise funds for two beneficiary organisations, and more recently, exploring the historic city of Hoi An with my young daughter and working with my Malaysian counterparts on the 2015 Titian Budaya[10] project, have rekindled my love for all things Southeast Asian. Sitting proudly in a prominent corner of my living room, the *kapah* (or field basket) from the Attapeu Province in Southern Laos is but one daily reminder of the colourful tapestries of diverse cultures in a region that am proud to be associated with.

---

[10] A 3-month cultural festival in Kuala Lumpur to commemorate the 50th anniversary of the establishment of Singapore-Malaysia diplomatic relations: Titian Budaya: Bridging Cultures, http://titianbudayasg.com/

The Silly Little Girl and The Funny Old Tree, commissioned for Titian Budaya and premiered at the Dewan Filharmonik PETRONAS, Kuala Lumpur, Malaysia, 8 December 2016. This piece was adapted and composed by Malaysian composer Yii Kah Hoe, from Singaporean playwright Kuo Pao Kun's play of the same title, for Malaysian wayang kulit master Eyo Hock Seng (foreground) and the Singapore Chinese Orchestra (background). (Image courtesy of CultureLink and the Ministry of Culture, Community and Youth, Singapore.)

It is worth concluding on an important qualifying note. Most of the above examples relate to culture as expressed through the arts, heritage and history. But culture is not just about its expressions — its art forms, or its artefacts. Culture is more than that. Culture is our way of being, a way of living and a way of relating to others.

It strikes me that I am writing on my way to Vientiane for my annual meeting with my ASEAN friends. If my past encounters are any indication — I recall being involved in the ASEAN-China FTA negotiations almost two decades ago — cultural differences will likely manifest themselves in big and small, but always interesting ways. Singapore officials have, unfortunately or otherwise, earned ourselves a no-nonsense reputation for combing through documents, dotting the "*i*"s and crossing the "*t*"s. On the other hand, our friends are perhaps more easy-going, or just simply more tactful.

Regardless, when we meet, it is about more than just making our way down a check-list. It is a chance for mutual understanding and discovery, and an opportunity for a meeting of cultures. I believe I speak for all my ASEAN friends in the culture sector when I say that every host country takes its hosting responsibilities *very* seriously — we seize upon every meeting to roll out our best artists and cultural performances, in our best cultural destinations. It is no wonder that all of us always leave inspired with wonderful memories and lasting friendships.

It is on such foundations that true cultural affinity is built.

YEO Whee Jim is currently Senior Director (Arts and Heritage) at the Singapore Ministry of Culture, Community and Youth (MCCY). He is a Board Member of the Singapore Art Museum and the Singapore-Tyler Print Institute, and is the Trust Secretary to the Cultural Matching Fund. He has had postings to the Ministry of Foreign Affairs; the Singapore Embassy in Beijing; the Public Service Division; the Ministry of Information, Communications and the Arts; the Ministry of Defence and the Public Service Commission Secretariat.

He is greatly indebted to Ms. Gayle Goh, Ms. Natasha Mano, Ms. Yeow Ju Li, and Mr. Christiaan Haridas for helping with the research and identifying the pictures that accompany this essay. Above all, he is grateful for their untiring efforts and numerous suggestions that have helped to make this essay a better piece. He would also like to thank Dr. Eugene Tan, Director of the National Gallery Singapore; Mr. Kennie Ting, Director of the Asian Civilisations Museum of the National Heritage Board and my numerous other colleagues for generously sharing their knowledge and expertise.

ASEAN Intergovernmental Commission on Human Rights (AICHR): Some Personal Reflections

Richard MAGNUS

✦ ✦ ✦

Brief History

AICHR and its terms of reference was established pursuant to Article 14 of the ASEAN Charter and adopted by the ASEAN Foreign Ministers' Meeting in July 2009. On 23 October 2009, the ten AICHR Representatives, one each from each Member State, were appointed and AICHR was inaugurated at the 15th ASEAN Summit in Cha-am, Hua Hin, Thailand. I became the first AICHR Representative from Singapore.

The Cha-am Declaration stated, inter-alia, that:

— *the establishment of AICHR presents to the region and the global community, ASEAN's strong commitment to the promotion and protection of human rights and fundamental freedoms;*
— *the establishment of AICHR is ASEAN's commitment to pursue forward-looking strategies to strengthen regional cooperation on human rights.*

AICHR was designed to be an integral part of ASEAN's organisational structure and an overarching institution with a cross-cutting mandate for the promotion and protection of human rights in ASEAN with other ASEAN bodies, as well as with external partners and stakeholders.

Drafting the ASEAN Human Rights Declaration

In 2011, AICHR began to focus on the drafting of the ASEAN Declaration on Human Rights (the Declaration) which was adopted by the ASEAN Heads of State Government on 18 November 2012. The Declaration is a landmark political document in terms of human rights in the region, reflecting the aspirations of the people of ASEAN. The Declaration contained three generations of human rights: the General Principles on the free and equal dignity of all persons et al; the Civil and Political Rights; the Economic, Social and Cultural Rights; the Right To Development; and the Right To Peace.

Singapore played a significant role in providing the initial draft of the Declaration for discussion and gently guided the subsequent caucuses, corridor and side discussions, and AICHR formal meetings to arrive at a consensus of the Declaration. The timing for the discussion on the Declaration was right; we wanted to meet the deadline of the 2012 Heads of State/Government meeting. There was a common mind among the Representatives to present a human rights document by then. The discussions on the Declaration within AICHR as well as with ASEAN sectoral bodies and civil society organisations were serious, hard but collegial. There was great camaraderie among the Representatives; the relationships were warm; there was a purpose, mission and an opportunity to benefit our people in ASEAN. This ameliorated the processses within AICHR.

It was a personally satisfying moment when the ASEAN Heads of State/Government adopted the Declaration. I have spoken and written elsewhere on how Singapore contributed significantly to the Declaration and how we ensured the safekeeping of our national interests and values.

Developing our Views

From the outset, I was concerned that AICHR, whose Representatives, come from distinct and different levels of social and political systems, should have a common understanding of the corpus and interpretation of (universal) human rights; in particular, the need to balance the enjoyment of human rights and fundamental freedoms with corresponding neighbourly and societal duties and responsibilities.

A couple of opportunities arose to have this conversation. One was the study visit to the United States in November 2010 at the invitation of US President Barack Obama. There were two primary agenda for this Programme: first to make known ASEAN's commitment to human rights matters and secondly to exchange views on human rights as understood by the United States as well as the stakeholders involved.

We came away with a few perspectives: that United States' national interests drove their agenda on human rights in other countries; that human rights when advocated by the United States for other countries were an unqualified right in themselves — without regard to corresponding duties and responsibilities — that is human rights were interpreted *in extremis*. In our discussion with a variety of United States civil society groups, we were surprised to learn that some of them received some sort of federal funding with an unspoken understanding that they are not to be concerned with domestic matters. These were valuable lessons for the Representatives.

The purists among us tempered their views on the reality of the application on human rights. We were determined to have an ASEAN-centric declaration and began contemplating the careful balancing of these rights with social duties and responsibilities which are within our ASEAN cultural ethos.

In May 2011, AICHR visited three European cities: Brussels, Strasbourg and Vienna and had conversations with various European institutions dealing with human rights, including civil society organisations. These institutions were: the European Court on Human Rights, the European External Action Service of the European Union, the European Commission, their relevant divisions of the Council of Europe, and the Fundamental Rights Agency and the Organization for Security and Cooperation (OSCE), especially those dealing with the freedom of media, and the OSCE Special Representative and Coordinator for Combating Trafficking in Human Rights.

We learned much also in this European study. The above Court's officials told us that they were bogged down with inordinate delay of the resolution of cases which were filed by individuals against European member states. Within the ASEAN way, such a court could not be contemplated in our human rights framework. There was much discussion on the Civil and Political Conventions. The OSCE highlighted the need for the media to be free to report stories and events; they learnt a bitter lesson when the press was restrained and did not report Hitler's plans. Again, we learned from the civil society groups we met that they received some funding to report on human rights abuses in other countries.

AICHR also had an interface meeting with the then United Nations High Commissioner for Human Rights, Ms. Navanetham Pillay in our seventh AICHR meeting in November 2011 in Bali, Indonesia. It was an uneventful meeting in my recollection.

Back Story

In 1993, the UN convened the World Conference on Human Rights in Vienna, Austria. The Conference adopted the Vienna Declaration and Program of Action. The ASEAN Foreign Ministers, in their Joint Communiqué at the 26th ASEAN Ministerial Meeting (AMM) in July 1993, stated the following, inter alia:

> …The Foreign Ministers …reaffirmed ASEAN's commitment to and respect for human rights and fundamental freedoms as set out in the Vienna Declaration of 25 June 1993…
> …They stressed that human rights are interrelated and indivisible comprising civil, political, economic, social and cultural rights. These rights are of equal importance…
> …They emphasised that the protection and promotion of human rights in the international community should take cognizance of the principles of respect for national sovereignty, territorial integrity; and non-interference in the internal affairs of states.
> …They were convinced that freedom, progress and national stability are promoted by a balance between the rights of the individual and those of the community, through which many individual rights are realized, as provided for in the Universal Declaration of Human Rights…

The ASEAN Human Rights Declaration

So the Vienna Declaration as well as the Universal Declaration of Human Rights (UDHR) and the views of the ASEAN Foreign Ministers' Joint Communique became our basic texts for working out the Declaration. This is now carried in the General Principles, Civil and Political Rights and the Economic and Cultural Rights.

The Declaration, in its current text, made reference to the UDHR and the Vienna Declaration and reaffirmed our commitments accordingly.

The Right To Development and the Right To Peace are unique to the Declaration. They speak for themselves. They find support in the ASEAN Blueprints and in the many ASEAN instruments.

Conclusion

The ASEAN Heads of State/Government commended AICHR for developing a comprehensive Declaration. This was the beginning. Giving the Declaration substance and practicality is the next. The vehicle which AICHR had adopted to do this is the five year rolling work plans. The Declaration is another critical piece to build up our ASEAN one vision, one identity, one community as we celebrate the 50th Anniversary of ASEAN!

Richard MAGNUS is retired Chief District Judge. The World Bank acknowledged him as the "architect" of judicial reforms in the lower judiciary. For his excellent service, he was awarded the Meritorious Service Medal and later the Public Service Star. He was the first Singapore Representative to the ASEAN Inter-Governmental Commission of Human Rights. Besides being a jurist and editor of several law books in the practitioner Series, Richard is a regulator, bioethicist, sits on some public companies and involved in several community engagements. He is also a member of the Public Service Commission and Vice Chairman of the UNESCO's expert (International Bioethics) group.

Promoting and Protecting Women's and Children's Rights in ASEAN — Some Observations on the ACWC

Aline WONG

I was Singapore's government representative for Women's Rights on the ASEAN Commission on the Promotion and Protection of the Rights of Women and Children (ACWC) from 2010 to 2014, serving a term of four and a half years as one of the Commission's inaugural representatives from the ASEAN Member States (AMS).[1] The ACWC was inaugurated at the ASEAN Leaders' 16th Summit held in Hanoi, April 2010. It held its first official meeting in February 2011.

Before ACWC was established, there had been various government and non-governmental institutions in ASEAN working on and advocating for women and children, e.g. the ASEAN Committee on Women (ACW) and the ASEAN Confederation of Women's Organizations (ACWO). As early as 2004, when the ASEAN Leaders adopted the Vientiane Action Programme (VAP) at their tenth Summit, there was already a call for the establishment of an ASEAN Commission on the promotion and protection of the rights of women and children. Soon after the ASEAN Charter was signed and ratified in 2007, a Roadmap for the ASEAN Community (2009–2015) was drawn up for the three Community pillars to accelerate their work under their respective Blueprints, towards establishing the ASEAN Community earlier than previously envisaged.

---

[1] Singapore's inaugural Representative for Children's Rights was Mr. Koh Choon Hui, Chairman of the Singapore Children's Society.

The background work on establishing this Commission which started in 2008 thus gathered momentum. Within a year after the Blueprints were published, ACWC was inaugurated in 2010.

Under its Terms of Reference (TOR), the ACWC is an intergovernmental body and an integral part of the ASEAN organisational structure under its Socio-Cultural Community pillar. It is a consultative body, and its mandate to promote and protect the rights of women and children covers many functional areas, including the upholding of the implementation of the Concluding Observations of the Convention on the Elimination of all Forms of Discrimination Against Women (CEDAW) and the Convention on the Rights of the Child (CRC), to which all the AMS are signatories.

ACWC is composed of two representatives from each AMS, one for Women's Rights and one for Children's Rights. Hence, the total composition of the ACWC is 20 representatives, with their respective support personnel from the government ministries concerned. Each member's term is for three years, except for one of the two inaugural representatives from each AMS who would serve for an initial four and half years.

Many of the representatives are government officials in charge of social welfare and development, with particular reference to women and children. Some are academics, and some have previously held political office. One or two are activists in NGOs who are now appointed as their government's representatives on the Commission.

As an entirely new organisation within ASEAN, ACWC representatives were able to draft our own Rules of Procedure. We also had the authority to set up our own Fund, although its utilisation would be subject to the same financial rules and regulations as those set up by the ASEAN administration.

Bearing in mind that the primary responsibility to promote and protect the fundamental freedoms and rights of women and children rests with each Member State (as stated in ACWC's TOR 3.5), and that we should adopt an evolutionary, collaborative and consultative approach to advancing the rights of women and children in ASEAN, the 20 representatives set about enthusiastically to craft our first Five-Year

Work Plan. There was a great deal of camaraderie and sharing of expertise by the representatives.

It was quite exciting and satisfying for me to have actively participated in the agenda-setting process and the drawing up of the First Work Plan 2012–2016. We first identified the thematic areas we wanted to concentrate on, followed by the AMS coming forward to be lead countries in certain projects of their choice.

Since there was no funding provision within the ASEAN structure for the work of ACWC, and no dedicated secretariat support for ACWC, the first priority task in our Work Plan was to strengthen the institutional capacity of ACWC. An initial or startup ACWC Fund was to be set up, with each AMS contributing a certain amount on an equal contribution basis. Along with this start-up Fund, each project to be undertaken is expected to be self-financing, with support to be sought from government/partner agencies/organisations within or outside ASEAN.

The second priority thematic area is the elimination of violence against women (VAW) and violence against children (VAC). This theme is in synchrony with the international movement now, led by the UN itself, against violence targeted at women and children in all kinds of vulnerable situations.

A third thematic area is in education — the promotion of gender equality in education, and for early childhood education. Other areas of concern are: women and children affected by HIV and AIDS, early marriage and reproductive health for women, adolescent physical and mental health, and an integrated child protection system. Climate change, natural disasters and armed conflicts with their major impacts on women and children, are another cluster of themes identified for study and action. Finally, the elimination of stereotypes and cultural practices harmful to the rights of women and children, the mainstreaming of women in policy measures, as well as the right of children to participate in all affairs affecting them, provide the foundation themes in the Action Plan.

Following the identification of the above thematic areas for ACWC to work on, specific project titles were listed with various AMS volunteering to be lead countries. For the 26 projects proposed and adopted,

Concept Papers were prepared, with rounds of inputs and discussions at subsequent ACWC meetings. ACWC has to make annual progress reports on these projects to the Senior Officials Meeting (SOMSWD) and the Ministerial Meeting on Social Welfare and Development (AMMSWD).

Singapore initiated a long-term project on building an ACWC Network of Social Service Agencies (NOSSA) which aims to enhance the capability of social service providers throughout ASEAN for victims of VAW and VAC, by means of exchange of experts and information, technical assistance, training and research. It also aims to provide direct assistance to the victims through rehabilitation, education and skills training, micro-finance, referrals and repatriation. All the AMS have joined this project with Singapore as the lead country.

Following the adoption of the ASEAN Human Rights Declaration in November 2012, and riding on the on-going public anti-violence campaigns across the world, members of the ACWC worked tirelessly on drafting a Declaration on the Elimination of Violence against Women and Elimination of Violence against Children in ASEAN in mid-2013. Our efforts were rewarded by the Leaders' expeditious adoption of the Declaration at their 23rd Summit in October 2013. The Declaration specifically mentioned the network of social service agencies as one of the measures to be taken to strengthen the prevention, protection and assistance to women and children victims of violence in ASEAN.

The implementation of NOSSA met with various challenges from the beginning, including funding support from partner agencies, identification of the service agencies from each AMS to form the initial list in the NOSSA network and which would be strengthened to become role-models for the others. To kick-start the project, Singapore organised a Special Taskforce meeting in Jakarta in April 2013, as well as a Training course for frontline social workers from ASEAN held in Singapore in April 2014.

Challenges such as funding and commitment from AMS were common to many of the ACWC projects. Progress was quite slow throughout its first Work Plan period. The lack of political will of some

AMS to support ACWC was at times obvious. The mood of optimism and enthusiasm among the representatives waned towards the middle of this period. Some cheer reappeared towards the end, when funding was at last available for certain major projects from international partner agencies.

There were other challenges as well. From the beginning, ACWC adopted an approach — which is commonly practised among ASEAN bodies, (like a "cultural trait" within ASEAN) — that of "co-opting" projects that are already on-going in some AMS (e.g., workshops, conferences, research publications), which are then "grafted" onto the ACWC Work Plan as some "low hanging fruits" or projects that can be readily accomplished. On the surface, such projects are related to the main themes that ACWC is concerned about. Upon closer look, this may not be so; this approach may not be right either. First, adopting ready-made projects might cause ACWC to lose focus and freshness of view in its work. Second, some of the on-going projects are not necessarily conceived according to the same assumptions and concepts employed by ACWC. Accordingly, the recommendations coming from such on-going projects are not necessarily representative of the views of ACWC. Unfortunately, given the polite culture of ASEAN, it is very difficult to raise objections or voice strongly critical comments on each other's work.

The issue of ultimate alignment with the ASEAN Intergovernmental Commission on Human Rights (AICHR) — as stipulated in ACWC's TOR article 7.7 — also turned out to be a great challenge for ACWC during its initial years. Although ACWC proposed reasonable grounds for a gradual, iterative approach to alignment with AICHR, these were not appreciated by AICHR, which had a different interpretation of its position as the "overarching" human rights institution within ASEAN. Much time and energy was also lost on account of some conflicting strong personalities on the two Commissions. That constituted a major distraction, which at times became quite distressful to the representatives on both sides.

Finally, as all decisions are made by consensus — "the ASEAN way" — it is possible that one AMS alone can cause a failure in arriving at consensus. This has happened, and ACWC is no exception. The convention within ASEAN to rotate the Chair according to alphabetical order of the AMS, does not guarantee that a strong Chair will emerge at crucial junctures, who can mediate behind the scenes cajole or charm the members, keep meetings short and sharp, and produce faster progress.

At the time of writing, ACWC is drafting its Second Work Plan 2017–2021. Of the original 26 projects in its First Work Plan, ten are considered completed or very soon to be completed. The rest may be carried over to the Second Work Plan, and some of these have by now received funding support from external partner agencies. It has been a struggle although progress is on the horizon. ACWC held its 13th Meeting in October 2016 back to back with the 15th Meeting of the ASEAN Committee on Women (AWC) which also met in Singapore. This would have offered an excellent opportunity for the two bodies to discuss how to reduce the amount of program overlaps between the two institutions.

Overall, a fundamental problem with ACWC's role is the overlapping of themes and programs between the various ASEAN bodies. There are significant overlaps with the ACW, the Senior Officials Meeting on Health and Development (SOMHD), the Senior Officials Meeting on Labour (SLOM) and with the SOMSWD itself, whose ASEAN Strategic Framework on Social Welfare and Development (2011–2015) essentially covers several major areas of ACWC's Work Plan already. However, overlapping areas occur not entirely because of the pre-existing areas of work done by the other ASEAN bodies. The problem with ACWC's role — at least in my view — lies in the lack of a distinctive human rights approach to the issues confronting women and children in ASEAN. And in the absence of a Human Rights Mechanism or even a monitoring mechanism, it is perhaps inevitable that the work of ACWC in social, cultural and economic areas would be perceived as being "subsumed" under the work of the other pre-existing sectoral bodies. A case in point is NOSSA which, unfortunately, had to be "aborted" by the end of 2016 partly because of the reason of overlap. It remains to be seen whether ASEAN's current restructuring effort in trimming down the complex structure and overlapping activities will put a clearer focus on ACWC for upholding the rights of women and children and helping the AMS to fulfil their obligations under CEDAW and CRC.

Aline WONG is the current Chancellor of the new Singapore University of Social Sciences (SUSS). Prior to this appointment, she had served as Academic Advisor of SIM University (2005–2015) which was the predecessor of SUSS.

Dr. Wong holds an MA and a PhD in Sociology from the University of California, Berkeley. Her academic career as Professor in Sociology spanned nearly 30 years at the National University of Singapore. She entered politics in 1984 and was appointed Minister of State for Health and for Education (1990–2001). She then served as Chairman of the Housing and Development Board (2003–2007).

Her public service to education, women's rights and social policies has been acknowledged through a number of local and international awards. She also served as Singapore's Representative for Women's Rights on the ASEAN Commission on the Promotion and Protection of the Rights of Women and Children (2010–2014).

ASEAN's Future

Thinking Realistically about ASEAN

Bilahari KAUSIKAN

It is utterly pointless to criticise a cow for being an imperfect horse.

I start with that rather cryptic pronouncement because too much discussion about ASEAN amounts to just that. ASEAN is 50 years old. Yet it is still an ill-understood organisation. The peoples of its member states are generally not conscious of ASEAN. Academics who study ASEAN and journalists who ought to be informing the public about ASEAN, do not really help dispel ignorance and improve public knowledge. Too often their suggestions on how to improve ASEAN amount to fervently wishing that a cow ought to be a horse.

I am not singling out academics and journalists for a special thrashing, let me hastily add that Secretariat officials and the policymakers of ASEAN Member States sometimes make such statements too. I have done so myself. However, our motives are usually quite different. We don't always believe what we say because what we say is sometimes only an instrument to achieve other goals that are usually left unsaid. This is the essence of ASEAN diplomacy.

ASEAN is far from perfect. It certainly needs improvement and there are many areas where its workings can be improved. But a cow will never become a horse. We have to accept a cow as a cow. A cow is quite a useful animal. So is a horse. But the usefulness of a cow is different from that of a horse. We should consider how we can improve the bovine breed; how we can make a better cow, rather than scolding it for not being able to run as fast as a horse.

ASEAN faces many challenges. Going forward, lack of public understanding of what ASEAN is and, equally important, what ASEAN is not, is going to be a very serious liability. A new generation of Southeast Asians who take the current stability of the region for granted need to be educated about the importance of ASEAN and must have a realistic appreciation of how ASEAN really works.

We have to take the world — or even that little part of it we call Southeast Asia — as it is and not mistake our hopes and wishes for reality. This does not mean that we should not aspire to change things in accordance with our ideals. But such an effort is doomed to failure unless it starts from an unsentimental understanding of reality.

So let me briefly outline what I consider the four most important things about real-world ASEAN.

ASEAN — An Organisation of Sovereign States

First and most fundamentally, *ASEAN is an organisation of sovereign states* who act through their respective governments.

Of course we often speak about a "people-oriented" or "people-centred" ASEAN. But the agency, the instrument, through which the "people" act are governments and the modality through ASEAN seeks to serve the 'people' whoever they may be — and this is not always obvious — are states and governments.

This means that the Charter notwithstanding, ASEAN has no autonomous existence apart from the will of its member states. This fact is sometimes obscured by talking about "community", a term that implies something that is more than the sum of its parts — supra-nationality.

We copied the term "community" from the EU lexicon at a time when the EU's feet of clay were not so evident. But semantics apart, supra-nationality — the pooling of sovereignties which is what in theory the EU is all about and the gap between theory and practice is widening even in the EU — is not on any part of ASEAN's agenda: past, present and for the foreseeable future, except in a very limited sense in the economic dispute settlement mechanism which has not been tested and I suspect, may never be tested.

ASEAN is not a happy band of brothers; if we were a happy band of brothers, there would be no need for ASEAN because ASEAN's fundamental and enduring purpose is to ensure a modicum of order and civility in a region where neither is to be taken for granted.

From this point of view, whatever our other limitations, ASEAN has been quite successful in maintaining peace in Southeast Asia for almost half a century. There have been tensions, skirmishes and even minor conflicts but no war. This may not seem very much. But if you think back to what Southeast Asia was like in 1967 when ASEAN was formed, this is not an inconsiderable achievement.

In a sense, whatever ASEAN does in any field is primarily a means to this end: the creation and maintenance of order and civility through a process of working together. This process of working together is at least as important as, and often more important than, whatever goal that may be the ostensible reason for the process. This is one of the fundamental realities of ASEAN.

It does not mean that goals are not important; it does not mean that we can just spin wheels forever without going anywhere. If we just spin wheels forever without caring about getting somewhere, disillusionment must eventually set in and ASEAN may well break up. But equally, if we push the goal — whatever goal, however desirable — too hard, ASEAN may also well break up. It is not always easy to maintain a balance or even know where the balance should lie.

And this brings me to the second point.

ASEAN Consensus

ASEAN works by consensus and can only work by consensus. This is because Southeast Asia is a very diverse region and ASEAN Member States differ in levels of economic development; we differ in types of political systems; we differ in our core identities of race, language and religion; and hence we differ in how each of us defines our national interests within the ASEAN framework even though we all have come to accept that framework as an important shared interest.

Working by consensus means ASEAN often privileges form over substance. We often set goals we are unable to fulfil or have no intention of fulfilling. We do this not because we are all utter hypocrites, but because we need to reach some form of agreement, even if it is just agreement over words, in order to keep the process going until circumstances change and what was once regarded as not in one member or another's interest perhaps becomes possible.

ASEAN's basic consensus is a consensus on always having some sort of consensus even if it is only a consensus on words or on not discussing issues that may break consensus because any other mode of decision-making among very diverse sovereign states risks even small rifts becoming major splits.

In practice, consensus need not mean unanimity. We now have a consensus that at least in some areas, consensus need not mean the agreement of all ten members but can mean those who are ready going ahead, while leaving the door open to others to join in when they are ready or when their definition of interests changes. But at present this mainly applies to economic cooperation.

The corollary to consensus decision-making is non-interference. This is now in practice often modified, particularly in functional areas where it is, however grudgingly, accepted that in a relatively compact area like Southeast Asia one country's policies can affect other countries and economic "community" must entail some acknowledgement of interdependence. But the principle of non-interference remains sacrosanct. Better to avert our eyes from the disagreeable than to openly disagree because who knows where disagreement may take us.

And this brings me to my third point: "ASEAN centrality", a phrase more often used than understood.

ASEAN Centrality

This idea of not pushing things too hard — of maintaining consensus even if it is only consensus over form — not only applies to intra-ASEAN relations; to relations amongst and between ASEAN members. It also applies to ASEAN's external relations; to relations with ASEAN's Dialogue Partners.

This is what lies behind the idea of "ASEAN centrality"; another aspect of ASEAN that is not well understood. Before we adopted the term "ASEAN centrality", we used to talk about "ASEAN being in the driver's seat". Sounds rather important, doesn't it? But remember sometimes the person in the driver's seat is only the chauffeur.

ASEAN centrality is not a boast about ASEAN's strategic weight. Rather, it is an acknowledgement of ASEAN's relative weakness vis-à-vis the major powers and a means of turning that weakness into some modicum of advantage.

If ASEAN has been able to set some regional norms; if the major powers have found some ASEAN-led forum such as the ASEAN Regional Forum and the East Asia Summit, of occasional use and worth their time, and if the major powers have graciously conceded a "central" role to ASEAN, it is precisely because they are confident that if push comes to shove, ASEAN cannot frustrate their most vital interests. In other words, in its relations with external powers, ASEAN works best when it does not work too well.

There is nothing particularly unique about this and ASEAN has this in common with all inter-state organisations including the UN. The veto which is the privilege of the Permanent Members of the Security Council is a safeguard to ensure that the UN cannot be used in any meaningful way against the interests of the principal members. And this is why the UN has survived whereas its predecessor the League of Nations, did not.

This is not an equal world and even the largest member of ASEAN is not equal to the major powers. "Sovereign equality" is one of the myths of international relations which it suits everybody to pretend to believe. But the concept of sovereign equality is not merely absurd if taken too seriously; if taken too seriously it is downright dangerous. But acceptance of the harsh reality of inequality within the polite slogan of "ASEAN centrality" gives ASEAN a modicum of influence amidst the treacherous swirls and eddies of great power politics where otherwise there would be none. This is better than nothing. It allows us to preserve some autonomy.

And this brings me to my fourth and final point. Which is really the summation of the preceding three points.

ASEAN Is Not a Substitute

Since ASEAN is an inter-state organisation that works by consensus between its members, what is key is national political will, national competence and national capability. When national will, competence and capability are present, ASEAN can act as a multiplier for national policies. ASEAN can help its members build capability and competence. But ASEAN is not a substitute for national political will, national capability and national competence.

This is clear if we consider the challenges of the next stage of ASEAN's development. In 2015, we reached the end of one phase of ASEAN's "community-building" effort and proudly announced the establishment of an ASEAN community. But it is not as if on the stroke of midnight on the 31st of December 2015, there was a blinding flash of light and all we ugly toads awoke in the New Year, magically and forever transformed into a new and superior class of being.

This is only the end of one phase. We did not reach a hundred percent of the targets we set ourselves for this phase, but we achieved enough of them to credibly declare victory, at least in the economic community where our goals for this phase were modest.

But we cannot stop. We would already have done the easy things. Henceforth we would have to reach consensus on more difficult issues. Last year we also adopted ASEAN 2025 which is a blueprint for the next decade of ASEAN's community-building effort. The vision did not lack ambition. The question mark, as always, is over implementation. The primary constraint will be the domestic politics of several key ASEAN Member States, some of whom are undergoing profound systemic transformations, some of whom are facing key elections or leadership changes, and hence several of whom are becoming less internally coherent.

Conclusion

Foreign policy always and everywhere must rest on a firm foundation of domestic politics. This is ASEAN's greatest challenge. I hope those who think about ASEAN will not lose sight of this simple fact which underlies

ASEAN's greatest successes as well as its greatest failures and on which ASEAN's future hangs.

I am not denigrating ASEAN and mine is a counsel of realism, not despair. Imperfect though it may be, there is no substitute for ASEAN. But ASEAN's continued survival is not to be taken for granted and will not be ensured by wishful thinking.

The major powers are now seeking a new modus vivendi between themselves and with the states of Southeast Asia. ASEAN is an indispensable instrument to help us all manage the strategic challenges and complexities of this period.

But the major powers are also seeking to capture and harness ASEAN to their ends. We are going to undergo a period of great stress. Already some ASEAN Member States have shown themselves unwilling to resist the lucrative temptations of lending themselves to the designs of some major powers.

To minimise such temptations, and to build a consensus for the next stage of ASEAN integration, ASEAN cannot remain as it presently is: an elite construct. To build consensus within each ASEAN Member State for the politically difficult next stage of ASEAN integration or "community-building", we need a broad and deep foundation of realistic and not idealised public understanding of what ASEAN can and cannot do. Thus far no ASEAN Member State has done a particularly good job of explaining ASEAN to their publics. This is not a sustainable situation.

Bilahari KAUSIKAN is currently Ambassador-at-Large in the Ministry of Foreign Affairs of Singapore.

From 2001 to May 2013, he was the second Permanent Secretary and subsequently Permanent Secretary of the Ministry of Foreign Affairs.

He had previously served in a variety of appointments in the Ministry and abroad, including as the Permanent Representative to the United Nations in New York and as Ambassador to the Russian Federation.

He has been awarded the Public Administration Medal (Gold) and the Pingat Jasa Gemilang (Meritorious Service Medal) by the Singapore Government.

Raffles Institution, the University of Singapore and Columbia University in New York all attempted to educate Mr. Kausikan.

ASEAN and Singapore: 50 Years of Partnership

Tommy KOH, Sharon SEAH Li-Lian and CHANG Li Lin

We wish to thank the 50 friends who have contributed essays to this book. We wish also to thank the Foreign Minister of Singapore, Dr. Vivian Balakrishnan for his foreword. We would like to thank our colleagues in the Ministry of Foreign Affairs and the Centre for International Law for their advice and help. Finally, we wish to thank our editor, Kim Tan and the book's designer, Jimmy Low.

We decided to edit this book for three reasons. First, we believed that ASEAN's 50th Anniversary is an event worth celebrating. Second, we wanted to use this book to explain to Singaporeans why ASEAN is so important to Singapore's foreign policy. Third, we wanted to record the many contributions which Singaporeans have made to ASEAN's development during the past 50 years.

Bangkok Declaration

It is hard for young Singaporeans to imagine the situation in Southeast Asia in 1967. The region was in turmoil. There was a danger that the war in Vietnam would spread to other countries. There was a deficit of trust between neighbours. The pundits were not wrong when they predicted that ASEAN would not survive. The five men who signed the Bangkok Declaration on the 8th of August 1967 took a leap of faith. We thank them for doing so. As a result of their action, we have a regional organisation,

ASEAN, which is often regarded as the second most successful regional organisation in the world.

ASEAN's Achievements

ASEAN has made three important achievements in the last 50 years.

First, ASEAN has helped to keep the peace in Southeast Asia for 50 years. Kishore Mahbubani and Jeffery Sng, in their book *The ASEAN Miracle,* describes ASEAN's "durable ecosystem of peace" as nothing short of a "modern miracle".[1] Indeed, ASEAN has had its share of trials and tribulations, such as the Cambodian crisis, the Vietnamese boat people crisis, the Boxing Day Tsunami, Cyclone Nargis, and the SARS pandemic crisis. In these crises, ASEAN had proven its unity, resilience and effectiveness. When Cambodian and Thai troops clashed along the Cambodian-Thai border, near the Prear Vihear Temple, ASEAN was able to play a positive role. Through ASEAN's intervention, the two sides were persuaded to come to the negotiating table and, with the United Nations' support, peace was restored to the border. Cambodia also made a successful application to the International Court of Justice to interpret its 1962 judgement.

Second, ASEAN's economic achievement is its second most important achievement. ASEAN has succeeded in merging its ten economies into a single market and production platform. Although the realities on the ground suggest that the journey is still incomplete, the political will to complete the economic integration of ASEAN is strong. ASEAN has a combined GDP of US$2.5 trillion that is expected to grow to US$4 trillion by 2030. With a population of 630 million, ASEAN is one of the most exciting growth regions in the world. It is today the world's seventh-largest economy and is projected to be the fourth largest by 2030. The economic growth experienced by ASEAN has contributed to rising standards of living and the reduction of poverty across Southeast Asia.

Third, ASEAN has become the indispensable convener, facilitator and chairman of the various regional organisations. The organisations

---

[1] Kishore Mahbubani and Jeffery Sng, *The ASEAN Miracle: A Catalyst for Peace* (Singapore: NUS Press), 75.

include the ASEAN Regional Forum (ARF), ASEAN Plus One, ASEAN Plus Three, East Asia Summit (EAS) and ASEAN Defence Ministers' Meeting Plus (ADMM Plus). ASEAN has been able to play this role because it is united, independent and neutral. ASEAN's Leaders should remember that they should not allow the great powers to divide them. A divided ASEAN means the end of the central role which ASEAN plays in the regional architecture.

ASEAN's Future

We have good reason to celebrate the 50th anniversary of ASEAN. We should however, not become complacent. ASEAN's future will depend on whether we can maintain our unity and independence. It will also depend on whether we will be able to re-invent ourselves in order to stay relevant and to respond to a changing world. ASEAN should also be mindful of the need to anchor ASEAN in the hearts and minds of the citizens of ASEAN. ASEAN should not be seen by our people as an elitist organisation serving the interests of the urban elite and of big businesses. ASEAN's integration must bring tangible benefits to the people of ASEAN. Singapore will be the chairman of ASEAN in 2018. Singapore will do its best to strengthen the family and to augment its relations with all its Dialogue Partners.

About the Editors

Tommy KOH is currently Ambassador-at-Large at the Ministry of Foreign Affairs; Special Adviser to the Institute of Policy Studies; and Chairman of the Governing Board of the Centre for International Law at the National University of Singapore (NUS). He is the Chairman of the International Advisory Panel of the Asia Research Institute (NUS) and Chairman of the Advisory Committee of the Master's Degree on Environmental Management (NUS). He is also the Co-Chairman of the Asian Development Bank's Advisory Committee on Water and Sanitation. He is Rector of the Tembusu College, National University of Singapore, and Chairman of the Board of Directors of the SymAsia Foundation of Credit Suisse.

He had served as Dean of the Faculty of Law of NUS, Singapore's Permanent Representative to the United Nations in New York, Ambassador to the United States of America, High Commissioner to Canada and Ambassador to Mexico. He was President of the Third UN Conference on the Law of the Sea and the Chairman of the Preparatory Committee for and the Main Committee of the UN Conference on Environment and Development. He was the founding Chairman of the National Arts Council, founding Executive Director of the Asia-Europe Foundation and former Chairman of the National Heritage Board. He was also Singapore's Chief Negotiator for the US-Singapore Free Trade Agreement. He acted as Singapore's Agent in two legal disputes with Malaysia. He has chaired two dispute panels for the WTO. He is the Co-Chairman of the China-Singapore Forum, the Japan-Singapore Symposium and the India-Singapore Strategic Dialogue.

In 2006, Prof. Koh received the Champion of the Earth Award from UNEP and the inaugural President's Award for the Environment from Singapore. He was conferred with honorary doctoral degrees in law by

Yale and Monash Universities. Harvard University conferred on him the Great Negotiator Award in 2014.

Sharon SEAH Li-Lian is Associate Director at the National University of Singapore's Centre for International Law. She oversees the Centre's strategic planning and external engagements. Prior to joining the Centre for International Law, she was with the Ministry of Foreign Affairs of Singapore from 2001 to 2012. She served a posting as First Secretary at the Singapore Embassy in Bangkok, Thailand from 2003 to 2007 and in the International Organisations Directorate of the Ministry from 2008 to 2012. She later joined Singapore's National Environment Agency as Deputy Director for International Relations from 2013 to 2015 handling transboundary environmental issues. She maintains a keen interest in anthropology, foreign policy, ASEAN and environmental issues. She is currently pursuing an LLM in Public and International Law at the University of Melbourne, Australia.

CHANG Li Lin is a civil servant. Prior to her current appointment in the public service, she was Deputy Director for Public Affairs at the Institute of Policy Studies (IPS) at the Lee Kuan Yew School of Public Policy, National University of Singapore. In the first half of her career at IPS, she was covering policy research in the areas of international relations. Thereafter, she took over the public affairs portfolio which included managing donor and media relations, and special projects. A graduate of the University of Reading and University of Kent at Canterbury, in the UK, Li Lin has a Masters in International Relations (IR) and a BA in Sociology and IR. She has written articles and edited a number of publications on Singapore's foreign policy, peacekeeping and domestic politics including *The Little Red Dot* series of essays by Singapore and foreign diplomats (co-edited with Tommy Koh) and *50 Years of Singapore and the United Nations* (co-edited with Tommy Koh and Joanna Koh).

Index

World Health Organization (WHO),
64–65
WTO principles, 117
Wunna Maung Lwin, 99

X
Xi Jinping, 190

Y
Yeo, George, 94, 102, 105, 221, 231,
293, 300, 338, 340, 356
"Yoshida Doctrine", 179

Z
Zain Azraai, 27
Zone of Peace, Freedom and
Neutrality (ZOPFAN), 24, 28, 32,
140
zoonotic diseases, risk of, 63–64
ZOPFAN. *See* Zone of Peace,
Freedom and Neutrality

www.ingramcontent.com/pod-product-compliance
Lightning Source LLC
Chambersburg PA
CBHW052149280326
41926CB00110B/4395